48th EDITION

Warman's®

Antiques&
Collectibles
2015

NOAH FLEISHER

Published by

Krause Publications, a division of F+W Media, Inc.
700 East State Street • Iola, WI 54990-0001
715-445-2214 • 888-457-2873
www.krausebooks.com

To order books or other products call toll-free 1-800-258-0929
or visit us online at www.krausebooks.com.

ISBN-13: 978-1-4402-3943-4
ISBN-10: 1-4402-3943-6

Cover Design by Nicole MacMartin
Designed by Jana Tappa, Sandi Carpenter, and Nicole MacMartin
Edited by Mary Sieber

Printed in China

On the cover, clockwise from upper left:

1970s wing lounge chair, Vladimir Kagan Designs, Inc., **$10,000;** *Roseville brown Water Lily basket,* **$250-$350;** *Tiffany Studios flowerform vase,* **$64,900;** *"A Refreshing Break" beverage advertisement by Arnold Armitage,* **$4,687.**

On the back cover:

Tiffany Studios Alamander chandelier, **$212,400;** *Pendant La Bretonne, circa 1900, signed Vever for Henri Vever, Paris.* **$400,000-$600,000.**

Contents

Introduction
Looking Back to the Future

By Noah Fleisher

T he ultimate collector fantasy is the time machine, to be able to summon the vessel, punch a button or two and open the door onto the past, wherever it may be.

Me? Late May 1938 and late April 1939, respectively, when Action Comics #1 (Superman's first appearance) and Detective Comics #27 (the first appearance of "The Batman") first hit the newsstands – first remembering to bring a few coins with an earlier date than those years on them – where I would buy a big stack of each. I'd also find Siegel and Shuster and ask them if I could buy the original art from that Action Comics #1 cover.

Noah Fleisher

Not that I've put *that much* thought into it….

The truth is, and it's one of the things that makes antiques and collectibles so interesting, we can never know at the time something debuts whether it will morph into something priceless.

Eras shift, generations age in and out of collecting; tastes change and the values of so many things rise and fall with seemingly little logic; what is deemed important now was unthinkable a decade ago. Compare and contrast the ups and downs of comic books vs. Beanie Babies, if you will.

Change is the only constant; some of us will be north of the line, some south.

Is there a way to hedge against a turkey? Or to divine the next niche?

Of course not. As we all learn in elementary school, though, an educated guess can get you a lot closer.

Let's look at the past, then, in an effort to formulate that guess:

Where is the market strong right now, and where has it been strong? Comic books continue to be gangbusters. Early horror movie posters are still the gold standard in that corner. High-end fashion accessories are seeing a boom in their respective markets, and first generation home computer technology is simply soaring.

All of these, respectively, reflect the time and place of their creations and all of them, respectively, were viewed as having little value when they began.

Comics books? Blamed for corrupting American youth in the early 1940s, rounded up and used for paper drives during World War II, and burned *en masse* with the advent of the comics code in 1954.

Horror movie posters? They were the harbingers of the end of society in the early 1930s,

NOAH FLEISHER received his Bachelor of Fine Arts degree from New York University and brings more than a decade of newspaper, magazine, book, antiques and art experience to his position as Public Relations Director of Heritage Auctions, one of the country's foremost auction houses. He is the former editor of *Antique Trader, New England Antiques Journal* and *Northeast Antiques Journal,* is the author of *Warman's Modern Furniture,* and has been a longtime contributor to *Warman's Antiques and Collectibles.*

responsible in part for bringing about the Hollywood Code, and the paper was never meant to be more than a throw-away…$300,000+ for a vintage *Dracula* or *Frankenstein* poster, anyone?

Luxury accessories? Long seen as a foible of high society women, an overpriced trinket, high-end handbags from Hermes to Channel and beyond are firmly entrenched in the public imagination. An entire new segment of collector has been born, and the best examples bring well into six figures.

First generation home computer technology? Look at the headlines in the last six years, browse eBay or check the databases of any number of auction houses – especially Breker, in Germany – and you'll see high six-figure price tags for things that a generation ago were not known to exist, which was fine, as nobody really cared. What's a bunch of wires, a few tubes and a keyboard anyway?

Computer equipment is the most recent of these phenomenon, made infinitely interesting to the modern mind by its very abstraction and its "newness," so let's look a little closer at this category as we get out the divining rod.

As an aside and in truth, however, that abstraction I mention above is present across every category I mention along with it. By themselves, these things are paper, or leather, or bits of metal and glass.

With the proper context and time to view them, however, meaning is imparted via nostalgia and distance. They are not empty at all. Comic books have meaning as relics of pop culture, movie posters graphically represent the shifting national mood and taste, handbags represent power and position in society and have intrinsic value based on quality.

We look back at each one; they are broadly popular in the culture at the time, but not seen as serious, until they emerge a decade or two later as valuable treasures.

If I'm looking back today, then, seeing these markets as they're established, I see the future in technology, in the machines that were built in my childhood in the 1970s, in the computer games and cartridges that entertained me through the summers of my youth on Atari and Nintendo and Apple IIe, and which are now selling for tens of thousands of dollars – in 2010 a California man sold a copy of the Activision game *Air Raid*, found in a storage unit, for more than $33,000.

In mid-2012 Sotheby's sold a working Apple 1 unit from 1976, one of only 200 made in the heady early days of the tech giant, for $374,000, double the $180,000 estimate. A few months later, in November of the same year, Auction Team Breker in Germany sold another Apple I machine for double *that* price, $630,000.

Before the antiques and auction world had time to catch its breath, Breker came back in May 2013 and sold *another* working Apple I for $671,400, breaking its own record, double the $390,000 estimate placed on the machine by the house. Then, in July 2013, Christie's – on an online-only auction, I might add – sold one more of these machines for $388,000. Not as much as the Breker sales but still a massive price.

That recent past, friends, is where the market is and is going to be. We are seeing it happen. It's only a matter of time before one of the first Apple computers brings $1 million. Or a game system goes for $100,000. Mark my words. Nothing but upside going out, right?

Maybe…

That market already has players and exposure in the mainstream.

Let's look deeper then.

At the bottom of it all, what drives the technology that is selling so well right now is, to borrow from the film *The Matrix*, all just a bunch of ones and zeroes. What it will all come down to, in the end, are the very words that define the ideas, whether they are made physically manifest or not.

"There are more than 252 million registered domain names as of April 2013," said Aron Meystedt, director of Intellectual Property Auctions at Heritage Auctions and a longtime veteran of the world of buying and selling domain names. "New registrations of all domains grew by 26.6 million year over year from 2012 through 2013. The domain industry and business is in excess of $1 billion annually, easily."

Intellectual property is about to become the Wild West. As I write this, we are not far out from the release of 1,800 Global Top Level Domains (GTLDs), domains that will expand the usual .com, .net, .biz, and .org by potentially millions of permutations. It's mind-boggling to think about, yet it's the milieu in which Meystedt naturally moves.

How does he make the very ethereal idea of selling words that represent ideas in the virtual world real?

Here's how he puts it simply: "There are a very finite number of meaningful words and identifiers, and these words and phrases are highly coveted by companies looking to establish an online presence."

By companies, by nations, by cities, by groups, and by consumers. There is an incredible amount of big business interest in this Internet expansion, and do not doubt that there are hundreds of millions of dollars about to flow to control some of these names.

"The future is split 50/50 between people who think the GTLDs will bring confusion and people who think what's to the right of the dot will mean less and less as years pass," Meystedt said. "Either way, the industry is exploding and more people and companies are entering the space now than ever before."

Either way, by the bare bones aspect of its essential nature, it's difficult for me to fully grasp what exactly it really means. I know, though, intuitively, that it's important.

What will it mean to the pursuit of collecting that means so much to all of us?

Well, that's where my crystal ball grows cloudy. I am a man interested in the physical, after all, and this is a book about the wonderful things produced by humans in the physical world.

Perhaps, though, the time is not far off when it will not be necessary for you – or your heirs – to actually have to possess the physical item, the Eames chair or the signed Babe Ruth baseball, but just to have the idea stored somewhere. The world will long have done away with the need of actual "reality," so simply controlling the digital code that indicates ownership of the idea, hence the item, will be enough.

I wouldn't bet the bank on that, of course, but it's fun to think about. Just keep an eye on that old PC gathering dust in your garage. It could be your future fortune....

In the meantime, keep collecting with passion and buying with your heart and you will never go wrong. Welcome to the 2015 edition of *Warman's Antiques & Collectibles*.

Sit back, read on and enjoy the great size of this volume and how it feels – good, heavy, and absolutely real – in your hands.

Michaan's Auctions

Tiffany Studios Apple Blossom window depicting apple tree in full bloom with limbs covered in flowers, cloud-streaked sky, and body of water, panel with metal tag impressed Tiffany Studios New York, circa 1915, 50" high x 20 1/2" wide, 60 1/4" high x 30 1/2" wide with museum frame. **$118,000**

Warman's: Who We Are

Edwin G. Warman was an entrepreneur in Uniontown, Pennsylvania. He dabbled in several ventures, including ownership of a radio station. He was also an avid antiques collector who published his price listings in response to requests from friends and fellow collectors. The first modest price guide was published in 1948 as *Warman's Antiques and Their Current Prices*. It was a bold move. Until then, antiques were sold primarily through dealers, antiques shops, and at auctions. The sellers and buyers negotiated prices and were forced to do their own research to determine fair prices. Under Warman's care, the price guide changed all that forever. Warman also published some specialized price guides for pattern glass and milk glass, as well as his "Oddities and Curiosities" editions, under the banner of the E.G. Warman Publishing Co.

Although the name varied slightly over the years, *Warman's Antiques and Their Current Prices* covered such collectible areas as mechanical banks, furniture, and silver, just like the Warman's of today. His pages consisted of a brief statement about the topic, either relating to the history or perhaps the collectibility of the category. A listing of current prices was included, often containing a black and white photograph.

E.G. Warman died in 1979. His widow, Pat Warman, continued the tradition and completed work on the 15th edition after his death. The estate sold the E.G. Warman Publishing Co. to Stanley and Katherine Greene of Elkins Park, Pennsylvania, in 1981. Chilton Books bought the Warman Publishing Co. in the fall of 1989. With the 24th edition, Warman's was published under the Wallace-Homestead imprint. Krause Publications purchased both the Warman's and Wallace-Homestead imprints in 1997.

We are proud to continue the rich tradition started 66 years ago by Mr. Warman, a man driven by his love of antiques and collectibles and by a thirst for sharing his knowledge.

The Warman's Advantage

The Warman's Advantage manifests itself in several important ways in the 2015 edition. As we reviewed past volumes, we wanted to make this book as easy to use as possible. To that end, we've consolidated and reorganized how we present several key categories. Our new mantra is, "What is it first?"

For instance, an antique clock may also have an advertising component, an ethnic element (like black memorabilia), reflect a specific design theme (like Art Deco), and be made of cast iron. But first and foremost, it's a clock, and that's where you'll find it listed, even though there are other collecting areas involved.

There are a few categories that remain iconic in the collecting world. Coca-Cola collectibles cross many interests, as do folk art, Asian antiques, and Tiffany designs, to name just a few. These still have their own broad sections.

In addition to handbags and maritime collectibles, newly expanded sections include art, ceramics, jewelry, toys, books, and glass.

Prices

The prices in this book have been established using the results of auction sales across the country, and by tapping the resources of knowledgeable dealers and collectors. These values reflect not only current collector trends, but also the wider economy. The adage that "an antique (or collectible) is worth what someone will pay for it" still holds. A price guide measures value, but it also captures a moment in time, and sometimes that moment can pass very quickly.

Beginners should follow the same advice that all seasoned collectors will share: Make mistakes and learn from them; talk with other collectors and dealers; find reputable resources, including books and websites; and learn to invest wisely, buying the best examples you can afford.

Words of Thanks

This 48th edition of the *Warman's* guide would not be possible without the help of countless others. Dozens of auction houses have generously shared their resources, but a few deserve special recognition: Heritage Auctions, Dallas; Backstage Auctions, Houston; Woody Auction, Douglass, Kansas; Greg Belhorn, Belhorn Auction Services LLC, Columbus, Ohio; Andrew Truman, James D. Julia Auctioneers, Fairfield, Maine; Anthony Barnes at Rago Arts and Auction Center, Lambertville, New Jersey; Karen Skinner at Skinner, Inc., Boston; Morphy Auctions, Denver, Pennsylvania; Susan Pinnell at Jeffrey S. Evans & Associates, Mount Crawford, Virginia; Rebecca Weiss at Swann Auction Galleries, New York; and Leslie Hindman Auctioneers, Chicago. And, as always, special thanks to Catherine Saunders-Watson for her many contributions and continued support.

Read All About It

There are many fine publications collectors and dealers may consult about antiques and collectibles in general. Space does not permit listing all of the national and regional publications in the antiques and collectibles field; this is a sampling:

Heritage Auctions

Dennis Stock (American, 1928-2010), "Audrey Hepburn While Filming 'Sabrina'," 1954, gelatin silver, printed later, 14" x 9 1/2", ed. 20/200, signed, titled, dated, and numbered in pencil in margin on recto. **$2,375**

- *Antique Trader,* published by Krause Publications, 700 E. State St., Iola, WI, 54990
  www.antiquetrader.com
- *Antique and The Arts Weekly,* 5 Church Hill Rd., Newton, CT 06470
  www.antiquesandthearts.com
- *AntiqueWeek,* P.O. Box 90, Knightstown, IN 46148
  www.antiqueweek.com
- *Maine Antique Digest,* P.O. Box 358, Waldoboro, ME 04572
  www.maineantiquedigest.com
- *New England Antiques Journal,* 24 Water St., Palmer, MA 01069
  www.antiquesjournal.com
- *The Journal of Antiques and Collectibles,* P.O. Box 950, Sturbridge, MA 01566
  www.journalofantiques.com
- *Southeastern Antiquing & Collecting* magazine, P.O. Box 510, Acworth, GA 30101
  www.go-star.com/antiquing

Let Us Know What You Think

We're always eager to hear what you think about this book and how we can improve it. Contact:

Paul Kennedy, Editorial Director, Antiques & Collectibles Books
Krause Publications
700 E. State St.
Iola, WI 54990-0001
715-445-2214, Ext. 13470
Paul.Kennedy@fwmedia.com

Visit an Antiques Show

One of the best ways to enjoy the world of antiques and collectibles is to take the time to really explore an antiques show. Some areas, like Brimfield, Massachusetts, and Manchester, New Hampshire, turn into antiques meccas for a few days each summer when dealers and collectors come for both specialized and general antiques shows, plus auctions.

Here are a few of our favorites:
- *Brimfield, Massachusetts, shows,* held three times a year in May, July, and September, *www.brimfield.com*
- *Round Top, Texas, antique shows*, held spring and fall, *www.roundtop.com/antique1.html*
- *Antiques Week* in and around Manchester, New Hampshire, held every August, *www.antiquesweeknh.com*
- *Palmer/Wirfs Antique & Collectible Shows*, including the Portland, Oregon, Expos, *www.palmerwirfs.com*
- *The Original Miami Beach Antique Show, www.dmgantiqueshows.com*
- *Merchandise Mart International Antiques Fair,* Chicago, *www.merchandisemartantiques.com*
- *High Noon Western Americana Show and Auction,* Phoenix, *www.highnoon.com*

Ask an Expert

Many contributors have proved invaluable in sharing their expertise during the compilation of the 48th edition of the *Warman's* guide. For more information on their specialties, call or visit their websites.

Caroline Ashleigh
Caroline Ashleigh Associates, LLC
1000 S. Old Woodward, Suite 105
Birmingham, MI 48009-6734
248-792-2929
www.auctionyourart.com
Vintage clothing, couture and accessories, textiles, western wear

Tim Chambers
Missouri Plain Folk
501 Hunter Ave.
Sikeston, MO 63801-2115
573-471-6949
E-mail: plainfolk@charter.net
Folk art

Tara Ana Finley, ISA AM
Anubis Appraisal & Estate Services, Inc.
1406 Milan Ave.
Coral Gables, FL, 33134
305-446-1820
www.anubisappraisal.com
E-mail: tarafinley@gmail.com,
tarafinley@anubisappraisal.com
African, Oceanic, Pre-Columbian, antiquties,
toys, trains, dolls, lead soldiers, militaria

Noah Fleisher
E-mail: noah.fleisher@yahoo.com
Modernism

Reyne Haines
Reyne Gallery
4747 Research Forest Dr. #180-274
The Woodlands, TX 77381
513-504-8159
www.reyne.com
E-mail: reyne@reyne.com
20th century decorative arts, lighting,
fine jewelry, wristwatches

Ted Hake
Hake's Americana & Collectibles Auctions
P.O. Box 1444
York, PA 17405
717-848-1333
E-mail: auction@hakes.com
Pop culture, Disneyana, political

Leslie Holms
Antique Purse Club of California
55 Ellenwood Ave.
Los Gatos, CA 95030
408-354-1626
E-mail: cree56@comcast.net
Antique handbags of all kinds

Mark Ledenbach
www.halloweencollector.com
E-mail: Marlede@sbcglobal.net
Halloween collectibles

Mary P. Manion
Landmarks Gallery & Restoration Studio
231 N. 76th St.
Milwaukee, WI 53213
800-352-8892
www.landmarksgallery.com
Fine art and restoration

Suzanne Perrault
Perrault Rago Gallery
333 N. Main St.
Lambertville, NJ 08530
609-397-1802
www.ragoarts.com
E-mail: suzanne@ragoarts.com
Ceramics

David Rago
Rago Arts and Auction Center
333 N. Main St.
Lambertville, NJ 08530
609-397-9374
www.ragoarts.com
Art pottery, Arts & Crafts

Dennis Raleigh Antiques & Folk Art
P.O. Box 745
Wiscasset, ME 04578
207-882-7821
3327 Cones Ct.
Midland, MI 48640
989-631-2603
www.dennisraleighantiques.com
E-mail: dgraleigh@verizon.net
Decoys, silhouettes, portrait miniatures

Henry A. Taron
Tradewinds Antiques
P.O. Box 249
Manchester-By-The-Sea, MA 01944-0249
(978) 526-4085
www.tradewindsantiques.com
Canes

Andrew Truman
James D. Julia, Inc.
P.O. Box 830
Fairfield, ME 04937
207-453-7125
www.juliaauctions.net
E-mail: atruman@jamesdjulia.com
Toys, dolls, advertising

Auction Houses

Sanford Alderfer Auction & Appraisal
501 Fairgrounds Rd.
Hatfield, PA 19440
215-393-3000
www.alderferauction.com
Full service

American Bottle Auctions
2523 J St., Suite 203
Sacramento, CA 95816
800-806-7722
www.americanbottle.com
Antique bottles, jars

American Pottery Auction
Waasdorp Inc.
P.O. Box 434
Clarence, NY 14031
716-759-2361
www.antiques-stoneware.com
Stoneware, redware

American Sampler
P.O. 371
Barnesville, MD 20838
301-972-6250
www.castirononline
Cast iron bookends, doorstops

Antiques and Estate Auctioneers
44777 St. Route 18 E.
Wellington, OH 44090
440-647-4007
Fax: 440-647-4006
www.estateauctioneers.com
Full service

Auctions Neapolitan
1100 First Ave. S.
Naples, FL 34102
239-262-7333
www.auctionsneapolitan.com
Full service

Backstage Auctions
448 West 19th St., Suite 163
Houston, TX 77008
713-862-1200
www.backstageauctions.com
Rock 'n' roll collectibles and memorabilia

Belhorn Auction Services, LLC
P.O. Box 20211
Columbus, Ohio 43220
614-921-9441
www.belhorn.com
Full service, American art pottery

Bertoia Auctions
2141 DeMarco Dr.
Vineland, NJ 08360
856-692-1881
www.bertoiaauctions.com
Toys, banks, holiday, doorstops

Bonhams
101 New Bond St.
London, England W1S 1SR
44-0-20-7447-7447
www.bonhams.com
Fine art and antiques

Brian Lebel's Old West Auction
451 E. 58th Ave.
Denver, CO 80216
480-779-9378
www.codyoldwest.com
Western collectibles and memorabilia

Brunk Auctions
P.O. Box 2135
Asheville, NC 28802
828-254-6846
www.brunkauctions.com
Full service

Caroline Ashleigh Associates, LLC
1000 S. Old Woodward, Suite 105
Birmingham, MI 48009-6734
248-792-2929
www.auctionyourart.com
Full service, vintage clothing, couture and accessories, textiles, western wear

Christie's New York
20 Rockefeller Plaza
New York, NY 10020
www.christies.com
Full service

Clars Auction Gallery
5644 Telegraph Ave.
Oakland, CA 94609
510-428-0100
www.clars.com
Full service

Coeur d'Alene Art Auction
8836 Hess St., Suite B
Hayden Lake, ID 83835
208-772-9009
www.cdaartauction.com
19th and 20th century Western and American art

Cowan's
6270 Este Ave.
Cincinnati, OH 45232
513-871-1670
www.cowanauctions.com
Full service, historic Americana, Native American objects

Doyle New York
175 E. 87th St.
New York, NY 10128
212-427-2730
www.doylenewyork.com
Fine art, jewelry, furniture

DuMouchelles Art Gallery
409 E. Jefferson Ave.
Detroit, MI 48226
313-963-6255
www.dumouchelle.com
Fine art and antiques,
art glass

Early Auction Co., LLC
123 Main St.
Milford, OH 45150
513-831-4833
www.earlyauctionco.com
Art glass

Elder's Antiques
901 Tamiami Trail (US 41) S.
Nokomis, FL 34275
941-488-1005
www.eldersantiques.com
Full service

Elite Decorative Arts
1034 Gateway Blvd. #108
Boynton Beach, FL 33426
561-200-0893
www.eliteauction.com
Fine artwork, porcelain,
bronze

Greg Martin Auctions
660 Third St., Suite 100
San Francisco, CA 94107
800-509-1988
www.gregmartinauctions.com
Firearms, edged weapons,
armor, Native American
objects

Great Gatsby's Antiques
and Auctions
5180 Peachtree Industrial Blvd.
Atlanta, GA 30341
770-457-1903
www.greatgatsbys.com
Fine art, fine furnishings,
lighting, musical instruments

Grey Flannel
8 Moniebogue Ln.
Westhampton Beach, NY
11978
631-288-7800
www.greyflannel.com
Sports jerseys, memorabilia

Guernsey's
108 E. 73rd St.
New York, NY 10021
212-794-2280
www.guernseys.com
Art, historical items,
pop culture

Guyette Schmidt & Deeter
24718 Beverly Rd.
St. Michaels, MD 21663
410-745-0485
www.guyetteandschmidt.com
Antique decoys

Hake's Americana &
Collectibles Auctions
P.O. Box 12001
York, PA 17405
717-434-1600
www.hakes.com
Character collectibles,
pop culture

Heritage Auctions
3500 Maple Ave., 17th Floor
Dallas, TX 75219-3941
800-872-6467
www.ha.com
Full service, coins, pop culture

Humler & Nolan
225 E. Sixth St., 4th Floor
Cincinnati, OH 45202
513-381-2041 or 513-381-2015
www.humlernolan.com
Antique American and European
art pottery and art glass

iGavel, Inc.
229 E. 120th St.
New York, NY 10035
866-iGavel6 or 212-289-5588
igavelauctions.com
Online auction, arts,
antiques and collectibles

Ivey-Selkirk
7447 Forsyth Blvd.
Saint Louis, MO 63105
314-726-5515
www.iveyselkirk.com
Full service

Jackson's International
Auctioneers and Appraisers
2229 Lincoln St.
Cedar Falls, IA 50613
319-277-2256
www.jacksonsauction.com
Full service, religious and
Russian objects, postcards

James D. Julia, Inc.
P.O. Box 830
Fairfield, ME 04937
207-453-7125
www.juliaauctions.net
Full service, toys, glass,
lighting, firearms

Jeffrey S. Evans
& Associates
2177 Green Valley Ln.
Mount Crawford, VA 22841
540-434-3939
www.jeffreyevans.com
Full service, glass, lighting,
Americana

John Moran Auctioneers, Inc.
735 W. Woodbury Rd.
Altadena, CA 91001
626-793-1833
www.johnmoran.com
Full service, California art

Keno Auctions
127 E. 69th St.
New York, NY 10021
212-734-2381
www.kenoauctions.com
Fine antiques, decorative arts

Lang's Sporting Collectibles
663 Pleasant Valley Rd.
Waterville, NY 13480
315-841-4623
www.langsauction.com
*Antique fishing tackle
and memorabilia*

**Leland Little Auctions
& Estate Sales, Ltd.**
246 S. Nash St.
Hillsborough, NC 27278
919-644-1243
www.llauctions.com
Full service

Leslie Hindman Auctioneers
1338 W. Lake St.
Chicago, Il 60607
312-280-1212
www.lesliehindman.com
Full service

**Litchfield County
Auctions, Inc.**
425 Bantam Rd. (Route 202)
Litchfield, CT 06759
860-567-4661
212-724-0156
www.litchfieldcountyauctions.com
Full service

McMasters Harris Auction Co.
5855 John Glenn Hwy
P.O. Box 1755
Cambridge, OH 43725
740-432-7400
www.mcmastersharris.com
Dolls and accessories

Michaan's Auctions
2751 Todd St.
Alameda, CA 94501
510-740-0220
www.michaans.com
Antiques, fine art

**Michael Ivankovich
Auction Co.**
P.O. Box 1536
Doylestown, PA 18901
215-345-6094
www.wnutting.com
Wallace Nutting objects

Morphy Auctions
2000 N. Reading Rd.
Denver, PA 17517
717-335-3435
www.morphyauctions.com
*Toys, banks, advertising,
pop culture*

Mosby & Co. Auctions
5714-A Industry Ln.
Frederick, MD 21704
240-629-8139
www.mosbyauctions.com
Mail, phone, Internet sales

Neal Auction Co.
4038 Magazine St.
New Orleans, LA 70115
504-899-5329
800-467-5329
www.nealauction.com
*Art, furniture, pottery,
silver, decorative arts*

New Orleans Auction Gallery
1330 St. Charles Ave.
New Orleans, LA 70130
800-501-0277
www.neworleansauction.com
Full service, Victorian

**Noel Barrett Vintage Toys
@ Auction**
P.O. Box 300
Carversville, PA 18913
215-297-5109
www.noelbarrett.com
*Toys, banks, holiday,
advertising*

Old Town Auctions
P.O. Box 91
Boonsboro, MD 21713
240-291-0114
301-416-2854
www.oldtownauctions.com
*Toys, advertising, Americana;
no Internet sales*

Old Toy Soldier Auctions USA
P.O. Box 13324
Pittsburgh, PA 15243
Ray Haradin
412-343-8733
800-349-8009
www.oldtoysoldierauctions.com
Toy soldiers

Old World Auctions
2155 W. Hwy 89A, Suite 206
Sedona, AZ 86336
800-664-7757
www.oldworldauctions.com
Maps, documents

Past Tyme Pleasures
39 California Ave., Suite 105
Pleasanton, CA 94566
925-484-6442
www.pasttyme1.com
Internet catalog auctions

Philip Weiss Auctions
1 Neil Ct.
Oceanside, NY 11572
516-594-0731
www.prwauctions.com
Full service, comic art

Pook & Pook, Inc.
463 E. Lancaster Ave.
Downingtown, PA 19335
610-629-4040
www.pookandpook.com
Full service, Americana

**Professional Appraisers
& Liquidators, LLC**
16 Lemington Ct.
Homosassa, FL 34446
800-542-3877
www.charliefudge.com
Full service

**Quinn's Auction Galleries
& Waverly Auctions**
360 S. Washington St.
Falls Church, VA 22046
703-532-5632
www.quinnsauction.com
www.waverlyauctions.com
*Full service, rare books
and prints*

Rago Arts and Auction Center
333 N. Main St.
Lambertville, NJ 08530
609-397-9374
www.ragoarts.com
*Arts & Crafts, modernism,
fine art*

Red Baron's Antiques, Inc.
8655 Roswell Rd.
Atlanta, GA 30328
770-640-4604
www.rbantiques.com
*Full service, Victorian,
architectural objects*

Rich Penn Auctions
P.O. Box 1355
Waterloo, IA 50704
319-291-6688
www.richpennauctions.com
*Advertising and country
store objects*

**Richard D. Hatch
& Associates**
913 Upward Rd.
Flat Rock, NC 28731
828-696-3440
www.richardhatchauctions.com
Full service

Robert Edward Auctions, LLC
P.O. Box 7256
Watchung, NJ 07069
908-226-9900
www.robertedwardauctions.com
Baseball, sports memorabilia

Rock Island Auction Co.
7819 42nd St. West
Rock Island, IL 61201
800-238-8022
www.rockislandauction.com
*Firearms, edged weapons
and accessories*

St. Charles Gallery, Inc.
1330 St. Charles Ave.
New Orleans, LA 70130
504-586-8733
www.stcharlesgallery.com
Full service, Victorian

Samuel T. Freeman & Co.
1808 Chestnut St.
Philadelphia, PA 19103
215-563-9275
www.freemansauction.com
Full service, Americana

Seeck Auctions
P.O. Box 377
Mason City, IA 50402
641-424-1116
www.seeckauction.com
Full service, carnival glass

Skinner, Inc.
274 Cedar Hill St.
Marlborough, MA 01752
508-970-3000
www.skinnerinc.com
Full service, Americana

Sloans & Kenyon
7034 Wisconsin Ave.
Chevy Chase, MD 20815
301-634-2330
www.sloansandkenyon.com
Full service

Swann Auction Galleries

*Theodore de Bry, "Americae pars,
nunc Virginia," Frankfurt, 1590.*
$8,400

Slotin Folk Art
Folk Fest Inc.
5619 Ridgetop Dr.
Gainesville, GA 30504
770-532-1115
www.slotinfolkart.com
Naïve and outsider art

Sotheby's New York
1334 York Ave.
New York, NY 10021
212-606-7000
www.sothebys.com
*Fine art, jewelry,
historical items*

**Strawser Auctioneers
& Appraisers**
P.O. Box 332, 200 N. Main
Wolcottville, IN 46795
260-854-2859
www.strawserauctions.com
Full service, majolica, Fiesta

Susanin's Auctions
900 S. Clinton
Chicago, IL 60607
312-832-9800
www.susanins.com
*Fine art, Asian, fine
furnishings, silver, jewelry*

Swann Auction Galleries
104 E. 25th St., #6
New York, NY 10010-2999
212-254-4710
www.swanngalleries.com
*Rare books, prints,
photographs, posters*

**Ted Owen and Co. Auctions /
The Fame Bureau**
Suite 71
2 Old Brompton Rd.
SW7 3DQ London,
United Kingdom
http://famebureau.com

Theriault's
P.O. Box 151
Annapolis, MD 21404
800-638-0422
www.theriaults.com
Dolls and accessories

Tom Harris Auction Center
203 S. 18th Ave.
Marshalltown, IA 50158
641-754-4890
www.tomharrisauctions.com
Full service, clocks, watches

John Toomey Gallery
818 North Blvd.
Oak Park, IL 60301
708-383-5234
www.treadwaygallery.com
*Arts & Crafts, modernism,
fine art*

**Tradewinds Antiques
& Auctions**
24 Magnolia Ave.
Manchester-By-The-Sea, MA
01944-0249
978-526-4085
www.tradewindsantiques.com
Canes

Treadway Gallery
2029 Madison Rd.
Cincinnati, OH 45208
513-321-6742
www.treadwaygallery.com
*American Arts & Crafts,
1950s decorative art*

Turkey Creek Auctions
13939 N. Highway 441
Citra, FL 32113
352-622-4611
800-648-7523
antiqueauctionsfl.com
Full service

Victorian Casino Antiques
4520 Arville St. # 1
Las Vegas, NV 89103
702-382-2466
www.vcaauction.com
Coin-operated devices

Waverly Auctions
360 S. Washington St.
Falls Church, VA 22046
703-532-5632
www.quinnsauction.com
www.waverlyauctions.com
*Full service, rare books
and prints*

Woody Auction
P.O. Box 618
317 S. Forrest
Douglass, KS 67039
316-747-2694
www.woodyauction.com
Glass

SPECIAL CONTRIBUTORS

*John Adams-Graf
Tom Bartsch
Eric Bradley
Brent Frankenhoff
Kyle Husfloen
Paul Kennedy
Karen Knapstein
Mark B. Ledenbach
Kristine Manty
Michael Polak
Antoinette Rahn
Barry Sandoval
Ellen T. Schroy
Mary Sieber
Susan Sliwicki
David Wagner
Martin Willis*

Advertising

By Noah Fleisher

The enduring appeal of antique advertising is not hard to understand. The graphics are great, they hearken back to a simpler time and a distinct American identity and – perhaps best of all – are available across all price levels. That means buyers from all tax brackets and walks of life.

"It's like anything in collectibles and antiques," Dan Matthews, president and owner of Matthew's Auction in Moline, Illinois, one of the nation's top auctioneers of petroliana and the author of *The Fine Art of Collecting and Displaying Petroliana.* "The best stuff, the very top, sells no matter what. Right now the medium-market is doing okay and the lower continues to drag a bit behind."

The most reliable value in Matthews' market continues to be top-of-the-line petroliana – names like Harbo Petrolium, Keller Springs, Quiver, or Must-go can command tens of thousands of dollars – but there is a definite hierarchy at play and, if you are thinking of expanding your collecting horizons to include antique signage, you would do well to know the market.

Noah Fleisher

Seasoned collectors will warn, with good reason, that money should not be the motivating factor in the hobby, so it may be somewhat deceptive to start this discussion with the idea of monetary value. The true value of antique advertising signs, from gas stations to country stores to soda pop, lies in the context of their production and the nostalgia they evoke of that time.

The best antique advertising evokes the meat of the first half of the 20th century, when signs were the most effective ways to catch the eyes of car culture consumers. The signs and symbols evolved to reflect the values and styles of the regions where they were posted and the products they reflected. A sign with bold color, great graphics, and a catchy slogan can transport a collector back decades in an instant. Collectors feel a rapport with a piece; they don't see dollar signs.

"Buy it because you like it," said Matthews, "because you can live it with it and it means something to you. Never get into something because you think you'll make money."

Look at the market for one of the most collectible and popular markets: Coca-Cola. Fifteen years ago the best Coke pieces in the middle market could reliably command several thousand dollars. Coca-Cola manufactured hundreds of thousands of signs and related ephemera, millions even, and they began to come out of the woodwork. There is little more evocative of classic Americana than the red and white of Coke, but as everybody sold their pieces and everybody acquired their bit of nostalgia, the market cooled and prices went

NOAH FLEISHER received his Bachelor of Fine Arts degree from New York University and brings more than a decade of newspaper, magazine, book, antiques and art experience to his position as Public Relations Director of Heritage Auctions, one of the country's foremost auction houses. He is the former editor of *Antique Trader*, *New England Antiques Journal* and *Northeast Antiques Journal*, is the author of *Warman's Modern Furniture*, and has been a longtime contributor to *Warman's Antiques and Collectibles.*

Whistle Soda tin sign, 1920s, beveled edge tin over cardboard easel-back, "Thirsty? Just [Whistle bottle image] / Get the Handy Bottle," manufactured by American Art Works, Coshocton, Ohio, scarce version, does not include orange, blue, and white Whistle Soda logo, near mint condition, 9" wide x 6 1/4" high. **$948**

down significantly. Pieces that had routinely brought $500-$1,000 could suddenly be had for significantly less, and people stopped selling.

Now, however, with several years of very quiet action in the books, the cycle seems to be turning around. New collectors have entered the market and older collectors are leaving. Those collections are finding new owners at a decent price.

"Coca-Cola does seem to be coming back," said Matthews. "It's been stagnant for the past five years, but good clean signs are finding good homes at good prices."

As with any category, the very best antique advertising will bring top dollar no matter what, as a look through the recent advertising sales database of prices realized at an auction house like Morphy's will attest to. In those sales it can be seen that that the rarest of Coca-Cola paper and tin routinely bring tens of thousands of dollars.

Antique advertising provides a tangible place for collectors to put real money. Looking through recent prices realized at the top auction venues – like Matthews, Morphy Auctions, and William Morford – it's obvious that top dollar can be had for the true rarities in the business and that the middle market provides a solid outlet for design-minded collectors as opposed to those who collect to amass a sizable grouping.

There are opportunities everywhere for the educated collector – from the country auction to the flea market. Going head to head, out of the blocks, with the top collectors in the business at the top auctions can result in frustration. Rather, if you're just getting your feet wet, research online, email experts and ask for resources, do your due diligence in seeing what the market is bringing and, then, take those skills to unlikely places and see what turns up.

"All the fields we deal in seem to be doing quite well right now," said Matthews. "Gas and oil, which there's more of than anything else, keeps going up more and more. The best thing to do is buy from reputable auction houses and dealers, from people who guarantee your product."

Barring the finds you can make at small antiques shows, shops and markets, expect to go into an auction ready to spend an average of $500 for a quality piece of petroliana, for pieces like rare oil and gas cans. A sharp and patient buyer can grab a steal for $10 or a masterpiece for a $1,000. As with anything else, a seasoned and practical eye comes with practice. The prices broaden greatly when the market is expanded to include country store advertising and specific brand advertising, like Campbell's Soup.

"Like most kinds of collectibles, everybody starts out buying middle grade stuff and graduates to the higher stuff," said Matthews. "Collectors in this hobby are very dedicated; prices on the best stuff haven't peaked yet, that's for sure."

A lot of the steadiness in the market is coming from the exposure antique advertising is getting in places like cable television, via shows like "American Pickers" and "Pawn Stars," where a premium is placed on supreme objects.

"These kinds of shows are only helping the hobby get bigger," Matthews added. "Take Ford Oil cans, for instance. Before these shows, the market was dominated by a handful of players. The prices ran way up. Those guys all got out, cans went down to $500 or so from $1,000 or more. Then these shows premiered, oil cans got some attention, and now a lot more collectors are back in at $1,000."

Factor in the pop culture value, as blue collar treasures are increasingly regarded as art , and the horizon is bright for this working-man's collectible.

"I see younger generations continuing to get into this hobby more and more," said Matthews. "As long as we have to put gas in our cars and food in our mouths, people will collect this stuff."

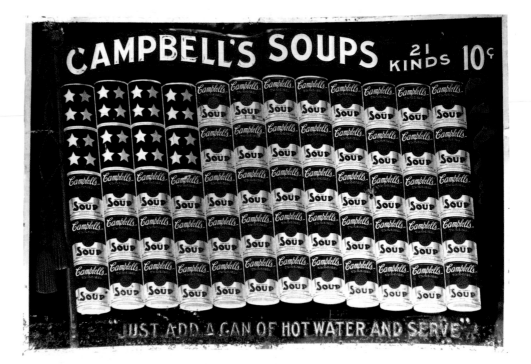

Showtime Auction Service

Campbell's Soup embossed tin sign, "21 Kinds" version, H.D. Beach Co., Coshocton, Ohio, four mounting holes in each corner, good condition, rust mostly on bottom area, 39 1/2" x 27 1/2". **$25,000-$75,000**

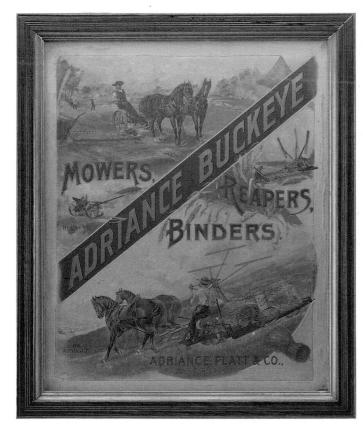

James D. Julia, Inc.

▲ *Mazda Lamps lithographed two-sided tin advertising display, wooden base has 11 electrified lightbulb sockets for displaying variety of lamps made by National Lamp Works Division of General Electric, base has gilt decals that state, "How are you fixed for lamps?," tin display panels near-excellent condition, original cord frayed, 27 1/4" wide x 13" high.* **$920**

James D. Julia, Inc.

Adriance, Platt & Co. Buckeye farm machinery lithographed poster with variety of vignettes illustrating mowers, reapers and binders at work in field. The company manufactured machinery under that name from 1866 until 1913, when it was bought by Moline Plow Co. **$1,066**

James D. Julia, Inc.

Twenty tin advertising items, companies from late 19th century to mid-20th century, selection includes three pot scrapers from Penn Stoves, Ward's Remedies, Sharples Cream Separator; three book ledgers from National Fire Insurance Co. and Guardian Assurance Co.; five die-cut De Laval Cream Separators cows and calves; two shoehorns for Princess and Shinola shoes; Nabisco letter opener; Patton's Sun Proof Paints match striker; Listerine toothbrush holder; Ceresota Flour advertising mirror; Calumet Baking Powder bank; and Armour's Vigoral dice set, varying sizes, good to very good condition. **$829**

James D. Julia, Inc.

Duke's Mixture porcelain door push, circa 1915, cobalt blue version with lithographic transfer process, captioned "The Roll of Fame," 4 1/4" wide x 8 1/2" high. The granulated or loose tobacco of Duke's Mixture became a popular medium- to low-priced brand of tobacco in the late 19th century. **$592**

Omaha Auction Center

New Haven wall clock advertising Valvoline Motor Oil, painted dial and tin panel on lower section of door, works, 17" wide x 42" high. **$650**

James D. Julia, Inc.

Three pre-war Lionel train advertising pieces and catalog, 1940, Manual of Lionel Instructions, foldout full-color brochure for 153 different gauge Lionel trains and accessories, full-color hardbound book, varying sizes. **$533**

James D. Julia, Inc.

Red Goose Shoes figural store displays, cast iron bank embossed on both sides with Red Goose Shoes name (4 1/2" high) and three chalkware displays, 4 1/2" high, 8" high, and 11 1/2" high. Red Goose Shoes was in operation from 1869 to 1911, when it was absorbed by another shoe manufacturer in a merger. It wasn't until 1904, during the St. Louis World's Fair, that red was added to the image of the goose, which was trademarked in 1906. **$414**

James D. Julia, Inc.

▲ *Tin candy displays, Life Saver counter display with embossed folding rear marquee, Chiclets three-tier wire shelf display, and three-tiered Life Saver counter display. Life Saver entered the market in 1912 with the introduction of the Pep O Mint flavor, but it wasn't until 1935 that the five-flavor roll pack was unveiled; Chiclets appeared on the scene in its original peppermint flavor in 1906.* **$474**

Morphy Auctions

▶ *Phoenix Pure Paint curved porcelain sign, circa 1910 to 1920, manufactured by Ingram-Richardson, rare, scarce, depicts young Native American admiring his application of war paints in hand mirror, excellent condition, small edge chips and two small surface chips/nicks near top of sign, old clear coat, slightly out of true curve at bottom due to past stress on piece, 20 1/4" x 12".* **$15,600**

James D. Julia, Inc.

◀ *Lewis Rye seldom seen reverse on glass advertising clock from Strauss Pritz & Co. of Cincinnati (1875-1918), promoting Lewis 66 rye whiskey, reverse lettering includes areas of silver foil highlights, scalloped perimeter edge has a few chips, clock mechanism not working and may not be original, 12" diameter.* **$1,185**

Bonhams

Pair of hand-painted signs, Nantucket and Clams, American, early 20th century, Nantucket hand-painted with black lettering and red and green borders, Clams hand-painted in black and white, "Dressed" or "Undressed" for 5¢ each, 15" x 35 1/2". **$687**

Morphy Auctions

Lorelei Beer poster from Helena, Montana, 1900 to 1910, matted and framed under glass, light wear, random light surface marks or rubs, minimal soiling or wear, excellent-plus condition, 27 x 21 1/2" framed. **$3,900**

James D. Julia, Inc.

▶ *Dooling Bros. post-war tether car and advertisement, two-piece die-cast maroon enamel car with Dooling Bros. tires, period advertisement shows car with knee action front suspension, full ball bearings at each wheel, original price of $45, 17" long. Dooling Bros. tether cars were available to the public from the late 1930s to the late 1950s and sparked the tether car racing hobby.* **$1,244**

Morphy Auctions

Frazer Axle Grease self-framed tin sign, lithography by The Meek Co., Coshocton, Ohio, mounted over original wooden rear framework, excellent-plus condition, faintly ambered tone and minor surface scratches and marks, black light inspection reveals traces of minute border area expert restoration, 25 1/2" x 37 3/4". **$4,800**

Showtime Auction Service

The Commonwealth Distillery reverse glass sign, Lexington, Kentucky, depicting factory scene with inlaid mother-of-pearl, American Railway and Commerce Advertising Co., Cincinnati, very good condition, some lifting around perimeter, original tiger-striped oak frame, 43 1/2" x 31 1/2" overall. **$15,000-$25,000**

Eveready Flashlights tin cutout flange, circa 1920s, rare, very good to excellent condition, light crazing and soiling with small marks, edge nicks, shallow crimp in bottom sign, 10" x 10 1/4". **$6,000**

Yellow Kid county fair full-size salesman's sample poster, produced by Donaldson Litho Co. of Cincinnati, "Me an Me Yellow Kid is goin to the Tenth Annual 1897 Tioga County Fair at Umpsville. Wat do you tink of dat. Come an' see me and me' folks!," bulk pricing information for poster displayed at bottom indicates 25 posters cost $1.75 while 1,000 copies could be purchased for $20, vertical tear at bottom, 28 1/2" wide x 42 1/2" high. **$575**

James D. Julia, Inc.

Mobiloil Pegasus porcelain signs, two identical one-sided die-cut Pegasus signs, one facing left, other facing right, no manufacturing marks or year of production information, 3 1/2" long. Red Pegasus logo started appearing on Mobiloil products in 1911. **$592**

James D. Julia, Inc.

De Laval Cream Separators tin sign, one of the most desirable of all De Laval advertising items, depicts farm family processing cream from fresh milk, includes mark at bottom "The H.D. Beach Co., Coshocton, O.," sign shows light mottling in lighter areas, 25 1/2" diameter. The De Laval cream separator was invented in Sweden in 1878. **$4,147**

Morphy Auctions

Boston Locomotive Works builder's print, dated 1858, full margins, not trimmed, cleaned and mounted on acid-free heavy paper, four-color stone chromolithograph in black, red, green, and brown: "Boston Locomotive Works / Formerly Hinkley & Drury, No. 380 Harrison Avenue, Boston, Mass. / J.H Bufford's Litho – 313 Washn. St. Boston," "Drawn by R.C. Wright," "Holmes Hinkley Pres.," and "O.W. Bayley, Principal of Mechanical Department"; excellent condition, archival-repaired 6" tear at left edge and archival-repaired 2" tear at right edge, wood acid burn in background on right side, custom mat, Foam-Core backer board, frame, 29 1/2" x 42". **$4,200**

Americana

By Noah Fleisher

T he collecting field of historical Americana is so broad and diverse, so infinitely parsible, that entering it with confidence can prove a daunting task to both neophyte and experienced collectors alike. For the purposes of this introduction and this section, we've chosen to keep the focus on historical Americana as it applies to key figures in American history – presidents, politicians and assorted prominent thinkers; artifacts that are, in this writer's estimation, easily identifiable and therefore easier to relate to.

For Tom Slater, formerly of Slater's Americana and currently the director of Americana Auctions at Heritage Auctions, there is a conflict in the Americana market currently between an abundance of good material and a lack of erudition among "new" collectors.

Noah Fleisher

"You don't see new collectors getting into Americana the same way that you see it in categories like comics or sports, which are more in-tune with current pop culture trends," he said. "New generations in these types of categories are being created by osmosis, inheriting their love of collecting – and often parts of their collections – from family members and friends, being influenced by what's clicking in the popular imagination and current public zeitgeist. When you get into more esoteric subjects, they require more commitment to develop working knowledge to be an effective collector."

Key trends in historical Americana are easy to read: signatures, ephemera, and artifacts directly related to early popular American figures – think George Washington, Thomas Jefferson and Abe Lincoln – will always command solid prices; a search through the prices realized anywhere from independent dealers, eBay and a variety of auction houses will confirm this.

A little deeper into the market, and a little further into the roster of historical figures from whom artifacts can be found and acquired, and the story begins to play out a little differently.

"At a certain point and a certain level, you can't tell what's going to sell or at what price," said Slater. "In the last five to 10 years we've seen a somewhat weaker, leaner and meaner stripe of collector emerge than we used to have. They're simply more discriminating now in how they spend and what they spend on. They're looking for the right pieces and the right values."

While that might necessarily mean that you're going to have serious competition and have to dig a little deeper into your bank account to acquire that George Washington compass, book plate or signed letter, it also means that – if you do your homework and know what you are looking for – there is tremendous opportunity.

NOAH FLEISHER received his Bachelor of Fine Arts degree from New York University and brings more than a decade of newspaper, magazine, book, antiques and art experience to his position as Public Relations Director of Heritage Auctions, one of the country's foremost auction houses. He is the former editor of *Antique Trader, New England Antiques Journal* and *Northeast Antiques Journal*, is the author of *Warman's Modern Furniture*, and has been a longtime contributor to *Warman's Antiques and Collectibles*.

Sotheby's

Reuben Sikes Revolutionary War powder horn, Nov. 6, 1775, inscribed, "REUBEN: SIKES: HIS: HORN: MADE: BY: HIM: IN: ROCKSBURY: CAMP: NOVM: Ye: 6: 1775," 15" long. **$10,000**

"Quality is key at whatever level you are collecting," said Slater. "Spend on quality, on what you love, and you'll never be disappointed with how much you enjoy something, what you pay for it or what it may bring when the time comes to sell it."

In terms of the broader market, there's a plethora of good material available, which may be a factor in the current price pause seen. The fact is that – though Americans love their history and have always actively coveted pieces of it – there is relatively little "brand new" material being found, unlike newer specialty categories like comics, sports and entertainment memorabilia. Twenty and 30 years ago, dealers and collectors alike were pulling significant pieces of historical Americana out of shows, shacks, attics and yard sales at incredible rates. Those glory days are done and picked over for the most part. You're not likely to find a William Stone lithograph of The Declaration of Independence in a garage sale anymore.

"When you get into areas where there aren't constantly new discoveries being made, you need to have a much deeper sense of going on," said Slater. "It seems there's a direct relationship between that and attracting new people, which is not necessarily the case in Americana right now."

Say you have done your research, read your history and have developed a fascination with the Founding Fathers. You'll have to look far and wide, and spend a pretty penny, for pieces that come directly from Washington, Adams, Jefferson, Madison or Monroe. If you know what you like, however, there is plenty to be had from those that surrounded those men, their families and their lives. Context becomes all-important, as does understanding what you're looking at when it looks at you.

"Attention spans are decreasing, which means fewer collectors are willing to undergo what can be a long and steep learning curve," said Slater. "The categories that are thriving are the ones that are more easily accessible. That, however, means greater competition down the line. For collectors willing to put in the time, the reward can be significant."

What is influencing the market right now? An aging collector population, for one, and a somewhat jaded collector base at the very top of the market, for another.

Collectors that have been in the market for 40 or 50 years are aging out of active buying and are selling off their core collections. In many cases they simply have no heirs that are following

Skinner, Inc., www.skinnerinc.com

Ephemera and two pamphlets including seven printed documents, late 18th and early 19th century, filled out and signed by hand, mostly judgments of court in Suffolk County; and approximately eight written indictments, same period, with tears, stains, and other faults, together with Address to Citizens of Massachusetts, on the Causes and Remedy of our National Distresses, by a Fellow Sufferer; Boston: printed at Repertory Office, 1808, 13 pps., octavo, stab-sewn, stained, holes with loss; and John Quincy Adams' "An Address Delivered at the Request of the Committee of Arrangements for Celebrating the Anniversary of Independence," Cambridge: University Press, by Hilliard and Metcalf, 1821, 34 pps., octavo, in blue paper wraps, water stained throughout, contemporary signatures on title. **$200**

them in their pursuit or they have too much in their collections for their families to efficiently and profitably disperse.

We are also living in a much more disposable culture these days. As subsequent generations come of age in an increasingly paperless society, less appreciation is created for the material culture of the past. A prime is example is the current cooling in the realm of John F. Kennedy and Camelot collecting.

"Kennedy had been a touchstone for almost three generations," said Slater. "Now those collectors, those people who were born and raised on Camelot and its attendant glamour, are aging out and the polish has faded somewhat on the perspective of those times. This has created, simultaneously, a leveling off in prices for JFK memorabilia and a golden opportunity for smart collectors willing to hold on to something for the duration. If history has taught us anything, it's that eventually everything comes around again and is eventually seen as being new."

Do your homework, learn what's scarce and what's in demand and know a treasure when it's in front of you. Be patient with your purchases and diligent in your pursuit of the material you want. Right now your purchases – be they with a major auction house or a reputable dealer – may have an air more of stewardship than of investment, but the popularity of television shows and books on antiques and collectibles points to an increased awareness in the potential value of historical material, if not its inherent value simply as a piece of history.

"That wider recognition of value that seems to be dawning in the general public is the thing that is encouraging," said Slater. "The smart, educated collector that will endure the vagaries of the market will, in time, realize the full potential not only of their investment but also of their passion for the subject."

Pictorial hooked rug, circa 1930, brown, beige, green, and black thread with figures of rooster and pig, inscribed "A Worthy Wife is She Who Can / Fry a Chicken, Boil a Ham / Gracious Hostess Tho You Be / Lose Not Your Practicality," 31" x 48". **$2,500**

History of the Indian Tribes of North America *by Thomas L. McKenney and James Hall. With biographical sketches and anecdotes of principal chiefs, with 120 portraits, from Indian Gallery in Department of War at Washington. Philadelphia: Daniel Rice and James G. Clark (1842-1844). Three volumes, folio, 20" x 14 1/4", 120 hand-colored lithographed plates.* **$81,250**

Sotheby's

Molded copper standing Massasoit weathervane, J. Harris & Co., Boston, third quarter 19th century, full-length, three-dimensional standing figure of Massasoit (chief of Wampanaog Indians, a tribe that lived in what is now southern Massachusetts) with feather headdress, in traditional attire, beads around neck, holding arrow with cast-iron head in right hand and bow in left hand, arm outstretched, quiver across back, molded foliage bush to Indians' rear, standing on copper rod, retains much original gilding, with natural highlights of verdigris patination overall, 31" high. **$122,500**

Sotheby's

Magnalia Christi Americana: Or, the Ecclesiastical History of New-England, from Its First Planting in the Year 1620, unto the Year of Our Lord, 1698, *by Cotton Mather. In seven books. London: printed for Thomas Parkhurst, 1702, folio, 12 3/8" x 7 3/4". Double-page map of New England and New York, final leaf of publisher's advertisements.* **$6,875**

Figures of African-American lawyer and wife by Lavinia Walker, 1876, beeswax, wool thread, silk, satin, wool tweed, and glass; paper affixed to back states, "These negros, a lawyer and his wife, were made of beeswax. They were created by great aunt Lavinia Walker, Grandma Babbitt's sister, in 1876, and presented to Nora Campau Babbitt, now Nora Babbitt Harsh, singing teacher in Chicago, at Fine Arts Bldg. 410 So. Michigan Ave. These negros were made in Ypsilanti, Michigan." Each 7" to 8" high, 11 1/4" x 10 3/8" overall. **$7,500**

The Illustrated Text Volume and the Rare Atlas for Perhaps the Greatest Work on the Grand Canyon, *Clarence Dutton. Tertiary History of the Grand Canon District. Washington: Government Printing Office, 1882. [2], xiv, 264 pages, illustrated with two chromolithograph views after W.H. Holmes, four heliotype plates after photographs, 36 other plates including color double-page map, several other double-page charts.* **$3,000**

Federal carved and giltwood eagle-form wall bracket, 19th century, 11 1/2" high x 18" wide x 10" deep. **$8,750**

Sotheby's

Painted tinware house lantern, dated 1863, pitched roof fitted with "chimney" and carrying handle, body with glass door and punched geometric decoration, painted green and bearing the word "Union" four times, with stars; 18" high. **$7,500**

Sotheby's

Rare salt-glazed stoneware jug decorated with cobalt blue-filled full-bodied incised bird on branch, attributed to Jonathan Fenton or Frederick Carpenter, Boston, 1793-1796, ovoid form with tooled neck impressed with numeral 2, front with large incised bird perched on scrolling leafage with stylized feathers, 14 1/2". **$18,750**

Sotheby's

Bronze figure of Benjamin Franklin after a model by Jean-Antoine Houdon, second half of 19th century, mounted on rouge griotte marble base; bronze bust of George Washington, possibly France, early 20th century, mounted on red marble plinth with bronze plaque engraved "First in war, First in peace, / and / First in the hearts of his Countrymen"; Washington bust 10" high, Franklin 16 1/4" high. **$5,625**

Dessert plate from White House service ordered by President James K. Polk in 1846; American shield with 27 stars, center decorated with yellow roses, 9". **$20,315**

Heritage Auctions

George Bissell, bronze bust of Abraham Lincoln, impressed on rear of plinth "Geo. E. Bissell, Sc. Copyright Gorham Co. Founders," 18". **$8,962**

Heritage Auctions

"Up at Bat," oil on Masonite, Aug. 10, 1940 Saturday Evening Post cover by Douglass Crockwell (American, 1904-1968), signed lower left, 30 x 23 1/2". **$40,625**

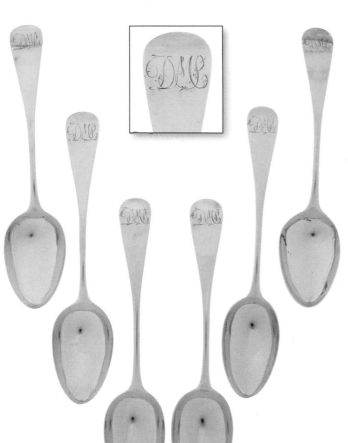

Heritage Auctions

Set of six silver tablespoons made by American patriot Paul Revere, circa 1790-1800, all with down-turned rounded-end handle with engraved monogram "DMS" in foliate script for prominent colonial Massachusetts couple Daniel Sargent and Mary Turner Sargent; each spoon with slightly more than 2 oz. silver, bowls approximately 1 3/4" at widest point; each bowl approximately 3" long, 8 3/4" long overall, "Revere" marked on back. **$83,650**

Heritage Auctions

▼ *Rare ferrotype jugate of Major Gen. George B. McClellan and George H. Pendleton, who ran for president and vice president, respectively, on Democratic ticket in 1864; defeated by Abraham Lincoln and Andrew Johnson; jugate with original red and blue paint highlights and T-bar pin attachment on verso, 1 1/4" x 1 1/4".* **$29,825**

Sotheby's

African-American circus scene, circa 1930, oil on canvas, 19 1/4" x 25 1/2". **$7,500**

Sotheby's

Henry Fullerton, 19th century portrait of George Washington, ink on paper, signed H. Fullerton, painter; depicts Washington in military uniform, fort flying American flag in left background, eglomise mat, back signed Jn A Trumbull, 3" diameter. **$2,125**

Sotheby's

Anna Claypoole Peale (American, 1781-1878), self-portrait, painted circa 1815, oil on canvas, in original frame, 30" x 24". **$11,250**

Sotheby's

Rare needlework sampler, Bathesheba Copeland (1796-1842), Northampton, Massachusetts, dated 1805, worked in silk threads and crinkled silk floss on linen, with satin, couched satin, split, outline and cross-stitches, inscribed "Then o divine benevolence be nigh/O teach me how to live & how to die Bathsheba/Copeland aged 9, 13" x 13 1/4". **$6,250**

Heritage Auctions

William Henry Harrison museum piece silk bandanna, possibly best-designed Harrison bandanna of 1840, borders with series of cider barrels and drinking mugs with slogan "Harrison and Reform," extreme outer border with repeat of slogan "W. H. Harrison Hero of Tippecanoe," central vignette of Harrison log cabin, farmhouse, candidate himself, and two veterans who have come to visit; 28 1/2" x 24 1/2. **$14,340**

Heritage Auctions

Trademark suit and string bow tie of American icon Colonel Harland Sanders, founder of Kentucky Fried Chicken (KFC). **$21,510**

Women's suffrage folk art doll figurine holding flag of North American Women's Suffrage Association, felt and cotton sash reads, "Don't Tread on Me," metal, fabric, paper, wood and human hair, 15" high. **$2,032**

Theodore Roosevelt safari beer stein, tapered form, depicts Roosevelt riding atop elephant and repelling lion's attack, lions throughout landscape, including handle and lid finial, other beasts perched in trees, three inscriptions all in German, one encircling bottom translates to "By Day and By Night, the Hunter Watches," 13" high and 1 1/2 liters. **$1,553**

ART

American Art

By Noah Fleisher

American art is an area that is ever-evolving, as diverse and varied as the country that inspires it. It is as easy to pin down as mercury. What's selling these days and for what price? Does that even matter when it comes to your American art?

There are names at the top of the art market that are "American" by necessity of their name, but they transcend and bring tens of millions of dollars at auction – Andy Warhol, Jackson Pollock, Robert Rauschenberg, Cy Twombly, to name a few – but those aren't necessarily our concern.

When you summit Everest, there is room for only one or two people; that is some rarified air that high. Canvases that bring eight and nine figures do not play into everyday reality, so let's not concern ourselves with those.

Brian Roughton is a 30-year veteran of the art business, the founder of Roughton Galleries and currently the Director of Fine Art at Heritage Auctions. He has made a career of furthering American art and artists, has sold to museums, universities, private collectors, and corporations. He knows the nuances of American art, past and present, as few of us possibly could.

I asked him for an overview of the American art market as it applies to work that ranges in price from $5,000 to $5 million.

Like the best experts do, he took a moment to correct my characterization before answering.

Noah Fleisher

"I disagree with the words 'art market,'" he said, "because paintings are unique and have intrinsic value rather that extrinsic value, like stocks, currency, etc. The best answer is that, concerning traditional, historical, genre, and impressionist paintings – unless they are 10s, or coming from a private, well-known collection, sales are weak. There's a rise in popularity for WPA, post-war modernist, and important high-end contemporary paintings. The new generation of collector is not interested in the traditional American school."

Roughton's assessment points to relative strengths and weaknesses exhibited at auction houses and galleries across the spectrum, with the main strength being shown at auction, and the possible deals and steals they can represent, and the struggle among dealers to gain significant foothold against the large scale buying opportunities auctions offer.

Within that context, then, is the market strong? Weak? Improving? And where, currently, are the best buying opportunities?

"Things continue to improve for auctions, I don't see that changing too quickly," Roughton said. "Keep in mind, though, that the market is cyclical and will, eventually, change so that the best opportunity is buying what was previously popular but weak today, meaning historical, traditional genre and impressionist paintings. I also suggest buying works on paper – watercolors, drawings, etc. – by important American artists."

NOAH FLEISHER received his Bachelor of Fine Arts degree from New York University and brings more than a decade of newspaper, magazine, book, antiques and art experience to his position as Public Relations Director of Heritage Auctions, one of the country's foremost auction houses. He is the former editor of *Antique Trader, New England Antiques Journal* and *Northeast Antiques Journal*, is the author of *Warman's Modern Furniture*, and has been a longtime contributor to *Warman's Antiques and Collectibles*.

The definition of "important" shifts greatly style to style and region to region, as borne out by prices realized at auctions across the country. Roughton points to several areas in particular that represent solid buying opportunities right now: post-war modernist art, WPA artists, important modern and contemporary paintings, drawings and sculpture.

"Illustrators, too, have been showing enormous growth of late," he added.

This is a good point, as many names traditionally associated with only illustration art – J.C. Leyendecker, Tom Lovell, Gil Elvgren, Rolph Armstrong, Douglas Crockwell – have been seeing their "real" paintings sell for very solid prices, well into six figures in some cases. This is partially due to the fact that illustration art has made real inroads into "fine art" in the last four years and partially due to the fact that, simply put, these are just good paintings. When collectors can get past their traditional ideas of what constitutes fine art – which they seem to be doing, at auction, at least – then the world of illustration and illustrators shows that these are some good artists who produced some brilliant work.

There is also a marked rise in the market for regional painters, especially painters from Southwestern and Western schools in Texas, New Mexico, California and well beyond. Painters from established areas in the northeast – Hudson River Valley, Cape Cod, New England – are very well-established. Look west and you may well find a gold mine.

Rising prices for the best individual regional artists show the trend is real. Overall totals for prices realized at auction at houses like Heritage and Coeur D'Aline saw record years in 2012 and 2013, with many artists previously relegated to "regional" status suddenly seeing significant upticks in interest and price. It's not unheard of anymore, in fact, to have an artist – someone like Texas painters Julian Onderdonk and Olin Travis – make the crossover from "Texas" painters to just "American" painters and to have their work appear in plain old "American fine art" auctions.

With so much information, then, and a rapidly shifting market, does this make it a good time to start buying art?

"It's always good to be cautiously buying important works, considered 10s on a scale of 1 to 10, when they are not in vogue," said Roughton. "I always feel that a person should buy and collect what they like. Art was never meant as an investment."

He's absolutely right, as most of us know or have been taught.

Heritage Auctions

Sam Francis (American, 1923-1994), "Untitled (69-008)," 1969, acrylic on paper, 43" x 31", signed and dated verso. **$65,500**

All the same, look closely for good buys in the genres that he mentions above as not having the spotlight right now: historical paintings, traditional genre and impressionist paintings, works on paper – watercolors, drawings – by important American artists.

If you're experienced and knowledgeable, then the market is ready and waiting.

What if you're just getting into it, though? What is the best way to go about building a collection?

"Visit galleries, museums, stay away from trends, ask questions, attend auctions, research what you like to find lesser known artists from a school of art that you have a particular interest in collecting," said Roughton. "When you find something that you have a serious interest in buying, take a breath and think about it overnight. It will more than likely be there tomorrow."

Heritage Auctions

▶ *Julian Onderdonk (American, 1882-1922), "Bluebonnets at Sunrise," oil on board, 13 1/2" x 9 1/2", signed lower right: Julian Onderdonk.* **$65,725**

Heritage Auctions

▼ *Charles Marion Russell (American, 1864-1926), "Kickover of Morning Coffee Pot," 1896, watercolor on paper, 19" x 28", signed and dated lower left: CM Russell / 1896 (with artist's cipher).* **$482,500**

Josef Albers (American, 1888-1976), "Study for Homage to the Square: Stucco Setting," 1958, oil on board, 29 1/2" x 29 1/2", initialed and dated lower right; titled, signed, dated and inscribed in ink on reverse. **$262,900**

Frederic Sackrider Remington (American, 1861-1909), "Apache Signal Fire," circa 1891, oil en grisaille on canvas, 34" x 24", signed lower right: Remington. **$262,900**

Heritage Auctions

▲ *John Frederick Kensett (American 1816 - 1872), "Scene near Greeley, Colorado," circa 1870-1872, oil on canvas, 36" x 60". Kensett was the most influential member of the second generation Hudson River School painters.* **$191,200**

Heritage Auctions

Joseph Christian Leyendecker (American, 1874-1951), "Honeymoon," The Saturday Evening Post cover, July 17, 1926, oil on canvas, 28.25" x 21.25", monogrammed lower right. This Leyendecker was a wedding gift from the artist to a family friend on her wedding day in 1932. **$194,500**

Heritage Auctions

Olin Travis (American, 1888-1975), "The Bay at Rockport," circa 1950, oil on canvas board, 12" x 16", titled and signed verso: The Bay at Rockport / by Olin Travis. **$8,963**

Heritage Auctions

▶ *Howard Chandler Christy (American, 1872-1952), "Nymphs in Summer," 1946, oil on canvas, 60.5" x 72", signed lower left. Commissioned from the artist by Commander Oliver Colvin, New York.* **$179,250**

Heritage Auctions

▼ *Martin Johnson Heade (American, 1819-1904), "Cherokee Roses in a Glass Vase," circa 1883-1888, oil on canvas, 19" x 12", signed lower right: M.J. Heade. Heade painted Cherokee roses (Rosa laevigata) for 12 (1883-1895) of the last 20 years of his artistic career (1883-1904).* **$170,500**

Heritage Auctions

▲ *Joseph Henry Sharp (American 1859-1953), "Winter at Crow Reservation, Montana," 1905, oil on canvas, 16 1/4" x 24 1/4", signed and dated lower right.* **$155,350**

Heritage Auctions

Grandma Moses (American, 1860-1961), "The Old Checkered House in Cambridge Valley," 1943, oil on Masonite, 21 3/4" x 29 3/4", signed lower center: MOSES.; also titled "The Old Checkered House in Cambridge Valley," dated 1943 and numbered 466 on original Grandma Moses label affixed verso. The Old Checkered House in Cambridge Valley derives from one of Grandma Moses's most famous series of a historic inn on the Cambridge Turnpike in Washington County near her childhood home. **$134,500**

Heritage Auctions

Roy Lichtenstein (American, 1923-1997), "The assimiboins attacking a blackfoot village at fort mckenzies - 28 august 1833," circa 1951, oil on canvas, 18" x 24", signed lower right. **$95,600**

Heritage Auctions

Walt Kuhn (American 1877 - 1949), "Untitled (Still Life)," 1932, oil on panel, 18 5/8" x 21 1/2", signed and dated at lower right, Walt Kuhn 1932. In addition to the images of circus performers for which he is best known, the 20h century American modernist also produced still lifes and landscapes in a vivid, highly plastic style. **$92,613**

Heritage Auctions

Maxfield Parrish (American, 1870-1966), "Sheep Pasture, Cornish, New Hampshire," 1936, oil on panel, 25" x 30", signed and dated lower right: Maxfield Parrish 1936, inscribed verso: Sheep Pasture / Cornish: New Hampshire / Maxfield Parrish / 1936 / M.P. Jr. No. 79. **$74,500**

Heritage Auctions

John Marin (American, 1870-1953), "Shapes—Colors, Delaware Country, Pa.," 1916, watercolor on card stock, 16 1/4" x 19 1/4", signed and dated lower right: Marin 16. **$41,825**

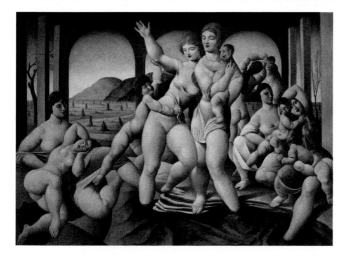

Heritage Auctions

Lorser Feitelson (American, 1898-1978), "Bathers," 1923, oil on canvas, 44 1/2" x 60", signed lower left: Feitelson 1923, inscribed canvas verso: FEITELSON / 59 RUE REAUMOR / PARIS / 1923. Feitelson co-founded Post-Surrealism with Helen Lundeberg and was also the supervisor of murals for the New Deal's Federal Art project from 1937-1943. **$38,838**

Heritage Auctions

▶ *Guy Carleton Wiggins (American, 1883-1962), "The Empire State Building, Winter," oil on canvas board, 12" x 9", signed lower left: Guy Wiggins; titled and signed verso: The Empire State Building / Winter / Guy Wiggins NA.* **$44,813**

Heritage Auctions

▼ *Edward Henry Potthast (American, 1857-1927), "Children at the Shore," oil on canvas, 24" x 30", signed lower left: E Potthast. Beloved by audiences from the 19th century through the present for his vibrant, sunlit depictions of carefree beachgoers enjoying leisurely holidays on the coast, Edward Potthast is considered one of the most prominent of the American Impressionists.* **$242,500**

Heritage Auctions

◄ *Paul Calle (American, b. 1928), "Mountain Monarch," 1976, pencil on paper, 37 1/2" x 27 1/2", signed and dated lower right: Paul Calle 1976. From the Hogan Family Collection.* **$25,000**

Heritage Auctions

▼ *Edna Reindel (American, 1894-1990), "The Bull Fight," circa 1936, oil on canvas, 25" x 30 1/4", signed upper left: Reindel.* **$35,000**

▲ *Frederick Judd Waugh (American, 1861-1940), "Sunset," oil on canvas, 24 1/2" x 50", signed lower right: WAUGH. From the Jean and Graham Devoe Williford Charitable Trust.* **$23,750**

▶ *Everett Spruce (1908-2002), "The Night Watchman," 1941, oil on canvas, 25" x 28 1/4", signed lower right: Spruce. This important historic painting was exhibited at the Museum of Modern Art in 1942.* **$22,705**

Edward Emerson Simmons (American, 1852-1931), "Winter Twilight on the Charles River," oil on canvas, 13 1/4" x 21 1/2", signed lower right: Edward E. Simmons. Simmons was a member of the Ten American Painters, who, as a group, seceded from the Society of American Artists. **$27,500**

Emile Albert Gruppe (American, 1896-1978), "Busy Harbor," Gloucester, circa 1945, oil on canvas, 30" x 25", signed lower right: Emile A Gruppe. **$17,500**

Ivan Gregorovitch Olinsky (American, 1878-1962), "The Song," 1916, oil on canvas, 36" x 32", signed and dated upper left: Ivan G. Olinsky / 1916. **$20,000**

Maurice Braun (American, 1877-1941), "Cumulous Clouds and California Trees," oil on canvas, 26" x 30", signed lower left: Maurice Braun. **$18,750**

Heritage Auctions

David Bates (American, b. 1952), "Crab Line," 1989, oil on board, 21 1/2" x 17 1/2", signed and dated lower right: Bates 89.
$17,500

Heritage Auctions

John Philip Falter (American, 1910-1982), "Saturday Night at the Longhorn," 1976, oil on canvas, 30" x 40", signed and dated lower left: John Falter '76; titled, signed and dated verso: Saturday Night at the Longhorn / John Falter 1976. From The Hogan Family Collection.
$16,250

Heritage Auctions

Bror Alexander Utter (American, 1913-1993), "Vessels and Fish," 1953, oil on canvas, 24" x 30", signed and dated lower right: Bror Utter 11'53. **$15,625**

Dickson Reeder (American, 1912-1970), "Portrait of Joe Harris," circa 1938-1939, oil on canvas, 26" x 17". **$10,755**

▼ *Frank Reaugh (American, 1860-1945), "Untitled," pastel on grit paper, 4 1/2" x 8 1/2", signed lower right: F. Reaugh. Born in 1860, Reaugh was an artist who devoted a great deal of his artistic skills to impressionistic depictions of West Texas and its legendary longhorns and is often referred to as the "Dean of Texas Artists."* **$8,963**

Tom Lea (American, 1907-2001), "Santa Elena Canyon, Big Bend," 1994, pastel on paper, 25 1/4" x 19 1/4", signed and dated lower left: Tom Lea / 94. **$7,648**

Ila Mae McAfee (American, 1897-1995), "Golden Clouds," oil on artists' board, 13" x 16", signed lower left: Ila McAfree, inscribed verso: "Golden Clouds." **$7,500**

Peter Hurd (American, 1904-1984), "Pennsylvania Landscape," circa 1928, oil on canvas laid on board, 16" x 20", signed lower left: Peter Hurd, inscribed verso: Peter Hurd / circa 1928? / painted at Chadford, PA / while studying with N.C. Wyeth. **$7,500**

Harry Shokler (American, 1896-1978), "The Town Pump (Small Town Activity)," 1921, oil on canvas, 18" x 22", signed and dated lower right: H Shokler / 21. **$7,500**

Deforrest Hale Judd (American, 1916-1992), "Ghost Town," 1954, oil on Masonite, 24" x 36", signed and dated lower right: Deforrest Judd 54. **$7,170**

Eric Sloane (American, 1905-1985), "Barn on the Hillside," oil on Masonite, 24 1/2" x 29", signed and inscribed lower right: To Brass / Bugle / Eric Sloane. **$5,860**

Heritage Auctions

Herman Dudley Murphy (American, 1867-1945), "Low Tide," oil on canvasboard, 10" x 14", signed, titled, and priced verso: Herman Dudley Murphy, Winchester, Mass / Low Tide / $125; monogrammed lower edge left of center. **$5,313**

Heritage Auctions

▶ *Jon Flaming (American, b. 1962), "Abandoned Silos," oil on Masonite, 24" x 36", monogrammed and signed lower left: Jon Flaming.* **$4,780**

Heritage Auctions

▼ *Clementine Hunter (American, 1886-1988), "Saturday Night at the Honkey Tonk," oil on board, 16" x 24", initialed lower right: CH.* **$5,078**

Heritage Auctions

Rockwell Kent (American, 1882-1971), "Adirondack Landscape," oil on panel, 12" x 16", signed lower right: Rockwell Kent, inscribed lower left: To our dear friend, Larissa -- S & R. **$15,535**

Heritage Auctions

Thomas Hart Benton (American, 1889-1975), "Train Out West," circa 1951, ink, sepia wash, and pencil on buff paper, 8 7/8" x 11 7/8", signed lower right in ink: Benton. **$9,560**

Heritage Auctions

▲ *Mel Ramos (American, b. 1935), "Georgia Peach," 1964, oil on canvas, 18 1/2" x 15 1/2", signed, titled and inscribed verso.* **$158,500**

Heritage Auctions

▲ *Maynard Dixon (American, 1875-1946), "Modern Man and Woman," 1934, gouache on paper, 28" x 25", signed and dated lower left: Maynard Dixon / 1934. This watercolor is a preliminary work for one of eight original panels created for the Rotunda Dome of the Palace of Fine Arts in San Francisco.* **$23,900**

Heritage Auctions

▼ *Wolf Kahn, (American, b. 1927), "Early Spring in New Jersey," 1976, oil on canvas, 18" x 30", signed lower right: W. Kahn, dated and titled on stretcher verso: 1976 Early Spring in NJ, numbered and dated verso: #49 1976.* **$13,145**

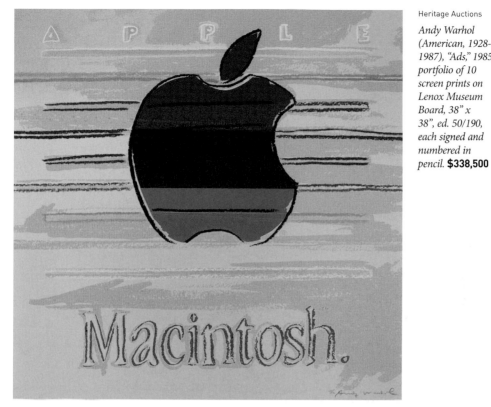

Andy Warhol (American, 1928-1987), "Ads," 1985, portfolio of 10 screen prints on Lenox Museum Board, 38" x 38", ed. 50/190, each signed and numbered in pencil. **$338,500**

Ed Ruscha (American, b. 1937), "Rustic Pines," 1967, gunpowder on paper, 13 1/4" x 21 3/4", signed and dated lower left: Ed Ruscha 1967 and noted lower right: gp. **$290,500**

Original Comic and Comic Strip Art

By Noah Fleisher

O riginal comic book and comic strip art is a market that's driven in large part by nostalgia," according to Todd Hignite, vice president of Heritage Auctions and a leading authority on the market for comic art. "You have collectors that buy it because they love it, because it takes them to a specific place and time in their lives."

Hignite is quick to relate, however, that the market for original book and strip art is undergoing something of a change in recent years, that the art is performing different functions, and a new generation of buyers is entering the market at the very moment that another generation is starting to get out.

The result?

"You have a group of younger buyers, in their 40s and 50s, who have always wanted the comic books they've seen growing up," said Hignite. "The early Spider-Man, X-Men, Fantastic Four, Hulk comics. Only now they see that the original art from these books is available. Suddenly they don't have to have just one of the copies of a book that is out there, they can actually get the original art. It's largely focused on Silver Age comic books."

Noah Fleisher

At the same time, the older generation of collectors – the ones that completed their comic book pursuits decades ago, graduating to the pursuit of the original Golden Age art from the books they grew up on – are beginning to liquidate their collections and slow down their purchasing. This has created relatively predictable prices across Golden Age comic art, anywhere from $100 up to $100,000 and beyond for the truly iconic cover art of DC greats like Joe Kubert, Jerry Robinson, Jack Kirby, and Mac Raboy.

As an aside, the Holy Grails of Golden Age comic art would easily be the covers for Action Comics #1 or Detective Comics #27, the first appearances of Superman and Batman, respectively. That artwork, along with all the art from those books, is considered to have disappeared long ago.

One of the most interesting things to consider when looking at this shift toward higher prices for Silver Age and even Modern Age work is to look at the sheer magnitude of the prices realized for the work of Silver Age and especially Modern masters – see the $400K+ paid for the Dark Knight Splash Page, the $657,250 for Todd McFarlane's original cover art for 1990's Spider-Man #328, or the $155,350 paid for Jack Kirby's iconic 1960s Silver Surfer page from Fantastic Four #55.

"These are prices that were unthinkable a decade ago, or even five years ago," said Hignite. "Now, however, for a variety of reasons, key artwork that is little more than 20 years old is steadily

NOAH FLEISHER received his Bachelor of Fine Arts degree from New York University and brings more than a decade of newspaper, magazine, book, antiques and art experience to his position as Public Relations Director of Heritage Auctions, one of the country's foremost auction houses. He is the former editor of *Antique Trader, New England Antiques Journal* and *Northeast Antiques Journal*, is the author of *Warman's Modern Furniture*, and has been a longtime contributor to *Warman's Antiques and Collectibles*.

commanding six figures at auction while regular pages, which you could pick up for a song a few years back, are routinely bringing a few hundred apiece. It's a very good return."

The shift is generational, in one sense, but also symbolic in another. The collectors coming into money and time to gather the Modern and Silver Age material right now are making a statement with their collecting. The great pieces of the 1970s, 1980s and 1990s are among the last pieces of comic art done the old fashioned way: with black and white drawings, penciled, inked and colored on board and sent to a press for printing. Digital technology has taken over the business of comic art, so the choicest nuggets from what could be the last great age of original hand-drawn comic art are commanding prices that, more and more, are in line with traditional fine art.

What about original comic strip art? What has the market brought in recent years for the masters of the daily, and what has the decline of the newspaper done to collectors and prices?

"There are certain names that are evergreen original comic strip art – all the big guys of the heyday of daily and Sunday strips," said Hignite. "Names like Charles Schulz, Gary Larson, George Herriman, Hal Foster, Winsor McCay, and Alex Raymond, they've consistently drawn strong prices and look to continue doing so."

What does that mean in the rest of the market? What about the masses of other strips from the 1920s to the 1990s? Looking at prices at auction over the last several years, it seems to mean that there are a lot of opportunities for those titles, along with their contemporaries, for the collectors whose fancy they tickle. In other words:

"In original comic strip art, unless you're spending $5,000 to $50,000 on one of the top names," said Hignite, "you should buy it because you love it and it appeals to you. If you want to live with it, then it's the right piece, at whatever level you're buying."

Which opens up another avenue for original strip art – as well as interior page original art from more general and mid-run comic books – that of original comic art as design.

"Bought, framed and hung, the original art from daily strips and comics is more and more appealing for the sheer design elements they bring," said Hignite. "They're great conversation pieces, yet they aren't so big or ostentatious that they dominate a room. We see more and more that these original pieces are being acquired at very fair prices and used to very good effect hung on a wall."

So where can you find prime examples of original

Heritage Auctions

Bil Keane, "The Family Circus" daily comic strip dated 5-11-67 (Register and Tribune Syndicate, 1967), excellent condition, 8" x 9 1/2", 11" x 14" matted. **$215**

comic strip and book art? At any reputable dealer, at any reputable auction house, and at almost any reputable antiques and/or collectibles show. The operative word here is "reputable," which means doing your homework, not being afraid to ask questions and buying with confidence once you are sure what piece you want and what price you are willing to spend.

"Always do your research," said Hignite. "You may pull a gem out of a dusty bin at an antiques festival or you may pounce on an overlooked treasure for nothing in an auction. The thing is to recognize the opportunity and to be ready and willing when it comes."

Heritage Auctions

Joe Simon (American, b. 1913), hero line-up group portrait illustration (undated), ink on illustration board, very good condition, 19 1/2" x 17 1/2". From the Joe Simon Estate. **$1,374**

Heritage Auctions

▶ *Joe Simon (American, b. 1913), Captain America "Last Man Standing" color illustration (1998), mixed media on illustration board, signed lower right, very good condition, 10 1/2" x 16 1/2". From the Joe Simon Estate.* **$550**

Heritage Auctions

Gerald Brom, "Hemah Angel" painting (1995), mixed media on board, signed and dated lower right by fantasy and "Magic: The Gathering" trading card game artist Brom, excellent condition, 7 1/4" x 11 1/4". Chemah (or Hemah) is one of the six angels of death, said to be the angel of wrath, fury and destruction who governs the death of domestic animals. **$860**

Heritage Auctions

▲ Milton Caniff, "Terry and the Pirates" daily comic strip dated 12-7-42 (News Syndicate, 1942), very good condition, overall paper aging, fold between panels two and three, 21 1/2" x 5". **$568**

Curt Swan (American, 1920-1996), Dick Giordano, and Frank McLaughlin, Superman #275, page 23 (DC, 1974), signed by Swan in last panel, very good condition, tape stains in margins, tape attaching title logo, overall paper aging, 10" x 15". **$478**

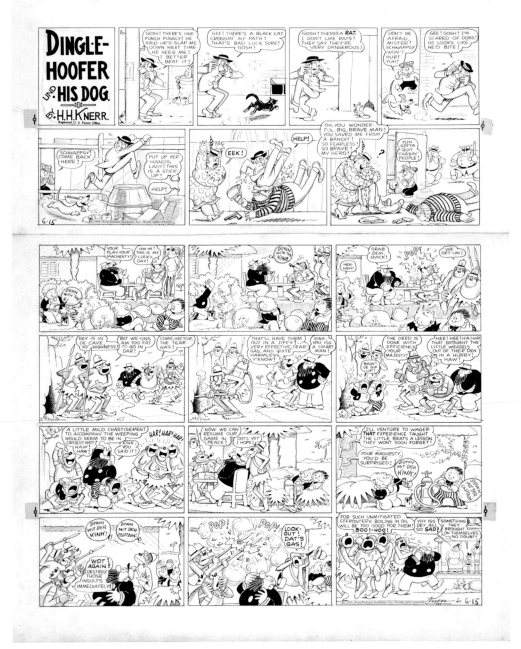

Harold Knerr, "Katzenjammer Kids" Sunday comic strip with matching "Dinglehoofer and his Dog" Adolph Topper original art dated 6-15-41 (King Features, 1941), excellent condition, combined image area 17" x 22". **$3,107**

Heritage Auctions

Irv Novick and Murphy Anderson, The Flash #201, page 11 (DC, 1970), from Robert Kanigher's "The Million-Dollar Dream," excellent condition, 10" x 15". **$448**

Heritage Auctions

◄ *Sal Buscema, Spectacular Spider-Man #197, page 31 (Marvel, 1993), final-page splash from the story "Power Play!," several missing text box paste-ups, art in very good condition, 10" x 15".* **$956**

Heritage Auctions

▼ *Chester Gould, "Dick Tracy" daily comic strip group dated June 24, 1960 and June 25, 1960 (Chicago Tribune, 1960), two consecutive 1960 strips focusing on the murder of Li'l Halakahiki's parents in Hawaii, excellent condition, matted together, 28" x 20" overall, each strip approximately 16 1/2" x 5".* **$275**

▲ *Jose Luis, "Salinas Cisco Kid" daily comic strip dated 3-19-66 (King Features, 1966), signed by artist in last panel, yellowing glue areas where old Zipatone film has slipped off, art in very good condition, 20" x 5 3/4".* **$418**

◄ *Ramona Fradon, The Brave and the Bold #66 cover art re-creation (undated), signed at lower right, excellent condition, 11 1/4" x 16 1/2". Fradon was inducted into the Comic Book Hall of Fame in 2006.* **$553**

▼ *Walt Kelly, "Pogo" daily comic strip dated 2-6-61 (Hall Syndicate, 1961), very good condition with light soiling, 18 1/2" x 5 1/4".* **$478**

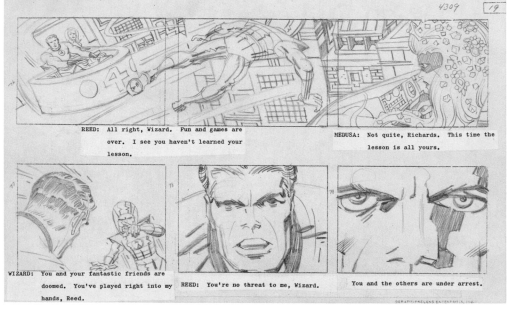

Heritage Auctions

Jack Kirby (American, 1917-1994), Fantastic Four "The Frightful Four" storyboard #19 (DePatie-Freleng, 1978), graphite on paper, excellent condition, crease in upper right corner, approximately 13" x 7". **$1,076**

Heritage Auctions

Floyd Gottfredson, "Mickey Mouse" daily comic strip dated 8-25-34 (King Features, 1934), early pie-eyed Mickey Mouse daily, "Walt Disney" signature on strip itself and another just above strip, neither signing by Disney himself, ink and blue pencil on board, excellent condition, 26 1/2" x 5 3/4", professionally matted to 32" x 10" overall. **$10,158**

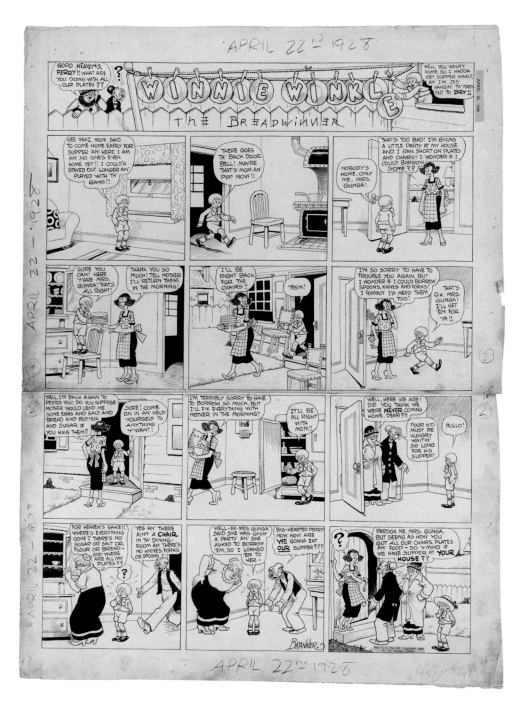

Heritage Auctions

Martin Branner, "Winnie Winkle" Sunday original art dated April 22, 1928 (Chicago Tribune, 1928), very good condition, 19" x 26". **$508**

Heritage Auctions

John Buscema and Alfredo Alcala, The Savage Sword of Conan #20, page 11 (Marvel, 1977), from "The Slithering Shadow," signed in upper left margin, excellent condition, 10 1/2" x 15". **$4,780**

Heritage Auctions

Bob Larkin, Crazy #19 preliminary King Kong cover art (Marvel, 1975), watercolor, includes original concept drawing by Stan Lee and two other concept drawings rendered in marker, each in very good to excellent condition, drawings on 8 1/2" x 11" paper, watercolor on 8 3/4" x 11 1/2" illustration board.
$1,135

Heritage Auctions

Herb Trimpe and Sal Buscema, The Incredible Hulk #136, title page 1 (Marvel, 1971), opener for Roy Thomas' Moby Dick adaptation, "Klaatu the Behemoth From Beyond Space!," very good condition, production process stains, 10" x 14. **$1,793**

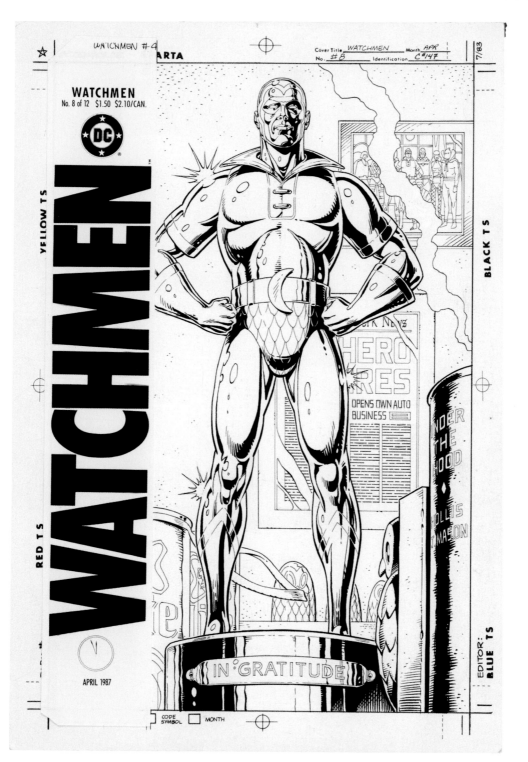

Heritage Auctions

Dave Gibbons, Watchmen #8, "Statuette of Nite Owl I" cover art (DC, 1987), for eighth Watchmen chapter, "Old Ghosts," excellent condition, 10" x 15". From the Shamus Modern Masterworks Collection. **$31,070**

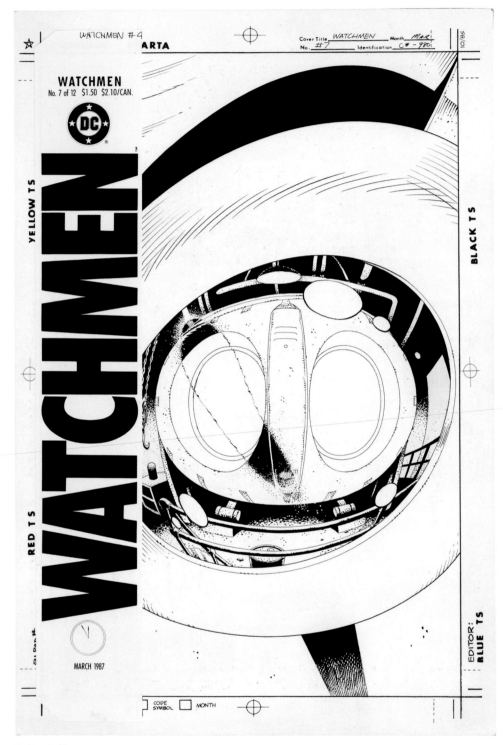

Heritage Auctions

Dave Gibbons, Watchmen #7, Nite Owl's Hovercraft cover art (DC, 1987), for seventh Watchmen chapter, "A Brother to Dragons," excellent condition, 10" x 15". From the Shamus Modern Masterworks Collection. **$38,838**

Heritage Auctions

Murphy Anderson (American, b. 1926), Justice League of America #14 cover art, first JLA appearance of the Atom (DC, 1962), ink and graphite on DC/Sparta Bristol board, includes copy of Justice League of America #14, excellent condition, minor staining, 12 1/2" x 18 1/2". **$44,813**

Heritage Auctions

Al Capp, "Li'l Abner" Sunday comic strip dated 12-31-50 (United Feature Syndicate, 1950), ink, graphite, and blue pencil on four strips of Bristol board taped together, art in good condition, combined image area 19" x 21 3/4". **$837**

Heritage Auctions

Roy Crane, "Captain Easy" Sunday comic strip, hand-colored original art dated Dec. 9, 1934 (NEA Services, 1934), ink on Bristol board affixed to backing sheet of cardboard, watercolor added, possibly by Crane himself, overall good condition with numerous tears, edge wear, and tanning, 20 1/2" x 27 1/2". **$3,585**

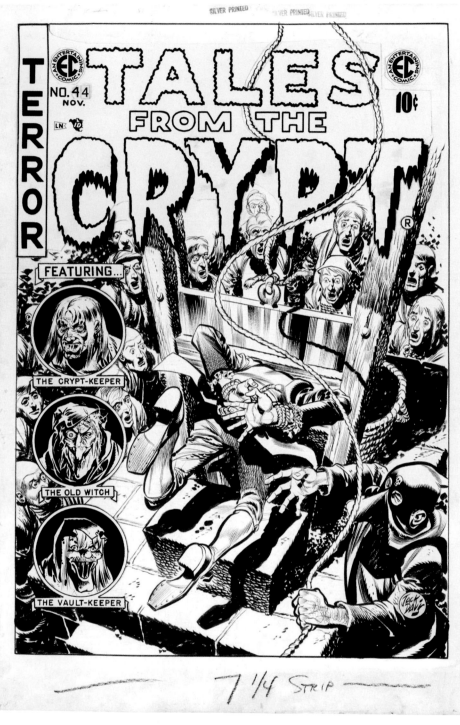

Heritage Auctions

Jack Davis, Tales From the Crypt #44, cover art (EC, 1954), "The Sliceman Cometh," ink on Bristol board, excellent condition, handling wear along outer borders, 13 1/2" x 19 1/2". **$44,813**

Jim Davis (American, b. 1945), "Garfield" daily comic strip dated 8-5-78 (United Feature Syndicate, 1978), very early daily, dated less than two months after strip's June 19, 1978 debut, ink and Zipatone shading film on Bristol board, excellent condition, 14" x 4", matted to 17 1/2" x 7 1/4" overall. **$1,912**

Hal Foster (Canadian-American, 1892-1982), "Prince Valiant" Sir Gawain Sunday comic strip #170 panel art dated May 12, 1940 (King Features, 1940), inscribed and signed by Foster, panel spotlights Sir Gawain, very good condition, 9" x 10 3/4" overall. **$837**

Dan DeCarlo, Humorama comic gag panel by longtime Archie Comics artist, circa 1950s, with hand-written caption that reads, "Now there's a dress design that's guaranteed to cut your cleaning bill in half!," ink, gray wash, and white paint on illustration board, very good condition, 9" x 12". **$657**

Bud Counihan, "Betty Boop" daily comic strip dated 11-10-34 (King Features, 1934), from first year of strip, very good condition, pinholes outside image area, pieces of tape on back, 20" x 4 3/4". **$1,793**

Heritage Auctions

Al Feldstein (American, b. 1925), Weird Science #6 cover art (EC, 1951), bizarre vision of mist-shrouded planet up-close, courtesy of series editor Feldstein, India and red ink, excellent condition, logo and type stats are recent replacements, scattered stains along bottom of image area and in outer borders, 13 1/2" x 19 1/2". From the Jerry Weist Collection. **$20,315**

Heritage Auctions

Frank Frazetta (American, 1928-2010), Vampirella #5 cover painting titled "Cornered" (Warren Publishing, 1970), Frazetta's second cover ever to appear on the Vampirella title, oil on masonite, signed lower left, excellent condition, 16" x 24" overall. In Frazetta's May 10, 2010 obituary, The New York Times *noted, "Frazetta helped define comic book and fantasy heroes like Conan, Tarzan, and John Carter of Mars. His signature images were of strikingly fierce, hard-bodied heroes and bosomy, callipygian damsels."* **$286,800**

Fine Art

F ine art, created for aesthetic purposes and judged by its beauty rather than its utility, includes original painting and sculpture, drawing, watercolor, and graphics. It is appreciated primarily for its imaginative, aesthetic, or intellectual content.

Today's fine art market is a global one, currently estimated to be worth $56.5 billion. After being dominated by Chinese and Asian buyers in 2010 and 2011, the 2012 fine art market recorded the entrance of major buyers from Russia and the Middle East.

Fine art remains a solid investment as well. Christie's, the world's largest seller of fine artworks, recorded record sales in 2012. Edvard Munch's "The Scream" sold for $120 million in May 2012, the priciest artwork ever sold at auction.

The Coeur d'Alene Art Auction

Richard Schmid (b. 1934), "White Roses" (1967), oil on canvas, signed lower right, 30" x 24". **$17,550**

Skinner, Inc.; www.skinnerinc.com

▲ *Marc Chagall (Russian/French, 1887-1985), "Village à l'âne Rouge" (1984), color lithograph on paper, edition of 50 (Mourlot, 1025), signed "Marc Chagall" in pencil lower right, numbered "38/50" in pencil lower left, image size 10 7/8" x 13 1/2", framed.* **$6,000**

Bonhams

◄ *Sergei Bongart (Russian/American, 1918-1985), "Still Life With Sunflowers in a Vase," oil on board, signed "Sergei Bongart" upper right, 40" x 30".* **$11,875**

The Coëur d'Alene Art Auction

▲ *Antoine Blanchard (1910-1988), "Paris, Notre Dame at les Bouquinistes," oil on canvas, signed lower right, 18" x 22".* **$14,040**

Pook & Pook, Inc.

▲ *Melissa Strawser (American, 20th century), copper sculpture of waterstrider, 18 1/2" high x 45" wide x 31" long.* **$652**

Pook & Pook, Inc.

▼ *Walter Emerson Baum (American, 1884-1956), oil on board, winter landscape, signed lower left, 18" x 22".* **$4,977**

Pook & Pook, Inc.

Elihu Vedder (American/Italian, 1836-1923), "Lion of the Nile," charcoal, initialed lower left and dated 1888, 10 1/2" x 19 1/4". **$7,110**

Skinner, Inc.; www.skinnerinc.com

Jules Louis Machard (French, 1839-1900), "Meditation," oil on canvas, signed "Jules Machard" lower right, identified on presentation plaque, lined, scattered retouch, craquelure, 40" x 30", framed. **$6,000**

Ludwig Thiersch (German, 1825-1909), "Elegant Couple Sketching and Reading by a Lake," oil on canvas, signed and dated "L. Thiersch 1874" lower left, small repaired tear to center corresponding to patch reinforcement on reverse, small tear to background in lower left quadrant, craquelure, minor paint losses, mild surface grime, 32 3/4" x 48 7/8", framed. **$15,600**

Guy Carleton Wiggins (American, 1883-1962), "Near Gloucester," oil on academy board, signed "Guy C. Wiggins" lower right, titled and signed on reverse, minor losses upper right, craquelure, 12" x 16", framed. **$7,800**

Short-horned bull sculpture, American School, 19th century, inscribed "by Frank Moscow" on base, fully carved walnut figure on relief-carved base with vegetation and rocky terrain, very good condition, minor shrinkage cracks on base, 18 1/2" high x 8" wide x 24" long. Provenance: It is reported that the sculpture was carved by Moscow, a decorative wood carver employed by a couple to ornament furniture purchased for their new home in Stoughton, Massachusetts, circa 1928. Moscow gave the couple the carving of the bull in thanks for letting him stay at their home during the time it took to ornament their furniture. **$4,200**

Skinner, Inc.; www.skinnerinc.com

Heinrich Hirt (German, 1841-1902), "The Little Peasant Girl," oil on canvas, signed and inscribed "H. Hirt/ München" lower left, retouch, minor paint loss, craquelure, 14 1/2" x 11 1/4", framed. **$2,460**

Pook & Pook, Inc.

Joan Miró (French/ Spanish, 1893-1983), "Femme Dans la Nuit," watercolor and crayon on paper, signed lower right, 9 3/4" x 11 3/4". Provenance: Ross L. Peacock Gallery, New York, 1974; certificate of authenticity from Daniel LeLong, Director of Gallery Maeght, Paris, Maeght's number 11944. **$33,180**

Bonhams

◄ *Granville Redmond (American, 1871-1935), "Rocky Point, Laguna," oil on canvas, signed "Granville Redmond" lower right, 22" x 30", 29" x 37" overall.* **$96,100**

Skinner, Inc.; www.skinnerinc.com

▼ *Louis Icart (French, 1888-1950), "Fanny & Cat" (1926), color etching with aquatint and stencil coloring on paper, signed "Louis Icart" in pencil lower right, numbered "207" in pencil lower left, identified within plate, artist's dry stamp lower left, light toning, faint water stains in right margin, plate size 14 3/8" x 13 1/8", framed.* **$1,020**

Bonhams

▲ *Granville Redmond (American, 1871-1935), "Moonrise Beyond the Bay" (1903), oil on canvas, signed and dated "G. Redmond '03-" lower left, 26" x 48", 32 1/2" x 54 1/2" overall.* **$80,500**

Bonhams

Francisco Zúñiga (1912-1998), "Dolores Sentada," (1977), lithograph in colors on wove paper, signed in pencil, dated and numbered 13/50 (plus five artist's proofs), published by Brewster Editions, New York, with blindstamp of printer, Kryon, S.A., Mexico D.F., sheet 30 1/4" x 22". **$1,500**

Bonhams

Raphael Soyer (American, 1899-1987), "Untitled" (portrait of a woman smoking), oil on canvas, signed "RAPHAEL SOYER" lower left, 12 1/2" x 16 1/4". **$5,625**

Bonhams

Eduardo Kingman (Ecuadorian, 1913-1997), "Untitled" (1973), gouache heightened with white on paper, signed and dated "Kingman 73" lower right, 18 7/8" x 26". **$1,875**

Bonhams

Antoine Blanchard (French, 1910-1988), "Théâtre des Variétés," oil on canvas, signed "Antoine Blanchard" lower right, 13" x 18". **$7,500**

The Coeur d'Alene Art Auction

Edouard Cortes (1882-1969), "Les Grands Boulevards, Theatre du Gymnase," oil on canvas, signed lower right, 18" x 21.5". **$32,175**

Pook & Pook, Inc.

Edmond Darch Lewis (American, 1835-1910), oil on canvas, landscape, signed lower left and dated 1870, 24" x 38". **$15,405**

The Coeur d'Alene Art Auction

Peder Severin Kroyer (1859-1909), "Autumn Forest at Skagen (Höstlandskap fi an Skagen)" (1908), oil on canvas, signed and dated lower left, 21.5" x 25.5". **$20,000**

Bonhams

▶ *Georges Braque (French, 1882-1963), "Les Fleurs Violets" (not in Vallier), circa 1960, etching and aquatint in colors on Arches paper, signed in pencil and numbered 164/200, with blindstamp of printer, Crommelynck, Paris, with full margins, framed, 18 3/4" x 11 1/2", sheet 26" x 19 1/2".* **$812**

Bonhams

Grant Wood (1891-1942), "Fruits" and "Wild Flowers," (1939), ("Fruits" shown) lithographs with hand-coloring on Rives paper, each signed in pencil, from editions of 250, published by Associated American Artists, New York, with full margins (2), 7 1/4" x 9 3/4"; 6 3/4" x 10", sheet 11 3/4" x 15 7/8"; 11 7/8" x 16". **$1,875**

Figural Bronzes

Bonhams

▶ *Frederic Remington (American, 1861-1909), "The Cheyenne," bronze, inscribed "copyright / Frederic Remington" on front side of base, "Roman Bronze Works" on back side of base, and "No. 84" on underside, 19" high.* **$80,500**

The Coeur d'Alene Art Auction

◀ *Charles M. Russell (1864-1926), "The Bucker and the Buckaroo," bronze, 15" high, stamped in base "C. M. Russell / Roman Bronze Works N-Y."* **$438,750**

A copy of a November 1989 letter from Rudy Wunderlich authenticating this as a lifetime cast accompanied the lot. Wunderlich states, "This letter will confirm that I am familiar with and have examined the original casting of Charles M. Russell's bronze entitled The Bucker and Buckeroo. This was first copyrighted in 1911 under the name of The Weaver. It is a scarce and very fine bronze by Russell, and according to Mrs. Russell's records there were only 19 casts made of this, many of them posthumous or after Russell's death. The one that you have, is, in my opinion, a lifetime cast, made by Roman Bronze Works N.Y. ... and is in excellent condition."

Bonhams

Harry Jackson (American, 1924-2011), "Trapper," bronze with brown patina on marble base, inscribed "© Harry Jackson 1970" and "33." on base, 22 1/2" high with base. **$7,500**

The Coeur d'Alene Art Auction

Earle E. Heikka (1910-1941), "Trophy Hunters," bronze, no. 27/30, 15.75" x 49.25" x 6.875". **$10,530**

The Coeur d'Alene Art Auction

Harry Jackson (1924-2011), "Cowboy's Meditation" (1964), bronze, stamped in base "Harry Jackson 64 10, P.," 22.5" high. **$21,060**

Harry Jackson wrote, "For the first time with these figures [Gunsil and Cowboy's Meditation] I had the irresistible urge to paint them, starting with the oldest of them, the man on horseback, the most complete of them [Cowboy's Meditation]. I wanted to get him in fine focus, I didn't want him to be the same color as his horse, or his vest the same color as his shirt, or his white forehead with the sun kept off by his hat the same color as his weathered face. I wanted to use everything I could in order to articulate and bear witness to this man. All of a sudden I had to state everything there, to construct the three dimensions and put in the shade and light, to create a fully realized form. I really cared about every bit. Every detail was like a universe in and of itself."

The Coeur d'Alene Art Auction

Harry Jackson (1924-2011), "Frontiersman" (cast 1972), bronze, no. 14/20, painted, stamped in base "© Harry Jackson 1965 / 14.P. / Pennsylvania Woodsman," with notarized Certificate of Origin indicating sculpture was cast at Wyoming Foundry Studio in Camaiore, Italy, 20" high. **$23,400**

◀ *Démetre H. Chiparus (Romanian, 1886-1947), "Three Girls Under an Umbrella," gilt bronze and ivory, circa 1925, signed CHIPARUS, impressed 5757, on onyx base, 7 3/4" high.* **$10,000**

Démetre Chiparus (Romanian/French, 1886-1947), "Scarf Dancer," bronze, breche violette marble base, signed "D.H. (Demetre Haralamb) Chiparus," 26.5" high x 6.25" square base. **$32,670**

G.I. Joe limited edition bronze statue #1/30 (Hasbro, 1994), rare variant version of G.I. Joe statue originally offered in resin, with added marble base, painted detail, excellent condition, approximately 14.5" high. **$388**

DuMouchelles

◀ *Démetre Chiparus (Romanian/French 1888-1950), "Starfish," bronze, signed on onyx base, 29" high.* **$6,150**

The Coeur d'Alene Art Auction

▼ *Richard Greeves (b. 1935), "Kickapoos" (May 22, 1804), bronze, stamped in base "Corps of Discovery 1804-1806 / Kickapoos, May 22nd 1804 / R. V. Greeves / 2003 20/30," 37" high.* **$12,870**

Elite Decorative Arts

▲ *Hans Keck (German, active circa 1920-1922), cold painted bronze and ivory figure depicting dancing woman standing on round plinth with three figural seated elephant feet with ivory tusks, mounted on green marble fitted base, signed "H. Keck fec." to round plinth, 12" high plus 1" base.* **$2,783**

Susanin's Auctioneers & Appraisers

◀ *A.C. Ladd, bronze figural group, 1916, 30" high.* **$1,216**

Bonhams

◄ *Démetre Chiparus (Romanian, 1886-1947), "Echo," enamel and gilt-bronze, carved ivory, marble, inscribed "Chiparus," 15 1/2"* high. **$11,250**

Bonhams

▼ *Ronnie Wells (American, b. 1944), "The Covey," bronze with polychrome patina, titled, signed, and numbered "The Covey by Wells 23/40" on base along with copyright insignia, 26 1/2" high.* **$625**

Bonhams

Démetre H. Chiparus (Romanian, 1886-1947, wk. 1914-1933), "Favorite," gilt-bronze and marble, signed in bronze "Chiparus" and numbered 1703, 14 1/4" high figure, 17 1/2" high overall. **$3,300**

Bonhams

Douglas Van Howd (American, b. 1935), "Texas Ranger," bronze with light brown patina on wooden base, inscribed "© Van Howd / 1/50" on left of base and "Texas Ranger" on front of base and on figure's chest, 45" high with base. **$2,000**

Bonhams

Démetre H. Chiparus (Romanian, 1886-1947), "Cleopatra," cold painted bronze, inscribed "D.H. Chiparus," plaque impressed "CLEOPATRE par D.H. Chiparus/ Laureate du Salon des Beaux-Arts," 9 1/2" high x 16 1/2" long. **$17,500**

Bonhams

◀ *French patinated bronze figure after model by Duchoiselle (French, 19th century), 12 1/2" high.* **$750**

Bonhams

▶ *French patinated bronze figure of dancer, Zingara, after model by Jean-Baptiste Clésinger (French, 1814-1883), late 19th century, inscribed "J. CLESINGER ROME 1858" and "F. BARBEDIENNE.FONDEUR," impressed "A. Collas Réduction Mécanique pastille," ink inscription to underside "34797 ga.," 22" high.* **$1,125**

Bonhams

Démetre H. Chiparus (Romanian, 1886-1947), "Clara," cold painted, parcel gilt and silvered bronze and carved ivory, onyx base, signed "Chiparus" in onyx, together with champlevé enamel and bronze mounted double column pedestal, sculpture 21 1/2" high x 28 1/2" long x 7 1/2" deep. **$98,500**

The Coeur d'Alene Art Auction

Bill Owen (b. 1942), "Sacking Out a Bronc" (1983), bronze, no. 25/45, stamped in base "© Bill Owen CA 25/45 1983," 33" high. **$8,190**

The Coeur d'Alene Art Auction

Kenneth Bunn (b. 1938), "Serengeti Lion" (2000), bronze, no. 8/35, stamped in base "©2000 / Bunn / 8/35," 19" high. **$9,945**

The Coeur d'Alene Art Auction

▲ *Cyrus Dallin (1861-1944), "Appeal to the Great Spirit," bronze, stamped in base "©CE Dallin 1913" (top), "Gorham Co Founders #203 9 x 9" (side), 9" high.* **$5,265**

Illustration Art

By Brent Frankenhoff and Maggie Thompson

Collectors, whether looking for a distinctive decoration for a living room or seeking a rewarding long-term investment, will find something to fit their fancy — and their budget — when they turn to illustration art.

Pieces of representational art — often, art that tells some sort of story — are produced in a variety of forms, each appealing in a different way. They are created as the source material for political cartoons, magazine covers, posters, story illustrations, comic books and strips, animated cartoons, calendars, and book jackets. They may be in color or in black and white. Collectible forms include:

Maggie Thompson & Brent Frankenhoff

• **Mass-market printed reproductions.** These can range from art prints and movie posters to engravings, clipped advertising art, and bookplates. While this may be the least-expensive art to hang on your wall, a few rare items can bring record prices.

• **Limited-run reproductions.** These range from signed, numbered lithographs to numbered prints.

• **Tangential items.** These are hard-to-define, oddball pieces. One example is printing plates (some in actual lead; some in plastic fused to lightweight metal) used by newspapers and comic-book printers to reproduce the art.

• **Unique original art.** These pieces have the widest range of all, from amateur sketches to finished paintings. The term "original art" includes color roughs produced by a painter as a preliminary test for a work to be produced, finished oil paintings, animation cels for commercials as well as feature films, and black-and-white inked pages of comic books and strips. They may be signed and identifiable or unsigned and generic.

Swann Galleries

Ludwig Bemelmans, "Madeleine," watercolor and ink, signed, 11" x 8 1/2". **$6,600**

"Illustration art" is often differentiated from "fine art," but its pop culture nature may increase the pool of would-be purchasers. Alberto Vargas (1896-1982) and Gil Elvgren (1914-1980) bring high prices for pin-up art; Norman Rockwell (1894-1978), James Montgomery Flagg (1877-1960), and J.C. Leyendecker (1874-1951) were masters of mainstream illustration; and Margaret Brundage (1900-1976) and Virgil Finlay (1914-1971) are highly regarded pulp artists.

MAGGIE THOMPSON was among the pioneering amateurs who formed the foundation in the 1960s of today's international anarchy of comic-book collecting. With her late husband, Don, she edited *Comics Buyer's Guide* and remains active as a collector and essayist. **BRENT FRANKENHOFF** is a lifelong collector and former editor of *Comic's Buyer's Guide*.

Swann Galleries

▲ *Thomas Ray, "Roast Beast,"* How the Grinch Stole Christmas, *pencil on paper, signed in pencil in full lower right, circa 1966, 10" x 12". Original illustration from the 1966 animated television production of Dr. Seuss's children's classic with Boris Karloff as the voice of the Grinch. Thomas Ray was a member of the animation team under the direction of Chuck Jones. Depicts the final triumphant banquet scene.* **$1,680**

Swann Galleries

◄ *Hilary Knight, illustration for* Eloise: The Business World, *pencil, crayon, and watercolor on paper, sight line, signed and dated [19]88, lower left, matted and framed, 12" x 10".* **$7,200**

Swann Galleries

Eleanor Campbell, "Dick and Jane," watercolor on thick card, maunscript production notes on recto margins and pencil notations on verso in unknown hand(s), some pinholes at upper edge, light smudging, 8 1/2" x 11". **$3,120**

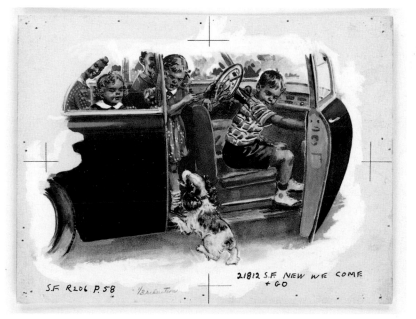

Swann Galleries

Eleanor Campbell, "Dick and Jane," original watercolor and whiteout on thick card, 1955, maunscript production notes on recto margins and publisher's rubberstamp on verso, some pinholes along margins not affecting image, 7 1/4" x 9 3/4". **$3,360**

Swann Galleries

Walt Disney Studios, "The Art of Skiing," hand-painted animation cel featuring Goofy from "The Art of Skiing," 1941, matted with affixed caption below, reading "Eyes should be kept to the front because objects sometimes appear with amazing suddenness," Courvoisier Galleries label and Disney Productions rubberstamp on verso, 9" x 7 1/2". **$1,200**

Swann Galleries

Walt Disney Studios, "Happy Birthday to Pooh," pen, ink, and watercolor, finished illustration possibly for the British edition of Disneyland Magazine, *7 1/2" x 11 1/4".* **$2,400**

Swann Galleries

Lawson Wood, advertisement for Ovaltine, pen and watercolor illustration showing group of Lawson's animals eyeing Ovaltine cups on tray held by elephant, signed lower left, printer's marks and comments around borders, marginal soiling and chipping, 12 1/2" x 15". **$1,680**

Swann Galleries

Michael Hague, "The Boy and the Velveteen Rabbit," watercolor illustration for The Velveteen Rabbit or How Toys Become Real, *signed lower left, matted and framed, New York: Holt, Rinehart and Winston, 1983, 14 3/4" x 23 1/2".* **$1,920**

Swann Galleries

Walt Disney Studios, "Grumpy," graphite and color pencil, sheet, animation drawing for Snow White and the Seven Dwarfs, *circa 1937, 10" x 12".* **$720**

Swann Galleries

*Denman Fink, "Gardeners Both,"
pen, ink, and pencil on illustration
board, signed and dated 1911 lower
right, magazine illustration for
Woman's Home Companion with
label on verso with title and dated
May 12, 1911, production notes in
pencil along margins, spotting and
finger-soiling outside image, 11" x
21 1/2".* **$960**

Swann Galleries

*James Thurber, "Rites of Spring,"
pen and ink with watercolor on
illustration board, drawing for
The New Yorker cover, signed
lower right, published as The New
Yorker cover on April 27, 1940,
14" x 9".* **$14,400**

Swann Galleries

*William E. Hill, society gents
ogling reclining woman, mixed
media, heightened with white,
signed lower left and dated
[19]14, matted and framed,
14 1/4" x 21 1/2".* Hill drew
the dust jacket art for the first
editions of F. Scott Fitzgerald's
This Side of Paradise *and*
Flappers and Philosophers. *His
work also appeared in* Life *and*
Puck *and in his own popular
weekly page of illustrations,
titled "Among Us Mortals," in
the Sunday* New York Tribune,
which ran in the 1920s. **$1,080**

Swann Galleries

*Constantin Alajalov, "Blithe Spirit,"
pencil and watercolor drawing for
poster and souvenir book for the
first American production of Noel
Coward's "Blithe Spirit," signed
lower right, 1941, 16" x 12 1/4".*
$2,880

Swann Galleries

James Thurber, "He Doesn't Believe a Single Word He's Read in the Past Ten Years," ink cartoon, image on tan paper, signed by Thurber, lower right, typed caption in window below image, framed in black plastic and matted, 4 1/4" x 7 1/2". **$10,200**

Swann Galleries

Charles Addams, Clifton Webb as Gulliver, watercolor and ink, cartoon illustration, signed lower right, 2" closed tear along lower right margin just into "C" of signature and similarly sized triangular portion excised from upper right corner not affecting image, 6 3/4" x 9 3/4". **$960**

The Little House in the Big Woods

Swann Galleries

Helen Sewell, two illustrations from Little House in the Big Woods: *pen and ink on paper, full page illustration showing Pa Ingalls as a boy in the big woods, 8 1/4" x 6 1/4; text vignette illustration showing Cousin Charlie jumping up and down on a nest of yellow-jackets, 4" x 3"; both with stamp on verso reading "Please return to/Harper & Brothers/Juvenile Department." Helen Sewell was the first person to illustrate Laura Ingalls Wilder's "Little House" series before Garth Williams.* **$2,400**

CALLING THE CLUB TO ORDER.

Swann Galleries

Thomas Nast, "Calling the Club to Order," watercolor and ink, signed and dated April 12, 1890, 16 1/4" x 13 1/4". **$660**

Swann Galleries

*Garth Williams,
"Stuart Little," two signed ink
drawings providing alternate techniques for
image appearing on chapter I heading of* Stuart Little
*by E. B. White, 5" x 6 1/4" images, including signature,
on wide-margined cream paper, some light marginal
creasing to first image, separate sheets with penciled
captions, signed by Williams, circa 1945.* **$16,800**

*Williams's first image is of the family with the parents,
the boy George, and cat Snowball looking down at Stuart
sleeping in his tiny bed with Williams's comment in pencil
in the lower corner, "Cat not good? Don't like boy's face?"
The second drawing is the same scene, but just of the
parents, drawn much older, without the boy and cat. The
comment on the separate sheet states, "Style Nº 2 lighter
drawing and people more comic."* Stuart Little *was White's
first book; for it, along with* Charlotte's Web, *he won the
Laura Ingalls Wilder medal in 1970.*

Swann Galleries

Leonard Leslie Brooke, "When it fell, there among its roots sat a goose, with feathers of pure gold," watercolor and ink illustration for The Golden Goose, *signed with initials lower left hand corner, London: Frederick Warne, 1905, 9 3/4" x 7 1/2".* **$1,800**

Swann Galleries

Ludwig Bemelmans, "Holiday House," watercolor, gouache, and ink wash on illustration board, published as Holiday Magazine *cover May 1951, with rubberstamp on verso, signed lower right, 27" x 21 1/2".* **$5,760**

Swann Galleries

▲ *Charles M. Schulz, "Peanuts," original three-tiered Sunday comic strip, pen, ink, and pencil on stiff paper; "Peanuts" logo pastedown, signed "Schulz" in final panel, dated March 1, 1953, some mild discoloration in margins, 16 3/4" x 23 3/4". This is an early strip featuring Charlie Brown and Patty (not to be confused with Peppermint Patty, who wouldn't be introduced by Schulz until years later). Patty was the only female character in the strip's earliest days, and the two characters appeared together in the first Peanuts strip. She would be seen less frequently in the ensuing years, making her last official appearance on April 11, 1976.* **$22,800**

Swann Galleries

◀ *Charles Addams, couple passing giant birdhouse, watercolor cartoon on illustration board, signed lower left, blank borders soiled, image clean, published in The New Yorker, Jan. 17, 1948, 16" x 13" on larger board.* **$6,000**

◀ *Ronald Searle, "Anatomy of an Antiquarian Bookseller," color lithograph showing Searle's insightful version of a bookseller, signed and dated 1967 lower right, one of 50 (?) copies, 26" x 19".* **$1,020**

▼ *Juan Carlos Barberis, "The Witch," gouache on illustration board, signed and dated "J.C. Barberis, N.Y. 29/10/59," 13" x 9 1/2".* **$360**

◀ *Ronald Searle, New York World's Fair, "Tower of Light," pen, ink, watercolor, and wash drawing on illustration board, full sheet, signed and dated 1964, lower left, 20" x 15".* **$3,840**

George Booth, "This meeting was called to order...," ink and wash on stiff paper for The New Yorker *cartoon,* The New Yorker *stamps on verso, signed "Booth" lower right and in full beneath caption, 10" x 9" on larger sheet.* **$960**

Dr. Seuss (Theodor Geisel), "A Pair of Llamas in Peru," pen, ink, and watercolor on board, inscribed and signed in pen, lower right, "For Hope Morris, That Llama Fancier - Dr. Seuss" with large ink and pencil study on verso, showing llamas, boy, rooster, and tile-roofed dwelling in background (marked "void"), professionally matted and framed with double-sided acrylic and gray wood to show both images, few scuffs to frame edges, very good condition, 9 1/2" x 8 3/4". **$21,600**

Wildlife Art

By Eric Bradley

Americans' love affair with wildlife art began long before there was a United States. Sir Walter Raleigh, planning his first expedition to the new world, requested artist John White to accompany the trip as a vital crewmate and fellow history maker. If he could show all of England the wonderful and profitable beasts and flowers to be found in the New World, Raleigh knew future trips would be all but certain. Images of flora and fauna equaled fame and fortune.

White's lifelike watercolors of brown pelicans, land crabs, and loggerhead turtles delivered beyond Raleigh's wildest dreams. Those early works from the late 1500s are the start of a genre of art uniquely American in subject, artistry, and political power. American wildlife art has inspired kings, presidents, and the public.

In the last 20 years, American wildlife art has established itself as a legitimate genre in both antique and postmodern art. A genre that had been taken for granted for so long has come into its own as a form of art both respectable and politically powerful. The market for wildlife art is surging. A single hand-colored engraving by John James Audubon, arguably the biggest name in American wildlife art, sold for $105,000 by the Neal Auction Co. while the Julius Bien reissue folio of Audubon's The Birds of America sold for $230,000.

Although Audubon's name has become synonymous with American wildlife (he portrayed some 2,000 birds and hundreds of animals and plants), his work was built on nearly 200 years'

Coeur d'Alene Art Auction

Brent Cotton (b. 1972), "The Refuge at Dawn" (2013), oil on canvas, signed lower right, 36" x 60". **$11,700**

According to the artist, "I witnessed this scene in January while I was deer hunting on a local waterfowl refuge near my home in western Montana. The early morning light shining through the mist and the ducks peacefully swimming made for a magical setting."

Coeur d'Alene Art Auction

Bob Kuhn (1920-2007), "Battle on the Burn – The Lion's Share," acrylic on board, 30" x 48". **$128,700**

worth of his predecessors' endeavors. The demand for wildlife art was solidified during the Age of Enlightenment, when collectors themselves funded expeditions for new discoveries.

"This was the age of discovery and enlightenment," said David Wagner, author of the groundbreaking book *American Wildlife Art* (Marquand Books, 2008). "A time when big science was interested in collecting and collecting information: data, words, pictures and numbers."

This pursuit sparked a tsunami of immigration that rushed to document all the unique living things to be found in the new world. Sadly, one price was to be paid by the creatures themselves, as in the case of the American passenger pigeon, of which Audubon himself marveled: "The air was literally filled with Pigeons; the light of noon-day was obscured as by an eclipse."

"The art certainly presented wildlife as a means to drive economic investment in the New World," Wagner said. "And art did play a role in the demise in what had been." Wagner's book documents for the first time the history and contemporary impact of American wildlife art. Its manuscript grew out of his 1992 PhD dissertation, and its 395 pages represents but one-third of his total research on the topic. He shows that up until the 1850s, wildlife art had largely been something of a pursuit for the wealthy.

In the 1850s cheaper printing methods made the art accessible to the middle class. Wildlife art became less about scholarly illustration and more about depicting the average hunting camp. That's when a 39-year-old New York publisher, Nathaniel Currier, hired his brother-in-law, James Ives, to launch a company advertised as "Print-Makers to the American People." At first the Currier & Ives Co. focused on sporting and hunting art in subscription form. The hardscrabble life of the early American was easing, and hunting and fishing took on less of an importance for survival than it did for sport and leisure.

In this era artists such as Arthur Fitzwilliam Tait (1819-1905), William Ranney (1813-1857) and William Harnett (1848-1892) celebrated the outdoors as a resource to be relished. One sculptor in particular, Edward Kemeys (1843-1907), has the distinction of being the first major figure in American wildlife art to be born in the United States. Kemeys found patrons for his sculptures of mountain lions for New York's Central Park and the iconic lions guarding the entry to Chicago's Art Institute.

By the dawn of the 20th century artist Carl Rungius (1869-1959) had begun honing a unique approach to depicting big game and sporting scenes. "After Audubon, who was larger than life, no one emerged to take his place," Wagner said. "There was a vacuum. Tait was hugely popular, as was Currier & Ives. With Rungius, his images had the subject of sportsmen but rendered from the perspective of an artist. America was just learning about Impressionism and Modernism. Rungius' paintings were large and he used color to achieve his Impressionism. It was chunkier and used different types of color."

The style of Louis Agassiz Fuertes, a contemporary of Rungius, is steeped in Audubon's scientific rendering with a mix of human-like emotions to his subjects. "His wood ducks almost smile at you in a folksy way. He wanted to know the inner self of the animal," Wagner said.

Rungius' and Fuertes' work modernized American wildlife painting and established it as a legitimate profession. It also created a standard of excellence throughout the 20th century, according to Wagner.

The 20th century exploded with a proliferation of wildlife art. From the National Wildlife Federation to the Federal Duck Stamp Competition, the oversupply of limited edition collectible prints to car companies naming products after the cougar, the mustang, and the ram, wildlife art touches every aspect of our collective modern popular culture.

By the late 20th century, painter Robert Bateman had become America's most influential living wildlife artist, Wagner said, because his aesthetic was purposefully integrated with ecological ideology and the enterprise of publishing. His painting "Mossy Branches – Spotted Owl" was released as a limited edition print in 1990 by Mill Pond Press. The edition of 4,500 prints sold out within a month of its release – during the height of an effort to preserve land in the Pacific Northwest to protect the endangered spotted owl.

What does the future of American wildlife art hold?

"I can make one prediction," Wagner said. "New heroes will jump out and will become icons in their own right," he said. "It won't be a one-shot phenomenon. It's going to be an artist with a whole body of work. Someone will come out and be the next James Audubon or Robert Bateman, someone with a signature style."

ERIC BRADLEY is public relations associate at Heritage Auctions, the world's third largest auction house. He is former editor of Antique Trader magazine and is the author of *Antique Trader 2013 Antiques and Collectibles Price Guide,* America's no. 1-selling guide to the antiques and collectibles market. An award-winning investigative journalist with a degree in economics, Bradley has written hundreds of articles about antiques and collectibles and has made several media appearances as an expert on the antiques market at MoneyShow San Francisco, on MSN Money, Nasdaq.com and on AdvisorOne.com. His work has received press from *The New York Times* and *The Philadelphia Inquirer.*

DAVID J. WAGNER is a leading wildlife art author, curator and lecturer. He organizes and promotes wildlife art exhibitions and educational programs to museums nationwide. Wagner received his PhD from the University of Minnesota and wrote his dissertation on American wildlife art, which served as the basis of his book, *American Wildlife Art.* He is the president of David J. Wagner, LLC, Milwaukee, which produces traveling exhibitions for museums throughout the United States and Canada.

Coeur d'Alene Art Auction

▲ *Bob Kuhn (1920-2007), "Tough Guys" (1989),*
acrylic on board, signed lower right, verso: signed
with title and date, 14 1/2" x 18 1/2". **$64,350**

Kuhn wrote, "Buffalo have a hard time not
looking menacing. They usually run from the
intruder, but not always, and that's what you
have to bear in mind during any confrontation.
Libby and I have twice been charged by ill-
tempered old bulls, unprovoked by us, but each
time we were on wheels. For anyone on foot,
the possibility of getting hurt is real. One of
those charging episodes afforded me the chance
to photograph a bull coming flat-out; it's as
dramatic a picture as any I've seen."

Swann Galleries

◄ *John James Audubon, "White-breasted Eagle,"*
Plate CXXVI, circa 1838, hand-colored engraved
plate from double elephant folio edition of
The Birds of America, on full sheet, 37" x 24".
$12,000

Coeur d'Alene Art Auction

Owen J. Gromme (1896-1991), "Pheasants," oil on canvas, signed lower left, 30" x 40". **$17,550**

Coeur d'Alene Art Auction

Edmund H. Osthaus (1858-1928), "Hunting Dogs," watercolor on paper, signed lower left, 15" x 21". **$22,230**

Coeur d'Alene Art Auction

Carl Rungius (1869-1959), "White Flag," etching on paper, signed lower right, 8" x 11". **$7,605**

Coeur d'Alene Art Auction

John Clymer (1907-1989), "Early Morning – White Tails and Tamarack," oil on board, signed lower right, label on verso: Grand Central Art Galleries, Inc., New York, New York, 20" x 30". **$23,400**

Coeur d'Alene Art Auction

John Banovich (b. 1964), "Approaching Masai" (2013), oil on canvas, signed and dated lower right, 44" x 32". **$64,350**

According to the artist, "No one likes having their afternoon catnaps interrupted...this male leopard has been disturbed by something in the distance. Masai and their cattle are fast approaching...a common story in a continent of over one billion people. There are fewer and fewer places for wild animals to find refuge. The human animal conflict has escalated to unprecedented levels, and the animal always loses in the end. I painted this cat in a pose as if he is being watched from below. It is an unusual position to paint, but I wanted to capture a moment as if the viewer were invisible to his intense, distant stare."

Coeur d'Alene Art Auction

Richard Friese (1854-1918), "Deer in a Forest Glade" (1912), oil on canvas, signed and dated lower right, 43" x 62 1/2". **$52,650**

Coeur d'Alene Art Auction

Hermann Herzog (1832-1932), "Elk Below the Glacier," oil on canvas, signed lower left, labels on verso: F. Weber & Co., Philadelphia; The Pittsburgh Art Co., 27" x 35". **$5,558**

Coeur d'Alene Art Auction

Luke Frazier (b. 1970), "North Country Grizzlies" (2013), oil on board, signed lower right, 30" x 36". **$22,230**

According to the artist, "Grizzly bears need a lot of area to roam, and there are still a few areas in North America [that] provide that habitat – Glacier National Park in Montana is one of them. Adult grizzlies, being at the top of the food chain, have little to fear from other wild creatures. In my opinion, sow grizzlies (momma bears) are the most dominant force in the wild. When they have cubs and food to protect, they are at their most dangerous. As the old saying goes, 'If momma isn't happy, ain't nobody happy.'"

Coeur d'Alene Art Auction

▲ *Robert Bateman (b. 1930), "Hoary Marmot" (1991), acrylic on board, signed and dated lower right, 12" x 24".* **$38,025**

Coeur d'Alene Art Auction

David Shepherd (b. 1931), "The Lagoon" (1990), oil on canvas, signed and dated lower right, 9" x 13". **$18,720**

Skinner, Inc.; www.skinnerinc.com

Frank Weston Benson (American, 1862-1951), "Yellowlegs," watercolor on paper, framed, signed and dated "F.W. Benson '2..." at lower right, 14 1/4" x 19 3/4". **$27,600**

Coeur d'Alene Art Auction

Thomas Hill (1829-1908), "Deer in a Thicket" (1892), oil on canvas, signed and dated lower left, 24" x 20". **$33,930**

Pook & Pook, Inc.

Pierre Jules Mene, bronze stag, signed on base, 13 1/2" high. **$1,304**

Skinner, Inc.; www.skinnerinc.com

Marguerite Kirmse (American, 1885-1954), "Flushed," etching on paper, framed, signed "Marguerite Kirmse" in pencil at lower right, titled in pencil at lower left, monogrammed within plate, 7 1/4" x 11 1/8". **$540**

Skinner, Inc.; www.skinnerinc.com

Roland Clark (American, 1874-1957), "Evening Flight," etching and drypoint on paper, framed, signed "Roland Clark" in pencil at lower right, 12" x 14 7/8". **$270**

Skinner, Inc.; www.skinnerinc.com

◄ *Solon Hannibal Borglum (American, 1868-1922), "Buffalo," bronze with green patina, integrated base, signed "S Borglum" in bronze base between back legs, 3 3/4" x 5" x 1 3/4".* **$2,040**

Pook & Pook, Inc.

▼*Richard Bishop, "Whistling Swan," pencil signed engraving, 11 3/4" x 14 1/2".* **$365**

Coeur d'Alene Art Auction

▼ *Harry Adamson (1916-2012), "Ballet – Black-Bellied Whistling Ducks" (1984), oil on canvas, signed and dated lower left, with framed limited edition print of this painting with remarque, artist's proof #1/30, 24" x 36".* **$14,040**

Coeur d'Alene Art Auction

Philip R. Goodwin (1881-1935), "Moose at Lake McDonald" (1910), oil on canvas, signed and dated lower right, 16" x 22". **$32,175**

Coeur d'Alene Art Auction

Harry Adamson (1916-2012), "Mallards," oil on canvas, signed lower left, 18" x 22". **$5,558**

Asian

Art and antiques from Asia have fascinated collectors for centuries because they are linked with the rich culture and fascinating history of the Far East. Their beauty, artistry and fine craftsmanship have lured collectors through the ages.

The category is vast and includes objects ranging from jade carvings to cloisonné to porcelain, the best known of these being porcelain.

Large quantities of porcelain have been made in China for export to America from the 1780s. A major source of this porcelain was Ching-te-Chen in the Kiangsi province, but the wares were also made elsewhere. The largest quantities were blue and white.

Prices for Asian antiques and art fluctuate considerably depending on age, condition, decoration, etc.

Bonhams

▲ *Pair of Chinese porcelain reticulated wedding lanterns in famille verte palette, late Ching dynasty, each hexagonal form with pierced panels enclosing foliate reserves, raised on separate conforming stand, inset with light, 12 1/4" high.* **$1,063**

Bonhams

◄ *Chinese export lacquer tea caddy, second quarter 19th century, shaped top with downswept sides over conforming case all-over decorated with figures in pavilion, interior fitted with two engraved pewter covered canisters, all on winged dragon feet, 5 1/2" high x 7 1/2" long.* **$1,000**

Bonhams

▲ *Satsuma porcelain vase, Meji period, decorated with figural cartouche including Samurai warriors and beauties, marked on underside "satsuma Hanrin-ga," 24 1/2" high.* **$875**

Elite Decorative Arts

▲ *Chinese yellow glazed footed and handled rectangular vessel with etched and slightly raised archaic beast design throughout, bottom holds etched Tongzhi reign mark, 6 3/8" high x 12 1/2" long x 8" deep.* **$4,719**

Elite Decorative Arts

▲ *Large antique Chinese Huanghuali wood scholar desk brush pot, circa Qing dynasty period, 18th/19th century, 9 1/4" high x 9 3/4" diameter.* **$6,353**

Elite Decorative Arts

◄ *Pair of Chinese hand-painted enameled porcelain square form vases, Qing dynasty period, 18th/19th century, depicting birds and flowers with urns to verso, sides having calligraphy poems and figural foo lion handles with rings, bottoms hold red seal marks, 16" high x 6 3/4" wide x 5 1/2" d.* **$1,331**

Bonhams

◀ *Gold and black lacquered portable writing chest, 19th century, decorated on roiro exterior in gold and silver hiramakie and e-nashiji with stalks of leafy bamboo and scattered with family crest of kashiwa (oak), further mon to interior of hinged door and two large interior drawers, lower drawer with removable interior compartment with sliding lid and secondary drawer to front fashioned with ink stone and receptacle for suiteki, with bronze fittings, 10 1/4" x 9 5/8" x 15 5/8".* **$500**

Bonhams

▼ *Chen Zhifo (1896-1962), peonies and peach blossoms hanging scroll, ink and color on silk, signed Xueweng with one seal of artist reading Chen Zifo yin, 34 5/8" x 16".* **$1,375**

Bonhams

▲ *Pair of lacquer decorated iron stirrups, Edo period, each curved front decorated in gold hiramakie, takamakie, and kirikane with scattered kite-string spools on roiro ground, suspension strap pierced with silhouette of swallow below hishi mon (diamond-form family crest), interior lacquered red, 12" long.* **$438**

Bonhams

▲ *Two Korean blue-glazed porcelain water droppers, each molded in shape of leaping carp with fins and scales in shallow relief beneath mottled cobalt blue wash and colorless glaze that stops along edge of unglazed base, 3 1/8" long.* **$313**

Bonhams

Wu Ruizhen (1915-2003) Chrysanthemums and Zhu Kongyang (1892-1986) Prunus, chrysanthemums mounted for framing, ink and color on paper, inscribed and dedicated, signed Wu Ruizhen, followed by one square seal of artist reading Rui Zhen Shu Hua, additional inscription by Liao Jingwen, 25 1/4" x 29"; Prunus hanging scroll, ink and color on paper, inscribed and signed Yong Wen, followed by six seals of artist, 42 3/4" x 13 1/4". **$625**

Bonhams

▶ *Ruby zoisite snuff bottle of rounded square form with flat lip, dark green stone with rose highlights, carved with lotuses emerging from waves, all on low ovular foot rim surrounding shallow recessed base, 1 7/8" high.* **$500**

Bonhams

◀ *Turquoise matrix snuff bottle, peach-form bottle with patches of green and bluish turquoise on iron brown-colored ground with raised curling leaves and tendrils at top, 2 1/2" high.* **$1,063**

Bonhams

▶ *Two jadeite models of ducks, both depicted as if on water and surrounded by aquatic plants and flowers, one surrounded by ducklings and the other grasping a fish in its mouth with a frog on its back; stone of lavender hue with patches of pale green, with green patches at top, back, and underside of carvings, 8 1/2" and 7" high.* **$4,375**

Bonhams

Chinese silk ground embroidered calligraphy panel, black thread on beige silk ground, framed and glazed, 52 1/8" x 15 1/4" (frame). **$813**

Bonhams

Polychrome painted figure of Daoist female immortal, late Ming/early Qing dynasty, possibly depicting Xiwangmu as suggested by phoenix ornament on her elaborately dressed coiffure as she sits dressed in layered garments and holding rank stick in her covered hands, 29" high. **$1,250**

Bonhams

Jadeite lidded vase, hu-form with domed lid surmounted by lion form finial and flanked by ring handles, main body centered with cartouche containing taotie decoration, with lion head handles flanking neck supporting free-moving ring handles, all raised on flared foot; stone of pale lavender hue with patches of apple green and a vein of russet hue, 16" high. **$4,375**

Bonhams

Pair of cinnabar lacquer-covered vases, late Qing/ Republic period, each of inverted pear form displaying scholars and young servant gathered in rural landscape, metal plates finishing feet, rims, and collars to domed covers, 11" high. **$1,000**

Bonhams

Pair of four-sectioned cloisonné enameled metal containers, Jingtai marks, late Qing dynasty, each section combined to form profile of archaistic hu with classic lotus flower and leaf scroll pattern encircling upper neck section, squirrels and grapes covering shoulder section, band of lions and ribboned balls around body, and four horses prancing above waves around spreading base bearing four-character Jingtai mark inlaid to underside, decoration in colored enamels with subsidiary wires of cloud-scroll shape on deep turquoise ground, interior of each section also covered in layer of dark turquoise enamel, 15" high. **$2,000**

Bonhams

Carved jadeite basket of flowering plants, basket issuing blossoming branches of peony, chrysanthemum, and other flowers with peaches, pomegranates, grape clusters, citron, insects, and birds all backed with woven ovoid panel; stone of pale green and lavender hue with apple green veining throughout, 20" high. **$5,625**

Bonhams

Pair of jadeite models of vases with flowering branches issuing multiple flowering branches including peony and chrysanthemums with pomegranates, peaches, and grape clusters with bird resting in front of vase; stone of pale gray and green hue with apple green veining and dark gray and black speckles throughout, 26" high. **$8,125**

Bonhams

▲ *Porcelain snuff bottle, Yongzheng mark, 19th century, compressed ovoid bottle with flared rim and decorated with dragon in underglaze blue and copper red, underside containing underglaze blue six character mark, 2 1/4" high.* **$813**

Bonhams

▶ *Cobalt-glazed ground bottle vase with famille rose enamel decoration, late Qing/Republic period, exterior walls of cylindrical neck and oval body covered with cobalt wash beneath colorless glaze that continues on interior walls and recessed base while opaque white and colored enamels form two phoenix birds in flight amid red sun and rainbow-colored clouds, 8 1/2" high.* **$1,250**

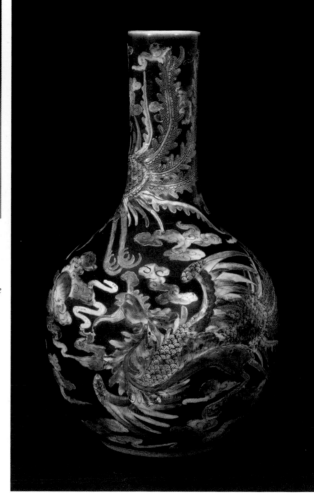

Bonhams

▶ *Pair of Chinese hardstone trees on cloisonné bases, 18" high.* **$500**

Bonhams

Pair of Chinese iron red and gilt painted "Dragon" vases with garlic-head mouths, late 19th century, each with apocryphal Wanli reign marks, each 15 3/4" high. **$2,750**

Bonhams

Famille rose enameled porcelain brush pot with landscape decoration, Guangxu mark, cylindrical vessel painted with continuous landscape scene of mountains with winding rivers, pavilions, and walled structure, with figures at various tasks including boating, bearing six-character mark in iron red regular script, 7 1/2" high. **$1,500**

Heritage Auctions

Chinese natural double gourd snuff bottle, China, Qing Dynasty, snuff bottle with dyed bone stopper, fitted in original silk lined box, 4 3/4" high x 2" wide. **$625**

Heritage Auctions

Pair of Imari porcelain jars on gilt bronze mounts, circa 1900, each of ginger jar-form with gilt bronze mounted fu dog finial to lid, over band of blue with orange medallions to shoulder, floral decoration on body, set on reticulated gilt bronze base raised on scroll and acanthus leaf toes, 23 1/2" high. **$5,625**

Heritage Auctions

Chinese carved hardstone Gu vase, China, Qing Dynasty, vase with carving throughout, raised on conforming carved wood stand, 10 1/2" high. **$30,000**

Heritage Auctions

Chinese cinnabar peach-form box, China, Qing Dynasty, shaped bisected oval box with two figures in landscape to center and carved decoration of stylized medallions, flowers and foliate throughout, 3 3/4" high x 5" wide. **$2,000**

Elite Decorative Arts

▲ *Antique Chinese light blue crackle glaze bowl having lotus form, bottom holds blue zhuanshu Qianlong reign mark (1736-1795), is of the period, 1 5/8" high x 4 3/4" diameter.* **$8,470**

Heritage Auctions

◄ *Chinese Tang Dynasty painted pottery court lady, circa 618-907 A.D., standing "fat lady" with elaborate coiffure wearing long-sleeved voluminous robe and slippers, her hands clasped in front, traces of pigment over white slip preserved throughout, on wood base, 12 1/2" high.* **$1,875**

Heritage Auctions

▶ *Four-piece Japanese lacquered box in stand, circa 1900, round box in four parts with figures in landscape scenes to exterior, set in circular stand with handle having splayed sides and raised on six feet, iron mounts throughout, 29 1/2" high.* **$469**

Elite Decorative Arts

▲ *Antique Chinese porcelain Forbidden City yellow ground planter, circa Qing dynasty period, 19th century, depicting bird in tree with flowers over yellow ground, includes fitted base, each marked with red calligraphy to bottom, 6 1/8" high, plus 1 1/4" base height x 11 1/2" long x 7" deep. Provenance: From the Estate of Count and Countess Claes-Eric de Lewenhaupt of Sweden.* **$2,299**

Elite Decorative Arts

▲ *20th century Chinese hand-painted enameled Emerald Rose bottle form vase after 18th century design, depicts tree with leaves, flowers and flying butterflies, bottom holds blue six-character calligraphy Yohngzheng reign mark, 13 1/4" high.* **$12,100**

Elite Decorative Arts

▶ *Pair of Qing dynasty period Chinese Sancai glaze sculptures, circa 18th/19th century, depicting seated foo lions on reticulated pedestals, each approximately 13" high.* **$1,210**

Autographs

By Zac Bissonnette

In *The Meaning and Beauty of Autographs*, first published in 1935 and translated from the German by David H. Lowenherz of Lion Heart Autographs, Inc. in 1995, Stefan Zweig explained that to love a manuscript, we must first love the human being "whose characteristics are immortalized in them." When we do, then "a single page with a few lines can contain the highest expression of human happiness, and... the expression of deepest human sadness. To those who have eyes to look at such pages correctly, eyes not only in the head, but also in the soul, they will not receive less of an impression from these plain signs than from the obvious beauty of pictures and books."

John M. Reznikoff, founder and president of University Archives, has been a leading dealer and authority on historical letters and artifacts for 32 years. He described the current market for autographs as "very, very strong on many fronts. Possibly because of people being afraid to invest in the market and in real estate, we are seeing investment in autographs that seems to parallel gold and silver."

Reznikoff suspects that Civil War items peaked after Ken Burns' series but that Revolutionary War documents, included those by signers of the Declaration of Independence and the Constitution are still undervalued and can be purchased for under $500.

Currrently, space is in high demand, especially Apollo 11. Pop culture, previously looked at as secondary by people who dealt in Washingtons and Lincolns, has come into its own. Reznikoff anticipates continued growth in memorabilia that includes music, television, movies and sports. Babe Ruth, Lou Gehrig, Ty Cobb and Tiger Woods are still good investments but Reznikoff warns that authentication is much more of a concern in sports than in any other field.

The Internet allows for a lot of misinformation and this is a significant issue with autographs. There are two widely accepted authentication services: Professional Sports Authenticator (PSA/DNA) and James Spence Authentication (JSA). A dealer's reliability can be evaluated by seeing whether he is a member of one or more of the major organizations in the field: the Antique Booksellers Association of America, UACC Registered Dealers Program, and the National Professional Autograph Dealers Association (NPADA), which Reznikoff founded.

There is an additional caveat to remember and it is true for all collectibles: rarity. The value of an autograph is often determined less by the prominence of the signer than by the number of autographs he signed.

ZAC BISSONNETTE is a consignment director for Heritage Auctions and has been featured on The Today Show, The Suze Orman Show, CNN, and National Public Radio. In addition to his work in the antiques field, he has served as a financial journalist for *Glamour*, *The Daily Beast*, *The New York Times*, *The Huffington Post*, and *AOL Money & Finance*. He has a degree in art history from the University of Massachusetts.

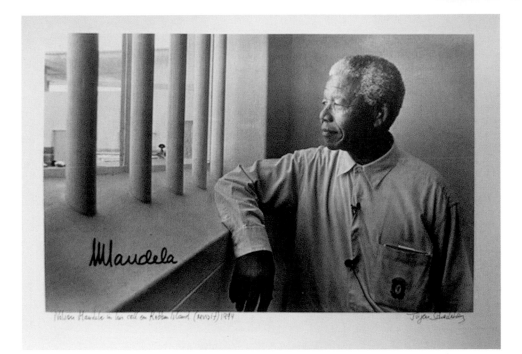

Ted Owen and Co. Auctions

Nelson Mandela, Robben Island 1994 (revisited), one of only a few official silver gelatin prints signed by both Nelson Mandela (front) and Jurgen Schadeberg (lower right), dated 1994 and inscribed with title (lower left); extensively inscribed (verso), "This was Mandela's first official visit after his release from prison in 1990 and obviously an emotional visit when he returned to the cell he spent 17 years of his 27 year sentence. He looked out of the bars and when he thought I had finished taking pictures, relaxed somewhat, and turned around to smile." (Jürgen Schadeberg). **$4,000-$8,000**

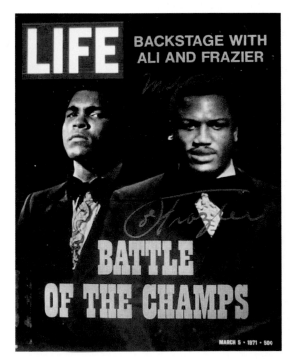

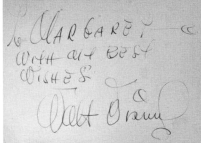

Bonhams

Walt Disney autograph book containing inscription and signature, signed and inscribed in blue ballpoint pen, "To Margaret – With all Best Wishes, Walt Disney," circa mid-20th century. **$554**

Ted Owen and Co. Auctions

Muhammad Ali and Joe Frazier, March 5, 1971 Life magazine "Battle of the Champs," signed on front cover by Muhammad Ali and Joe Frazier in gold pen, good condition with light wear. **$1,287**

Ted Owen and Co. Auctions

Pele, limited edition number 0006 of 2,500 produced, hand-signed by Pele on initial page, bound in brown silk, 636 pages with 1,700 images detailing life and career of Pele taken from newspaper and magazine articles, transcripts, articles from books, and personal memorabilia as well as from leading sportswriters; with original presentation box imprinted with "Pele" and his full name, Edson Arantes do Nascimento, "Carnival" version with color print hand-signed by all surviving members of three-time World Cup-winning 1970 Brazilian team, approximately 55.5cm x 45.5cm framed and glazed. **$3,200-$5,500**

Bonhams

Elvis Presley, ticket for Lido Cabaret-Restaurant Bar, signed on back in red ink by Presley, Champs-Elysees, Paris, 1959, accompanied by Sylvia Peters publicity card and letter concerning provenance, 5" x 4". According to the vendor, who was a dancer at the time, she was friends with Sylvia Peters when she had a fleeting affair with Presley, having met him in Paris on a rest and relaxation break from his military service in Germany. Sylvia obtained the signature and gave it to her friend, whom she knew to be a great fan of the singer. **$1,088**

Ted Owen and Co. Auctions

Queen autographed album page, Freddie Mercury, Brian May, and John Deacon signed in blue pen and Roger Taylor signed in black pen, with two unpublished concert photographs, excellent condition. **$508**

*Paul McCartney,
original British
European Airways
(BEA) travel
bag signed by
McCartney over
central logo, bag
shows some wear.*
$540-$750

◄ *The Rolling Stones/Keith Richards, white
canvas straight jacket with Velcro restraints
to waist and chest and shoulders, decorated
with various motifs and doodles by Keith
Richards, with annotation "Herrods
Knightsbridge," Union Jack, "Make piece
at war" and "I [heart with arrow] Mum!"
and signed in black pen by Keith Richards.*
$2,709

*Princess Diana autographed photograph,
signed in black Sharpie, excellent condition,
8" x 10".* **$270**

Elvis Presley inscription and autograph on record-album sleeve. **$300-$500**

▶ *Alexander Hamilton letter, United States Founding Father; first Secretary of the Treasury (1789-1795), autograph letter signed, one page, 9.25" x 7.5", March 3, 1794, Treasury Department, addressed to George Gale, Supervisor for the District of Maryland, requesting the state reimburse $128 to Nathaniel Rochester for supplies furnished by him to recruits at Hagers Town (now Hagerstown), Maryland; toning, scattered stains, and full separation at center fold, piece missing along centerfold that impacts one word, framed and glazed.* **$2,350**

From an archive of 31 original historical documents pertaining to 1798 Fries Rebellion in Pennsylvania, written appointment of Capt. William Rodman of the Bucks County Troop of Light Dragoons to post of Deputy Marshall. **$3,000-$5,000**

Ted Owen and Co. Auctions

John Lennon, autographed 3" x 5" page, dedicated in black ink, "To Steve love from John Lennon" with smiley doodle and date 1976, mounted with color photograph, 9" x 12". **$1,016**

Bonhams

▶*Eric Clapton, promo 45 for "Change of Address From June 23rd 1969," Island, no catalog number, 500 only, one side with details of new address, other with sales office address, sleeve signed and inscribed in black marker by Clapton, "To Max best wishes, Eric Clapton" and dated "88."* **$1,286**

Cowan's Auctions

Neil Armstrong (1930-2012) signed program, Apollo 11 crew member and first man to set foot on the moon (July 1969), original program from March 11, 1972, Conferment of the Freedom of the Burgh, held in Langholm, Scotland, in recognition for Armstrong's achievements in space exploration, signed on back cover in black ink by Armstrong, 5" x 8", small tear extends to front page, small tea stain on top left-hand corner of front page. **$1,057**

▲ Original Peanuts Sunday comic, 3-1-1964, personalized "To Susie and George with friendship, Charles Schulz." **$36,000**

◄ President Harry S. Truman, signed black and white photograph dated November 1948, two days after election, holding up copy of Chicago Daily Tribune with banner headline incorrectly stating, "Dewey Defeats Truman," bent inward slightly, minor damage to upper right corner, 10" x 8". Truman was returning to Washington from Missouri when he stepped to the rear of the train at St. Louis Union Station and was handed the paper. Across the newspaper, Truman has inscribed: "Too bad!" **$10,157**

◄ John F. Kennedy, on Senate letterhead, dated 2/28/1957, "I appreciate receiving your letter concerning my position with respect to sanctions against Israel. In the thought that you might be interested, I am enclosing a copy of the remarks I made in Cleveland last Sunday evening on the subject of the Middle East situation," signed and inscribed, "The situation seems to be improving!," with original envelope and copy of Kennedy's remarks. **$1,650**

Heritage Auctions

Mark Twain/Samuel Clemens, one page, 2.75" x 1.5", found on verso of calling card for Dr. Isaiah Frank, author placed both real name and pen name on card: "Truly yours / Sl. Clemens / (Mark Twain)"; fine condition, with 4" x 5.5" color image of Twain. **$2,031**

Heritage Auctions

▶ *Postcard from Renoir to his son, Jean, with unaddressed postcard signed by Renoir, autograph postcard signed, dated March 12, 1913, location Nice, front depicting photograph image of DOZY— Ruines de l'Eglise du Pre, verso: "I embrace you (hug you), AR"; with autograph postcard signed, depicting landscape with lake photograph, signed on verso Renoir, some staining.* **$3,750**

Heritage Auctions

◀ *Agatha Christie, British crime novelist, typed letter, signed as Agatha Mallowan, very good condition, horizontal crease, some toning, small stain.* **$300**

Antiques & Collectibles | *Warman's*

Heritage Auctions

◀ *James Dean-signed black and white photograph, circa 1955, glossy finish, depicting classic headshot of actor in costume as Jim Stark from "Rebel Without a Cause," signed in turquoise fountain pen ink in upper right corner "To Pat / with my best wishes / James Dean," verso displays photographer's credit stamp reading, in part, "Photograph / by / Floyd McC...Warner...," remainder obscured by typed press snipe glued over stamp reading "James Dean -- soon to be seen in Warner Bros.' Rebel Without a Cause," 10" x 8".* **$8,750**

Heritage Auctions

▼ *Original artwork signed by 26 NASA astronauts, including 10 moonwalkers, from personal collection of astronaut "den mother" Lola Morrow, excellent condition, sight 18" x 16", framed to 20" x 18" overall.* **$3,883**

Banks

By Eric Bradley & Karen Knapstein

Banks that display some form of action while accepting a coin are considered mechanical banks, and those that have no mechanical action are known as still banks. Mechanical banks date back to ancient Greece and Rome, but the majority of collectors are interested in those made between 1867 and 1928 in Germany, England, and the United States. More than 80 percent of all cast-iron mechanical banks produced between 1869 and 1928 were made by J. & E. Stevens Co. of Cromwell, Connecticut. Tin banks are usually of German origin.

The mechanical bank hobby continues to catch headlines as some of the best examples of rare banks head to the auction block. Morphy Auctions is a world leader in selling mechanical and still banks most desired by collectors; the firm has offered more than 6,000 mechanical banks in the last 12 years, and nearly 2,700 still banks.

Dan Morphy, owner and founder of Morphy Auctions, says condition – like in all other categories of collecting – is king. "Banks in top condition seem to be the trend these days," he said.

It's not uncommon for desirable banks to earn four and five figure results. During Morphy's June 2013 sale of toys and banks — a sale that tallied more than a half million dollars — seven of the top 10 lots were banks made during the late 19th and early 20th centuries. Among them was a near-mint figural cast iron bank depicting the muscular Greek god Atlas with the world hoisted onto his back, which settled at $12,000.

During the same sale, an all-original example of a beady-eyed pelican still bank in near-mint-plus condition landed at $11,400.

You don't need to be able to fill a bank to start collecting toy and mechanical banks. Auctions abound with more affordable character banks and premium banks from the mid-20th century. Designs are as varied as your imagination and cover a number of historical events, political figures, and landmarks. Unlike other collecting areas, many rare forms of mechanical and still banks (banks with no mechanical action) are highly valued, even if they are not in perfect condition. However, one should always buy the best condition afforded; when investing in a collection, quality should always outweigh quantity.

Those interested in mechanical banks are encouraged to learn more about the Mechanical Bank Collectors of America (www.mechanicalbanks.org), a non-profit organization consisting of around 400 members from the United States and several foreign countries. Organized in 1958, it is dedicated to expanding the knowledge and availability of antique mechanical banks. The MBCA can be reached at info@mechanicalbanks.org or by writing to Mechanical Bank Collectors of America, P.O. Box 13323, Pittsburgh, PA 15242.

Another valuable resource is the Still Bank Collectors Club of America (www.stillbankclub.com), a non-profit organization founded in 1966 that now consists of nearly 500 collectors from the United States, Canada, Germany, Denmark, Australia and England. Learn more about the SBCCA by writing to SBCCA Membership Chairman, 440 Homestead Ave., Metairie, LA 70005.

ERIC BRADLEY is the former editor of *Antique Trader* magazine and an award-winning investigative journalist with a degree in economics. Bradley's work has received press from *The New York Times* and *The Wall Street Journal*. He also served as a featured guest speaker on investing with antiques. A member of Heritage Auctions public relations department, Bradley has a passion for tramp art, ceramics and art pottery.
KAREN KNAPSTEIN is the Print Editor of *Antique Trader* magazine. A lifelong collector and student of antiques, she has written dozens of articles on antiques and collectibles. She lives in Wisconsin with her husband and daughter.

Skinner, Inc.; www.skinnerinc.com

Five fruit-form pottery banks, late 19th century, polychrome painted, three apples and two pears, scattered glaze loss, 2 1/4" to 4 1/8" high. **$400**

Skinner, Inc.; www.skinnerinc.com

Cast iron "Shell Out" shell-form still bank, J. & E. Stevens Co., circa 1882, original paint, impressed 1882 patent mark on bottom, paint wear, 2 1/2" high x 5 1/4" wide. **$540**

Noel Barrett Auctions

Clown on Globe mechanical bank, painted cast iron, J. & E. Stevens Co., excellent to near mint condition, paint chip on hat band, which strikes ball finial when activated, 9" high in seated position. **$16,000**

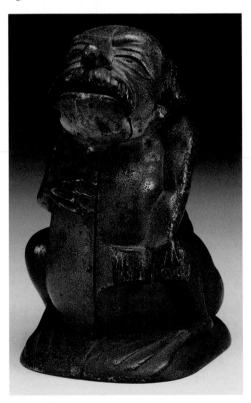

James D. Julia, Inc.

General Butler still bank modeled after Civil War general, caricature of Butler's face with frog body, rare and difficult to find, original as-found condition including trap, overall fair to good condition, 6 1/2" high. **$1,035**

Morphy Auctions

Hall's Lilliput mechanical bank, J. & E. Stevens Co., original near mint condition, 4 1/2" high. **$3,600**

Morphy Auctions

Home Savings Safe still bank, all original, near mint condition, 4 1/2" high. **$330**

Morphy Auctions

Pelican cast iron still bank, man thumbs nose variation, original example with stunning paint, near mint-plus condition, 8" high. **$11,400**

Morphy Auctions

Blackpool still bank, John Harper & Co., beautiful japanning, excellent-plus condition, 7 1/2" high. **$450**

Noel Barrett Auctions

Darktown Battery mechanical bank, J. & E. Stevens Co., painted cast iron, circa late 1800s, very good condition, missing trap, some small areas of corrosion on base plate bottom, 9 3/4" long x 7" high. **$1,000**

Noel Barrett Auctions

Chocolat-Menier kiosk vending bank, embossed lithographed tin chocolate dispensing mechanical bank in form of French advertising kiosk, elaborate early version from 1920s, appears fully functional, very good condition, some wear, missing spire, 8 1/2" high. **$500**

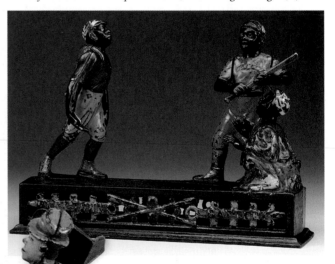

James D. Julia, Inc.

▲ *Darktown Battery mechanical bank, J. & E. Stevens Co.; when coin is placed in pitcher's hand it is tossed to catcher's mitt while batter swings his bat; overall good condition with even wear throughout, 9 3/4" long.* **$1,534**

Morphy Auctions

◄ *Mason mechanical bank, Shepard Hardware Co., all original, excellent-plus condition, 7 1/2" long.* **$2,040**

Noel Barrett Auctions

Noel Barrett Auctions

Frog on Stump mechanical bank, painted cast iron, J. & E. Stevens Co., strong color on tree and foliage, excellent condition, 4" long. **$800**

Teddy & Bear mechanical bank, painted cast iron, J. & E. Stevens Co., flawless Teddy face, minor chips on hat, coat and thigh, 10" long. **$2,500**

Noel Barrett Auctions

Owl Turns Head mechanical bank, J. & E. Stevens Co., painted cast iron, strong gold and green foliage, excellent condition, 7 1/2" high. **$425**

Morphy Auctions

▶ *Owl Turns Head mechanical bank, J. & E. Stevens Co., original paint with gold highlights in grass, near mint plus condition, 7 1/2" high.* **$4,500**

James D. Julia, Inc.

Hubley Elephant & Howdah cast iron mechanical bank; when coin is placed in elephant's trunk and tail is pulled, coin is deposited in front of howdah; original aluminum tail, good condition with heavy crazing and wear throughout, 9" long. **$118**

Mark Mussio, Humler & Nolan

Uncle Sam bank, early 1900s, gloss brown glaze with golden highlights, marked Rozane RPCo., 4 1/4" high. **$225**

James D. Julia, Inc.

Speaking Dog mechanical bank, J. & E. Stevens Co.; girl sits on Victorian sofa with large brown dog, one hand holds paddle, other is raised, when coin is placed on girl's paddle and lever is pushed, coin is dropped into sofa and dog's mouth opens and tail wags; paint in above average condition, little wear, minor chipping, bank shows minor wear, missing trap, 7 1/2" long x 7 1/2" high. **$2,300**

Noel Barrett Auctions

Mammy & Child mechanical bank, painted cast iron, Kyser & Rex, Philadelphia, strong color, original locking trap but lacking key, excellent condition, repaired original spoon, paint losses to child's dress, 7 1/4" high. **$2,500**

Noel Barrett Auctions

*Bad Accident
mechanical bank,
painted cast iron,
J. & E. Stevens Co.,
very good condition,
cart repainted and
repaired, 10 1/4" long.*
$700

Morphy Auctions

*Lighthouse cast iron
mechanical bank with
detailed red brick
tower, near mint-plus
condition, 10 1/2"
high.* **$10,800**

James D. Julia, Inc.

*Lighthouse cast iron mechanical bank, rocky outcropping
and lighthouse building are japanned, tower painted red,
coin slot in building, slot in top of tower stacks nickels,
which can be seen in cutout windows, overall very good
condition with some oxidation to base and minor paint
chipping throughout, 10 1/2" high.* **$2,242**

Morphy Auctions

Two Frogs mechanical bank, J. & E. Stevens Co., working, all original, excellent condition, 8 1/2" long. **$3,600**

Morphy Auctions

Magic cast iron mechanical bank, J. & E. Stevens Co., pistachio green with red version, excellent condition, crack in roof, 5" high. **$8,400**

Morphy Auctions

▼ *Eagle and Eaglets mechanical bank, J. & E. Stevens Co., working excellent condition, 8" long.* **$660**

James D. Julia, Inc.

▲ *Eagle and Eaglets mechanical bank, J. & E. Stevens Co., American eagle perched on mound feeding her two eaglets; when coin is placed in eagle's mouth and lever is pushed, eagle lurches forward and drops coin into receptacle as baby eagles rise up; complete with working bellows that represents peeping sound of eaglets, originally marketed as American Eagle bank, eagle appears to be original and in good condition, base and nest with restoration and repair, 8 1/2" long.* **$575**

Morphy Auctions

Two-faced Devil still bank, A.C. Williams Co., all original, very good to excellent condition, 4 1/2" high. **$660**

Noel Barrett Auctions

◄ *Cat & Mouse mechanical bank, painted cast iron, J. & E. Stevens Co., strong color, excellent condition, small hairline crack in base, 11 1/2" high extended.* **$8,500**

James D. Julia, Inc.

Rare cast iron French Mickey Mouse bank, all original, sanctioned by Walt Disney and produced in France in 1930s; pie-eyed Mickey with watermelon mouth and hands on hips, enameled in typical Mickey Mouse colors of red, white and black, overall very good-plus condition, all original paint, heavy alligatoring, most notable to white surfaces, raised lettering on underside of feet, embossed lettering to rear of each ear, 8 1/2" high. **$4,313**

James D. Julia, Inc.

Tammany mechanical bank, also known as Boss Tweed bank representing corrupt New York City politician of late 1800s, J. & E. Stevens; when coin is placed in his hand, arm pivots, depositing coin in pocket while nodding his head in thanks; near excellent condition with minor paint chips, 6" high. **$690**

Yellow Cab still bank, Arcade, advertising for "Canal 2100" on top of roof, all original, near mint condition, 8" long. **$1,920**

Rooster mechanical bank, all original including lever, excellent condition, 6" high. **$780**

Atlas cast iron mechanical bank, original example, difficult to find with globe complete, near mint condition, 8 1/4" high. **$12,000**

Books

By Noah Fleisher

J oe Fay is the manager of the Rare Books Department at Heritage Auctions. He's a young man, a devoted husband and father of two, an obsessive film buff and VHS tape aficionado. He also has an encyclopedic knowledge of the printed word.

He can wax poetic about the mysteries of incunabla, then turn around a breath later and extol the virtues of Stephen King or Sherlock Holmes, his personal favorite, finding the common thread between them. He's got an eye for early copies of The Federalist Papers and can spot a rare first edition of J.K. Rowlings' *Harry Potter and the Philosopher's Stone*, reciting from memory exactly what makes it a true first edition.

We sat down for a conversation about the current market in rare books, which proved as entertaining as it did enlightening.

Warman's: Give me an overview of rare books as they relate to 2013 and 2014.

Joe Fay: As always, the top of the market is very stable. The market seems to be holding steady against a fairly violent public assault on the printed word.

Noah Fleisher

I hear the question all the time: "Will the Kindle kill the printed book?" Of course not. Folks bemoan the death of the printed word, but it's not going to happen anytime soon. It seems like every new technology that transmits information has called for the death of the book, but it hasn't happened yet and I don't think it will.

I think rare books will become increasingly more precious because of their physicality. People will come to interact with books in a different, more intimate way because of their relative scarcity.

Warman's: Is the market improving? Where are the best buying opportunities?

Joe Fay: The market is improving since the rather large hiccup of 2008. There is strength in special or unique books: examples with wonderful inscriptions, association copies, fine bindings, etc. Also, with the prevailing cultural obsession with superheroes and comic book-related material, there has never been a stronger market for science fiction and genre fiction.

You can also never go wrong with incunabula, books printed before 1500, or great copies of great works in the major collecting categories.

Early printed books are always strong, the incunabula I just mentioned. Important first editions in the major categories, such as history, science and medicine, natural history, travel, religion, maps and atlases, literature, economics, early American imprints, children's books, and illustrated books.

Fine press printing and artists' books seem to be on the upward trend, too, as books become

NOAH FLEISHER received his Bachelor of Fine Arts degree from New York University and brings more than a decade of newspaper, magazine, book, antiques and art experience to his position as Public Relations Director of Heritage Auctions, one of the country's foremost auction houses. He is the former editor of *Antique Trader, New England Antiques Journal* and *Northeast Antiques Journal*, is the author of *Warman's Modern Furniture*, and has been a longtime contributor to *Warman's Antiques and Collectibles*.

more of a specialty in the face of competing technologies.

Warman's: Is there room for new and younger collectors in rare books right now?

Joe Fay: I think it's a good market to get into at any time and any age. The rule I live by when talking about book collecting, as any expert in any category will tell you: Collect what you like. Find some focus within a subject area, author, printer or publisher, and collect everything you can.

Don't limit yourself to just the books, either. For a given author, seek out autograph material, posters, artifacts, original art if applicable, and so on. It can be very rewarding to walk into a person's personal library and not only see an incredible run of first editions by Ray Bradbury, but also find a *Fahrenheit 451* poster on the wall, next to a framed letter from the author. I guess this is a disguised version of diversification, in a way.

Warman's: It's a huge field. How do you go about starting or bolstering a collection if you've been out for a while?

Joe Fay: Vigilance. It's a great time to be a buyer of rare books because they are so readily available to be bought.

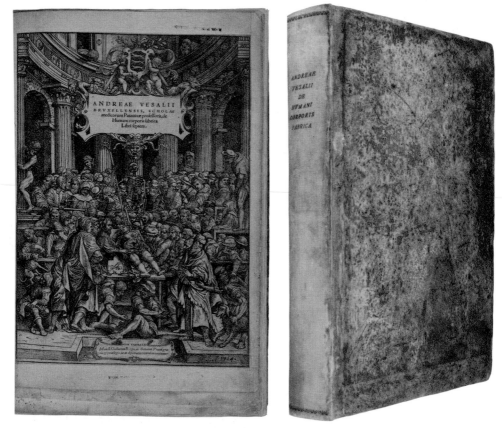

Heritage Auctions

Andreas Vesalius, De Humani Corporis Libri Septem. *[Basile: Johannes Oporinus, June, 1543]. First edition of famous medical book and most important anatomical work; also considered to be the most beautiful anatomical book of all time. Folio in sixes, approximately 17" x 11", [viii], 659 (actually 663), [1, errata], [36] pp., woodcut title in first state, possibly supplied from another copy and mounted onto another leaf with no loss of image.* **$122,500**

Build a relationship with a reputable dealer, save keyword searches at online sites like eBay and Heritage, places where you get email reminders when material matching your interests becomes available.

Warman's: What is it that draws people to rare books?

Joe Fay: That's a really big question. I think the desire to collect rare books started with a thirst to converse with the great minds of the past, which encompasses really anything. There are practically limitless possibilities for a subject area to collect in rare books.

If you want to assemble the best collection of books bound in yellow cloth, you can do that. You want to collect signs made by homeless panhandlers? Let me introduce you to Michael Zinman, who already does that. You want to collect pamphlets and other imprints dealing with early 20th century American Communism? I hope you have a lifetime to devote to it and I would love to see your collection someday.

For me, personally, the allure of rare books comes down to both what they are, physically, and what they represent. Books are wonderful to handle. If a book is well put together, it fits nicely in the hand or lies well when opened on a table, it stimulates both the eye to flip through and the mind to read and is a pleasure to look at on the shelf. Even the smell of a book is a unique phenomenon that evokes myriad emotions and memories.

A rare first printing of a given important novel is rare in itself, but it also represents a viewpoint and a cultural zeitgeist that is usually universal, that mattered both when the book was published and today. They are a window into the minds of people long gone, markers of our evolution as humans. This is not something you get with many other collecting categories.

Warman's: Looking back 10 years and looking ahead 10 years, how does/will the market look in comparison?

Joe Fay: A couple of generations ago everyone had books in their house. For 550 years books have been the primary method by which people learned. Now, there are so many competing delivery systems for information that print culture has obviously taken a hit.

I think the number of collectors 10 years from now will be smaller in number but more intense in terms of who is collecting. Rare books have become a bit of a niche market, but you can see the contraction markedly at regional book fairs. More people used to come to fairs than they do now. High-end fairs like the New York Antiquarian Book Fair are still going strong, and will likely to continue to do so, because the top end of the market

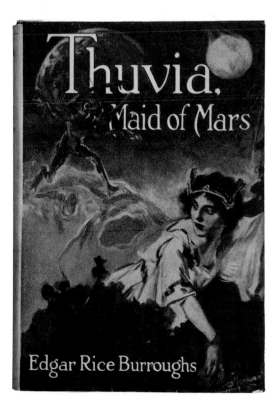

Heritage Auctions

Edgar Rice Burroughs, Thuvia, Maid of Mars. *Chicago: A.C. McClurg & Co., 1920, first edition, inscribed and signed by Burroughs on front free endpaper, 256 pages plus 12-page publisher's catalog.* **$9,560**

is not going anywhere. Truly valuable rarities always bring premium prices.

Warman's: You hear how technology has hurt books. Tell me how it has helped.

Joe Fay: The Internet and the eReader have certainly had an effect on the trade, no doubt – we have fewer and fewer bookstores these days – but the web has also opened up thousands upon millions of avenues for finding books, especially those that people once thought were very rare or even unique. The Internet has also had a positive effect on some titles by reinforcing their rarity.

The Internet helped to stratify the rare book world. With so much information, no one can pay – and no one will ask – unreasonable prices for common books. I talk to book dealers all the time who say something to the effect of, "I used to be able to get $500 for that book, now I can't give it away." Then they turn around and say, "You know that book I sold in your Internet weekly auction for $1,000? I've had that book on my table at book fairs for 10 years for $150 and barely anyone looked at it."

Obviously, the web can now help actually identify rarity instead of proving commonness.

Warman's: How much homework should a collector do before entering the category, or is it best to consult experts and let them fill in the gaps?

Joe Fay: Do a lot of homework. Many people have been burned by casually starting to collect books or by trusting the wrong dealer. Don't just do homework on the books; check out the dealer, the auction house, or whatever entity you might do business with.

Call other dealers and talk to them about a given dealer. Check with the Better Business Bureau. Call the auction house and talk to the book department.

Book dealers and rare books auctioneers, once trusted, can be a very important source of information for collectors, and can often "fill in gaps," as you say.

Heritage Auctions

Book of Hours, *Artois [St.-Omer] France, circa 16th century, small quarto, approximately 8.5" x 5.75", 76, lacking one leaf after fol. 31, otherwise complete.* **$68,500**

Heritage Auctions

◄ *Charles Darwin*, On the Origin of Species by Means of Natural Selection, or The Preservation of Favored Races in the Struggle for Life. *London: John Murray, 1859, first edition, two quotations on p. [ii]. Octavo in twelves (7 13/16" x 4 15/16"). ix, [1], 502 pages, plus 32-page publisher's catalog dated June, 1859. One of the most influential scientific works of the 19th century. From the James and Deborah Boyd Collection.* **$83,500**

Heritage Auctions

▶ *John Gould*, The Birds of Europe. *London: Richard and John E. Taylor, [1832-] 1837. Five imperial folio volumes, 21.5" x 14.25" each, 449 hand-colored illustrations on 448 lithographed plates printed by Charles Hullmandel, majority of plates by Elizabeth Gould from sketches by Gould, with remainder by Edward Lear.* **$80,500**

Heritage Auctions

▶ *Galileo Galilei*, Dialogo... Doue ne I congressi di Quattro giornate si discorre sopra I due Massimi Sistemi del Mondo Tolemaico, e Copernicano... *Florence: Giovanni Batista Landini, 1632, first edition, quarto.* **$65,725**

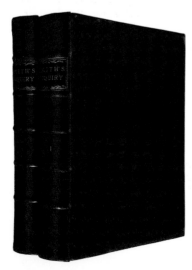

Heritage Auctions

◄ *Ernest Hemingway,* Three Stories & Ten Poems. *Paris: Contact Publishing Co., 1923, first and only edition of Hemingway's first book, one of only 300 copies printed, with inscription from author to editors of The Little Review, the "little magazine" in Paris that published his first mature prose work the same year: "For j.h. and Margaret Anderson with love from Hemingway" ("j.h." being Jane Heap). Twelvemo, 58 pages plus printer's imprint.* **$68,500**

Heritage Auctions

▲ *Joseph Smith, Junior,* The Book of Mormon: An Account Written by the Hand of Mormon, Upon Plates Taken From the Plates of Nephi. *By Joseph Smith, Junior, Author and Proprietor. Palmyra, [New York]: Printed by E. B. Grandin for author, 1830, first edition, John Wesley Brackenbury's copy, with his name on front pastedown: "J. W. Brackenbury / His Book / White Cloud / Kansas" written in pencil by Brackenbury. The Book of Mormon, rare in the first edition, is one of the most collectible books on religion issued in the United States.* **$47,800**

Heritage Auctions

◄ *Adam Smith,* An Inquiry into the Nature and Causes of the Wealth of Nations. *London: Printed for W. Strahan; and T. Cadell, 1776, first edition, two large quarto volumes, approximately 10.75" x 8.25". Smith (1723-1790) spent 10 years writing and perfecting The Wealth of Nations.* **$80,500**

Heritage Auctions

▲ *Thomas L. M'Kenney and James Hall,* History of the Indian Tribes of North America. *Philadelphia: Daniel Rice & James G. Clark, 1842-1842-1844, first edition.* **$43,750**

Heritage Auctions

◄ *Sir Isaac Newton,* Opticks, or, A Treatise of the Reflexions, Refractions, Inflexions and Colours of Light. *Also* Two Treatises of the Species and Magnitude of Curvilinear Figures. *London: Printed for Sam. Smith, and Benj. Walford, 1704, first edition, two parts in one quarto volume. Opticks provided the scientific framework for the study of optics, collecting together all of Newton's researches for the first time.* **$43,750**

Heritage Auctions

▲ Treaties of Amity and Commerce, and of Alliance Eventual and Defensive, between his most Christian Majesty and the Thirteen United States of America. *Philadelphia: John Dunlap, 1778, first edition. First edition of the Treaty of Alliance with France, a milestone in American history, the first treaty between the United States and another country, and the decisive event of the American Revolutionary War.* **$43,750**

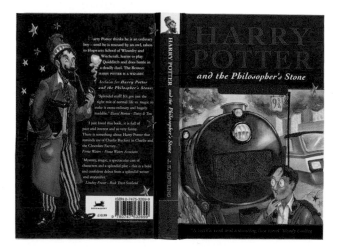

Heritage Auctions

◄ *J. K. Rowling,* Harry Potter and the Philosopher's Stone. *London: Bloomsbury, [1997], first edition, first issue (with "Joanne Rowling" and complete number line on copyright page, as well as "1 Wand" listed twice on page 53, superb condition.* **$43,750**

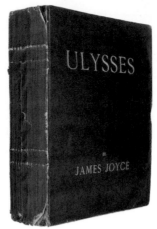

Heritage Auctions

Heritage Auctions

Heritage Auctions

The Whole Byble, that is the holy scripture of the Olde and Newe testament faythfully translated into Englyshe by Myles Couerdale, and newly ouer sene and correcte. *London: "Prynted For Andrewe Hester" (actually printed in Zurich by Christopher Froschover), 1550, reprint of the famous* Coverdale Bible, *first printed in 1535, and the last to appear in Coverdale's lifetime.* **$40,625**

James Joyce, Ulysses. *Paris: Shakespeare and Co., 1922, first edition, number 513 of 750 numbered copies printed on handmade paper (total edition 1,000 copies).* **$35,000**

Johannes Kepler, Strena Seu De Nive Sexangula. *Frankfurt: Gottfried. Tampach, 1611, first edition, quarto, woodcut printer's device, three woodcut illustrations in the text.* **$20,000**

Heritage Auctions

▼ *William Shakespeare,* Mr. William Shakespear's Comedies, Histories and Tragedies. *London: Printed for H. Herringman, E. Brewster, and R. Bentley, 1685, the Fourth Folio edition of Shakespeare's Plays, Folio, approximately 13.25" x 8.75".* **$16,250**

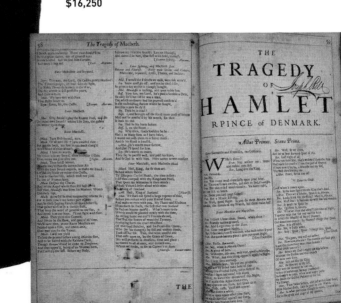

Edgar Allan Poe, Tales of the Grotesque and Arabesque. Philadelphia: Lea and Blanchard, 1840, first edition, one of 750 printed, very good complete copy, rare in original cloth with original critical notices and flyleaves present. **$21,850**

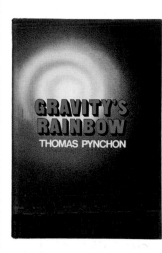

▲ *Thomas Pynchon, Gravity's Rainbow. New York: Viking, 1973, first edition, first printing, inscribed and signed by Pynchon on half-title page, "10/86 / To Michael Urban, / Best Wishes, / Thomas Pynchon," 760 pages.* **$16,250**

▶ *Noah Webster, An American Dictionary of the English Language: Intended to exhibit, I. The origin, affinities and primary signification of English words, as far as they have been ascertained. II. The genuine orthography and pronunciation of words, according to general usage, or to just principles of analogy. III. Accurate and discriminating definitions, with numerous authorities and illustrations. To which are prefixed, an introductory dissertation on the origin, history and connection of the languages of western Asia and of Europe, and a concise grammar of the English language. In two volumes. New York: Published by S. Converse, printed by Hezekiah Howe, 1828.* **$34,655**

Heritage Auctions

◀ *H. A. Rey*, Curious George. *Boston: Houghton Mifflin, 1941, first edition, quarto, unpaginated, illustrations by author, publisher's brick red cloth with Curious George vignette in black on front board and lettering in black on spine, illustrated endpapers, original dust jacket with $1.75 price.* **$26,290**

Heritage Auctions

▶ *Herman Melville*, Moby-Dick; or, The Whale. *New York: Harper & Brothers, 1851, first American edition.* **$10,625**

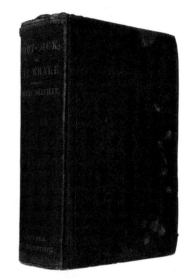

Heritage Auctions

J. M. Barrie, Peter Pan in Kensington Gardens *(from "The Little White Bird") with drawings by Arthur Rackham. London: Hodder & Stoughton, 1906, limited to 500 copies, this is number 49, numbered and signed by Arthur Rackham, 125 pages, 50 color plates mounted on brown paper with descriptive tissue guards.* **$10,158**

Heritage Auctions

L. Frank Baum, The Wonderful Wizard of Oz. Chicago and New York: George M. Hill Co., 1900, first edition, first state of the text. **$9,375**

Heritage Auctions

▼ *Jules Verne, The Green Ray, translated from the French by Mary de Hauteville. London: Sampson Low, Marston, Searle, & Rivington, 1883, first English edition.* **$8,125**

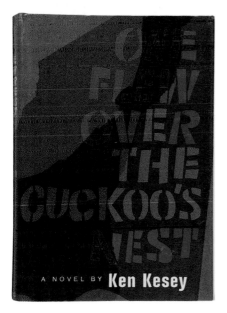

Heritage Auctions

▲ *Ken Kesey, One Flew Over the Cuckoo's Nest. New York: The Viking Press, 1962, first edition, first printing, inscribed by Kesey: "For / Darrel / Kesey / 1993," 311 pages.* **$8,365**

Heritage Auctions

▶ *Robert A. Heinlein,* Stranger in a Strange Land. *New York: G.P. Putnam's Sons, 1961, first edition, first printing.* **$7,768**

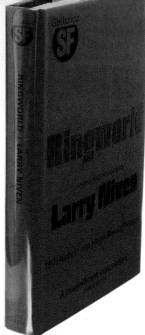

Heritage Auctions

▼ *J.R.R. Tolkien, The Lord of the Rings trilogy, including:* The Fellowship of the Ring. *London: George Allen & Unwin, 1954, first edition, signed by Tolkien on second free endpaper, 423 pages plus map attached to rear flyleaf.* **$7,768**

Heritage Auctions

▲ *Larry Niven,* Ringworld. *London: Victor Gollancz, 1972, first English edition, 288 pages, inscribed by author on title page, dated 1984, winner of the 1971 Hugo Award for best novel.* **$5,079**

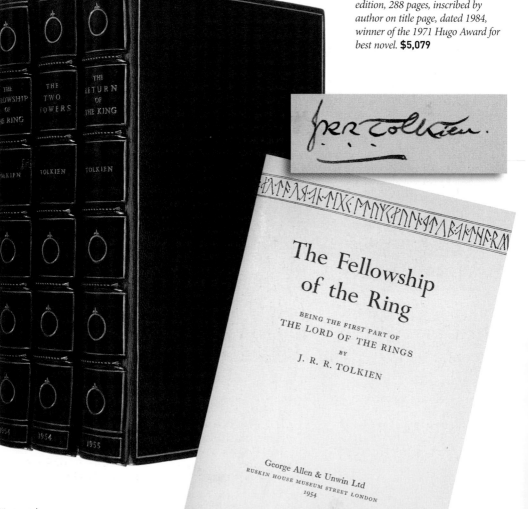

◀ *H.P. Lovecraft,* The Outsider and Others. *Collected by August Derleth and Donald Wandrei. Sauk City, Wisconsin: Arkham House, 1939, first edition of first collection of Lovecraft's writings, rare and important first book and first publication printed by Arkham House, one of only 1,268 copies printed, 553 pages.* **$5,079**

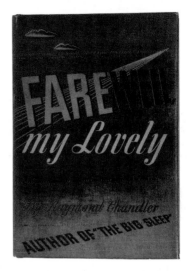

▲ *Raymond Chandler,* Farewell, My Lovely. *New York: Alfred A. Knopf, 1940, first edition, first printing of Chandler's second Philip Marlowe novel.* **$8,066**

George Orwell, Nineteen Eighty-Four *[1984]. London: Secker & Warburg, 1949, first edition, "First Published 1949" stated on copyright page, 312 pages.* **$4,482**

Harper Lee, To Kill a Mockingbird. *Philadelphia: J.B. Lippincott, 1960, first edition in first issue dust jacket, 296 pages, important and scarce book, only 5,000 copies printed. Lee's only novel won the 1961 Pulitzer Prize for Literature.* **$4,780**

John Kennedy Toole, A Confederacy of Dunces. *Foreword by Walker Percy. Baton Rouge: Louisiana State University Press, 1980, first edition signed by Walker Percy, 338 pages.* **$4,482**

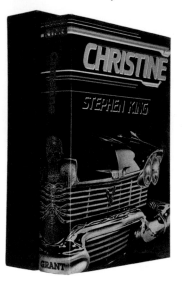

▶ *E.B. White,* Charlotte's Web. *New York: Harper and Brothers, 1952, first edition, pictures by Garth Williams, 1953 Newberry Award winning book.* **$1,554**

◀ *Stephen King,* Christine. *West Kingston: Donald M. Grant, 1983, first edition, limited to 1,000 numbered copies of which this is number 121, signed by King, 544 pages.* **$598**

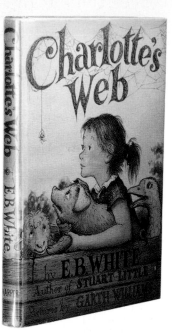

▶ *Charles Dickens,* Christmas Books, *including:* A Christmas Carol. *"In Prose. Being a Ghost Story of Christmas. With Illustrations by John Leech." London: Chapman and Hall, 1843, first edition, first issue. The first edition of* A Christmas Carol *went on sale Dec. 19, 1843 and by Christmas Eve every copy had sold out. Within weeks of publication, eight different stage adaptations were playing in London theatres.* **$16,250**

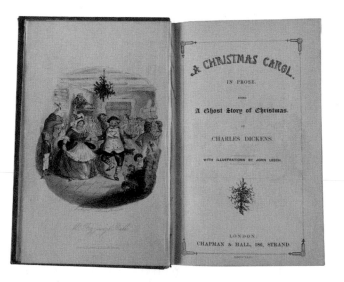

H.G. Wells, The Invisible Man, A Grotesque Romance. *London: C. Arthur Pearson Limited, 1897, first edition, 245 pages plus two pages of advertisements.* **$538**

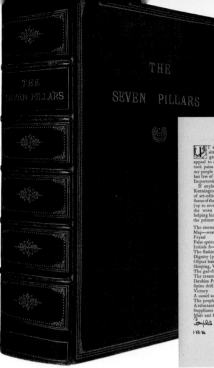

◀ *T.E. Lawrence,* Seven Pillars of Wisdom. A Triumph. *London: Printed for author by Manning Pike and H. J. Hodgson, 1926, scarce privately printed edition, one of only 170 complete copies, initialed by Lawrence at p. xix: "Complete copy i.xii.26 T. E. S." Quarto, 65 lithographic plates (61 bound at rear), frontispiece portrait of Feysal.* **$62,500**

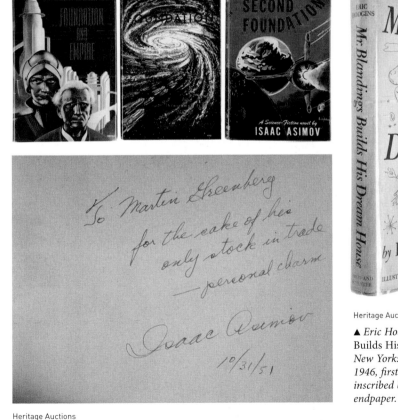

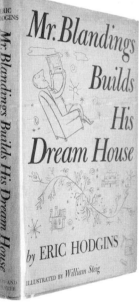

▲ *Eric Hodgins,* Mr. Blandings Builds His Dream House. *New York: Simon and Schuster, 1946, first edition, signed and inscribed by author on front endpaper.* **$538**

▲ *Isaac Asimov, The Foundation Trilogy, including:* Foundation, Foundation and Empire, *and* Second Foundation. *Garden City: Gnome Press, [1951-1953], all volumes first editions, each a presentation copy, inscribed by Asimov on front free endpaper.* **$21,250**

Heritage Auctions

Alexander Gardner, Gardner's Photographic Sketch Book of the War. *Washington, D.C.: Philp
and Solomons, [1865-66]. Two oblong folio volumes, approximately 12" x 16", 100 albumen prints
(approximately 7" x 9") mounted on larger sheets with lithographed frames and captions. The most
celebrated collection of Civil War photographs,* Gardner's Photographic Sketch Book of the War *contains
"many of the most graphic and memorable Civil War images that have come down to us" (ICP). The
photographs cover the entire conflict from Manassas in 1862 to the dedication of the monument at Bull Run
in June 1865.* **$194,500**

Bottles

By Michael Polak

G lass bottles are not as new as some people believe. In fact, the glass bottle has been around for about 3,000 years. In the late first century B.C., the Romans, with the assistance of glassworker craftsmen from Syria and Egypt, began making glass vials that local doctors and pharmacists used to dispense pills, healing powders, and miscellaneous potions.

The first attempt to manufacture glass in America is thought to have taken place at the Jamestown settlement in Virginia around 1608 by the London Co. The first successful American glass house was opened in 1739 in New Jersey by Caspar Wistar, who immigrated from Germany to Philadelphia in 1717.

Throughout the 19th century, glasshouses opened and closed because of changes in demand and technological improvements. Between 1840 and 1890, an enormous demand for glass containers developed to satisfy the demands of the whisky, beer, medical and food packing industries. Largely due to this steady demand, glass manufacturing in the United States evolved into a stable industry.

Unlike other businesses of the time that saw major changes in manufacturing processes, producing glass bottles remained unchanged. The process gave each bottle character, producing unique shapes, imperfections, irregularities, and various colors. That all changed at the turn of the 20th century when Michael J. Owens invented the first fully automated bottle making machine. Although many fine bottles were manufactured between 1900-1930, Owens' invention ended an era of unique bottle design that no machine process could ever duplicate.

The modern antique bottle collecting craze started in the 1960s with dump digging. Since then, interest in bottle collecting continues to grow, with new bottle clubs forming throughout the United States and Europe. More collectors are spending their free time digging through old dumps and foraging through ghost towns, digging out old outhouses where peopl often tossed empty bottles, exploring abandoned mine shafts, and searchir favorite bottle or antique shows, swap meets, flea markets, and garage sale: In addition, the Internet offers collectors numerous opportunities and resources to buy and sell bottles with many new auction websites. Many bottle clubs now have websites providing even information for the collector. These new technologies and resources helped bottle collecting to continue grow and gain interest.

Most collectors, however, still look beyond the type and value of a bottle to its origin and history. Researching the history of a bottle is almost as interesting as finding bottle itself. Both pursuits have close ties to the rich history of settling of the United States and the early methods of merchandising.

▶ *Mineral water bottle, "Deep Rock Spring – Oswego, N.Y.," medium teal blue green, quart, smooth base, American 1865-1875.* **$1,900-$2,000**

MICHAEL POLAK has collected more than 3,000 bottles since entering the hobby in 1976. He is a regular contributor to a variety of antiques publications and is the author of *Antique Trader Bottles Identification & Price Guide,* 7th edition.

Hutchinson bottle, "J. F. Deegan – Pottsville – PA.," medium yellow amber, tooled top, American 1885-1895, 6 3/4". **$450-$475**

Midwestern blown pattern molded flask, medium amber, folded lip, 24-rib-pattern to right, 1810-1820, 7 1/2". **$500-$550**

Hawaiian bottle, "Siphon Co. LTD. – Honolulu, T. H. – Contents 35 Fl. Oz.," 1935. **$1,800-$2,500**

*Inkwell, medium green, American
1840-1860, 2 1/2".* **$175-$200**

*Belle fruit jar, aqua, quart, sheared and
ground lip, original domed glass lid,
American 1869-1875.* **$1,200-$1,300**

*Charles Cordial London Gin
bottle, brilliant turquoise, applied
top, American 1860-1870, 8".*
$200-$225

*Medicine bottle, M.B. Robert's
Vegetable Embrocation, medium
teal blue, open pontil, American
1840-1860, 5-1/4".* **$300-$325**

*EHVB crosshatched pickle bottle
(E.H. Van Benschoten of New York),
light green, six-sided, American
1850-1860, 14".* **$600-$700**

Sarsaparilla bottle, Sands' Sarsaparilla, aqua green, applied top, American 1885-1895, 8". **$100-$125**

Soda bottle, L.C. Smith, cobalt blue, American 1840-1860, 7 3/8". **$300-$325**

Sunburst scent bottle, medium pink amethyst, American 1840-1860, 2 7/8". **$900-$1,000**

Fire grenade, "Rockford – Kalamazoo – Automatic And – Hand Fire Extinguisher – Patent applied For," cobalt blue, tooled lip, American 1875-1895, 11". **$500-$600**

Cobalt blue medicine bottle, USA Hospital, medium cobalt blue, applied square collar, 1865-1870, 9". **$1,600-$1,800**

"Bowman's Drug Stores – Poison," cobalt blue, original label, American 1890-1920, 7 1/2". **$550-$600**

Target ball (motif of man shooting on two sides), medium amethyst, English 1877-1895, 2 5/8" diameter.
$200-$250

Barber bottle, medium pink over white with fancy enameled decoration, pontiled base, tooled lip, American 1885-1920, 7-1/2".
$100-$125

Soda fountain syrup dispenser, Grape Crush, amethyst glass, American 1900-1930, 15". **$1,150**

◄ Beer bottle, "American Brewing Co. – West Berkley Cal. – This Bottle Not To Be Sold," medium amber, one-half pint (split), tooled top, 1890-1910. **$180-$200**

▲ Hair restorer bottle, "Mrs. S.A. Allen – Worlds Hair – Restorer – New York," lime green, applied double collar top, 1865-1875, 7 3/8". **$900-$1,000**

▶ Black glass onion shape wine bottle, medium olive green, Dutch 1720-1750, 6 7/8" x 5 1/2" diameter. **$250-$300**

▲ Two strapside whiskey flasks, "John Coyne – Cor. Fayette & Seneca Sts. – Utica, N.Y.," yellow green, pint, applied top, and "D.F. Flagg & Co. – 165 Blackstone St – Boston," tooled double collar top, American 1880-1900. **$250-$300**

▲ Midwestern pattern molded flask, medium yellow green, 24-vertical rib pattern, American 1815-1835, 6". **$1,000-$1,100**

Warner bottle, "Warner's Safe Cure – Trade Mark – London," English 1890-1900, 7 3/8" and 9 3/8".
$150-$250

Bitters bottle, "Suffolk Bitters – Philbrook & Tucker – Boston," light golden yellow amber, figural pig, smooth base, applied tapered collar top, 1865-1875, 10 1/8". **$800-$900**

Four A.G. Smalley & Co. milk bottles – half-pint, pint, quart, and half-gallon, patent April 5, 1898, Boston, Massachusetts, American 1900-1910. **$400-$425**

◄ *Back bar bottle, "Drink – Moonshine – Makes You Happy," dark amber, American 1895-1910, 11 1/4".* **$450-$500**

► *Rib-pattern chestnut flask, deep red amber, 24 rib-pattern swirled to left, American 1815-1835, 5-1/8".* **$225-$250**

CERAMICS

American Ceramics

Fiesta

The Homer Laughlin China Co. originated with a two-kiln pottery on the banks of the Ohio River in East Liverpool, Ohio. Built in 1873-'74 by Homer Laughlin and his brother, Shakespeare, the firm was first known as the Ohio Valley Pottery, and later as Laughlin Bros. Pottery. It was one of the first white-ware plants in the country.

After a tentative beginning, the company was awarded a prize for having the best white-ware at the 1876 Centennial Exposition in Philadelphia.

Three years later, Shakespeare sold his interest in the business to Homer, who continued on until 1897. At that time, Homer Laughlin sold his interest in the newly incorporated firm to a group of investors, including Charles, Louis, and Marcus Aaron and the company bookkeeper, William E. Wells.

Under new ownership in 1907, the headquarters and a new 30-kiln plant were built across the Ohio River in Newell, West Virginia, the present manufacturing and headquarters location.

In the 1920s, two additions to the Homer Laughlin staff set the stage for the company's greatest success: the Fiesta line.

Dr. Albert V. Bleininger was hired in 1920. A scientist, author, and educator, he oversaw the conversion from bottle kilns to the more efficient tunnel kilns.

In 1927, the company hired designer Frederick Hurten Rhead, a member of a distinguished family of English ceramists. Having previously worked at Weller Pottery and Roseville Pottery, Rhead began to develop the artistic quality of the company's wares, and to experiment with shapes and glazes. In 1935, this work culminated in his designs for the Fiesta line.

For more information on Fiesta, see *Warman's Fiesta Identification and Price Guide* by Glen Victorey.

Fiesta Colors

From 1936 to 1972, Fiesta was produced in 14 colors (other than special promotions). These colors are usually divided into the "original colors" of cobalt blue, light green, ivory, red, turquoise, and yellow (cobalt blue, light green, red, and yellow only on the Kitchen Kraft line, introduced in 1939); the "1950s colors" of chartreuse, forest green, gray, and rose (introduced in 1951); medium green (introduced in 1959); plus the later additions of Casuals, Amberstone, Fiesta Ironstone, and Casualstone ("Coventry") in antique gold, mango red, and turf green; and the striped, decal, and Lustre pieces. No Fiesta was produced from 1973 to 1985. The colors that make up the "original" and "1950s" groups are sometimes referred to as "the standard 11."

In many pieces, medium green is the hardest to find and the most expensive Fiesta color.

4 3/4" fruit bowls in turquoise, cobalt blue, ivory, yellow and light green, **$35 each.** *Red.* **$40**

#3 mixing bowl in red. **$175**
Bowl lids in light green, red, and yellow. **$1,250-$2,000 each**

Fiesta Colors and Years of Production to 1972

Antique Gold—dark butterscotch.. 1969-1972
Chartreuse—yellowish green 1951-1959
Cobalt Blue—dark or royal blue.. 1936-1951
Forest Green—dark hunter green 1951-1959
Gray—light or ash gray.. 1951-1959
Green—often called light green when comparing it
   to other green glazes; also called "Original" green............................ 1936-1951
Ivory—creamy, slightly yellowed... 1936-1951
Mango Red—same as original red 1970-1972
Medium Green—bright rich green 1959-1969
Red—reddish orange .... 1936-1944 and 1959-1972
Rose—dusty, dark rose... 1951-1959
Turf Green—olive.. 1969-1972
Turquoise—sky blue, like the stone... 1937-1969
Yellow—golden yellow.. 1936-1969

▲ *Two-pint jug in turquoise.* **$135**
Red. **$175**

Water tumblers in light green, cobalt blue, and turquoise. **$90 each**

Comport in cobalt blue. **$150**
Sauceboat in light green. **$80**

Carafe in red. **$395**

Medium teapot in turquoise. **$295**

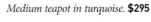

◀ *Disk water pitcher in red.* **$225**

▼ *Teacup and saucer in cobalt blue.* **$39/set**

Dessert bowls in cobalt blue and turquoise. **$65 each**
Red. **$75**

Unopened boxed set of two teacups in yellow. Boxes can double or triple overall value of piece. **$78-$117**

Demitasse coffeepot in green. **$600**

Demitasse cups and saucers in original colors. Cups: red, **$100;** *cobalt blue, ivory, and turquoise,* **$95 each;** *yellow and green,* **$85 each.** *Saucers: red and turquoise,* **$25 each;** *cobalt blue, ivory, yellow and green,* **$20 each.**

Demitasse cup and saucer in ivory. **$115/set** *Red.* **$125/set**

Tom & Jerry mugs: forest green and chartreuse. **$95 each** *Gray.* **$85**

Deep plate in chartreuse. **$75**

Oval platter in medium green. **$250**

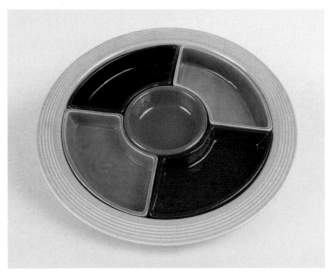

Relish tray in ivory with cobalt blue, light green, red, turquoise, and yellow inserts. **$425**

12" compartment plate in red. **$145**

Promotional juice tumbler in red. **$75**

▲ *7" plates in light green, cobalt blue, turquoise, and yellow.* **$15 each** *Red.* **$20**

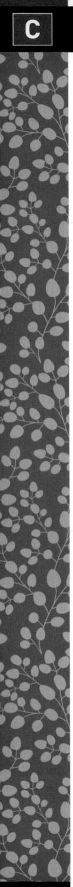

▶ *Special order promotional disk juice pitcher in red.* **$650**

◀ *Promotional French casserole in yellow with yellow cover.* **$275-$325**

Left to right: 8", 10", and 12" vases in turquoise, yellow, and cobalt blue. **$800, $1,150,** *and* **$1,950,** *respectively.*

Covered casserole in red. **$300**
Yellow. **$250**

Rare promotional salad bowl in cobalt blue, with Kitchen Kraft red spoon and yellow fork. This was the Promotional Salad Set that sold between 1940 and 1943. Bowls were usually yellow. **$2,000 for bowl**

Two covered onion soup bowls and lids in ivory. Lid on left is typical production style with flared knob and shorter flange ring; lid on right is early production style with more tapered knob and deeper flange ring. More common one on left is approximately **$775.** No established value for one on right.

Eggcup in yellow. **$70**
Ashtray in light green. **$85**

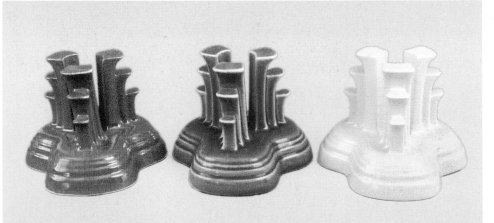

Tripod candleholders in yellow, light green, and ivory. **$725 each pair**

Fulper

T he firm that became Fulper Pottery Co. of Flemington, New Jersey, originally made stoneware pottery and utilitarian wares beginning in the early 1800s. Fulper made art pottery from about 1909 to 1935.

The company's earliest artware was called the VaseKraft line (1910-1915). Its middle period (1915-1925) included some of the earlier shapes, but it also incorporated Oriental forms. Its glazing at this time was less consistent but more diverse. The last period (1925-1935) was characterized by Art Deco forms.

FULPER in a rectangle is known as the "ink mark" and dates from 1910-1915. The second mark, which dates from 1915-1925, was incised or in black ink. The final mark, FULPER, die-stamped, dates from about 1925 to 1935.

Rago Arts & Auction Center

▼ *Tall rare urn, blue and ivory flambé glaze, 1916-1922, raised racetrack mark, 14 1/2" x 9".* **$3,250**

Rago Arts & Auction Center

▶ *Flower jug, Copperdust Crystalline glaze, 1916-1922, incised racetrack mark, 12" x 8".* **$1,500**

Mark Mussio, Humler & Nolan

▶ *Vaz bowl in Mirror Black over cream flambé, marked with vertical Fulper ink stamp logo and Panama-Pacific Expo paper label, also bears remnants of another Fulper paper label, excellent original condition with slight crazing in bowl, 6 3/8" high.* **$180**

Mark Mussio, Humler & Nolan

▼ *"Bell pepper" vase in bluish-green mat glaze with yellow on top, incised racetrack mark, excellent condition, 4 1/4" high.* **$350**

Mark Mussio, Humler & Nolan

▼ *Tapered gourd vase in green mat glaze with tan at rim, incised racetrack mark, excellent condition, 5 5/8" high x 9" wide.* **$275**

Rago Arts & Auction Center

Two pairs of book blocks, Mission Bells and Chinese Gates, 1910-1916, Chinese Gates with vertical ink stamp, Mission Bells with paper label, 8" x 6 1/4", 7 1/4" x 5 1/2". **$1,250**

Mark Mussio, Humler & Nolan

◄ *Vase with cream flambé over Mirror Black glaze, raised vertical Fulper mark, several burst glaze bubbles and some tiny scratches, 16 1/2" high.* **$850**

Mark Mussio, Humler & Nolan

▲ *Handled compote on raised base coated with mustard mat glaze, paler yellow interior encircled with streaks of brown-gray, center has splash of red-brown, unmarked, crazed interior, excellent original condition, 5" high x 12 1/2" wide.* **$200**

Rago Arts & Auction Center

▶ *Rare VaseKraft lamp, Flemington Green flambé glaze, circa 1908, glazed ceramic, leaded glass, two sockets, base with rectangular ink stamp, patent pending, no. 22, shade numbered 22/33/28, 22" x 16".* **$13,750**

Pook & Pook, Inc.

▲ *Art pottery candle sconce, 20th century, 10 3/4" high.* **$395**

Rago Arts & Auction Center

▶ *Baluster vase, Chinese Blue flambé glaze, 1916-1922, vertical incised racetrack mark, 11 1/2" x 8 1/2".* **$1,750**

Rago Arts & Auction Center

▼ *Jardiniere, Mirror Black glaze, 1910-1916, vertical black ink stamp, 8 1/4" x 10".* **$3,000**

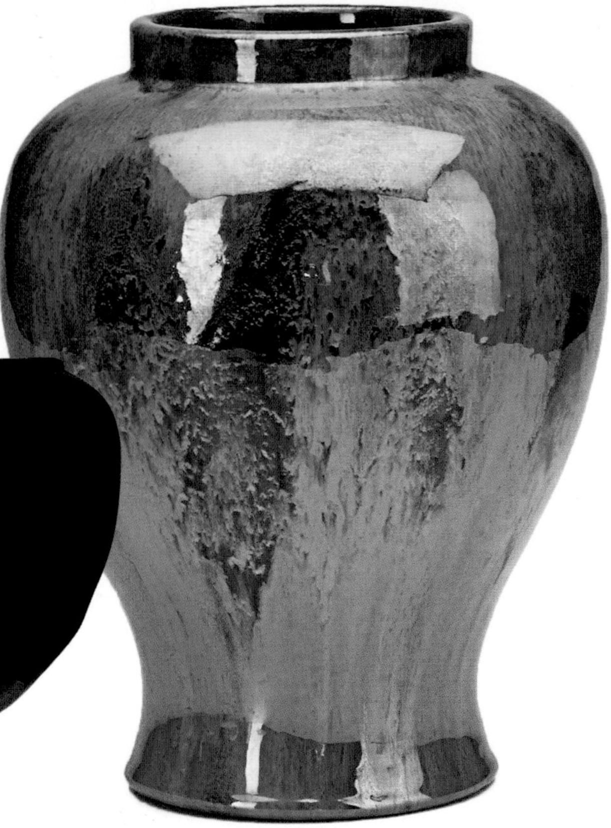

Mark Mussio, Humler & Nolan

▲ *Flambé Chinese sleeping cat doorstop in flambé Mirror Black with ivory glaze, rectangular Fulper stamp, stilt pull off bottom, excellent condition, 5 1/8" x 9 3/4".* **$1,200**

Rago Arts & Auction Center

▲ *"Bum" glazed ceramic doorstop, 1910s, unmarked, 8" x 9 1/2" x 6".* **$1,375**

Rago Arts
& Auction Center

▶ *Rare VaseKraft lamp, Cat's Eye flambé glaze, circa 1908, glazed ceramic, leaded glass, two sockets, VaseKraft stamp, vertical rectangular ink stamp, patent pending, 17 1/2" x 14".* **$9,375**

Rago Arts & Auction Center

▼ *Urn, Green Crystalline glaze, 1910-1916, vertical rectangular ink stamp, 12" x 8 1/2".* **$1,000**

Rago Arts & Auction Center

▼ *Jar with pedestal, Cucumber Green crystalline glaze, 1916-1922, raised racetrack mark, 11 1/4" x 10 1/2".* **$4,063**

Mark Mussio, Humler & Nolan

▲ *Pair of pillar candlestick vases with glossy and mat glazes in several shades of green with touches of brown at rim, ink stamp racetrack logo, excellent original condition, 8 1/2" high.* **$425**

Mark Mussio, Humler & Nolan

Handled vase with blue snowflake crystals over lilac gray, ink stamp racetrack mark, excellent original condition, 6" high. **$200**

Mark Mussio, Humler & Nolan

Squatty gourd vase with green glaze over blue with small patches of cobalt, Prang mark on bottom, 3 3/4" high x 6 3/8" diameter. **$400**

Mark Mussio, Humler & Nolan

Necked vase with mat Aqua Green Crystalline glaze, racetrack logo, excellent condition, 7 3/4" high. **$150**

Mark Mussio, Humler & Nolan

Vase with blue snowflake crystals, impressed oval Fulper logo, glazed over kiln kiss on fat part of vase, two uneven areas at rim, also glazed over, 9 1/2" high. **$190**

Mark Mussio, Humler & Nolan

Handled vase in Mirror Black over butterscotch glaze, vertical racetrack ink stamp logo, small open glaze bubble on inside of rim, some kiln pulls on base, 11 3/4" high. **$425**

Grueby

William Grueby was active in the ceramic industry for several years before he developed his own method of producing matte-glazed pottery and founded the Grueby Faience Co. of Boston in 1897.

The art pottery was hand thrown in natural shapes, hand molded and hand tooled. A variety of colored glazes, singly or in combinations, was produced, but green was the most popular. In 1908, the firm was divided into the Grueby Pottery Co. and the Grueby Faience and Tile Co. The Grueby Faience and Tile Co. made art tile until 1917, although its pottery production was phased out about 1910.

Rago Arts &
Auction Center

Vase with leaves and buds, rare matte mauve glaze, circa 1900, circular Faience stamp, CP, 7 1/4" x 5".
$1,875

Mark Mussio, Humler & Nolan

▶ *Tile decorated with white and brown swan against green grass and blue sky by Ruth Erickson, marked with artist's initials "RE" on back in blue slip, minor nicks at edges, 4" x 4".*
$2,600

Mark Mussio, Humler & Nolan

▲ *Matte glaze vase with five hand-tooled leaves and buds coming up from base, impressed Grueby Faience Co. Boston on bottom, excellent original condition, 7 3/8" high.* **$1,200**

Rago Arts & Auction Center

▶ *Massive, rare vase with leaves and buds, circa 1900, circular Faience stamp, 23" x 9".* **$21,250**

Rago Arts & Auction Center

▲ *Rare floor vase carved with leaves and buds, curdled green glaze, circa 1900, unmarked, 26" x 11 1/2".* **$6,875**

Rago Arts & Auction Center

◀ *Early Kendrick vase, matte green glaze, circa 1900, circular Faience stamp, paper label, 12" x 8 1/2".* **$31,250**

Rago Arts & Auction Center
Tile with yellow tulip, circa 1905, decorator's initials, 1" x 6" sq.
$2,125

Rago Arts & Auction Center
▼ *Rare and early vase carved with leaves, circa 1900, horizontal stamp GRUEBY BOSTON, MASS., 12" x 7 1/2".* **$5,313**

Rago Arts & Auction Center
▶ *Early bulbous vase carved with leaves, circa 1900, circular Faience stamp/152, paper label 1114, artist's cipher, 12" x 9".*
$5,000

Heritage Auctions
Squat, bulbous, ribbed art pottery vessel, circa 1900, matte yellow glaze, marked GRUEBY, BOSTON MASS (impressed), 3" high x 6" wide. **$500**

Hull Pottery

I n 1905, Addis E. Hull purchased the Acme Pottery Co. of Crooksville, Ohio. In 1917, the A.E. Hull Pottery Co. began making art pottery, novelties, stoneware and kitchenware, later including the famous Little Red Riding Hood line. Most items had a matte finish, with shades of pink, blue, and brown predominating.

After a flood and fire in 1950, the factory reopened in 1952 as the Hull Pottery Co. New pieces, mostly with a glossy finish, were produced. The firm closed in 1985.

Pre-1950 vases are marked "Hull USA" or "Hull Art USA" on the bottom. Many also retain their paper labels. Post-1950 pieces are marked "Hull" in large script or "HULL" in block letters.

Each pattern has a distinctive letter or number, e.g., Wildflower has a "W" and a number; Water Lily, "L" and number; Poppy, numbers in the 600s; Orchid, numbers in the 300s. Early stoneware pieces are marked with an "H."

For more information on Hull Pottery, see *Warman's Hull Pottery Identification and Price Guide* by David Doyle.

Belhorn Auctions, LLC

Blossom Flite console set with T10 bowl and T11 candleholders, all marked, all mint, bowl 17" long. **$35**

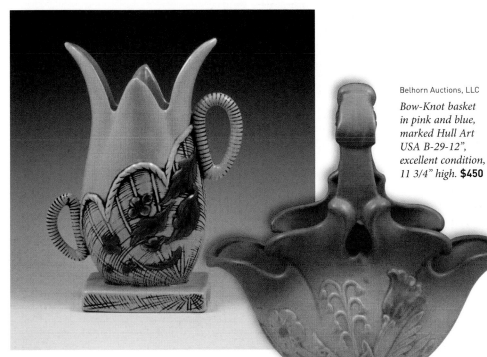

Belhorn Auctions, LLC

Bow-Knot basket in pink and blue, marked Hull Art USA B-29-12", excellent condition, 11 3/4" high. **$450**

Belhorn Auctions, LLC

Blossom Flite vase, marked Hull USA T7 © '55, mint condition, 10 1/2" high. **$30**

Belhorn Auctions, LLC

Bow-Knot cornucopia in blue and turquoise, marked Hull Art USA B-5-7 1/2", mint condition, 6 7/8" high. **$45**

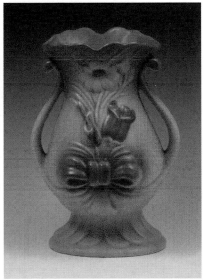

Belhorn Auctions, LLC

Bow-Knot vase in pink and blue, marked Hull Art USA B-7-8 1/2", mint condition, 8 3/4" high. **$55**

Belhorn Auctions, LLC

Bow-Knot wall plaque in pink, unmarked, small area of restoration on edge, factory pop near one flower, 10 1/2" across. **$90**

Belhorn Auctions, LLC

◄ *Bow-Knot vase in blue and turquoise, marked Hull Art USA B-10-10 1/2", mint condition, 10 3/4" high.* **$85**

Belhorn Auctions, LLC

Ebb Tide tea set, all marked, creamer and teapot in mint condition, lid to sugar has chip, seahorse has been broken and repaired, 3 3/4" to 6 1/4" high. **$55**

Belhorn Auctions, LLC

Large Hull Ebb Tide pitcher, marked Hull USA E-10, mint condition, 13 3/4" high. **$45**

Belhorn Auctions, LLC

Ebb Tide mermaid planter, unmarked, mint condition, 8 3/4" long. **$50**

Belhorn Auctions, LLC

Ebb Tide E-6 fish vase and E-13 candleholders, all marked, candleholders in mint condition, small nick to topmost point on fish vase, 9 1/4" and 2 1/2" high. **$45**

Belhorn Auctions, LLC

Ebb Tide tea set with lidded teapot, lidded sugar, and creamer, all marked, all mint condition, 3 1/2" to 6 1/4" high. **$85**

Belhorn Auctions, LLC

Little Red Riding Hood (LRRH) salt and pepper shakers, unmarked, excellent condition, 5" high. **$30**

Belhorn Auctions, LLC

Little Red Riding Hood (LRRH) lidded teapot, marked Pat. Des. No. 135889 USA, excellent condition, 8" high. **$40**

Belhorn Auctions, LLC

Magnolia cornucopia in dusty rose, marked Hull Art USA 19-8 1/2, mint condition, 8 3/4" high. **$21**

Strawser Auction Group

Pair of Magnolia vases, 2-8 1/2". **$52**

Belhorn Auctions, LLC

Hull Pottery Association commemorative Little Red Riding Hood planter from 1998, marked and dated, signed Linda Gill, mint condition, 7 1/2" long. **$60**

Belhorn Auctions, LLC

Parchment & Pine console set, unmarked, mint condition, bowl 11" long. **$30**

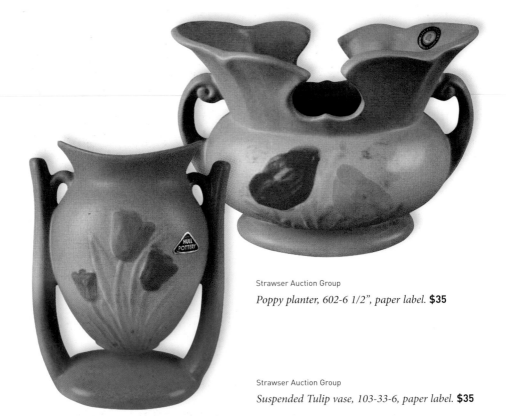

Strawser Auction Group

Poppy planter, 602-6 1/2", paper label. **$35**

Strawser Auction Group

Suspended Tulip vase, 103-33-6, paper label. **$35**

Strawser Auction Group
Water Lily, L-12-10 1/2". **$35**

Strawser Auction Group
Wildflower ewer, W-11-8 1/2. **$41**

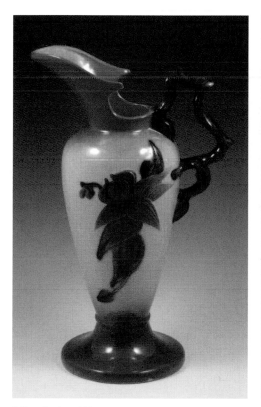

Belhorn Auctions, LLC
*Woodland Gloss ewer, marked Hull USA
W24-13 1/2", mint condition, 14 1/4" high.* **$40**

Belhorn Auctions, LLC
*Woodland Gloss basket, marked Hull USA
W9-8 3/4", mint condition, 9" high.* **$21**

Belhorn Auctions, LLC

Woodland Gloss console set, all marked, all mint, bowl 14 1/2" long. **$35**

Belhorn Auctions, LLC

Woodland Gloss tea set, all marked, all mint, 3 3/4" to 6 1/2" high. **$60**

Novelty Items

Belhorn Auctions, LLC

Hippo planter in green, marked Hull USA, excellent condition, 8 1/2" long. **$70**

Belhorn Auctions, LLC

◄ Bluebird clock, unmarked, excellent condition, 10 1/2" high. **$160**

Turkey Creek Auctions, Inc.

Pretzel jar, 9 1/2" high x 7 1/2" diameter. **$83**

Turkey Creek Auctions, Inc.

Planter, duck design, #104, 8 3/4" high x 10 1/4" wide. **$41**

Belhorn Auctions, LLC

Corky Pig bank in yellow and blue, fully marked and dated 1957, mint condition, 7" long. **$30**

McCoy Pottery

The first McCoy with clay under his fingernails was W. Nelson McCoy. With his uncle, W.F. McCoy, he founded a pottery works in Putnam, Ohio, in 1848, making stoneware crocks and jugs.

That same year, W. Nelson's son, James W., was born in Zanesville, Ohio. James established the J.W. McCoy Pottery Co. in Roseville, Ohio, in the fall of 1899. The J.W. McCoy plant was destroyed by fire in 1903 and was rebuilt two years later.

It was at this time that the first examples of Loy-Nel-Art wares were produced. The line's distinctive title came from the names of James McCoy's three sons, Lloyd, Nelson, and Arthur.

George Brush became general manager of J.W. McCoy Pottery Co. in 1909, the company became Brush-McCoy Pottery Co. in 1911, and in 1925 the name was shortened to Brush Pottery Co. This firm remained in business until 1982.

Separately, in 1910, Nelson McCoy, Sr. founded the Nelson McCoy Sanitary and Stoneware Co., also in Roseville. By the early 1930s, production had shifted from utilitarian wares to art pottery, and the company name was changed to Nelson McCoy Pottery.

Designer Sydney Cope was hired in 1934, and was joined by his son, Leslie, in 1936. The Copes' influence on McCoy wares continued until Sydney's death in 1966. That same year, Leslie opened a gallery devoted to his family's design heritage and featuring his own original art.

Nelson McCoy, Sr. died in 1945, and was succeeded as company president by his nephew, Nelson McCoy Melick.

A fire destroyed the plant in 1950, but company officials – including Nelson McCoy, Jr., then 29 – decided to rebuild, and the new Nelson McCoy Pottery Co. was up and running in just six months.

Nelson Melick died in 1954. Nelson, Jr. became company president and oversaw the company's continued growth. In 1967, the operation was sold to entrepreneur David Chase. At this time, the words "Mt. Clemens Pottery" were added to the company marks. In 1974, Chase sold the company to Lancaster Colony Corp., and the company marks included a stylized "LCC" logo. Nelson, Jr. and his wife, Billie, who had served as a products supervisor, left the company in 1981.

In 1985, the company was sold again, this time to Designer Accents. The McCoy pottery factory closed in 1990.

For more information on McCoy pottery, see *Warman's McCoy Pottery*, 2nd edition, by Mark F. Moran.

Kaminski Auctions

Ceramic teapot, Boston Ivy design, 8" high x 10" wide x 7" deep. Provenance: Property of Oprah Winfrey. **$125**

Victorian Casino Antiques

Indian head ceramic cookie jar, No. 50, marked "McCoy USA" on bottom, circa 1954-1956, crazing, small chip on hair. **$96**

Victorian Casino Antiques

Dalmatians in rocking chair ceramic cookie jar, marked "McCoy USA" on bottom, circa 1961, small chip near top of chair. **$75**

Victorian Casino Antiques

Popeye cylinder ceramic cookie jar, No. 222, unmarked on bottom, "Cookies" and "Popeye Copyright King Features Syndicate, Inc. 1965. World rights reserved" on front, circa 1971-1972, very good condition, some small blemishes. **$92**

Kaminski Auctions

Large Brush McCoy glazed stoneware jardinière, Amaryllis pattern, cream and green ivotint glaze, circa 1920s, 1/4" glaze chip to rim, 9 1/2" high x 11 1/2" diameter. **$180**

Victorian Casino Antiques

▼ *Barnum's Animal Crackers ceramic cookie jar, marked "152 USA" on bottom, copyright 1972, Nabisco, Inc., front is a transfer, some wear on transfer and some small blemishes, overall good condition.* **$108**

Victorian Casino Antiques

▲ *Teepee ceramic cookie jar, marked "McCoy USA 137" on bottom, slant top, small chip at teepee tip, some crazing.* **$108**

Skinner, Inc.; www.skinnerinc.com

Two aqua-glazed molded Flying Swallow-decorated art pottery jardinières, one glossy glazed and one matte glazed, hairline from rim on matte glazed item, 6 7/8" high. **$123**

Strawser Auctions

▶ *Vase, 14 1/2" high.* **$64**

Leslie Hindman
Auctioneers

▲ *Arts & Crafts pottery umbrella stand, Brush McCoy, cylindrical form, decorated with repeating stylized lotus stems in ivory glaze on brown reserve, 16 3/4" high.* **$281**

Mark Mussio, Humler & Nolan

Jewel jardinière enameled with green, pink and cobalt triangles with white enamel beadwork, excellent original condition, 6 3/4" x 7 1/2". **$225**

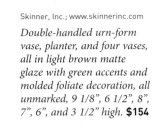

Skinner, Inc.; www.skinnerinc.com

Double-handled urn-form vase, planter, and four vases, all in light brown matte glaze with green accents and molded foliate decoration, all unmarked, 9 1/8", 6 1/2", 8", 7", 6", and 3 1/2" high. **$154**

Strawser Auction Group

Large jardinière, green with ivy bank rim, nick to bottom of one handle, 12" high. **$52**

Strawser Auction Group

El Ranchero Sombrero and bowl, 12" high x 12 1/2" diameter. **$75**

Strawser Auction Group

El Ranchero coffeepot and stand, pot 9 3/4" high, stand 4 1/2" high. **$75**

Red Wing Pottery

Various potteries operated in Red Wing, Minnesota, starting in 1868, the most successful being the Red Wing Stoneware Co., organized in 1877. Merged with other local potteries through the years, it became known as Red Wing Union Stoneware Co. in 1906 and was one of the largest producers of utilitarian stoneware items in the United States.

After a decline in the popularity of stoneware products, an art pottery line was introduced to compensate for the loss. This was reflected in a new name for the company, Red Wing Potteries, Inc., in 1936. Stoneware production ceased entirely in 1947, but vases, planters, cookie jars, and dinnerware of art pottery quality continued in production until 1967, when the pottery ceased operation altogether.

For more information on Red Wing pottery, see *Warman's Red Wing Pottery Identification and Price Guide* by Mark F. Moran.

Stoneware

Three-gallon churn-form store advertisement with "elephant ears," with original churn cover, 14 3/8" high including lid. **$7,500**

Two-gallon churn with Utah advertising, otherwise unmarked, 12 5/8" high. **$4,000**

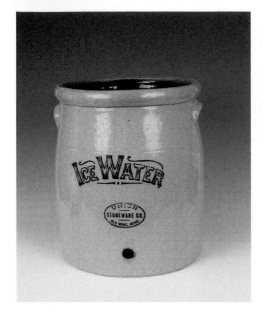

Unusual three-gallon stoneware ice water cooler in a glaze between tan and white, Albany slip interior, 11 3/4" high. **$900-$1,250**

Four-gallon salt-glaze churn with cobalt decoration of "lazy 8" and "tornado," circa 1890, and cover in Albany slip glaze, 16" high, unmarked. **$800-$900**

Five-gallon white stoneware "beehive" two-handle jug with advertising, 17" high, rare. **$4,000**

Three-gallon salt-glaze "beehive" jug with elaborate "3" and stylized leaf, circa 1890, with glaze drippings known as "turkey droppings," 14" high, unmarked. **$2,000**

Two stoneware eggs showing face of child emerging from one side and child's bare bottom emerging from other side, each also has vent hole, each 1 3/4" long. **$900 each**

Cow and calf in bisque, small base, 5" long, 4 1/4" high. **$3,000**

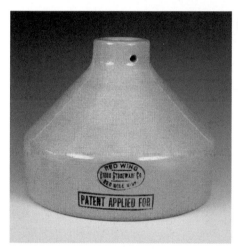

White stoneware Christmas tree holder rarely found in colored glaze, 8 1/2" high. **$800**

Hotel-size spittoon with blue sponge decoration, 6" high x 9 1/2" diameter. **$2,000**

Four-gallon white stoneware water cooler without gallon mark, lid impressed 3W, 12 3/4" high without lid, lid 9 1/2" diameter. **$800-$1,000**

Art Pottery

▲ *Flower bowl made for Ernest Sohn, a New York-area retailer, marked "ES USA," 14" diameter.* **$50+**

▼ *Candlesticks No. 233C in Nokomis glaze, part of console set with Bowl No. 233, each 7" high.* **$1,000 pr.**

▲ *"Cherub" Brushed Ware vase in "cement" finish, also found in green, No. 131, ink-stamped in circle: "Red Wing Union Stoneware Co.—Red Wing, Minn.," 12" high.* **$550**

Lion planter No. 917, 13" long, also raised mark, "Red Wing USA." **$400**

◀ *Baseball batter and catcher figurines designed by Charles Murphy, Nos. 1176 and 1177, batter holds wooden bat, 8" and 7" high.* **$600 each**

▶ *Statue titled "Woman in the Hand" No. 1178, designed by Charles Murphy, 1942, one of only three known, 12" high.* **$4,000**

◀ *Lamp base No. 806 (based on No. 200 vase) in Nokomis glaze, 9 1/2" high.* **$800-$1,200**

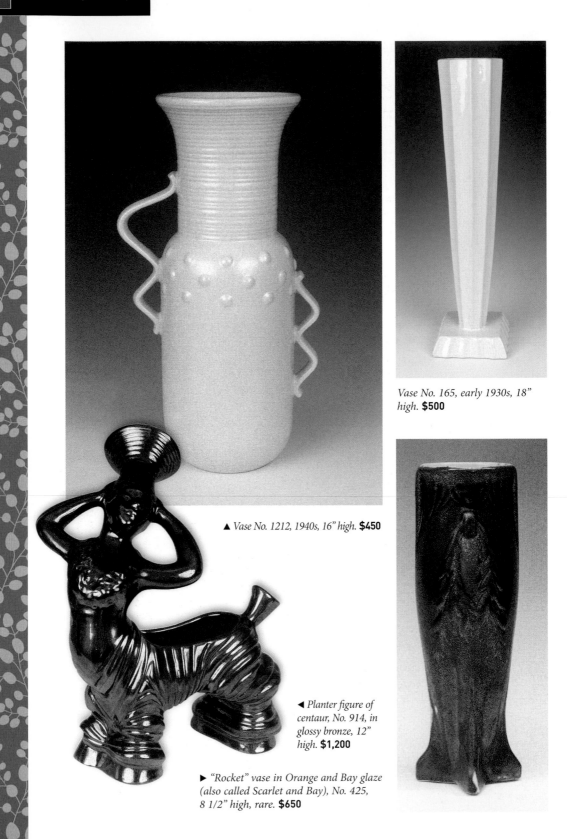

Vase No. 165, early 1930s, 18" high. **$500**

▲ Vase No. 1212, 1940s, 16" high. **$450**

◄ Planter figure of centaur, No. 914, in glossy bronze, 12" high. **$1,200**

► "Rocket" vase in Orange and Bay glaze (also called Scarlet and Bay), No. 425, 8 1/2" high, rare. **$650**

▲ *Decorator Line footed oval bowl No. M3017, 13 1/2" wide.* **$225**

◄ *Figure of a centaur No. 1123, in Bronze-Tan Engobe with yellow and black decoration, 9 1/4" high.* **$1,000**

▼ *"Woman with Two Tubes" double bud vase No. 1175, designed by Charles Murphy, 1942, 10 1/2" high.* **$1,200-$1,500 in these colors**

► *Vase No. 3019 in burnt orange crystalline glaze, designed by Charles Murphy, raised mark, "Red Wing U.S.A. 3019," 13" high x 13" diameter.* **$500**

Rookwood Pottery

Maria Longworth Nichols founded the Rookwood Pottery in 1880. The name, she later reported, paid homage to the many crows (rooks) on her father's estate and was also designed to remind customers of Wedgwood. Production began on Thanksgiving Day 1880 when the first kiln was drawn.

Rookwood's earliest productions demonstrated a continued reliance on European precedents and Japanese aesthetic. Although the firm offered a variety of wares (Dull Glaze, Cameo, and Limoges for example), it lacked a clearly defined artistic identity. With the introduction of what became known as its "Standard Glaze" in 1884, Rookwood inaugurated a period in which the company won consistent recognition for its artistic merit and technical innovation.

Rookwood's first decade ended on a high note when the company was awarded two gold medals: one at Exhibition of American Art Industry in Philadelphia and another later in the year at the Exposition Universelle in Paris. Significant, too, was Maria Longworth Nichols' decision to transfer her interest in the company to William W. Taylor, who had been the firm's manager since 1883. In May 1890, the board of a newly reorganized Rookwood Pottery Co. purchased "the real estate, personal property, goodwill, patents, trade-marks… now sole property of William W. Taylor" for $40,000.

Under Taylor's leadership, Rookwood was transformed from a fledgling startup to a successful business that expanded throughout the following decades to meet rising demand.

Throughout the 1890s, Rookwood continued to attract critical notice as it kept tradition of innovation alive. Taylor rolled out three new glaze lines—Iris, Sea Green and Aerial Blue—from late 1894 into early 1895.

At the Paris Exposition in 1900, Rookwood cemented its reputation by winning Grand Prix, a feat largely due to favorable reception of the new Iris glaze and its variants.

Over the next several years, Rookwood's record of achievement at domestic and international exhibitions remained unmatched.

Throughout the 1910s, Rookwood continued in a similar vein and began to more thoroughly embrace the simplified aesthetic promoted by many Arts & Crafts figures. Production of the Iris line, which had been instrumental in the firm's success at the Paris Exposition in 1900, ceased around 1912. Not only did the company abandon its older, fussier underglaze wares, but newer lines of pottery introduced also trended toward simplicity.

Unfortunately, the collapse of stock market in October 1929 and the ensuing economic Depression dealt Rookwood a blow from which it did not recover. The Great Depression took a toll on the company and eventually led to bankruptcy in April 1941.

Rookwood's history might have ended there were it not for the purchase of the firm by a group of investors led by automobile dealer Walter E. Schott and his wife, Margaret. Production started once again. In the years that followed, Rookwood changed hands a number of times before being moved to Starkville, Mississippi, in 1960. It finally closed its doors there in 1967.

For more information on Rookwood, see Warman's *Rookwood Pottery Identification and Price Guide* by Denise Rago and Jonathan Clancy.

Rago Arts and Auction Center

▲ *Ed Diers, scenic Vellum plaque, "Mountain Stream," Cincinnati, 1917, flame mark XVII/V and original price, mounted in original frame (painted), 8 1/2" x 11".* **$8,125**

Rago Arts and Auction Center

Maria L. Nichols, two-handled Limoges-style vase, Cincinnati, 1882, stamped 1882/MLN with anchor, 10 1/2" x 6 3/4". **$1,750**

Mark Mussio, Humler & Nolan

Dull Glaze pitcher with butterflies, A. R. Valentien, 1886, impressed Rookwood symbol with date, shape 308 X, and Y for yellow clay, incised with artist's monogram, professional restoration to rim and upper portion of handle where it attaches to body, 19 3/4" high. **$1,500**

Mark Mussio, Humler & Nolan

Standard Glaze ewer decorated in 1888 by Kataro Shirayamadani with dragon stretching around shoulder of vessel, impressed Rookwood symbol with date, shape number 62, S for sage clay body, incised with L for Light Standard Glaze, Japanese script signature, light crazing and restoration to chip beneath spout, 9 1/8" high. This ewer was decorated during Shirayamadani's second year at Rookwood. **$1,300**

Mark Mussio, Humler & Nolan

▲ *Vellum vase decorated in 1924 by Fred Rothenbush, tree-lined lake around circumference of vase, impressed Rookwood symbol, date and shape 1356 E, excellent original condition without crazing, two glaze skips at base, 7 1/2" high.* **$1,600**

Mark Mussio, Humler & Nolan

◄ *Limoges-style whiskey jug with clouds, grasses and fired on gold, thought to be the work of Maria Longworth Nichols in 1882, marks include Rookwood in block letters, date and initials MLN in black on bottom appear to be fired on, restoration to handle, 8 1/4" high.* **$2,000**

Mark Mussio, Humler & Nolan

Large Standard Glaze plaque, Old Master style, by Grace Young in 1903, depicting two Dutch gentlemen seated at a table, after a similar work by Jan de Bray, impressed on rear with large Rookwood insignia, date and shape X 1188 X, incised "After de Bray" and with Young's monogram, pinpoint burst glaze bubbles, oversprayed, 10" x 14 3/8". **$3,500**

Mark Mussio, Humler & Nolan

Standard Glaze pillow vase decorated in 1897 by William P. McDonald, portrait of gentleman, purportedly that of Judson Harmon, governor of Ohio from 1909 to 1913 and Attorney General under Grover Cleveland, when this portrait was done; impressed Rookwood logo with date and shape 707 X, incised with McDonald's monogram, fine crazing and some scratches, 11 5/8" high. **$1,200**

Mark Mussio, Humler & Nolan

Vellum landscape plaque painted by Carl Schmidt in 1919, stream flowing between two wooded banks, trees reflected in water with hills in background, impressed Rookwood symbol and date, typewritten label identifying work as "Evening Glow, C. Schmidt," Rookwood circular poster on backing, fine, overall crazing, excellent original condition, original frame, 9 3/8" x 12 1/4". **$5,000**

Mark Mussio, Humler & Nolan

Decorated mat glaze vase, produced by Elizabeth Lincoln in 1923, pine boughs with cones around circumference of vessel, impressed Rookwood symbol, date and shape number 1920, monogrammed by artist in black slip, uncrazed, excellent original condition, 9 3/8" high. **$1,200**

Mark Mussio, Humler & Nolan

Rare Dull Glaze plaque decorated by M. A. Daly in 1896 with portrait of cavalier, done in Old Master style, reverse of plaque bears incised menu for 1896 meeting of Cincinnati Art Club, proferring "Cream of Celery Soup, Olives, Pickles, Broiled Quails (sic), Stewed Potatoes, Roquefort and Camembert Cheese and Coffee"; signed "M.A. Daly '96" in lower right corner of front and incised "MENU C.A.C. 1896" along with menu components on back, without crazing and in excellent original condition in wooden frame, 6 3/8" x 4 1/2". **$2,600**

Mark Mussio, Humler & Nolan

Rookwood advertising sign with dark blue rook perched on branch with green leaves and name of pottery, made in 1915, impressed on back with Rookwood insignia, date and shape 1622, minor edge and corner chips, 4 1/4" x 8 1/2". **$5,250**

Mark Mussio, Humler & Nolan

Porcelain lidded coffee pot with spout stopper, decorated by Arthur Conant in 1933 with scene of wild hog peering through reeds, impressed Rookwood symbol, date and shape 6330, pot, lid and stopper in excellent original condition, 11 1/2" high. **$4,200**

Mark Mussio, Humler & Nolan

Early carved and painted mat glaze lamp, peacock feather design on four lobes, carved and painted by Anna Valentien in 1904, impressed Rookwood symbol, date and shape 1047, artist's monogram in black slip, original fittings, nick to one edge, 15" high. **$2,000**

Mark Mussio, Humler & Nolan

Three-piece inkwell modeled by Anna Valentien in 1902 with nude draped around opening, mat green glaze, impressed with Rookwood insignia, date and shape 156 Z, incised with artist monogram, ink cup has chip to one edge, tiny nick to interior edge that supports ink cup, both unseen when lid is in place, 4 1/4" high. **$1,200**

Mark Mussio, Humler & Nolan

Spanish water jug crafted by Albert Valentien in 1883, impressed designs around top and near bottom of vase, painted scene with large beetle and dragonfly in treed landscape, fired-on gold, impressed Rookwood name in block letters, date, shape 108, kiln mark, Y to indicate yellow clay, incised with artist's monogram, no crazing, tiny "in-the-making" indentations around foot, 9" high. **$2,100**

Mark Mussio, Humler & Nolan

Dull Glaze vase decorated by A.R. Valentien in 1884, incised patterns in bands around top and bottom, glazed gold, central portion of vessel encircled with landscape of birds flying above Oriental grasses, impressed Rookwood in block letters with date, shape 162 B, and a Y to indicate yellow clay, incised with artist's cipher, 10 1/2" high. **$2,200**

Mark Mussio, Humler & Nolan

Porcelain covered box decorated by Sara Sax in 1930, stylized flowers and geometric details in Art Deco tradition, impressed on base with Rookwood symbol, date, shape 6205 and fan-shaped esoteric mark, artist's monogram in black slip, no crazing, excellent original condition, 5" high x 7" x 4 1/2". **$2,300**

Mark Mussio, Humler & Nolan

Limoges-style vase decorated by Albert Valentien in 1883, two storks on front and another on back, standing in marshy terrain with grasses and trees, fired-on gold, impressed Rookwood in block letters, date, G for ginger clay, kiln mark on bottom, signed by artist in slip on side, restoration to foot, some wear to gilding, 28 1/4" high. **$3,000**

Mark Mussio, Humler & Nolan

Rare Rookwood production vase designed by Shirayamadani, produced in 1910, green over brown mat glazes, embossed lotus blossoms and flowers with egret perched on one pad, marks include company logo, date and shape number 1354, excellent original condition with no crazing, 11" high. **$1,100**

Mark Mussio, Humler & Nolan

Dull Glaze flat-sided jug decorated by Edward Pope Cranch in 1884, one side with quartet of owls perched on branch, opposite side with trio of buzzards on branches, incised and outlined in black against brown ground, impressed Rookwood in block letters, date, shape number 85, G to indicate ginger clay, artist's last name, without crazing, fine original condition, 6 1/2" high. **$2,100**

Mark Mussio, Humler & Nolan

Iris Glaze vase decorated by Carl Schmidt in 1905 with mushrooms encircling vessel, impressed Rookwood symbol, date and shape 900 E, incised with W for white (Iris) glaze, Schmidt's monogram, fine overall crazing, excellent original condition, 8 7/8" high. **$3,200**

Mark Mussio, Humler & Nolan

Tall Black Opal Glaze vase decorated in 1925 by Lorinda Epply, trailing flowers, impressed Rookwood symbol, date and shape 2785, incised with Epply's monogram, uncrazed with restoration to drill hole in base, minor glaze burn to shoulder, 13 5/8" high. **$1,500**

Mark Mussio, Humler & Nolan

Pair of Union Terminal bookends, designed by Arthur Conant, cast in 1933 and covered with Ivory Mat Glaze, impressed Rookwood symbol, date and shape 6378, uncrazed with fine detail, excellent original condition, 4 1/2" x 7". **$6,250**

Mark Mussio, Humler & Nolan

Standard Glaze portrait of Native American maiden done in 1898 by Artus Van Briggle, young girl with shoulder-length hair, marks include Rookwood logo, date, shape number 786 D, star-shaped mark, incised initials of artist, minor glaze scratches and very faint crazing, 8" high. **$8,000**

Mark Mussio, Humler & Nolan

Rare Standard Glaze full-length portrait of geisha by Grace Young in 1900, woman stands with fan in her right hand, marks include Rookwood logo, date, shape number 907 D and incised monogram of Young, faint crazing, excellent original condition, 10 1/4" high. **$7,750**

Mark Mussio, Humler & Nolan

Decorated porcelain vase with wisteria on exterior and lined in black, by Kataro Shirayamadani in 1926, impressed Rookwood emblem, date and shape 2789, incised with master's Japanese script signature, no crazing, minor color loss to interior of rim, 10 7/8" high. **$4,000**

Mark Mussio, Humler & Nolan

Vellum landscape vase decorated by Fred Rothenbusch in 1916, trees above misty valley, impressed Rookwood symbol, date, shape 1660 D, and V for Vellum, incised with Rothenbusch's monogram, fine overall crazing, 9 5/8" high.
$1,200

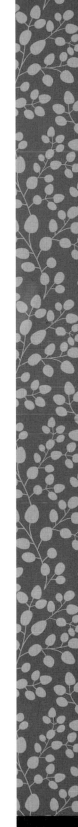

Mark Mussio, Humler & Nolan

Rare Iris Glaze plaque depicting four-masted ship near Kennebuck, Maine, by Sturgis Laurence in 1903, large ship sailing past domed-shaped island while other vessels, tiny on horizon, sail and steam past, plaque signed SL in lower left corner and marked on back with large Rookwood logo, date, notation X1168X, and incised notation "Mouth of Kennebuck Sturgis Laurence," uncrazed, 1/8" nick at top edge of tile, most likely factory, 10 1/8" x 14 3/8". **$23,000**

Mark Mussio, Humler & Nolan

Rookwood Butterfat Glaze vase painted by Janet Harris in 1931, possible repeating pattern of elephants, gray glaze, marks include Rookwood logo, date, shape number 6098 and Harris's monogram in black slip, uncrazed, 4 5/8" high. **$1,100**

Mark Mussio, Humler & Nolan

Rookwood Scenic Vellum vase painted in 1928 by E.T. Hurley, areas of water bracketed by birch trees with stands of timber in background, marks include Rookwood logo, date, shape number 614 C, incised V for Vellum glaze, Hurley's incised intitials, uncrazed, 13" high, accompanying original Rookwood sales brochure with a sticker from William Kendrick's Sons Jewelers in Louisville, retailer from whom consignor's family purchased vase in late 1920s. **$5,000**

Mark Mussio, Humler & Nolan

Rare Decorated Porcelain scenic vase constructed by Arthur Conant in 1921, thatch-roofed cottage near gnarled cherry trees with pink blossoms beneath blue sky, impressed Rookwood symbol, date and shape 925 C, incised with Conant's monogram, original condition with no crazing, 10 1/2" high. **$6,750**

Mark Mussio, Humler & Nolan

Vellum Glaze scenic vase painted by Fred Rothenbusch in 1922, forest with small house with red roof, lit windows, stars above, marks include Rookwood logo, date, shape number 546 C, impressed V for Vellum glaze body, incised monogram of artist, faint crazing 9 3/4" high. **$2,600**

Mark Mussio, Humler & Nolan

Rare Aerial Blue scenic vase of shepherdess holding her staff as she watches over her flock, by William P. McDonald in 1894, impressed with Rookwood insignia, date, shape 721 C and Aerial Blue mark, number 273 encased between two crescent moons, incised with McDonald's monogram, very fine light crazing, vase of blue clay, readily visible on bottom, 5 1/2" high. **$3,000**

Mark Mussio, Humler & Nolan

Painted Mat vase decorated by Harriet Wilcox in 1904, lotus flower stems and pads against dark background, impressed Rookwood symbol, date and shape 904 C, Wilcox's monogram in black slip, no crazing, excellent original condition, 12 1/4" high. **$12,500**

Mark Mussio, Humler & Nolan

Elegant Iris Glaze scenic vase with sailboats seen through tall trees, done in 1911 by Kataro Shirayamadani, people visible in boats with peach-colored sky, marks include Rookwood logo, date, shape number 1652 B, impressed V, wheel ground X and incised cypher of artist, uncrazed, several small glaze flaws at base account for X, professionally and invisibly restored, 14" high. **$9,750**

Mark Mussio, Humler & Nolan

Decorated Mat Glaze vase by Lisbeth Lincoln in 1925, large chrysanthemums, impressed Rookwood symbol, date, shape 614 B, triangular-shaped esoteric mark, artist's monogram in black slip, no crazing, excellent condition, 14 7/8" high. **$2,000**

Mark Mussio, Humler & Nolan

Yellow Vellum vase decorated with yellow chrysanthemums on brown ground by Lorinda Epply in 1929, impressed Rookwood symbol, date, shape 546 C, and V for Vellum, incised with Y for Yellow Vellum, artist's monogram, uncrazed, excellent original condition, 9 5/8" high. **$2,000**

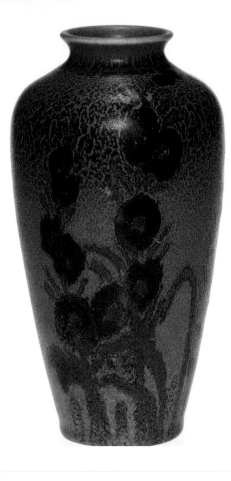

Mark Mussio, Humler & Nolan

Decorated Mat Glaze vase with tall plants with red flowers going around vessel, by Lisbeth Lincoln in 1922, impressed Rookwood symbol, date and shape 614 F, artist's monogram in black slip, no crazing, excellent original condition, 6 3/4" high. **$1,300**

Mark Mussio, Humler & Nolan

Decorated Mat Glaze vase encircled with white and blue irises against brick red ground, work of John Wesley Pullman in 1929, impressed Rookwood symbol, date and shape 900 B, artist's monogram in black slip, excellent original condition with no crazing, 10 1/2" high. **$2,600**

Mark Mussio, Humler & Nolan

Rare and important Modeled Mat or carved Painted Mat vase done by Albert Valentien in 1900, two brightly colored irises in relief carved and painted by artist, marks include Rookwood logo, date, shape number 909 C and Valentien's full signature, uncrazed, 8 5/8" high. **$11,000**

Mark Mussio, Humler & Nolan

Gardenware Faience statue depicting young lad grasping fountain, sitting on grapes and leaves, impressed on base "Rookwood Faience 3062 Y," 19 1/4" high. **$1,800**

Mark Mussio, Humler & Nolan

Dull Glaze ewer decorated by Rookwood's founder, Maria Longworth Nichols, in 1882, incised design around top and bottom of vessel with spooky landscape showing bats flying through a sky illuminated by full moon with somber landscape below, impressed Rookwood in block letters with date, shape number 101 and Y for yellow clay body, incised with Nichols' monogram, handle looks professionally reattached to body, 12 1/8" high. **$1,300**

Mark Mussio, Humler & Nolan

Rookwood porcelain scenic vase painted by Arthur Conant in 1918, white peonies on one side and red sparrow opposite, crosshatching surrounds collar, interior lined in salmon color, hints of water beyond reddish ground, marks include Rookwood logo, date, shape number 243 E, sideways P for porcelain body, incised monogram of Conant, uncrazed, 6 5/8" high. **$2,500**

Mark Mussio, Humler & Nolan

Wax Mat lamp vase decorated by John Dee Wareham, Clydesdale horse, trees and grasses, done in 1938 allegedly for Augustus Busch of Anheuser Busch Brewing Co., impressed Rookwood insignia, date and S to indicate Special shape, Wareham's cypher in blue slip, factory sticker indicates this is a Decorated Wax Mat with original price of $50; cast hole to bottom of vessel, without crazing and in excellent original condition, 14" high. Accompanying newspaper article indicates vase was made for "Gussie" Busch (1899-1989), whose brewery utilized Clydesdal horses to pull beer wagons during parades. **$1,000**

Roseville Pottery

R oseville is one of the most widely recognizable of potteries across the United States. Having been sold in flower shops and drugstores around the country, its art and production wares became a staple in American homes through the time Roseville closed in the 1950s.

The Roseville Pottery Co., located in Roseville, Ohio, was incorporated on Jan. 4, 1892, with George F. Young as general manager. The company had been producing stoneware since 1890, when it purchased the J. B. Owens Pottery, also of Roseville.

The popularity of Roseville Pottery's original lines of stoneware continued to grow. The company acquired new plants in 1892 and 1898, and production started to shift to Zanesville, just a few miles away. By about 1910, all of the work was centered in Zanesville, but the company name was unchanged.

Young hired Ross C. Purdy as artistic designer in 1900, and Purdy created Rozane—a contraction of the words "Roseville" and "Zanesville." The first Roseville artwork pieces were marked either Rozane or RPCO, either impressed or ink-stamped on the bottom.

In 1902, a line was developed called Azurean. Some pieces were marked Azurean, but often RPCO. In 1904 at the St. Louis Exposition, Roseville's Rozane Mongol, a high-gloss oxblood red line, captured first prize, gaining recognition for the firm and its creator, John Herold.

Many Roseville lines were a response to the innovations of Weller Pottery, and in 1904 Frederick Rhead was hired away from Weller as artistic director. He created the Olympic and Della Robbia lines for Roseville. His brother, Harry, took over as artistic director in 1908, and in 1915 he introduced the popular Donatello line.

Mark Mussio, Humler & Nolan

▲ *Early Velmoss jardiniere with embossed leaves and flowers, unmarked, minor scuffs on surface, 9 5/8" high x 13" diameter.* **$375**

Mark Mussio, Humler & Nolan

▶ *Experimental Bittersweet vase decorated on front with vining flowers for which line was named, incised on back "Bittersweet Open shells yellow orange Berries—Red Leaves—Lt. Green," excellent original condition, 9".* **$2,200**

By 1908, all handcrafting ended except for Rozane Royal. Roseville was the first pottery in Ohio to install a tunnel kiln, which increased its production capacity.

Frank Ferrell, who was a top decorator at the Weller Pottery by 1904, was Roseville's artistic director from 1917 until 1954. This Zanesville native created many of the most popular lines, including Pine Cone, which had scores of individual pieces.

Many collectors believe Roseville's circa 1925 glazes were the best of any Zanesville pottery. George Krause, who had become Roseville's technical supervisor, responsible for glaze in 1915, remained with Roseville until the 1950s.

Company sales declined after World War II, especially in the early 1950s when cheap Japanese imports began to replace American wares, and a simpler, more modern style made many of Roseville's elaborate floral designs seem old-fashioned.

In the late 1940s, Roseville began to issue lines with glossy glazes. Roseville tried to offset its flagging artware sales by launching a dinnerware line—Raymor—in 1953. The line was a commercial failure.

Roseville issued its last new designs in 1953. On Nov. 29, 1954, the facilities of Roseville were sold to the Mosaic Tile Co.

For more information on Roseville, see *Warman's Roseville Pottery, 2nd edition,* by Denise Rago.

Mark Mussio, Humler & Nolan

▲ *Experimental Geranium vase with pink flowers on front and incised "Geranium Flowers white pink rose" on back, marked "Flower 58 washed 168 8-34-103" in black grease pencil on bottom, excellent original condition, 9" high.* **$2,400**

Mark Mussio, Humler & Nolan

▶ *Della Robbia vase with stylized poppies done by artisan with initials "KO," four carved flowers and many seed pods encircle vase, marked with artist's initials on side, shape 27 in Della Robbia line, light overall crazing, excellent original condition, 14 1/4" high.* **$9,750**

Mark Mussio, Humler & Nolan

Olympic tankard titled "Triptolemos and the Grain of Wheat," three classic Greek figures with repeating bands at top and base, marked in black on bottom "Rozane Pottery Triptolemos and the Grain of Wheat," excellent condition with minor scratches, 11" high. **$2,000**

Mark Mussio, Humler & Nolan

Olympic vase on three feet, three full-length classical women with repeating bands around rim and foot, unmarked, red color with overspray, 13 1/8" high. **$1,200**

Mark Mussio, Humler & Nolan

Large Rozane Dark vase decorated by Arthur Williams, full-length figure of man in classical garb, impressed Rozane 954 RPCo 1 and cross on bottom, signed A Williams on side, overall crazing, small glaze bubbles and small firing separation on bottom, 21" high. **$1,000**

Mark Mussio, Humler & Nolan

Dealer advertising sign, 1940s, Roseville script mark in yellow matte against pink matte background, excellent original condition, 4 5/8" x 7 3/4". **$1,000**

Mark Mussio, Humler & Nolan

▲ *Blackberry faceted bowl, most of original Roseville sticker on bottom, excellent condition, 3 3/4" high x 10" wide.* **$200**

Mark Mussio, Humler & Nolan

▼ *Tourist vase depicting tourists on country road in red car, wide dark bands, unmarked, some crazing and two glaze bubbles, fine original condition, 12 3/8" high.* **$1,100**

Mark Mussio, Humler & Nolan

▲ *Carnelian I two-handled vase with dark blue over light blue matte glazes, shape 339-15", marked with RV inkstamp, regular crazing, some tiny glaze bursts, 15" high.* **$200**

Mark Mussio, Humler & Nolan

▶ *Rozane Mongol vase with copper red glaze, raised Rozane Mongol wafer, few short scratches, 10 7/8" high.* **$2,000**

▶ *Rare Aztec jardiniere and pedestal, circa 1915, artist's cipher on pedestal, 35 1/2" x 16" overall.* **$1,875**

▲ *Rare Egypto oil lamp base consisting of three elephants with riders providing support for font area, marked with Rozane Ware Egypto wafer seal on bottom, older restoration to large chip on flat base, 10 1/2" high.* **$1,000**

◀ *Futura Purple Crocus vase, shape 429-9", unmarked, professional restoration to chip at base.* **$700**

▶ *Carnelian II spherical vase in turquoise with silver-like mottling on shape 441, excellent condition, 8" x 9".* **$450**

▲ *Futura Bamboo Leaf ball vase, shape 387-7", Roseville Pottery foil label on bottom, overall crazing, 7 1/2".* **$400**

Mark Mussio, Humler & Nolan

▲ *Pair of tall slender candlesticks in blueberry glaze, one with triangle black Roseville sticker, excellent condition, 15" high.* **$225**

Mark Mussio, Humler & Nolan

◄ *Fudji vase in several shades of blue, unmarked, excellent original condition, 7 3/4" high.* **$2,600**

Mark Mussio, Humler & Nolan

▲ *Azurean vase decorated by Walter Myers with two fish observed through low hanging branch of flowering tree, impressed on bottom with large B, smaller B, and shape number 898, signed "W. Myers" by artist on foot, fine crazing and two pinpoint size nicks at base, 12 5/8" high.* **$1,700**

Mark Mussio, Humler & Nolan

Early Rozane jardiniere and pedestal with garlands of flowers against stippled backdrop, open glaze pop at inside bottom, early number mark on bottom, excellent condition, 30 1/4" high (combined). **$425**

Mark Mussio, Humler & Nolan

◄ *Wincraft buttress floor vase, shape 289-18" with pink tulips front and back, raised marks, good condition, 18 1/2" high.* **$325**

Mark Mussio, Humler & Nolan

Imperial I floor vase, excellent condition, 15 1/2" high. **$325**

Mark Mussio, Humler & Nolan

Ming Tree floor vase with branch handles, shape 585-14", raised marks, repair to chip on rim, 14 1/2" high. **$250**

Rago Arts and Auction Center

Tall rare Della Robbia vase with wild roses and cut-out rim, circa 1910, raised Rozane Ware seal, incised artist's signature on bottom and initials on side, 15 1/2" x 6". **$43,750**

Mark Mussio, Humler & Nolan

▼ *Florentine II sand jar with panels of clustered flowers, marked with raised "Roseville USA" and shape 297, overall crazing and some minor chips at base, 16 1/2" high.* **$100**

Mark Mussio, Humler & Nolan

▲ *Lamp with raised flowers and foliage in high glaze combination of turquoise, yellow, and pink over matte bronze glaze, original fittings, replaced double sockets and cord, metal base marked "Davrt, NY," excellent condition, ceramic portion 8" high.* **$600**

Mark Mussio, Humler & Nolan

◄ *Imperial II vase in green and orange, shape number 476-8, unmarked, excellent original condition, uncrazed, 8 1/4" high.* **$650**

Mark Mussio, Humler & Nolan

▲ *Pauleo vase in mottled two-tone blue matte glaze on tall form, incised number 234 on bottom, restoration to small glaze nicks on foot ring, 17 3/4" high.* **$700**

Mark Mussio, Humler & Nolan

▲ *Rosecraft Panel vase with nudes poised in four panels, glaze separation on rim and small clay bumps on one nude, stamped "Rv" on bottom, 10 1/4" high.* **$500**

Mark Mussio, Humler & Nolan

▲ *Rozane Royal Dark vase with life-size red and yellow irises painted by Josephine Imlay, signed by artist on side, marked with Roseville Rozane Ware wafer seal on bottom, completely oversprayed indicating some sort of professional repair, 15 5/8" high.* **$325**

Mark Mussio, Humler & Nolan

▶ *Scarce Mongol vase, circa 1904, with re-creation of ancient Chinese blood red glaze, raised Rozane Ware wafer with Mongol wing, old sticker that is illegible, sticker from White Pillars Museum in Norwich, Ohio, certificate verifying vase was part of Purviance Collection at White Pillars, shallow scratches, 10 7/8" high.* **$1,500**

Mark Mussio, Humler & Nolan

▶ *Crystalis oil lamp vase on Egypto form of three elephants with riders that form support for oil font holder, reddish orange Crystalis glaze covers inside and outside of vase, large crystals visible on flatter surfaces, marked with Rozane Ware Egypto wafer seal, restoration to small base chip, 10 5/8" high.* **$2,900**

Mark Mussio, Humler & Nolan

▲ *Rozane vase with two handles, English spaniel on vessel, decorated by Claude Leffler, impressed on base "Rozane 826 RPO 3 A B" and signed "C.L. Leffler" in slip on foot, overall crazing, two glaze bubbles, several chips at base, 21" high.* **$600**

Weller Pottery

Weller Pottery was made from 1872 to 1945 at a pottery established originally by Samuel A. Weller at Fultonham, Ohio and moved in 1882 to Zanesville, Ohio.

Weller's famous pottery slugged it out with several other important Zanesville potteries for decades. Cross-town rivals such as Roseville, Owens, La Moro, and McCoy were all serious fish in a fairly small and well-stocked lake. While Weller occasionally landed some solid body punches with many of his better art lines, the prevailing thought was that his later production ware just wasn't up to snuff.

Samuel Weller was a notorious copier and, it is said, a bit of a scallywag. He paid designers such as William Long to bring their famous discoveries to Zanesville. He then attempted to steal their secrets, and, when successful, renamed them and made them his own.

After World War I, when the cost of materials became less expensive than the cost of labor, many companies, including the famous Rookwood Pottery, increased their output of less expensive production ware. Weller Pottery followed along in the trend of production ware by introducing scores of interesting and unique lines, the likes of which have never been created anywhere else, before or since.

In addition to a number of noteworthy production lines, Weller continued in the creation of hand-painted ware long after Roseville abandoned them. Some of the more interesting Hudson pieces, for example, are post-World War I pieces. Even later lines, such as Bonito, were hand painted and often signed by important artists such as Hester Pillsbury. The closer you look at Weller's output after 1920, the more obvious the fact that it was the only Zanesville company still producing both quality art ware and quality production ware.

For more information on Weller pottery, see *Warman's Weller Pottery Identification and Price Guide* by Denise Rago and David Rago.

Mark Mussio, Humler & Nolan

Brighton butterfly with flesh tone body and wings in gray, white, and black, unmarked, excellent original condition, without pin, 2 1/4" x 3 1/2". **$110**

Rago Arts and Auction Center

Rare tall Cameo vase with birds and ferns, Fultonham, Ohio, stamped Weller 2P, 13 1/2" x 7". **$1,500**

Mark Mussio, Humler & Nolan

▲ *Rare Coppertone "Two Fish" vase, marked with Weller half-kiln ink stamp and marked with 2 and H in black slip, small chip to dorsal fin of smaller fish, good mold and color, 8".* **$1,300**

Mark Mussio, Humler & Nolan

▲ *Coppertone bud vase with fluted rim and frog clinging to side, marked on base with number 12 in slip, good mold and color, 9".* **$500**

Mark Mussio, Humler & Nolan

◄ *Coppertone Gardenware Pan with Rabbit figure, impressed on bottom with Weller Pottery script logo, excellent original condition, 13 5/8" high.* **$3,000**

Mark Mussio, Humler & Nolan

Cretone vase decorated in Art Deco style by Hester Pillsbury with leaping deer, flowers, leaves, and designs in white slip, applied via pastry bag, on satin black ground, impressed with Weller Pottery "script" mark and monogrammed by artist on side, fine crazing visible on interior and bottom, glaze inclusion at rim, 7" high. **$500**

Mark Mussio, Humler & Nolan

Eocean vase decorated with pair of life-size white lilies, bud and foliage painted and signed by artisan Lillie Mitchell, incised X404 on bottom, excellent condition, 16 1/4" high. **$1,900**

Mark Mussio, Humler & Nolan

Eocean vase displaying flock of mallard ducks landing at eventide, water reeds below them, duck on back, executed by Albert Haubrich, lavender blue and pink evening sky, inscribed Eocean Weller, impressed X476 and painted cipher of artist on side, fine overall crazing, excellent condition, 13" high. **$2,300**

Mark Mussio, Humler & Nolan

Large Eocean vase with red poppies front and back, painted by Charles Chilcote, inscribed Eocean Weller on bottom, light crazing, minor surface scratches, 11 3/4" high. **$550**

Mark Mussio, Humler & Nolan

▲ *Flemish hanging shade with garlands embossed in surface, impressed Weller inside, brass hanging hooks attached, electrical fixture inside with opaque globe in center of shade, wiring not operative, excellent original condition with minor rubs, 17 1/2" diameter.* **$550**

Mark Mussio, Humler & Nolan

◄ *Forest jardinière displaying meadow of mature trees in summer, impressed Weller on bottom, glazed over line at rim, 10 1/2" high, 12 1/4" diameter.* **$400**

Mark Mussio, Humler & Nolan

Hen with six chicks, impressed Weller incised logo, fine crazing, professional restoration to comb and some small chips at base, 7 3/4" high x 7 3/4" long. **$850**

Mark Mussio, Humler & Nolan

Gardenware rooster, naturalistic mat tones, incised Weller logo, fine crazing, professional restoration to comb, some small chips at base, 12 7/8" high x 13" long. **$1,000**

Mark Mussio, Humler & Nolan

▶ *Hudson vase with white and yellow hollyhock decoration by Hester Pillsbury, impressed Weller in large block letters on bottom, signed by artist on side, paper label reads "From the White Pillars Museum," glaze bubbles near base, 11 5/8" high.* **$600**

Mark Mussio, Humler & Nolan

Hudson twin-handled vase decorated with robin perched among blooms on tree branch, artist's initials, LBM, are at base of piece in black slip, bottom marked with Weller Pottery half-kiln stamp and possibly the letter "A" in green slip, light overall crazing, 7 3/4" high. **$2,200**

Mark Mussio, Humler & Nolan

Hudson vase decorated by Sara Reid McLaughlin with Dutch scene of several windmills, sailboats, and pink-roofed houses, signed by artist in black slip within scene and incised Weller Pottery and 15 on bottom, small glaze flake at base and fine overall crazing, 11 1/8" high. **$1,700**

Mark Mussio, Humler & Nolan

Jewell footed dresser box with cover, embossed face of maiden, mermaids/fish around base portion, cosmetic repair to nose of maiden, very good condition, 4 1/2" high x 5 1/2" diameter. **$400**

Mark Mussio, Humler & Nolan

▶ *LaSa vase encircled by scene of river flowing past shore with trees and clouds above, unmarked, few tiny scratches, good color, surface in excellent shape, 11 1/4" high.* **$550**

Mark Mussio, Humler & Nolan

▼ *Tall LaSa vase with tropical scene of palm trees, mountains and red sky, unmarked, 1/8" glaze chip at base and minor abrasions, 16" high.* **$650**

Mark Mussio, Humler & Nolan

▲ *Tall LaSa scenic vase with pine trees, clouds, mountains and red sky, signed Weller LaSa on side near base, excellent condition with minor abrasions, 16" high.* **$1,000**

Mark Mussio, Humler & Nolan

◀ *LaSa signed gourd vase with tropical view of palm trees and large lake with mountains in distance against evening sky, 9 1/4" high.* **$500**

Mark Mussio, Humler & Nolan

▶ *Louwelsa vase decorated with roses, sterling silver overlay, impressed on base Louwelsa Weller X 11, no artist mark or marks on silver, overall crazing, 7 3/4" high.* **$550**

Mark Mussio, Humler & Nolan

▲ *Large Louwelsa vase with red tulips done by Albert Haubrich, impressed Louwelsa Weller circular logo, incised F, impressed number 11 and number 46, overall crazing, glaze nick off base, 16 1/2" high.* **$900**

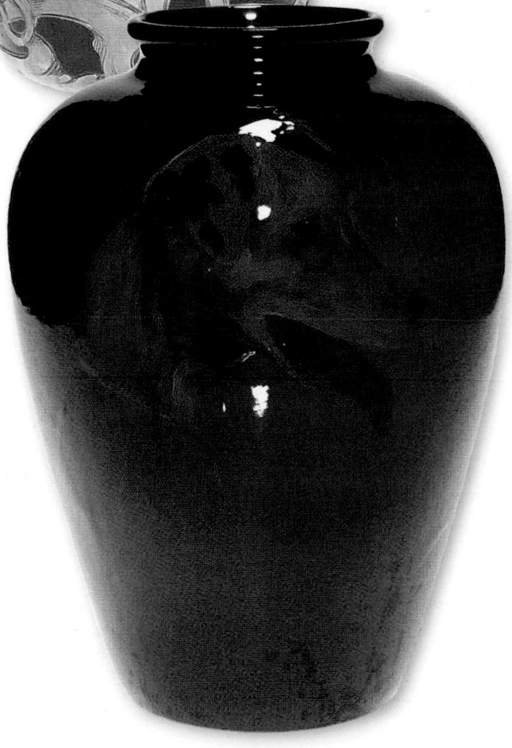

Mark Mussio, Humler & Nolan

▶ *Louwelsa vase displaying portrait of Dalmatian, impressed circular Weller Louwelsa symbol and X 485, no artist mark visible, overall crazing, scratches, and small burst glaze bubbles, 10 3/4" high.* **$450**

Mark Mussio, Humler & Nolan

Matt Ware vase decorated with three mushrooms in heavy slip, impressed Weller in small block letters on bottom, some crazing to slip-decorated portion, bruise at base, 6 5/8" high. **$550**

Mark Mussio, Humler & Nolan

▼ *Scenic vase showing Japanese lanterns hanging from tree after sunset, unmarked, fine crazing and minor glaze drips, 9" high.* **$1,100**

Mark Mussio, Humler & Nolan

Matt Ware vase with molded design of arrowroot plant, mat green glaze, impressed Weller in small block letters, no crazing, stilt pull to foot ring, 15 7/8" high. **$550**

Mark Mussio, Humler & Nolan

Rosemont vase, each side with bluebird and branches with pink flowers, one side also has yellow butterfly, impressed Weller in block letters, minor crazing and scratches, 7 5/8" high. **$150**

Mark Mussio, Humler & Nolan

▲ *Selma covered jar with repeating pattern of bluebirds in apple tree, impressed with WELLER on bottom, restoration to small chip on lid and fine overall crazing, 7 7/8" high.* **$650**

Mark Mussio, Humler & Nolan

Sicard vase with stylized floral decoration and fine coloration, marked Weller Sicard on side near base and incised 10 on bottom, tiny bubbles in glaze, 4 3/4" high. **$500**

Mark Mussio, Humler & Nolan

▲ *Sicard vase from Weller Theatre in Zanesville, Ohio, signed Weller Sicard in gold slip on bottom, label from White Pillars Museum, some restoration at rim, overall crazing and pinpoint glaze bubbles within decoration, larger open glaze bubbles around edge of bottom, 33" high.* **$6,750**

Rago Arts & Auction Center

Sicard vase with daisies, 1903-1917, signed Weller Sicard, 29M, 5 3/4" x 7 1/4". **$1,500**

Mark Mussio, Humler & Nolan

◄ *Sicard candlestick with swirls of green, gold, and purple, signed Weller and Sicard on opposite sides of base, excellent condition, 6 1/2".* **$500**

Mark Mussio, Humler & Nolan

▼ *Sicard vase decorated with ivy leaves in blue, purple, green, and gold, signed Weller and Sicard on opposite sides near base, 1/4" grinding chip at base, 7 1/4" high.* **$450**

Mark Mussio, Humler & Nolan

▲ *Sicard candlestick in green and gold with shamrock designs, signed Weller and Sicard on opposite sides near base, excellent condition, 7 1/2" high.* **$450**

Mark Mussio, Humler & Nolan

▶ *Sicard vase decorated with green and gold dandelion and leaves against purple background, signed Weller on side of piece, excellent condition with minor abrasions, 7 3/8" high.* **$425**

Mark Mussio, Humler & Nolan

▶ *Sicard vase with mistletoe decoration in green, purple, and gold, signed Weller Sicard on side near bottom, minor grinding chips at base and faint crazing, 7 1/4" high.* **$475**

Mark Mussio, Humler & Nolan

▲ *Sicard lobed vase decorated with nasturtiums in green and purple, signed Weller Sicard on body with impressed Weller on bottom and number 37, minor abrasions and fine overall crazing, 5 3/8" high x 7" wide.* **$850**

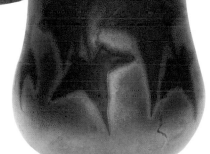

Mark Mussio, Humler & Nolan

◀ *Sicard pear-form vase decorated with English ivy over aqua, smooth surface with purplish blue coloration and green glazing, signed Weller Sicard on side, excellent condition, 4 1/2".* **$425**

Mark Mussio, Humler & Nolan

▶ **Far Right:** *Silvertone vase with four white calla lilies and green foliage against backdrop of lilac and blue with pale yellow, stamped Weller Ware with number 3 beneath, minor crazing, excellent condition, 11 3/4" high.* **$225**

Mark Mussio, Humler & Nolan

▶ *Silvertone Thistle vase, marked with Weller Pottery half-kiln logo and T and 12X in black slip (possibly a trial piece), excellent original condition, good mold and color, 7 3/4" high.* **$800**

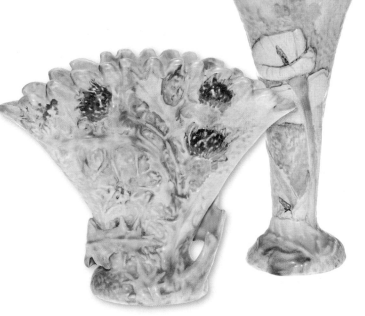

Mark Mussio, Humler & Nolan

Rare etched mat scenic tankard showing swans in wooded pond, work of Albert Wilson, swans and water are incised, trees in background are painted, typical Weller numbers on bottom, signed A. Wilson on side in white slip, uncrazed with small glaze chip on spout and pinhead nick at base, 16 5/8" high. **$600**

Mark Mussio, Humler & Nolan

Voile jardinière and pedestal presenting orchards bearing fruit, jardinière hand-marked 16 under glaze, excellent condition, combined height 32". **$500**

Mark Mussio, Humler & Nolan

White and Decorated vase featuring exotic bird perched on branch with flowering rose of Sharon blooms, impressed Weller in block letters on base, excellent original condition with fine light crazing, 13 1/8" high. **$1,200**

Mark Mussio, Humler & Nolan

Woodcraft wall pocket with two bluebirds, one in nest, one on branch, with red flowers and leaves, impressed Weller in block letters on rear, fine crazing with restoration to beak of bird on branch, minor firing separation to vine, 14 3/4" x 12". **$700**

European Ceramics

Select English, European Makers

The **Amphora Porcelain** Works was one of several pottery companies located in the Teplitz-Turn region of Bohemia in the late 19th and early 20th centuries. It is best known for art pottery, especially Art Nouveau and Art Deco pieces. Several markings were used, including the name and location of the pottery and the Imperial mark, which included a crown. Prior to World War I, Bohemia was part of the Austro-Hungarian Empire, so the word "Austria" may appear as part of the mark. After World War I, the word "Czechoslovakia" may be part of the mark.

Belleek is thin-bodied, ivory-colored, almost-iridescent porcelain, first made in 1857 in County Fermanagh, Ireland. Production continued until World War I, was discontinued for a period of time, and then resumed. The Shamrock pattern is most familiar, but many patterns were made, including Limpet, Tridacna and Grasses.

Several American firms made a Belleek-type porcelain. The first was Ott and Brewer Co. of Trenton, N.J., in 1884. Other firms producing this ware included The Ceramic Art Co. (1889), American Art China Works (1892), Columbian Art Co. (1893) and Lenox Inc. (1904). Irish Belleek bore specific marks during given time periods, which makes it relatively easy to date. Variations in mark color are important, as well as the symbols and words.

Capo-de-Monte

Capo-di-Monte: In 1743, King Charles of Naples established a soft-paste porcelain factory. The firm made figurines and dinnerware. In 1760, many of the workmen and most of the molds were moved to Buen Retiro, near Madrid, Spain. A new factory, which also made hard-paste porcelains, opened in Naples in 1771. In 1834, the Doccia factory in Florence purchased the molds and continued production in Italy.

Capo-di-Monte was copied well into the 20th century by makers in Hungary, Germany, France and Italy.

Figures (pair), Capo-di-Monte, classical females, one at desk with compass and scroll, other sculpting helmeted bust on stand, oval base, porcelain, Capo-di-Monte, 19th century, 6 1/2" high. **$510 pair**

In 1749, **Josiah Spode** was apprenticed to Thomas Whieldon and in 1754 worked for William Banks in Stoke-on-Trent, Staffordshire, England. In the early 1760s, Spode started his own pottery, making cream-colored earthenware and blueprinted whiteware. In 1770, he returned to Banks' factory as master, purchasing it in 1776.

Spode

Spode pioneered the use of steam-powered, pottery-making machinery and mastered the art of transfer printing from copper plates. Spode opened a London shop in 1778 and sent William Copeland there in about 1784. A number of larger London locations followed. At the turn of the 18th century, Spode introduced bone china. In 1805, Josiah Spode II and William Copeland entered into a partnership for the London business. A series of partnerships between Josiah Spode II, Josiah Spode III and William Taylor Copeland resulted.

Copeland

In 1833, Copeland acquired Spode's London operations and seven years later, the Stoke plants. William Taylor Copeland managed the business until his death in 1868. The firm remained in the hands of Copeland heirs. In 1923, the plant was electrified; other modernization followed.

In 1976, Spode merged with Worcester Royal Porcelain to become Royal Worcester Spode, Ltd.

Delftware is pottery with a soft, red-clay body and tin-enamel glaze. The white, dense, opaque color came from adding tin ash to lead glaze. The first examples had blue designs on a white ground. Polychrome examples followed.

The name originally applied to pottery made in the region around Delft, Holland, beginning in the 16th century and ending in the late 18th century. The tin used came from the Cornish mines in England. By the 17th and 18th centuries, English potters in London, Bristol and Liverpool were copying the glaze and designs. Some designs unique to English potters also developed.

Augustus II, Elector of Saxony and King of Poland, founded the Royal Saxon Porcelain Manufactory in the Albrechtsburg, **Meissen,** in 1710. Johann Frederick Boettger, an alchemist, and Tschirnhaus, a nobleman, experimented with kaolin from the Dresden area to produce porcelain. By 1720, the factory produced a whiter, hard-paste porcelain than that from the Far East. The factory experienced its golden age from the 1730s to the 1750s under the leadership of Samuel Stolzel, kiln master, and Johann Gregor Herold, enameler.

The Meissen factory was destroyed and looted by forces of Frederick the Great during the Seven Years' War (1756-1763). It was reopened, but never achieved its former greatness.

In the 19th century, the factory reissued some of its earlier forms. These later wares are called "Dresden" to differentiate them from the earlier examples. There were several other porcelain factories in the Dresden region and their products also are grouped under the "Dresden" designation.

Many marks were used by the Meissen factory. The first was a pseudo-Oriental mark in a square. The famous crossed swords mark was adopted in 1724. A small dot between the hilts was used from 1763 to 1774, and a star between the hilts from 1774 to 1814. Two modern marks are swords with a hammer and sickle, and swords with a crown.

Gouda and the surrounding areas of Holland have been principal Dutch pottery centers for centuries. Originally, the potteries produced a simple utilitarian, tin-glazed Delft-type earthenware and the famous clay smoker's pipes.

When pipe making declined in the early 1900s, Gouda turned to art pottery. Influenced by the Art Nouveau and Art Deco movements, artists expressed themselves with freeform and stylized designs in bold colors.

In 1842, American china importer **David Haviland** moved to Limoges, France, where he

Skinner Inc., www.skinnerinc.com

Plate, Delftware, England, 18th century, with polychrome decorated floral and bird designs, 11 3/4" diameter. **$444**

Dresden/Meissen

Gouda

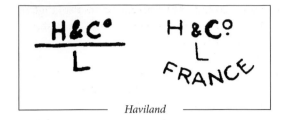

Haviland

began manufacturing and decorating china specifically for the U.S. market. Haviland is synonymous with fine, white, translucent porcelain, although early hand-painted patterns were generally larger and darker colored on heavier whiteware blanks than were later ones.

Haviland revolutionized French china factories by both manufacturing the whiteware blank and decorating it at the same site. In addition, Haviland and Co. pioneered the use of decals in decorating china.

Haviland's sons, Charles Edward and Theodore, split the company in 1892. In 1936, Theodore opened an American division. In 1941, Theodore bought out Charles Edward's heirs and recombined both companies under the original name of H. and Co. The Haviland family sold the firm in 1981.

Charles Field Haviland, cousin of Charles Edward and Theodore, worked for and then, after his marriage in 1857, ran the Casseaux Works until 1882. Items continued to carry his name as decorator until 1941.

Thousands of Haviland patterns were made, but not consistently named until after 1926. The similarities in many of the patterns make identification difficult. Numbers assigned by Arlene Schleiger and illustrated in her books have become the identification standard.

The **"KPM"** mark has been used separately and in conjunction with other symbols by many German porcelain manufacturers, among which are the Königliche Porzellan Manufactur in Meissen, 1720s; Königliche Porzellan Manufactur in Berlin, 1832-1847; and Krister Porzellan Manufactur in Waldenburg, mid-19th century.

Collectors now use the term KPM to refer to the high-quality porcelain produced in the Berlin area in the 18th and 19th centuries.

Creamware is a cream-colored earthenware created about 1750 by the potters of Staffordshire, England, which proved ideal for domestic ware. It was also known as "tortoiseshellware" or "Prattware" depending on the color of glaze used.

The most notable producer of creamware was Josiah Wedgwood. Around 1779, he was able to lighten the cream color to a bluish white and sold this product under the name "pearl ware." Wedgwood supplied his creamware to England's Queen Charlotte (1744-1818) and Russian Empress Catherine the Great (1729-1796), and used the trade name "Queen's ware."

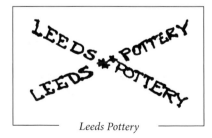

Leeds Pottery

The **Leeds Pottery** in Yorkshire, England, began production about 1758. Among its products was creamware that was competitive with that of Wedgwood. The original factory closed in 1820, but various subsequent owners continued until 1880. They made exceptional cream-colored ware, either plain, salt glazed or painted with colored enamels, and glazed and unglazed redware.

Early wares are unmarked. Later pieces are marked "Leeds Pottery," sometimes followed by "Hartley-Green and Co." or the letters "LP."

Liverpool is the name given to products made at several potteries in Liverpool, England, between 1750 and 1840. Seth and James Pennington and Richard Chaffers were among the early potters who made tin-enameled earthenware.

By the 1780s, tin-glazed earthenware gave way to cream-colored wares decorated with cobalt blue, enameled colors and blue or black transfers.

Bubbles and frequent clouding under the foot rims characterize the Liverpool glaze. By 1800, about 80 potteries were working in the town producing not only creamware, but soft paste, soapstone and bone porcelain.

The reproduction pieces have a crackled glaze and often age cracks have been artificially produced. When compared to genuine pieces, reproductions are thicker and heavier and have weaker transfers, grayish color (not as crisp and black), ecru or gray body color instead of cream, and crazing that does not spiral upward.

Skinner Inc., www.skinnerinc.com

Coffeepot and cover, creamware, England, circa 1780, attributed to Liverpool, pear shape with black transfer "tea party" and "shepherd" prints, strap handle and ball knop, 10" high. **$355**

Minton

In 1793, **Thomas Minton** joined other entrepreneurs formed a partnership to build a small pottery at Stoke-on-Trent, Staffordshire, England. Production began in 1798 with blueprinted earthenware, mostly in the Willow pattern. In 1798, cream-colored earthenware and bone china were introduced.

A wide range of styles and wares was produced. Minton introduced porcelain figures in 1826, Parian wares in 1846, encaustic tiles in the late 1840s, and majolica wares in 1850. In 1883, the modern company was formed and called Mintons Limited. The "s" was dropped in 1968.

Many early pieces are unmarked or have a Sevres-type marking. The "ermine" mark was used in the early 19th century. Date codes can be found on tableware and majolica. The mark used between 1873 and 1911 was a small globe with a crown on top and the word "Minton."

Mocha decoration usually is found on utilitarian creamware and stoneware pieces and was produced through a simple chemical action. A color pigment of brown, blue, green or black was made acidic by an infusion of tobacco or hops. When the acidic colorant was applied in blobs to an alkaline ground, it reacted by spreading in feathery designs resembling sea plants. This type of decoration usually was supplemented with bands of light-colored slip.

Types of decoration vary greatly, from those done in a combination of motifs, such as Cat's Eye and Earthworm, to a plain pink mug decorated with green ribbed bands. Most forms of mocha are hollow, e.g., mugs, jugs, bowls and shakers.

English potters made the vast majority of the pieces. Collectors group the wares into three chronological periods: 1780-1820, 1820-1840 and 1840-1880.

William Moorcroft was first employed as a potter by James Macintyre & Co. Ltd. of Burslem, Staffordshire, England, in 1897. He established the Moorcroft pottery in 1913.

The majority of the art pottery wares were hand thrown, resulting in a great variation

Moorcroft

among similarly styled pieces. Colors and marks are keys to determining age.

Walter Moorcroft, William's son, continued the business upon his father's death and made wares in the same style.

The company initially used an impressed mark, "Moorcroft, Burslem;" a signature mark, "W. Moorcroft" followed. Modern pieces are marked simply "Moorcroft," with export pieces also marked "Made in England."

Sanford Alderfer Auction & Appraisal

Bowl, Moorcroft, china with fruit motif, grapevine and leaves in blue, purple and yellow on green ground, 8 3/4" diameter, 2 3/4" high. **$184**

In 1794, the **Royal Bayreuth** factory was founded in Tettau, Bavaria. Royal Bayreuth introduced its figural patterns in 1885. Designs of animals, people, fruits and vegetables decorated a wide array of tableware and inexpensive souvenir items.

Tapestry wares, in rose and other patterns, were made in the late 19th century. The surface of the pieces feel and look like woven cloth.

The Royal Bayreuth crest used to mark the wares varied in design and color.

Royal Bayreuth

Skinner Inc., www.skinnerinc.com

Royal Crown Derby bone china cockerel, England, circa 1952, polychrome enamel decorated, modeled standing on a tree stump, printed mark, 11 3/4". **$207**

Derby Crown Porcelain Co., established in 1875 in Derby, England, had no connection with earlier Derby factories that operated in the late 18th and early 19th centuries. In 1890, the company was appointed "Manufacturers of Porcelain to Her Majesty" (Queen Victoria) and since that date has been known as "Royal Crown Derby."

Most of these porcelains, both tableware and figural, were hand decorated. A variety of printing processes were used for additional adornment.

Derby porcelains from 1878 to 1890 carry only the standard crown printed mark. After 1891, the mark includes the "Royal Crown Derby" wording. In the 20th century, "Made in England" and "English Bone China" were added to the mark.

Doulton pottery began in 1815 under the direction of John Doulton at the Doulton & Watts pottery in Lambeth, England. Early output was limited to salt-glazed industrial stoneware. After John Watts retired in 1854, the firm became Doulton and Co., and production was expanded to include hand-decorated stoneware such as figurines, vases, dinnerware and flasks.

In 1878, Doulton's son, Sir Henry Doulton, purchased Pinder Bourne & Co. in Burslem, Staffordshire. The companies became Doulton & Co., Ltd. in 1882. Decorated porcelain was added to Doulton's earthenware production in 1884.

Most Doulton figurines were produced at the Burslem plants, where they were made continuously from 1890 until 1978. After a short interruption, a new line of Doulton figurines was introduced in 1979.

Dickensware, in earthenware and porcelain, was introduced in 1908. The pieces were decorated with characters from Dickens' novels. Most of the line was withdrawn in the 1940s, except for plates, which continued to be made until 1974.

Character jugs, a 20th-century revival of early Toby models, were designed by Charles J. Noke for Doulton in the 1930s. Character jugs are limited to bust portraits, while Royal Doulton Toby jugs are full figured. The character jugs come in four sizes and feature fictional characters from Dickens, Shakespeare and other English and American novelists, as well as historical heroes. Marks on both character and Toby jugs must be carefully identified to determine dates and values.

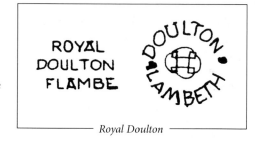

ROYAL DOULTON FLAMBE

Royal Doulton

Doulton's Rouge Flambé (Veined Sung) is a high-glazed, strong-colored ware.

Production of stoneware at Lambeth ceased in 1956.

Beginning in 1872, the "Royal Doulton" mark was used on all types of wares produced by the company.

Beginning in 1913, an "HN" number was assigned to each new Doulton figurine design. The "HN" numbers, which referred originally to Harry Nixon, a Doulton artist, were chronological until 1940, after which blocks of numbers were assigned to each modeler. From 1928 until 1954, a small number was placed to the right of the crown mark; this number, when added to 1927, gives the year of manufacture.

In 1751, the **Worcester Porcelain Co.**, led by Dr. John Wall and William Davis, acquired the Bristol pottery of Benjamin Lund and moved it to Worcester. The first wares were painted blue under the glaze; soon thereafter decorating was accomplished by painting on the glaze in enamel colors. Among the most-famous 18th-century decorators were James Giles and Jeffery Hamet O'Neal. Transfer-print decoration was developed by the 1760s.

A series of partnerships took place after Davis' death in 1783: Flight (1783-1793); Flight & Barr (1793-1807); Barr, Flight & Barr (1807-1813); and Flight, Barr & Barr (1813-1840). In 1840, the factory was moved to Chamberlain & Co. in Diglis, Worcester. Decorative wares were discontinued. In 1852, W.H. Kerr and R.W. Binns formed a new company and revived the production of ornamental wares.

In 1862, the firm became the Royal Worcester Porcelain Co. Among the key modelers of the late 19th century were James Hadley, his three sons, and George Owen, an expert with pierced clay pieces. Royal Worcester absorbed the Grainger factory in 1889 and the James Hadley factory in 1905. Modern designers include Dorothy Doughty and Doris Lindner.

The principal patron of the French porcelain industry in early 18th-century France was Jeanne Antoinette Poisson, Marquise de Pompadour. She supported the Vincennes factory of Gilles and Robert Dubois and their successors in their attempt to make soft-paste porcelain in the 1740s. In 1753, she moved the porcelain operations to **Sevres**, near her home, Chateau de Bellevue.

The Sevres soft-paste formula used sand from Fontainebleau, salt, saltpeter, soda of Alicante, powdered alabaster, clay and soap.

In 1769, kaolin was discovered in France, and a hard-paste formula was developed. The baroque designs gave way to rococo, a style favored by Jeanne du Barry, Louis XV's next mistress. Louis XVI took little interest in Sevres, and many factories began to turn out counterfeits. In 1876, the factory was moved to St. Cloud and was eventually nationalized.

Louis XV allowed the firm to use the "double L" in its marks.

Spatterware generally was made of common earthenware, although occasionally creamware was used. The earliest English examples were made about 1780. The peak period of production was from 1810 to 1840. Firms known to have made spatterware are Adams, Barlow, and Harvey and Cotton.

The amount of spatter decoration varies from piece to piece. Some objects simply have decorated borders. These often were decorated with a brush, requiring several hundred touches per square inch to achieve the spatter effect. Other pieces have the entire surface covered with spatter. Marked pieces are rare.

Collectors today focus on the patterns—Cannon, Castle, Fort, Peafowl, Rainbow, Rose, Thistle, Schoolhouse, etc. The decoration on flatware is in the center of the piece; on hollow ware, it occurs on both sides.

Aesthetics and the colors of spatter are key to determining value. Blue and red are the most common colors; green, purple, and brown are in a middle group; black and yellow are scarce.

In 1754, Josiah **Wedgwood** and Thomas Whieldon of Fenton Vivian, Staffordshire, England, became partners in a pottery enterprise. Their products included marbled, agate, tortoiseshell, green glaze and Egyptian black wares. In 1759, Wedgwood opened his own pottery at the Ivy House works, Burslem, Staffordshire. In 1764, he moved to the Brick House (Bell Works) at Burslem. The pottery concentrated on utilitarian pieces.

Between 1766 and 1769, Wedgwood built the famous works at Etruria. Among the most-renowned products of this plant were the Empress Catherine of Russia dinner service (1774) and the Portland Vase (1790s). The firm also made caneware, unglazed earthenwares (drabwares), piecrust wares, variegated and marbled wares, black basalt (developed in 1768), Queen's or creamware, and Jasperware (perfected in 1774).

Bone china was produced under the direction of Josiah Wedgwood II between 1812 and 1822 and revived in 1878.

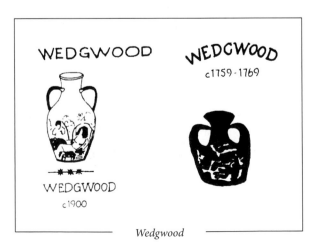

Wedgwood

Wedgwood solid black Jasper Dancing Hours bowl, England, 20th century, applied white classical relief with running laurel border above figures, impressed mark, 7" diameter. **$119**

Moonlight Luster was made from 1805 to 1815. Fairyland Luster began in 1920. All luster production ended in 1932.

A museum was established at the Etruria pottery in 1906. When Wedgwood moved to its modern plant at Barlaston, North Staffordshire, the museum was expanded.

Vilmos Zsolnay (1828-1900) assumed control of his brother's factory in Pécs, Hungary, in the mid-19th century. In 1899, Miklos, Vilmos' son, became manager. The firm still produces ceramic ware.

The early wares are highly ornamental, glazed and have a cream-colored ground. Eosin glaze, a deep, rich play of colors reminiscent of Tiffany's iridescent wares, received a gold medal at the 1900 Paris exhibition.

Originally, no trademark was used, but in 1878 the company began to use a blue mark depicting the five towers of the cathedral at Pécs. The initials "TJM" represent the names of Miklos' three children.

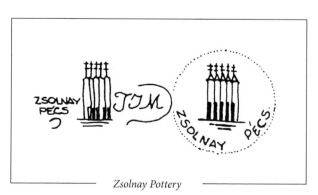

Zsolnay Pottery

KPM

By Melody Amsel-Arieli

K PM plaques are highly glazed, enamel paintings on porcelain bases that were produced by Konigliche Porzellan Manufaktur (KPM), the King's Porcelain Factory, in Berlin, Germany, between 1880 and 1901.

Their secret, according to Afshine Emrani, dealer and appraiser at www.some-of-my-favorite-things.com, is KPM's highly superior, smooth, hard paste porcelain, which could be fired at very high temperatures.

"The magic of a KPM plaque is that it will look as crisp and beautiful 100 years from now as it does today," he said. Even when they were introduced, these plaques proved highly collectible, with art lovers, collectors, tourists, and the wealthy acquiring them for extravagant sums.

KPM rarely marketed painted porcelain plaques itself, however. Instead, it usually supplied white, undecorated ones to independent artists who specialized in this genre. Not all artists signed their KPM paintings, however.

While most KPM plaques were copies of famous paintings, some, commissioned by wealthy Americans and Europeans in the 1920s, bear images of actual people in contemporary clothing. These least collectible of KPM plaques command between $500 and $1,500 each, depending on the attractiveness of their subjects.

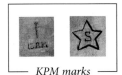
KPM marks

Gilded, hand-painted plaques featuring Middle Eastern or female Gypsy subjects and bearing round red "Made in Germany" stamps were produced just before and after World War I for export. They command between $500 and $2,000 each. Plaques portraying religious subjects, such as the Virgin Mary or the Flight into Egypt, command higher prices but are less popular.

Popular scenes of hunters, merrymakers, musicians, etc., generally fetch less than $10,000 apiece because they have been reproduced time and again. Rarer, more elaborate scenes, however, like "The Dance Lesson" and "Turkish Card Players" may be worth many times more.

Highly stylized portraits copied from famous paintings–especially those of attractive children or décolleté women–

Rago Arts and Auction Center

◄ *Pair of porcelain gourd vases with hand-painted reserves of hunting scenes with original velvet-lined box, 19th century, script mark KPM, 14 1/4" high* **$1,875**

MELODY AMSEI-ARIELI is a freelance writer and frequent contributor to *Antique Trader*. She is the author of *Between Galicia and Hungary: The Jews of Stropkov* as well as *Jewish Lives: Britain 1750-1950* (Pen & Sword, 2013). She lives in Israel.

allowed art lovers to own their own "masterpieces." These are currently worth between $2,000 and $20,000 each. Romanticized portrayals of cupids and women in the nude, the most desirable KPMs subjects of all, currently sell for up to $40,000 each. Portraits of men, it must be noted, are not only less popular, but also less expensive.

Size also matters. A 4" x 6" inch plaque, whose subject has been repeatedly reproduced, may sell for a few thousand dollars. Larger ones that portray the same subject will fetch proportionately more. A "Sistine Madonna" plaque, fashioned after the original work by Rafael and measuring 10" x 7 1/2", might cost $4,200. One featuring the identical subject, but measuring 15" x 11", might cost $7,800. A larger plaque, measuring 22" x 16", might command twice that price.

The largest KPM plaques, measuring 22" x 26", for example, often burst during production. Although no formula exists for determining prices of those that have survived, Afshine Emrani said that each may sell for as much as $250,000. Rare plaques like these are often found in museums.

The condition of a KPM plaque also affects its price. Most, since they were highly glazed and customarily hung instead of handled, have survived in perfect condition. Thus those that have sustained even minor damage, like scratches, cracks, or chips, fetch considerably lower prices. Those suffering major damage are worthless.

KPMs painted plaques arouse so much interest and command such high prices that, over the last couple of years, unscrupulous dealers have entered the market. According to dealer Balazs Benedek, KPM plaques are "the mother of all fakes. About 90 percent of KPM plaques are mid- to late-20th century reproductions. And about 70 percent are not hand painted."

Collectors should be aware that genuine KPM paintings always boast rich, shiny, glazes that preserve their colors, and though subject matter may vary, they typically feature nude scenes, indoor portraits of women, or group gatherings in lush settings. Anything wildly different should raise suspicion.

Genuine KPMs, on their backs or edges, feature small icons of scepters deeply set in the porcelain, over the letters KPM. These marks are sometimes accompanied by an "H" or some other letter, which may indicate their production date or size. Some are imprinted with the size of the plaque as well, which facilitated sorting or shipping. Shallow or crooked imprints may reveal a fake.

Heritage Auctions

◄ *Framed porcelain plaque painted by Liebmann after Gérard: Madame Racamier, depicting Madame Racamier seated on cushioned chair with background of drapery and columns, inscribed on reverse Madame Racamier n. François Gerard, v. Hugo Liebmann, circa 1900, carved gilt frame, decoration after François Gérard (French, 1770-1837), marks: (scepter) KPM, G, 237 – 158, plaque in good condition, frame with some loss to gilt ground, 9 3/8" high x 6 1/4" wide, frame 13 5/8" x 10 5/8".* **$3,125**

James D. Julia, Inc.

Plaque depicting mother and child sitting on balcony wall with mother pointing, clothed in white gown with red shawl draped over one arm, signed on back with impressed KPM with scepter mark and impressed T, gold frame, very good to excellent condition, plaque 5 1/2" x 8 1/2," 10" x 13" overall. **$1,150**

Heritage Auctions

Framed painted porcelain plaque after Le Brun by Brüdel: Madame Molé-Raymond, circa 1890, marks: (scepter) KPM, 237-145, signed A. Brüdel, inscribed on reverse Dame mit Muff, n. Lebrun, G.B. Brüdel, carved gilt frame, 9 1/2" high x 6 3/8" wide, frame 13 1/2" x 10 1/2". **$2,250**

Heritage Auctions

Framed painted porcelain plaque, 20th century, marks: (scepter) KPM, 158 237, W, carved gilt frame, good condition, frame with surface cracks, 9 1/4" high x 6 1/4" wide, frame 18 1/2" x 15 1/2". **$4,063**

Heritage Auctions

Framed porcelain plaque, Bacchanal scene of putti atop cloud in carved gilt and painted frame with velvet mat, circa 1910, marks: (scepter) KPM, H, 10 1/2 - 8 1/2, plaque in good condition, frame with minor surface loss and aging to mat, 10 7/8" x 8 3/4", frame 16 1/4" x 14". **$1,875**

Heritage Auctions

Set of 12 signed, floral-painted plates, reticulated rim with lattice and foliate design, circa 1900, marks: (scepter, globe) KPM, MADE IN GERMANY, signed W. Aidish, very good condition, 9 3/8" diameter. **$9,375**

Heritage Auctions

◄ *Porcelain and gilt metal temple-form mantel clock, circa 1890, allegorical panels depicting four seasons to sides, porcelain cupola decorated with allegorical depictions of three muses, gilt finial at each corner and on top, supported by four cobalt columns with gilt metal mounts on four gilt feet, marks to porcelain: (underglaze blue scepter), D, marks to mechanism: R.B. BREVETE, S.G.D.G., (bee), repair to front panel from top going down approximately 2", repair to top of one corner of approximately 4", loss to gilding commensurate with age, 14 1/8" high* **$5,000**

Doyle New York

Framed painted porcelain plaque titled "The Florentine Flower Girl," young woman wearing dark orange and white dress and gold headscarf, carrying a flower-filled basket, late 19th/early 20th century, rectangular form, stamped K.P.M. with scepter mark on reverse, 9 7/8" high x 7 5/8" wide **$5,000**

Heritage Auctions

Framed porcelain plaque after Kauffmann: "Vestal Virgin," circa 1900, veiled woman sitting with oil lamp, decoration after Angelica Kauffmann (Swiss, 1741-1807), marks: (scepter) KPM, H, plaque in very good condition, later carved gilt frame with minor indication of age, 12 3/8" high x 9 3/8" wide, frame 19 1/4" x 15 5/8". **$3,750**

Heritage Auctions

Framed porcelain plaque depicting courting scene in garden setting, circa 1920, later frame, marks: (scepter) KPM, F 6, plaque in very good condition, frame with some rubbing at edges, 13 1/2" x 11 1/2", frame 16 1/2 x 14". **$2,750**

Heritage Auctions

Framed porcelain plaque painted by Tenner: Shakespeare in the Court of Elizabeth I, Shakespeare entertaining Queen Elizabeth I and her court within draped garden setting with peacock in foreground, inscribed on reverse Shakespeare am Hofe d. K. Elisabeth, circa 1900, marks: (scepter) KPM, Sz, 375 – 315, signed upper left corner: F. Tenner, plaque in very good condition, later gilt frame with separation at miters, 12 3/8" high x 15 1/4" wide **$11,250**

Heritage Auctions

Framed porcelain plaque painted by R. Dittrich after Salomon Koninck (Dutch, 1609-1656): "The Hermit," circa 1900, bearded hermit reading in wooded setting, stamped marks: (scepter) KPM J.T, 203 145, underglaze marks: Erremith, R Dietrich (bee hive), plaque in very good condition, 8 1/2" high x 6 1/8" wide, later gilt frame with red velvet fillet 16 1/2" x 13 1/2". **$3,750**

Cowan's Auctions, Inc.

◄ *Hand-painted rectangular porcelain plaque depicting Bartolomé Esteban Murillo's "Grape and Melon Eaters," 1645-1646, ornate gilt frame, illegible signature, impressed KPM on verso, 15 1/4" x 12 1/4".* **$7,800**

Heritage Auctions

▼ *Framed, painted and transfer-printed porcelain plaque after Menzler: "Patrizierin," circa 1900, marks: (scepter) KPM, 9 3/4 - 7 3/8, plaque printed and over painted, inscribed 956, Patrizierin n/ Menzler, painted for Mermood, Jaccard Jewelry Co., St. Louis, presented in carved gilt frame, plaque in very good condition, frame with some loss and repair to carved foliage, some loss of gilding on surface, 9 1/4" high x 7" wide, frame 14 5/8" x 12 1/4",* **$1,750**

Heritage Auctions

◄ *Framed painted porcelain plaque after Nathaniel Sichel: "Foreign Girl," with stringed instrument, inscribed on reverse Mädchen aus der Fremde d'après N. Sichel, circa 1880, plaque in very good condition, frame with scuffs and nicks and some loss of gilt surface, 14 1/2" high x 9 1/2" wide, frame 23 3/4" x 18 3/4".* **$6,875**

Kaminski Auctions

▲ *Porcelain plaque after Joseph Coomans, portrait of young girl, original gilt gesso frame, 19th century, 16 1/2" x 10 1/2", frame 20" x 25 1/2".* **$10,000**

James D. Julia, Inc.

◄ *Plaque depicting young woman in white gown looking over back of pink chair into mirror, signed on back with impressed KPM, scepter mark, and impressed 824, gold frame, very good to excellent condition, plaque 5 1/2" x 8 1/2", 10" x 13" overall.* **$1,035**

Limoges

Limoges" has become the generic identifier for porcelain produced in Limoges, France, and the surrounding vicinity. Over 40 manufacturers in the area have, at some point, used the term as a descriptor of their work, and there are at least 400 different Limoges identification marks. The common denominator is the product itself: fine hard paste porcelain created from the necessary components found in abundance in the Limoges region: kaolin and feldspar.

Until the 1700s, porcelain was exclusively a product of China, introduced to the Western world by Marco Polo and imported at great expense. In 1765, the discovery of kaolin in St. Yrieixin, a small town near Limoges, made French production of porcelain possible. (The chemist's wife credited with the kaolin discovery thought at first that it would prove useful in making soap!)

Limoges entrepreneurs quickly capitalized on the find. Adding to the area's allure were expansive forests providing fuel for wood-burning kilns; the nearby Vienne River, with water for working clay; and a workforce eager to trade farming for a (hopefully) more lucrative pursuit. Additionally, as the companies would be operating outside metropolitan Paris, labor and production costs would be significantly less.

By the early 1770s, numerous porcelain manufacturers were at work in Limoges and its environs. Demand for the porcelain was high because it was both useful and decorative. To meet that demand, firms employed trained, as well as untrained, artisans for the detailed hand painting required. (Although nearly every type of Limoges has its fans, the most sought-after—and valuable—are those pieces decorated by a company's professional artists.) At its industrial peak in 1900, Limoges factories employed over 8,000 workers in some aspect of porcelain production.

Bonhams

Three Limoges porcelain ichthyological plates, retailed by Mansard, Paris, early 20th century, each decorated with fish swimming among waterweeds and shells with insects above, gilt heightened borders, green printed J.P./L factory mark and blue printed retailer's mark, 9 5/8" diameter, together with seven Wedgwood square form creamware dessert plates in the Wellesley pattern. **$250**

A myriad of products classified as Limoges flooded the marketplace from the late 1700s onward. Among them were tableware pieces, such as tea and punch sets, trays, pitchers, compotes, bowls and plates. Also popular were vases and flower baskets, dresser sets, trinket boxes, ash receivers, figural busts, and decorative plaques.

Although produced in France, Limoges porcelain was soon destined for export overseas; eventually over 80 percent of Limoges porcelain was exported. The United States proved a particularly reliable customer. Notable among the importers was the Haviland China Co.; until the 1940s, its superior, exquisitely decorated china was produced in Limoges and then distributed in the United States.

By the early 20th century, many exporters in the United States were purchasing porcelain blanks from the Limoges factories for decoration stateside. The base product was authentically made in France, but production costs were significantly lower: Thousands of untrained porcelain painters put their skills to work for a minimal wage. Domestic decoration of the blanks also meant that importers could select designs suited to the specific tastes of target audiences.

Because Limoges was a regional designation, rather than the identifier of a specific manufacturer, imported pieces were often marked with the name of the exporting firm, followed by the word "Limoges." Beginning in 1891, "France" was added. Some confusion has arisen from products marked "Limoges China Co." (aka "American Limoges"). This Ohio-based firm, in business from 1902-1955, has absolutely no connection to the porcelain produced in France.

The heyday of quality French Limoges lasted roughly into the 1930s. Production continues today, but after World War II, designs and painting techniques became much more standardized.

Vintage Limoges is highly sought-after by today's collectors. They're drawn to the delicacy of the porcelain as well as the colors and skill of decoration; viewing a well-conceived Limoges piece is like seeing a painting in a new form. Valuation is based on age, decorative execution and, as with any collectible, individual visual appeal.

Pook & Pook, Inc.

Painted porcelain footbath, 8" high x 22 1/2" wide x 15" diameter. **$91**

James D. Julia, Inc.

◄ *Ormolu mirror with Limoges enameled scene of maiden in distress being attacked by two bandits, maiden holding hand mirror high above her head and looking into distance as if signaling someone; enameled panel is artist signed, reverse side houses what appears to be original beveled glass mirror, mirror and enameled panel housed in ormolu frame that swivels in matching stand decorated with lion's paw feet and gargoyles; very good to excellent condition with some minor pitting to silvering on mirror; mirror 10 1/4" high overall; Limoges panel approximately 4" x 5 3/4".* **$5,036**

Skinner, Inc.; www.skinnerinc.com

▼ *Porcelain sugar and creamer with Great Seal of United States, Tressemanes & Vogt, France, 1892-1897, boat-shaped vessels with gilt foliate border, handles, and feet, one side decorated with polychrome and gilt seal, green "T & V LIMOGES FRANCE DEPOSE" backstamp, 2 7/8", 3" high.* **$480**

Sauceboat and undertray, footed boat-shaped vessel with scroll-molded rim and wide arched spout, ornate looped gold handle, hand painted with white roses on shaded pink, blue and green ground, matching décor on undertray, underglaze Elite factory mark 5, 5" long, 6" high. **$275 set**

Planter, round, upright waisted sides and slightly scalloped rim, raised on four gold scroll feet, decorated with large red and pink roses and green leaves on dark ground, underglaze green Tresseman & Vogt Mark 7, 8" diameter, 5 1/2" high. **$850**

Kaminski Auctions

Late Victorian dessert set marked AL/Limoges France, 11 3/4" x 15 5/8" oval platter with shell-molded scalloped rim with hand-painted colored daisies and heavy gold in center, and four matching plates, 8" diameter. **$70**

Skinner, Inc.; www.skinnerinc.com

Enamel on copper plaque depicting procession of the Magi, France, 19th century, after Benozzo Gozzoli (circa 1421-1497), in polychrome and gilt with raised "jewel" accents, back incised "France," metal frame, plaque 11" x 7". **$2,760**

Vases, Louis XVI style, round pedestal foot on four paw feet supporting baluster-form body with flaring neck, figural Grecian helmet handles at shoulder, deep gold ground with one side decorated with square reserve enclosing dockside scene with figures and sailing vessel, each reverse decorated with military trophies, circa 1900, 15 1/2" high. **$1,610 pr.**

Teapot, bulbous tapering ribbed body with wide domed cover with fancy loop finial, gold serpentine spout and C-scroll handle, star mark of Coiffe factory and Flambeau China mark of decorating firm, also Haviland & Co. mark, France, early 20th century. **$100**

Rago Arts and Auction Center

Six hand-painted chargers (three shown), late 19th/early 20th century, Orientalist scene by Morley, four avian scenes by Boumy, Puisoye, Valantin, and Dubois, and unsigned pastoral scene, largest 13 1/2" diameter. **$531**

Kaminski Auctions

French bronze gilt enameled box, 2 1/4" high x 7" wide x 4 1/4" deep. **$850**

Skinner, Inc.; www.skinnerinc.com

Pair of metal-mounted enamel vases, late 19th/early 20th century, each polychrome decorated with seated figure in landscape setting, 7 1/2" high. **$780**

Skinner, Inc.; www.skinnerinc.com

Hand-painted punch bowl, late 19th/early 20th century, raised gold foliage with polychrome enameled fruiting grapevines, printed factory mark, 14" diameter. **$215**

Elite Decorative Arts

Bawo & Dotter hand-painted covered handled tureen with matching floral serving platter, each with floral designs with crimson ground and gild accenting, bottoms have green Limoges mark with gold Bawo & Dotter mark, serving platter signed Ribes, 19th/20th century; tureen 10 1/2" high x 15" long, platter 19" long x 12 3/4" wide. **$610**

Kaminski Auctions

▶ *Eight-piece game set consisting of one platter and seven plates with hand-painted scenes of birds and forestry in center and gold decoration on borders, all stamped CFH/GDM on back, platter 18 1/4" long, plates 8 1/2" wide.* **$600**

Kaminski Auctions

▲ *French enamel on copper vase, 19th century, 4" high.* **$300**

Skinner, Inc.; www.skinnerinc.com

▶ *Eight porcelain Mary Bacon Jones-designed plates, circa 1905, each polychrome enamel-decorated design based on Rudyard Kipling's* The Jungle Book, *printed Wm. Guerin & Co. Limoges mark, 10 7/8" diameter.* **$2,400**

Bonhams

▲ *Porcelain game service, early 20th century, each piece decorated with different game bird in copse, signed de Solis, one two-handled oval platter, 18 1/2" long, and 12 plates, 9 1/2" diameter.* **$875**

Cowan's Auctions, Inc.

▶ *Twelve dinner plates, French, early 20th century, white ground with bands of blue and gold in scrolling floral design, all marked.* **$570**

Kaminski Auctions

Hand-painted punch bowl, 6 3/4" x 16" diameter. **$250**

Skinner, Inc.; www.skinnerinc.com

▲ *Eleven hand-painted porcelain plates depicting orchids, early 20th century, retailed by Ovington Bros., New York, each with gilded border decorated with floral garlands, polychrome enameled orchids in center, signed "L. Meage," Latin names for specimens on reverse, 9 3/8" diameter.* **$1,140**

Kaminski Auctions

▶ *Set of 12 French shellfish plates, 9" diameter.* **$225**

Majolica

In 1851, an English potter was hoping that his new interpretation of a centuries-old style of ceramics would be well received at the "Great Exhibition of the Industries of All Nations" set to open May 1 in London's Hyde Park.

Potter Herbert Minton had high hopes for his display. His father, Thomas Minton, founded a pottery works in the mid-1790s in Stoke-on-Trent, Staffordshire. Herbert Minton had designed a "new" line of pottery, and his chemist, Leon Arnoux, had developed a process that resulted in vibrant, colorful glazes that came to be called "majolica."

Trained as an engineer, Arnoux also studied the making of encaustic tiles, and had been appointed art director at Minton's works in 1848. His job was to introduce and promote new products. Victorian fascination with the natural world prompted Arnoux to reintroduce the work of Bernard Palissy, whose naturalistic, bright-colored "maiolica" wares had been created in the 16th century. But Arnoux used a thicker body to make pieces sturdier. This body was given a coating of opaque white glaze, which provided a surface for decoration.

Pieces were modeled in high relief, featuring butterflies and other insects, flowers and leaves, fruit, shells, animals, and fish. Queen Victoria's endorsement of the new pottery prompted its acceptance by the general public.

Elite Decorative Arts

Old English jardiniere and pedestal depicting flowers growing from trees over dark tones, bottom of pedestal has impressed "ENGLAND" mark, late 19th to early 20th century, 15 3/4" x 19 1/2" diameter, pedestal 30" high x 14 1/4" diameter, overall 46" high. **$726**

Strawser Auction Group

Gustafsburg tall compote supported by three storks, overlapping leaf and bull rush top, 10 1/2" high x 10 1/4" diameter. **$272**

When Minton introduced his wares at Philadelphia's 1876 Centennial Exhibition, American potters also began to produce majolica.

For more information on majolica, see *Warman's Majolica Identification and Price Guide* by Mark F. Moran.

Other Majolica Makers

John Adams & Co., Hanley, Stoke-on-Trent, Staffordshire, England, operated the Victoria Works, producing earthenware, jasperware, Parian, majolica, 1864-1873. (Jasperware is a fine white stoneware originally produced by Josiah Wedgwood, often colored by metallic oxides with raised classical designs remaining white.)

Another Staffordshire pottery, **Samuel Alcock & Co.**, Cobridge, 1828-1853; Burslem, 1830-1859, produced earthenware, china and Parian.

The **W. & J.A. Bailey Alloa Pottery** was founded in Alloa, the principal town in Clackmannanshire, located near Edinburgh, Scotland.

The **Bevington** family of potters worked in Hanley, Staffordshire, England in the late 19th century.

W. Brownfield & Son operated in Burslem and Cobridge, Staffordshire, England from 1850-1891.

T.C. Brown-Westhead, Moore & Co. produced earthenware and porcelain at Hanley, Stoke-on-Trent, Staffordshire, from about 1862 to 1904.

The **Choisy-le-Roi** faience factory of Choisy-le-Roi, France, produced majolica from 1860 until 1910. The firm's wares are not always marked. The common mark is usually a black ink stamp "Choisy-le-Roi" pictured to the right with a large "HBm," which stands for Hippolyte Boulenger, a director at the pottery.

William T. Copeland & Sons pottery of Stoke-on-Trent, Staffordshire, England, began producing porcelain and earthenware in 1847. (Josiah Spode established a pottery at Stoke-on-Trent in 1770. In 1833, the firm was purchased by William Copeland and Thomas Garrett. In 1847, Copeland became the sole owner. W.T. Copeland & Sons continued until a 1976 merger when it became Royal Worcester Spode. Copeland majolica pieces are sometimes marked with an impressed "COPELAND," but many are unmarked.)

Jose A. Cunha, Caldas da Rainha, southern Portugal, also worked in the style of Bernard Palissy, the great French Renaissance potter.

Julius Dressler, Bela Czech Republic, was founded 1888, producing faience, majolica and porcelain. In 1920, the name was changed to EPIAG. The firm closed about 1945.

Eureka Pottery was located in Trenton, New Jersey, circa 1883-1887.

Railway Pottery was established by S. Fielding & Co., Stoke, Stoke-on-Trent, Staffordshire, England, 1879.

There were two **Thomas Forester** potteries active in the late 19th century in Staffordshire, England. Some sources list the more famous of the two as Thomas Forester & Sons Ltd. at the Phoenix Works, Longton.

Established in the early 19th century, the **Gien** pottery works is located on the banks of France's Loire River near Orleans.

Joseph Holdcroft majolica ware was produced at Daisy Bank in Longton, Staffordshire, England, from 1870 to 1885. Items can be found marked with "J HOLDCROFT," but many pieces can only be attributed by the patterns and colors that are documented to have come from the Holdcroft potteries.

George Jones & Sons Ltd., Stoke, Staffordshire, started operation in about 1864 as George Jones and in 1873 became George Jones & Sons Ltd. The firm operated the Trent Potteries in Stoke-on-Trent (renamed "Crescent Potteries" in about 1907).

In about 1877, **Samuel Lear** erected a small china works in Hanley, Staffordshire. Lear produced domestic china and, in addition, decorated all kinds of earthenware made by other manufacturers, including "spirit kegs." In 1882, the firm expanded to include production of majolica, ivory-body earthenware, and Wedgwood-type jasperware. The business closed in 1886.

Robert Charbonnier founded the **Longchamp** tile works in 1847 to make red clay tiles, but the factory soon started to produce majolica. Longchamp is known for its "barbotine" pieces (a paste of clay used in decorating coarse pottery in relief) made with vivid colors, especially oyster plates.

Hugo Lonitz operated in Haldensleben, Germany, from 1868-1886, and later Hugo Lonitz & Co., 1886-1904, producing household and decorative porcelain, earthenware, and metalwares. Look for a mark of two entwined fish.

The **Lunéville** pottery was founded about 1728 by Jacques Chambrette in the city that bears its name, in the Alsace-Lorraine region of northeastern France. The firm became famous for its blue monochromatic and floral patterns. Around 1750, ceramist Paul-Louis Cyfflé introduced a pattern with animals and historical figures. Lunéville products range from hand-painted faience and majolica to pieces influenced by the Art Deco movement.

The **Massier** family began producing ceramics in Vallauris, France, in the mid-18th century.

François Maurice, School of Paris, was active from 1875-1885 and also worked in the style of Bernard Palissy.

George Morley & Co. was located in East Liverpool, Ohio, 1884-1891.

Morley & Co. Pottery was founded in 1879, Wellsville, Ohio, making graniteware and majolica.

Orchies, a majolica manufacturer in northern France near Lille, is also known under the mark "Moulin des Loups & Hamage," 1920s.

Faïencerie de Pornic is located near Quimper, France.

Quimper pottery has a long history. Tin-glazed, hand-painted pottery has been made in Quimper, France, since the late 17th century. The earliest firm, founded in 1685 by Jean Baptiste Bousquet, was known as HB Quimper. Another firm, founded in 1772 by Francois Eloury, was

Skinner, Inc.; www.skinnerinc.com

Hugo Lonitz model of swan, Germany, late 19th century, white glazed figure naturalistically modeled and seated atop stepped oval base, impressed mark, 4 3/4" high. **$600**

Skinner, Inc.; www.skinnerinc.com

Pair of Joseph Holdcroft vases, England, circa 1875, each with register of white flowers to foot and rim, central high relief scene of bird and butterfly among vine and flower motif on cobalt ground, impressed mark, professional restoration to body of each, 10 3/8" high. **$480 pr.**

known as Porquier. A third firm, founded by Guillaume Dumaine in 1778, was known as HR or Henriot Quimper. All three companies made similar pottery decorated with designs of Breton peasants, and sea and flower motifs.

The **Rörstrand** factory made the first faience (tin-glazed earthenware) produced in Sweden. It was established in 1725 by Johann Wolff, near Stockholm.

The earthenware factory of **Salins** was established in 1857 in Salins-les-Bains, near the French border with Switzerland. Salins was awarded with the gold medal at the International Exhibition of Decorative Arts in Paris in 1912.

Sarreguemines wares are named for the city in the Lorraine region of northeastern France. The pottery was founded in 1790 by Nicholas-Henri Jacobi. For more than 100 years, it flourished under the direction of the Utzschneider family.

Wilhelm Schiller and Sons, Bodenbach, Bohemia, was established 1885.

Thomas-Victor Sergent was one of the School of Paris ceramists of the late 19th century who was influenced by the works of Bernard Palissy.

St. Clement was founded by Jacques Chambrette in Saint-Clément, France, in 1758. Chambrette also established works in Lunéville.

The **St. Jean de Bretagne** pottery works are located near Quimper, France.

Vallauris is a pottery center in southeastern France, near Cannes. Companies in production there include Massier and Foucard-Jourdan.

Victoria Pottery Co. was located in Hanley, Staffordshire, England from 1895-1927.

Wardle & Co. was established 1871 at Hanley, Staffordshire, England.

Josiah Wedgwood was born in Burslem, Staffordshire, England, on July 12, 1730, into a family with a long pottery tradition. At the age of nine, after the death of his father, he joined the family business. In 1759, he set up his own pottery works in Burslem. There he produced cream-colored earthenware that found favor with Queen Charlotte. In 1762, she appointed him royal supplier of dinnerware. From the public sale of "Queen's Ware," as it came to be known, Wedgwood was able to build a production community in 1768, which he named Etruria, near Stoke-on-Trent, and a second factory equipped with tools and ovens of his own design. (Etruria is the ancient land of the Etruscans, in what is now northern Italy.)

Skinner, Inc.;
www.skinnerinc.com

Three-piece Royal Worcester candle set, England, late 19th century, each modeled as stylized Corinthian columns, one slightly larger with two sconces, impressed mark, two single sconces with professional restorations, both arms of double candelabra and center restored, to 10 1/4" high. **$123**

Minton bowl, England, date cipher for 1867, circular shape with pale pink exterior and orange interior, three frogs on faux cobblestone base, impressed factory mark and cipher marks, 4 1/8" high. **$984**

Minton stag head sweetmeat dish, England, 1864, polychrome enamel decorated and modeled with circular dish set atop cornucopia-shaped stem terminating at stag head, all set on raised oval base, impressed marks, areas of antlers professionally restored, 4 1/4" high. **$570**

English jardiniere in Egyptian taste, circa 1875, likely George Jones, square shape with canted corners and decorated with pharaoh busts and sphinxes on outset feet, unmarked, professionally restored hairline crack to one side, 2" hairline crack to base, two jardiniere feet professionally repaired, 8" high. **$584**

▶ *Minton pomegranate vase, England, date cipher for 1879, elongated neck, handle modeled as pomegranate tree branch with leaves and fruit radiating outward onto neck and body of vase, impressed mark, professional restoration to pomegranate and leaves, 21" high.* **$510**

Skinner, Inc.; www.skinnerinc.com

Minton chestnut bowl, England, circa 1870, polychrome decorated and modeled with chestnuts and leaves to scallop-edge shell-shaped bowl with robin's-egg blue interior, impressed mark, 10 1/2" long. **$180**

Skinner, Inc.; www.skinnerinc.com

▲ *George Jones jardiniere, England, late 19th century, decorated with low relief scene of birds and cherry blossoms between basketweave pattern register to rim and base, pad mark, lower side of body with hairline and restoration, 10 1/2" high.* **$840**

Skinner, Inc.; www.skinnerinc.com

◄ *Hugo Lonitz fish-form covered tureen, Germany, late 19th century, polychrome enameled and inset with glass eyes, impressed factory mark and numbered 1347, incised lowercase "b," blue underglaze "KY," 17 1/2" long.* **$861**

Skinner, Inc.; www.skinnerinc.com

George Jones fox tray, England, circa 1870, oval, leaf-molded dish adorned with fox head to one side, tail under rim, impressed and pad marks, repair to tip of one ear, 10" long. **$300**

Wedgwood jardiniere on pedestal base, England, circa 1893, allover marigold-colored ground with molded body decorated in panels of floral urns, impressed marks, jardiniere 17" high, pedestal base 24 1/4" high. **$1,200**

Wedgwood figural Trentham vase, England, 1873, modeled by Rowland Morris, polychrome enameled and modeled as two cherubs supporting vase on their backs, tools of agriculture applied to raised base, impressed mark, professional restorations to chips along top rim and to feet at either end of base, one end to foliate garland missing, cherubs stained, 10 1/2" high. **$510**

Tile and iron planter, possibly Italy, 19th century, rectangular form with paneled sides, two polychrome enamel decorated portrait tiles to either side, floral decorated tile to either end, 16 3/4" long overall. **$660**

Strawser Auction Group

St. Clement rooster and duck figural pitchers, 11" and 13" high. **$206**

Strawser Auction Group

▲ *Brown picket fence cheese keeper, repair to handle and rim of base, 9 1/2".* **$242**

Strawser Auction Group

◄ *Fielding turquoise shells and fishnet pitcher with coral handle, base chip to underside, 6 1/2" high.* **$303**

Strawser Auction Group

▲ *Wedgwood pitcher with Oriental motif, 7" high.* **$157**

Strawser Auction Group

◄ *Fielding shells and fishnet pitcher with coral handle, hairline crack on spout, minor surface wear, 7" high.* **$272**

Strawser Auction Group

Shells and coral on waves pitcher, 8" high. **$575**

Strawser Auction Group

Cottage figural pitcher with rare cobalt rooftop, 8" high. **$333**

Strawser Auction Group

Mottled unusual form teapot, 5" high. **$194**

Strawser Auction Group

▲ *Fielding wheat and daisy pewter top syrup pitcher, 5" high.* **$272**

Skinner, Inc.; www.skinnerinc.com

◄ *George Jones calla lily jardiniere, England, late 19th century, decorated in low relief on textured roulette turquoise ground with yellow rim, impressed and pad mark, 10 1/2" high.* **$300**

Strawser Auction Group

Rare Wardle three-piece tea set with matching tray, minor spout nick to teapot and creamer, staining to sugar bowl, tray 10 3/4" diameter. **$726**

Skinner, Inc.; www.skinnerinc.com

Minton cobalt blue decorated Amphora vase, England, 1862, gilded trim to base modeled with lion mask motifs and scrolled feet, impressed mark, 5 3/4" high. **$123**

Strawser Auction Group

◀ Pair of French asparagus and fern plates, 9 3/4" diameter. **$484**

Strawser Auction Group

Pond lily plate, 9 1/2" diameter. **$303**

Strawser Auction Group

French asparagus platter with rare cobalt ground, 14 1/2" long. **$393**

Strawser Auction Group

George Jones strawberry serving platter, 14 1/2" long. **$514**

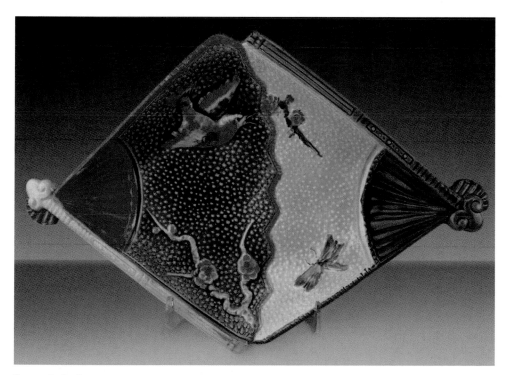

Strawser Auction Group

Eureka Pottery Co. bird and fan diamond-shaped tray, 16" long. **$194**

Meissen

Augustus II, Elector of Saxony and King of Poland, founded the Royal Saxon Porcelain Manufactory in Albrechtsburg, Meissen, in 1710. Johann Friedrich Bottger, an alchemist, and Tschirnhaus, a nobleman, experimented with kaolin from the Dresden area to produce porcelain. By 1720, the factory produced a whiter hard-paste porcelain than that from the Far East.

The Meissen factory experienced its golden age from the 1730s to the 1750s. By the 1730s, Meissen employed nearly 100 workers. It became known for its porcelain sculptures; Meissen dinnerware also won acclaim.

The Meissen factory was destroyed and looted by the forces of Frederick the Great during the Seven Years' War (1756-1763). It was reopened but never achieved its former greatness. By the early 1800s, Meissen's popularity began to wane. In the 19th century, the factory reissued some of its earlier forms.

Many marks were used by the Meissen factory. The famous crossed swords mark was adopted in 1724. The swords mark with a small dot between the hilts was used from 1763 to 1774, and a star between the hilts from 1774 to 1814.

Three vases, circa 1900, each with underglaze blue crossed swords mark, flanked by serpent handles centered by floral sprays or bunches of fruit, largest with double cancellation and impressed A148/67, pair impressed or incised E153, tallest 19" high.
$1,250

Pook & Pook, Inc.

Pair of fox head stirrup cups, 19th century, 3 1/4" high. **$1,778**

Pook & Pook, Inc.

Set of eight bird plates, 19th century, 8 1/2" diameter, together with two floral plates, 9 1/2" diameter. **$652**

Pook & Pook, Inc.

Reticulated floral bowl, 6" high, 10" diameter. **$59**

▶ *Figure group depicting elegant woman in 18th century dress standing over cherub reading book, surrounded below by ladies-in-waiting and two girls, ovoid naturalistic base, late 19th/early 20th century, 12" high.* **$6,463**

James D. Julia, Inc.

Porcelain figurine titled "Duck Sale," marked on underside with gray M and impressed numbers 720 62, very good to excellent condition, 6 1/2" high x 6" wide. **$830**

Bonhams

Porcelain group of Abduction of Prosperpine, circa 1900, underglaze blue crossed swords mark with double cancellation, incised 1787, impressed 125 and black painted 57, 8" high. **$750**

Skinner, Inc.; www.skinnerinc.com

Pair of porcelain vases, late 19th/early 20th century, scrolled snake handles, gilding to rim, handle terminals, lower body, and socle, crossed swords marks, 15 3/8" high. **$984**

Skinner, Inc.; www.skinnerinc.com

▲ *Pair of porcelain flower sellers, late 19th century, gilded and polychrome enamel decorated figures, man holding hat full of flowers, woman a basketful, each with underglaze blue crossed swords marks, 6 1/4", 6 5/8" high.* **$1,320**

Skinner, Inc.; www.skinnerinc.com

◄ *Four items, late 19th century, each polychrome enameled and gilded, including pair of figures of man and woman, each supporting floral garland, 6 1/4" high, 6 1/2" high; pair of covered urns with foliate festoons above figural landscape scenes, 5" high; crossed swords marks.* **$1,722**

Skinner, Inc.; www.skinnerinc.com

▲ *Five porcelain figures, 19th century, each gilded and polychrome enamel decorated, including youth playing shuttlecock, 5 7/8" high; youth playing flute, 5 3/4" high; young girl feeding chickens, 4 5/8" high; young boy with barrel of grapes, 3 5/8" high; and maiden riding back of steer, 3 3/8" high; crossed swords marks.* **$1,968**

Skinner, Inc.; www.skinnerinc.com

◀ *Five porcelain figures, 19th century, each gilded and polychrome enamel decorated, including male youth, 7 1/4" high; woman with bird in apron, 7 1/8" high; posing dandy, 6 3/4"; man hiking, 7"; and harlequin and maiden dancing, 7"; crossed swords marks.* **$3,900**

Pair of porcelain cobalt blue ground vases and covers, late 19th century, each with gilded scrolled foliage surrounding shaped cartouches, polychrome enamel decorated with courting figures on one side, floral bouquets on reverse, underglaze crossed swords marks, finial restored to one cover, 9 3/8" high. **$1,230**

Porcelain courting group, late 19th century, gilded trim with polychrome enameling to man and woman seated beneath tree, rabbit by their feet, underglaze crossed swords mark, first quality mark, loss and old repairs to numerous leaves, rabbit missing half of rear leg, restored to end of sword, 9 3/4" high. **$1,320**

Porcelain figural group, late 19th century, polychrome enamel decorated and gilded with figures of two boys supporting girl on stilts, all by sculpture of classical maiden, crossed swords mark, heavy losses to leaves and branches, restored to small scattered chips, basket on backside missing handle, 10 3/8" high. **$1,920**

Porcelain lover's group, late 19th century, polychrome enameled and gilded model depicting man and woman in amorous pose, lamb by their side, crossed swords mark, first quality mark, restoration to woman's hand by lamb and to ribbons of man's hat, scattered chips to flowers and leaves, 7 1/2" high. **$1,440**

Skinner, Inc.; www.skinnerinc.com

◀ *Pair of porcelain figures with garlands, late 19th century, each gilded and polychrome enamel decorated, man supporting garland atop his shoulders, woman holding garland across her chest, underglaze blue crossed swords marks, 6 3/8", 6 1/2" high.* **$960**

Skinner, Inc.; www.skinnerinc.com

▲ *Porcelain figural group, late 18th/early 19th century, gilded and polychrome enamel decorated, modeled as farmer with cow and milkmaid, underglaze blue crossed swords mark, 7 3/8" high.* **$1,140**

Skinner, Inc.; www.skinnerinc.com

▲ *Porcelain blue ground vase and cover, 19th century, bottle shape with gilded trim lines and decorated in white and black enamel with classical maiden on either side, underglaze blue crossed swords mark, 8 5/8" high.* **$1,968**

Skinner, Inc.; www.skinnerinc.com

◀ *Porcelain allegorical figural group, 19th century, gilded and polychrome enamel decorated, modeled as seated Cupid dressed in long coat and wearing hat and surrounded by three maidens, blue crossed swords mark, first quality mark, restorations to kneeling maiden's neck and arms, seated maiden's back of seat, cupid's legs, 7 1/4" high.* **$2,091**

Bonhams

Four porcelain busts, circa 1900, each with blue crossed swords mark, comprising three allegorical of the seasons, one with single cancellation mark, incised model numbers and bust of Renaissance maiden, incised L17, 8 1/4" to 11" high. **$2,750**

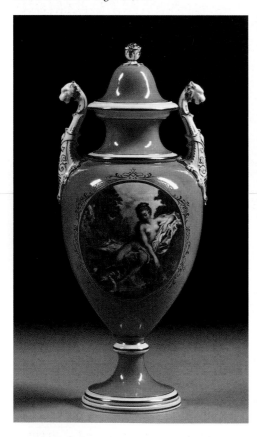

Skinner, Inc.; www.skinnerinc.com

Porcelain yellow ground vase and cover, early 20th century, gilded griffin head handles, polychrome enamel decorated oval cartouches with nude nymph to either side, underglaze crossed swords mark, slight hairline through figure on one side, 15 5/8" high. **$923**

Elite Decorative Arts

Porcelain blue onion three-tier cake plate with figural woman with flowers finial, bottom with blue crossed swords mark with number 2, circa 1860-1880, 21 1/2" high. **$1,936**

Skinner, Inc.; www.skinnerinc.com

Pair of porcelain cobalt ground plates, 19th century, each with pierced floret and ringlet border and polychrome enamel decorated cartouches, one depicting Triumph of Bacchus, the other Renaud and Armide, titled in French, crossed swords marks, 9 1/8" diameter. **$3,321**

Skinner, Inc.; www.skinnerinc.com

Skinner, Inc.; www.skinnerinc.com

Porcelain figural courting group, late 19th century, polychrome enameled and gilded model with three figures, maiden with suitor, another maiden grieving by her side, crossed swords mark, first quality mark, restoration to bow in maiden's hat, maiden's arm resting on shoulder of other maiden, basket of flowers, fingers of hand at basket, 12 1/4" high. **$2,400**

Porcelain figural courting group, late 19th century, polychrome enameled and gilded depiction of maiden centering male suitor, another kneeling by column with lovebirds in his hat, crossed swords mark, first quality mark, restoration to standing suitor's back hand, 12" high. **$2,583**

Elite Decorative Arts

▲ *Porcelain group of Venus and attendants, centered by Venus seated in shell chariot riding a wave, surrounded by attendants in form of putti, dolphins, and mermaids, underglaze blue crossed swords with single cancellation, late 19th century, incised D81, impressed 68 and red painted 41, 8 1/2" high.* **$2,057**

Skinner, Inc.; www.skinnerinc.com

▶ *Porcelain swan group, 19th century, gilded and polychrome enamel decorated, modeled as mother swan with two of her young, crossed swords mark, 4 5/8" high.* **$450**

Sèvres

S ome of the most desirable porcelain ever produced was made at the Sèvres factory, originally established at Vincennes, France, and transferred, through permission of Madame de Pompadour, to Sèvres as the Royal Manufactory about the middle of the 18th century. King Louis XV took sole responsibility for the works in 1759, when production of hard paste wares began. Between 1850 and 1900, many biscuit and soft-paste pieces were made again. Fine early pieces are scarce and high-priced. Many of those available today are late productions. The various Sèvres marks have been copied, and pieces in the "Sèvres Style" are similar to actual Sèvres wares but not necessarily from that factory.

Sèvres mark

Elite Decorative Arts

Pair of French porcelain six-arm candelabrum, 19th century, each with hand-painted scenes of courting couples and landscapes, signed A. Daret, each scene surrounded by cobalt ground, mounted on gilded bronze lion base with scrolled floral arms, each approximately 25 5/8" high. **$1,331**

Skinner, Inc.; www.skinnerinc.com

Pair of bronze-mounted porcelain urns, France, circa 1900, each with dark cobalt ground, gilt trim, and oval medallions, polychrome enamel decorated with cartouche of lovers to one side, cottage landscapes on reverse, 16" high. **$492**

Skinner, Inc.; www.skinnerinc.com

Pair of jeweled porcelain cabinet portrait plates, 19th century, with matching cobalt blue rims, enamel decorated with reserves of flowers and classical motifs, with gilt accenting and white, turquoise, and red jeweling, inner rim with flower garland wrapped in ribbon, each painted in center with portrait roundel in red jeweled surround, one depicting Pierre Corneille, the other Embegirde Femme de Pharamond, identified and with factory marks on reverse, 9 1/2" diameter. $2,829

Kaminski Auctions

▶ *Two cups and one saucer, French, 19th century, larger: cup 3" high, saucer 5" diameter. $750*

Elite Decorative Arts

▼ *French enameled portrait urn, late 19th to early 20th century, depicting shepherd courting young girl, signed J. Missant lower right of painting, cobalt ground with scrolled floral gilt accents, 11 3/4" high x 13 3/4" wide. $1,815*

Elite Decorative Arts

▶ *Pair of French porcelain cobalt ground urns depicting man and woman with floral scenes, 19th century, dore bronze rim mount with handles and base, each approximately 8 7/8" high. Provenance: From the estate of Count and Countess Claes-Eric de Lewenhaupt of Sweden. $787*

Kaminski Auctions

Pair of French urns, cobalt blue and gold decorated, 19th century, 22 1/2" x 9 1/2". **$1,900**

Kaminski Auctions

Pair of green urns with ormolu, late 18th/early 19th century, 10 1/4". **$1,100**

Kaminski Auctions

Cup with lid and saucer, 18th/19th century, 6" x 6 1/2". **$750**

Elite Decorative Arts

French porcelain mounted centerpiece bowl with figural cherub bronze-doré six-armed candelabra frame, 19th century, front of bowl has hand-painted scene depicting young family, verso depicts floral bouquet, oval hand-painted porcelain portrait plaque of aristocratic woman on front of base, crafted scrolled leaves, latticework and floral garlands, 31 1/2" high x 25 1/4" long x 14 3/4" deep. **$12,100**

Mark Mussio, Humler & Nolan

Large figure of fish in brown with gilded accents, marked with Sevres France M-N-F logo, chip to right rear corner of plinth, 9 1/4" high x 17 1/2" long. **$275**

Elite Decorative Arts

French porcelain sculpture depicting man holding hat, standing near stool, bottom has blue double L mark with A (used circa 1753 but possibly made as late as 19th century), 13" high. **$424**

Skinner, Inc.; www.skinnerinc.com

Pair of gilt-bronze-mounted porcelain urns and covers, France, circa 1900, each with multicolored lustre borders and central cartouches of allegorical subjects with landscapes on reverse, nymph handles, signed under covers, 17 1/4" high. **$11,070**

Mark Mussio, Humler & Nolan

Vase with mottled blue high glaze and gold trim at top and bottom, circa 1892-1893, stamped on base S 92 within oval and with Dore' a Sevres 93 logo, initials JT in green slip, excellent original condition, 9 1/2" high. **$160**

Elite Decorative Arts

Porcelain hand-painted box with top depicting woman with cherub, 19th century, signed "Rolle" lower left hand corner, body depicting floral bouquets with pink ground, bottom holds blue Sevres double L mark with red Chateau des Tuilieres mark, 5 5/8" high x 9 1/2" long x 6 1/4" deep. **$726**

Rago Arts and Auction Center

Porcelain Napoleonic military plate with gilded border, 19th century, artist signed Swebach, dated 1812, 9" diameter. **$1,375**

Rago Arts and Auction Center

Three porcelain Napoleonic military plates with gilded borders, 19th century, one artist signed L. Moreau, script signature M. Imple de Sevres, each 9 3/8" diameter. **$2,375**

Elite Decorative Arts

▲ *Pair of gilded French bronze and porcelain five-arm candelabrum, each with cobalt porcelain body with hand-painted landscape and courting couple scenes, 19th century, each approximately 27 1/4" high x 12 1/2" diameter.* **$2,178**

Mark Mussio, Humler & Nolan

◄ *Vase with crystalline glaze with large blue crystals on cobalt surface along with splashes of mustard and turquoise, made in 1902, marked with triangular logo featuring S and date, excellent original condition, 9 1/4" high.* **$500**

Mark Mussio, Humler & Nolan

Porcelain vase made in 1910 with crystalline glaze, featuring large blue crystals and smaller ivory crystals, brass mounts at top and bottom, attached to brass stand, marked with triangular logo showing S and date within, excellent original condition, 10" high. **$400**

Mark Mussio, Humler & Nolan

Crystalline vase with mushroom-colored crystals on green surface dripped over cobalt, 1919, Sevres ink stamp with date, gold colored holder, excellent original condition with two mounting holes drilled to bottom of vase to attach it to holder, ceramic portion 6 7/8" high. **$600**

Elite Decorative Arts

French gilded bronze and porcelain urn depicting courting couple in landscape scene with yellow ground, 19th century, signed lower right of painting, blue double "L" with "S" and "L," 26 1/2" high x 13" wide. **$2,420**

Rago Arts and Auction Center

Three Dresden and porcelain plates with hand-painted genre scenes and gilded borders, early 20th century, largest 9 1/4" diameter. **$1,500**

Rago Arts and Auction Center

Four porcelain items, 19th/20th century: covered center bowl with gilt and floral decoration, pair of covered urns, and lidded urn with ram's head handles, all marked, tallest 16 1/2". **$625**

Wedgwood

I n 1754, Josiah Wedgwood and Thomas Whieldon of Fenton Vivian, Staffordshire, England, became partners in a pottery enterprise. Their products included marbled, agate, tortoiseshell, green glaze, and Egyptian black wares.

Between 1766 and 1769, Wedgwood built the famous works at Etruria. Among the most-renowned products of this plant were the Empress Catherina of Russia dinner service (1774) and the Portland Vase (1790s). The firm also made caneware, unglazed earthenwares (drabwares), piecrust wares, variegated and marbled wares, black basalt (developed in 1768), Queen's or creamware, and Jasperware (perfected in 1774).

Bone china was produced under the direction of Josiah Wedgwood II between 1812 and 1822 and was revived in 1878. Moonlight luster was made from 1805 to 1815. Fairyland luster began in 1920. All luster production ended in 1932.

A museum was established at the Etruria pottery in 1906. When Wedgwood moved to its modern plant at Barlaston, North Staffordshire, the museum was expanded.

All images courtesy Skinner, Inc., www.skinnerinc.com.

Emile Lessore decorated Queen's Ware double urn, England, circa 1865, raised rectangular shaped plinth set with two attached urns, each with two covers, all enamel decorated in typical palette, plinth with hand-painted cartouches in landscapes, artist signed and impressed mark, 8 3/4" high. **$2,760**

Ivory Vellum potpourri and cover, England, late 19th century, globular shaped Queen's Ware body with pierced cover, gilded upturned loop handles, gold and enamel flowers and foliage, insert disc lid, impressed mark, 9 3/4" high. **$369**

Emile Lessore decorated Queen's Ware dish, England, circa 1865, oval shape with scalloped rim, polychrome enamel decorated with man serenading woman in landscape setting, titled on reverse The Duet, artist signed and impressed mark, 9 3/8" long. **$240**

Majolica jardiniere on pedestal base, England, circa 1893, allover marigold-colored ground with molded body decorated in panels of floral urns, impressed marks, jardiniere 17" high, pedestal base, 24 1/4" high. **$1,200**

Rosso Antico wine cooler, England, mid-19th century, barrel shape with handles of mask heads below leaf and berry headdress, molded body with fruiting grapevines, impressed mark, 9 3/4" high. **$246**

◄ *Wedgwood-mounted cut-steel and fruitwood patch box, England, circa 1800, circular box trimmed in tortoiseshell with multifaceted steel beadwork surrounding central octagonal dark blue medallion with applied white classical figure in relief, 2 5/8" overall diameter.* **$240**

▼ *Light blue jasper dip apotheosis of Virgil vase and cover, England, mid-19th century, applied white relief with snake handles terminating at Medusa masks, classical figures in relief surrounding body within foliate borders, Pegasus finial, impressed mark, 17 3/4" high.* **$12,000**

Dark blue jasper dip Portland vase, England, 19th century, applied undraped classical figures in white relief, man wearing Phrygian cap under base, impressed mark, 10" high. **$2,160**

▼ *Light blue jasper plaque, long narrow rectangular shape, applied white relief scene of Judgment of Hercules, impressed mark, 19th century, mounted in ebonized wood frame, some surface wear, 5 3/4" x 16".* **$1,763**

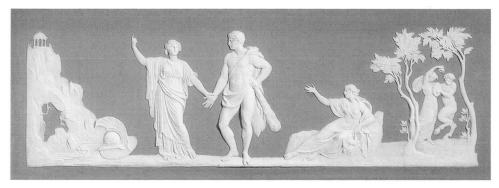

◀ *Fairyland Lustre "Picnic by a River" plaque, England, circa 1920, rectangular shape with blue sky and purple bat, printed mark, set in an ebonized wood frame, by sight 4 1/4 x 9 3/4".* **$7,200**

▼ *Fairyland Lustre pillar vase, England, circa 1920, shape 3451, blue to daylit sky with paneled sides, printed mark, 12" high.* **$12,000**

◀ *Fairyland Lustre lily tray, England, circa 1920, pattern Z4968 with Jumping Faun interior to daylit sky, exterior with mottled green ground and gilded birds, printed mark, 9" diameter.* **$9,600**

◀ *Fairyland Lustre leapfrogging elves fruit bowl, England, circa 1920, pattern Z5360 with flame sky, interior with Woodland Bridge Variation I and Mermaid center, signed MJ and printed mark, 11 1/4" diameter.* **$18,000**

Crimson jasper teapot, covered, squatty bulbous body with short angled spout and C-form handle, domed cover with button finial, applied white classical figures, circa 1920, restoration to figure and rim chips on cover, 5 1/4" high. **$400-$600**

Crimson jasper dip box and cover, England, circa 1920, scalloped rim with white applied classical figural group centering florets, box with classical figure groups, impressed mark, 3 3/4" long. **$720**

◀ *Crimson jasper dip Portland vase, England, circa 1920, applied classical figures in white relief, impressed mark, 6 1/8" high.* **$2,400**

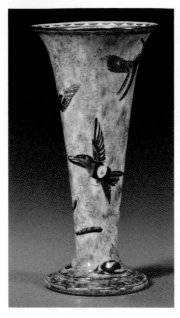

Hummingbird Lustre trumpet vase, England, circa 1920, mottled blue, pink, and green ground with gilded and polychrome decorated birds surrounding body, printed mark, 11" high. **$1,320**

Fairyland Lustre Melba center bowl, England, circa 1920, pattern Z5462, exterior with Woodland Elves IV–Big Eyes to dark blue sky, interior with Jumping Faun to pale orange sky, printed mark, 8" diameter. **$7,200**

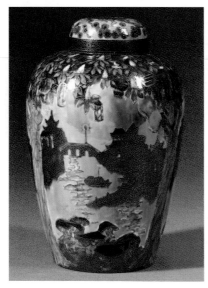

Fairyland Lustre vase, slightly tapering cylindrical body with flaring round foot and angled shoulder to short trumpet neck, decorated in Goblin pattern No. Z5367, brown goblins with red-spotted wings standing and kneeling on green grass alongside dark blue water with butterflies and fairies flying above, gold Wedgwood Portland vase mark, few glaze hairline cracks, small flake under foot, 8 1/2" high. **$6,500**

Fairyland Lustre Willow pattern vase and cover, England, circa 1920, shape 2410, pattern Z5228 to blue sky, printed mark, 9 1/2" high. **$9,000**

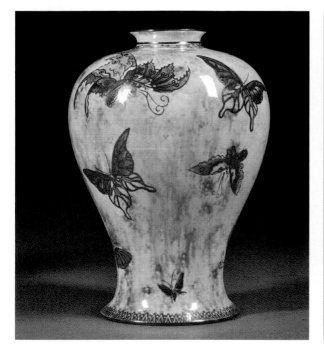

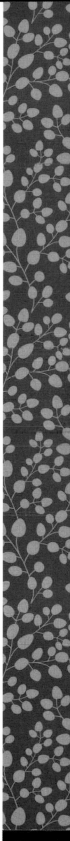

Butterfly Lustre vase, England, circa 1920, shape 2414, pattern Z4832 with gilded and polychrome enameled butterflies to mother-of-pearl ground, printed mark, 9 1/2" high. **$1,560**

Butterfly Lustre vase and cover, England, circa 1920, shape 2046, pattern Z4832 with gilded and polychrome enameled butterflies to mother-of-pearl ground, printed mark, 10 7/8" high. **$1,320**

Pair of Dragon Lustre vases, England, circa 1920, pattern Z4829, mottled blue ground with gilded and polychrome enamel decorated dragons coiling body, printed marks, 12 3/8" high. **$1,320**

Pair of three-color jasper vases, England, mid-19th century, solid white ground with applied lilac and green classical motifs and white classical figural groups, impressed marks, 5 1/4" high. **$492**

Three-color jasper dip barber bottle and cover, England, circa 1866, lilac ground with green medallions and applied white Bacchus heads to shoulders, classical figures and fruiting grapevine festoons in relief, impressed mark, 10 1/4" high. **$431**

Light green jasper dip Portland vase, England, 19th century, applied undraped classical figures in white relief, man wearing Phrygian cap under base, impressed mark, 10 1/2" high. **$720**

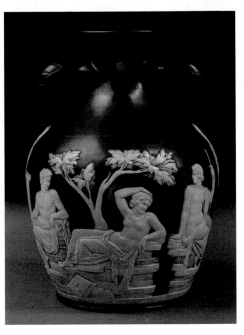

Yellow jasper dip biscuit barrel, England, circa 1930, cylindrical shape with applied black classical muses below fruiting grapevine festoons terminating at lion masks and rings, running grapevine at footrim, silver-plated rim, handle, and cover, impressed mark, 5 1/2" high. **$600**

Charles Bellows solid black jasper Portland vase, England, 1913, polished surface with applied classical undraped figures in white relief, man wearing Phrygian cap below base, inscribed "Executed for Charles Bellows at Etruria 1913 No. 2," impressed mark, 10" high. **$8,400**

Pair of slip-decorated white terra-cotta stoneware vases, England, late 18th century, each with white cut to brown with flower heads in relief to border, impressed marks, 6 3/4" high. **$720**

Civil War Collectibles

By Noah Fleisher

The Civil War, in its way, was the single most important event in American history. The nation's tortured relationship with slavery and abolition was kicked down the road by every founding father and every president until Lincoln had the courage to stand up to and stop it.

The ramifications of the conflict still play out today, though an increasingly large segment of the population has less and less familiarity with the particulars. Films like Spielberg's 2012 epic "Lincoln" help keep the conflict current in the broadest sense, but the true scope of the war, its players and battles, its massive reach and devastating effects, requires a healthy intellectual curiosity and the time to nurture it.

The War Between the States also left behind a rich material history to bolster any study of the era. From uniforms to guns to photographs, writings and various printed ephemera, the field of Civil War collecting is vast and intricate, with pieces from most every corner of the war available to serious collecting.

The market of Civil War collecting is a market, however, that is somewhat in flux.

Prices are down from a decade or two ago, when common and mid-range pieces were bringing high prices, respective to their previous comparables, and the very best material – those things tied to big names in the war, or important regiments, with impeccable provenance – were simply exorbitant.

Noah Fleisher

Things seemed to reach a bottom of sorts a few years ago and now, as we approach the sesquicentennial of the end of the war, the best material is experiencing a balancing out, perhaps even a comeback. No matter how you come at it, there are good opportunities if you know where to look.

"The Civil War market is evolving to meet the demands of a changing collector base," said Eric Smylie, noted historian and an expert in Civil War and Arms & Militaria at Heritage Auctions. "Most dealers and collectors have finally realized that if the market is going to grow and thrive, they need to cultivate a new generation of collectors to follow the current generation. The prospects for that happening are very good, even if it will be a smaller number of collectors. I've seen movement in the last few years of collectors from other areas moving into the Civil War market. They're generally buying high-quality, identified, and unique pieces."

The exuberance of a decade ago has worn off and with it, for several years, the exuberance of

NOAH FLEISHER received his Bachelor of Fine Arts degree from New York University and brings more than a decade of newspaper, magazine, book, antiques and art experience to his position as Public Relations Director of Heritage Auctions, one of the country's foremost auction houses. He is the former editor of *Antique Trader, New England Antiques Journal* and *Northeast Antiques Journal,* is the author of *Warman's Modern Furniture,* and has been a longtime contributor to *Warman's Antiques and Collectibles.*

Heritage Auctions

Civil War 11-star Confederate 1st National Flag from personal effects of Lt. Henry Bedinger Davenport, 2nd Virginia Infantry CSA, likely associated with that unit; 53" on hoist, 84 1/2" on fly, fly and canton composed of single layer of red, white, and blue wool challis. **$20,315**

collectors, which – as Smylie points out – has led to a contracted market and a generation of collectors that was almost passed over altogether. As current trends at auction seem to indicate, however, there is a younger generation of collectors (men and women in their 30s and 40s) beginning to show interest in the history. The prices also support Smylie's observation that the pool is smaller and that they are interested in paying good money for top-level material and let the bottom fall away.

"The market shows sustained strength of late led by high quality, well-provenanced weapons, uniforms, and more showy equipment," Smylie said. "The more common material, bullets, run-of-the mill cartridge boxes, U.S. belt plates, and ephemera have suffered in recent years."

The prices realized on the images that follow certainly seem to bear this out.

While the overall market, at the top end, follows the truism that quality will always sell, smart collectors would indeed do well to look at the more generic parts of the market because there are sure to be good deals on the areas that have "suffered," plenty of which are more than sufficient to start a collection, bolster an existing grouping, or hook a beginner who doesn't have the discretionary income yet to go after the big stuff.

"Indeed there are always opportunities," said Smylie. "There are many older collections coming on the market right now. You'll often see the large collections accompanied by fanfare, but there are smaller collections, with good material, coming out of rural attics and suburban

Heritage Auctions

▲ *Charleston, S. C. one sheet headed* The Charleston Mercury Extra, *dated "Saturday Evening April 14, 1861." Headlines at top: "The Battle of Fort Sumter! / End of the Fight! / Major Anderson Surrenders!" Large, bold, two-line pronouncement at bottom: "South Carolina / Is Independent!," only example of this date known to exist, 12" x 15 3/4".* **$9,560**

cellars and quietly slipping onto the market. Finding that hidden or overlooked treasure is often a matter of knowledge and lots of luck."

Most any Civil War dealer or auctioneer worth his salt is going to be happy to spend some time with you if you are new to the market, or thinking of getting back in after staying away for a while, and neophyte collectors should find someone they like and trust. That, coupled with some time spent in self-erudition on what you like – North? South? Uniforms? Correspondence? Battle field artifacts? – should lead you into a very rewarding and infinitely fascinating area.

"Study the items that interest you before you buy," said Smylie. "Go to shows, touch the material, ask questions, carefully read auction catalogs, and follow the prices realized prices. Buy from well-established and reputable dealers and auction houses, as they will stand by the material they sell. In time, you will recognize a genuine piece from a reproduction in a booth bulging with items.

"To all collectors, perhaps the best advice is to buy the best you can afford," he added. "Don't try to save a few dollars by purchasing a faded or repaired item if a better one is available. Buying quality is always better than settling for something less."

More than 650,000 soldiers died in the brutal bloodshed of the Civil War, in fighting that was obviously horrifying to endure and still shocking to learn about. The war nearly destroyed America and helped forge the union as it is today – infinitely diverse and prone to disagreement, as ever, but decidedly united when push comes to shove.

The artifacts of the conflict carry that heavy history; the rifle a soldier carried into battle, or the coarse wool tunic that provided scant protection from cold and was suffocating in the heat, they tie us to our past and thrill us with their immediacy to such a charged and important moment in time.

The important material is out there, waiting to be appreciated, almost 250 years after its intended purpose expired. Now it is waiting for a new generation to make it new again.

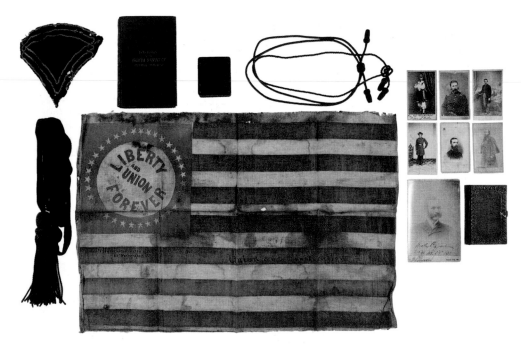

Heritage Auctions

Group of material associated with John C. Moseley (Mosly), 8th Kentucky Infantry U.S.; Mosely (spelled Mosly in records) joined the regiment on June 16, 1862, and served to the end of the war, reaching rank of sergeant major. **$21,510**

Three-piece coin silver coffee set, circa 1855, that belonged to Mr. and Mrs. Jefferson Davis, set by Hyde & Goodrich of New Orleans, given by Mrs. Davis to her granddaughter, Varina Howell Davis Hayes, Christmas 1887. **$26,680**

◀ *Confederate militia uniform worn by Capt. Peyton N. Hale, Co. F "Grayson Dare Devils," 4th Virginia Infantry, killed in action at First Bull Run.* **$23,900**

▶ *Civil War New Jersey marked 3 ordnance rifle on period carriage, tube for gun believed to have come from sea wall around Bannerman's Island in Hudson Valley, New York, approximately 11', 5" overall length to carriage trail. From the Michael Yeck Collection.* **$26,290**

Heritage Auctions

▲ *Rare 1863 uniform of the famed Keystone Zouaves worn by Pvt. Jediah K. Burnham, Co. A, 76th Pa. Vol. Inf., manufactured at Schuylkill Arsenal at direction of U.S. Army in the style of classic French zouave uniforms of the period.* **$65,725**

Heritage Auctions

▶ *Brig. Gen. Lloyd Tilghman's presentation flag, inscribed sword he was wearing when killed, and sword belt, descended for last 150 years through direct lineal descendants. Tilghman was killed at the Battle of Champion's Hill on May 16, 1863, by a shell fragment.* **$59,750**

Heritage Auctions

▼ *Original Civil War ammunition caisson and limber, rare, excellent condition, retaining much original period paint on wood and iron furniture, wooden spokes, iron rims, wheels approximately 58" diameter, wooden chest approximately 40" wide x 20" deep x 17" high, lid covered in sheet copper or brass, wood painted army green with black painted iron hardware.* **$47,800**

Heritage Auctions

◀ *Center section of pre-war presentation flag of "Mississippi Rifles," escort and honor guard to Jefferson Davis, accompanied by provenance and detailed research.* **$44,813**

Heritage Auctions

◀ *U.S. Model 1838 24 Pounder 8" Coehorn mortar, made by Cyrus Alger & Co., Boston, marked "C. A. & Co." and "T. J. R." on muzzle for Ordnance Officer Thomas Jefferson Rodman, who inspected this mortar on May 16, 1862. From the Michael Yeck Collection.* **$44,813**

Heritage Auctions

▲ *Half plate ambrotype of "The Gallant Pellham," John Pelham from Life, by Mathew Brady, taken in Brady's New York Studio, circa 1858, when Pelham was on leave from West Point.* **$41,825**

Heritage Auctions

◀ *Rare lock of Abraham Lincoln's hair in engraved gold locket, from the family of a Lincoln cabinet member, sewn to cloth with handwritten note, "Lock of Abraham Lincoln's Hair Given to Mary McCormick Cameron," locket 40mm wide x 50mm high, 70mm overall length including bale, exceptional condition.* **$38,838**

Heritage Auctions

Cased pair of inscribed 1851 Colt Navy pistols, Col. Charles Dare, 23rd Pennsylvania Volunteer Infantry, serial numbers 98925 and 98930, .36 caliber six-shot cylinders with naval engagement scene. From the Michael Yeck Collection. **$19,120**

Heritage Auctions

Rare Civil War artillery limber for 3" ordnance rifle, excellent condition, all wood and remaining paint period/original, limber chest retains all original furniture including handles, corner pieces, and lid hasp, 57" wheel diameter, wooden spokes, iron rims, chest approximately 42" wide x 20.5" deep x 16.75" high. From the Michael Yeck Collection. **$23,900**

Heritage Auctions

Confederate eight-star (Virginia) 1st National Flag, from a chapter of Daughters of the American Revolution, accompanied by history of ownership. **$16,730**

Heritage Auctions

Richmond Depot Confederate 2d National Pattern Flag, including implications of flag's use in battle, good condition. **$13,500**

Heritage Auctions

▲ *Rare Civil War Confederate waist belt plate (Mullinax 122), on original belt, accompanied by Mullinax letter of authenticity, untouched condition.* **$13,145**

Heritage Auctions

▼ *Eight South Carolina Civil War palmetto guards (Albert SC 17A) 24mm buttons, mint condition with 100% gilt and "Extra Gold Qualy" with lion at top, back mark.* **14,340**

Heritage Auctions

▲ *French import uniform identified to a member of 62nd Pa. Vol. Infantry, worn by Sgt. Robert N. Martin, Co. M, 62nd Pa. Vol. Infantry.* **$14,340**

Civil War Hanes hand grenade in mint overall condition with dark patina, no rust or pitting, 3 1/2" exterior diameter, interior explosive ball retaining all 14 original brass nipples, exterior shell marked on one side in 3/8" block letters "Excelsior" and on other, in a circle, "W. W. Hanes Pat. Aug. 26. 62," two halves screw together. This novel idea for a hand grenade proved to be dangerous to the user as well as the enemy, resulting in limited production and low survival rate. **$10,755**

Confederate cedar wood canteen captured in peach orchard at Gettysburg, July 2, 1863, M1858 pewter spout inserted and sealed with cotton gasket with possible original cork, initials ES carved in center of face, standing for Egbert Sinsabaugh, Co. H 141st Pennsylvania Vol. Infantry, who captured the canteen from a member of the 8th South Carolina Infantry "...a little south of the Peach Orchard"; with capture information on period ink tag attached to lower half of face of canteen, signed by Sinsabaugh. **$11,950**

Variant "Great Star" 34-star Civil War flag, double sided, cotton, 56" on hoist and 87" on fly. **$20,315**

Heritage Auctions

Grouping associated with Capt. John Christia Peterson, including Lincoln-signed commission. Peterson served with 15th U.S. Infantry from his commissioning in 1862 until his resignation on Aug. 11, 1864. **$10,755**

Heritage Auctions

Silk headquarters flag of 8th New Jersey Volunteer Infantry, likely the product of Tiffany & Co., embroidered below canton is 8th N. J. V., beneath that Col. Ramsey, who took command of the regiment on April 1, 1863, after the resignation of original regimental commander Adolphus Johnson. **$9,560**

▲ *Sharps New Model 1863 .52 caliber percussion carbine serial # C 46797, barrel with 98% original blue, very fine condition, minor wear at muzzle, frame and lock with strong bright case colors.* **$9,560**

▼ *Julian Scott, "Between Rounds," oil on canvas, 1887, 20" x 15.75", signed lower right "Julian Scott '87." Scott was only 15 at the outbreak of the Civil War. He lied about his age and enlisted in the Third Vermont Infantry. He became a drummer in Company E, which took part in the Battle of Lee's Mills during the Peninsular Campaign.* **$8,365**

◀ *Rare chasseur cap of New York's famed "14th Brooklyn," kepi worn by members of 14th New York State Militia, which later became 84th New York Infantry.* **$8,963**

▶ *Classic Civil War Confederate company grade officer's kepi, likely North Carolina, untouched.* **$9,560**

▲ *Albumen image of President Lincoln on battlefield of Antietam, 1862, photograph by first American photojournalist, Alexander Gardner: "President Lincoln on Battle-Field of Antietam, October, 1862." On Oct. 1, 1862, two weeks after the battle of Antietam, Lincoln visited the Army of the Potomac, encamped near Harper's Ferry. President Lincoln stands facing his reluctant general, George McClellan, who had finally achieved the victory that justified the issuance of the final Emancipation Proclamation.* **$8,365**

▲ *Quarter-plate ambrotype with period identification of Maj. William J. Alexander, 46th Texas "Frontier" Cavalry. The "Frontier" Cavalry, Texas State Troops, was organized in March 1862.* **$7,469**

◄ *Rare Civil War Jennifer Officer's saddle and martingale set, superb condition, effects of Union officer Lt. Henry B. Walker of 121st New York Infantry.* **$8,365**

Heritage Auctions

▶ 14K gold case pocket watch etched with "Pine Bluff Arkansas Volunteers" and engraved "J.R. Core"; Waltham, accompanied by two gold-filled watch chains totaling 27" long. **$2,390**

Heritage Auctions

▼ American folk art marquetry panel of C.S.S. Alabama overtaking Union merchant vessel Lydia, inscribed "THE ALABAMA OR 290 LYING TOO TO BOARD THE AMERICAN SHIP LYDIA FROM CALCUTTA BOUND TO HAVANA." **$2,390**

Heritage Auctions

▲ Rare Confederate copy of 2.20" Schenkl shell, an attempt by Confederate arsenals to copy a Federal Schenkl projectile for use in 2.25" mountain rifle; non-excavated projectile is one of only two known to exist; the other is located in West Point Museum. **$6,752**

Heritage Auctions

▶ Pickett's Charge, Battle of Gettysburg projectile relic, 10-pound Parrott shell, no fuse, script engraved on front "Pickett's Charge on Cemetery Hill Gettysburg 1863"; fine condition, early battlefield recovery, fired but retaining sabot. **$6,573**

▲ *Colt Model 1851 .36 caliber percussion Navy revolver identified to Sgt. Horace B. Greeley, Co G 13th Maine Infantry, matching numbers 108977, manufactured in 1861. Horace B. Greely enlisted in the 13th Maine Infantry on Dec. 12, 1861, and mustered out on Jan. 6, 1865.* **$2,390**

▼ *Charles Wellington Reed, Congressional Medal of Honor winner for bravery at Gettysburg, unbound book of 35 original sketches, graphite on paper, each page 5.75" x 3.75", some sketches signed "C. W. Reed."* **$2,390**

▲ *Samuel Kirk & Son castellated repoussé coin silver bowl presented to Mrs. Jefferson Davis by citizens of Macon, Georgia in 1887.* **$15,535**

Heritage Auctions

▲ *Large collection of GAR medals and ribbons.* **$508**

Heritage Auctions

▶ *Civil War crutches presented to Medal of Honor winner Gen. John C. Robinson by his son and A. D. C. Lt. Erastus Robinson; crutches show heavy use, inscription on silver plaque worn but legible. John C. Robinson served in the Mexican and Seminole Wars and commanded Fort McHenry at the outbreak of the Civil War.* **$1,195**

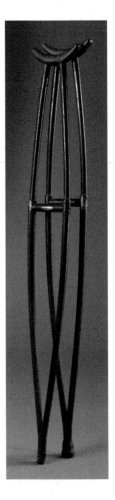

Heritage Auctions

◀ *Scarce, fine condition fired 3.67" caliber Hotchkiss bolt retaining complete lead sabot with rifling grooves, Hotchkiss patent information visible on underside of base, excellent condition, light pitting.* **$478**

Heritage Auctions

▲ *Confederate naval officer's sword patterned after U.S. M1852, by Firmin & Sons of London, descended in the family of Robert Baker Pegram, commander of the Confederate steamer CSS Nashville.* **$59,750**

Heritage Auctions

▼ *Civil War officer's red silk sash, 117" long x 4 3/8" wide, tight weave, terminates in two corded tassels 7 1/2" long, fine quality, excellent condition with minor stains, wear on tassels.* **$1,195**

Heritage Auctions

▶ *Coin silver presentation pitcher to Capt. Joseph Ellison, founder of Mistick Krewe of Comus, by members of New Orleans Confederate Guard, Louisiana Volunteer Infantry, March 20, 1862, engraved "Presented / Capt. Jos. Ellison / By the Officers and Members of / Co. C Confederate Regt./ Camp Caroline, March 20, 1862." Below presentation are engraved names and ranks of every member of unit and six honorary members, including Joseph's brother, William P. Ellison. Pitcher stamped with early Gorham company marks and "Coin / 250," excellent condition, 11.5" high.* **$22,705**

Heritage Auctions

▼ *Charles F. Allgower, "Untitled," graphite drawing on paper, mounted on board, circa 1862, 7.5" x 3.75", soldiers and military encampment outside walls of large compound. Allgower's regiment was serving in Grover's Division, Department of the Gulf, beginning on Dec. 20, 1862.* **$478**

Heritage Auctions

▶ *Bible flag made from Confederate flag captured at Columbus, Kentucky, June 14, 1861 by 8th Illinois Volunteer Infantry, approximately 3 1/2" x 1 1/2", constructed using four hand-sewn fragments of First National Confederate flag.* **$1,195**

Heritage Auctions

▲ *John Brown pike captured by Marine Maj. William Worthington Russell at Harper's Ferry on Oct. 18, 1859, produced by Charles Blair of Collinsville, Connecticut, on direct order from Brown for use in his slave insurrection.* **$7,768**

Heritage Auctions;

▼ *Grouping from Maj. James R. Brelsford, surgeon, 74th Ohio Vol. Inf., with Brelsford's diaries.* **$12,548**

Clocks

T he clock is one of the oldest human inventions. The word clock (from the Latin word clocca, "bell"), suggests that it was the sound of bells that also characterized early timepieces.

The first mechanical clocks to be driven by weights and gears were invented by medieval Muslim engineers. The first geared mechanical clock was invented by an 11th century Arab engineer in Islamic Spain. The knowledge of weight-driven mechanical clocks produced by Muslim engineers was transmitted to other parts of Europe through Latin translations of Arabic and Spanish texts.

In the early 14th century, existing clock mechanisms that used water power were being adapted to take their driving power from falling weights. This power was controlled by some form of oscillating mechanism. This controlled release of power – the escapement – marks the beginning of the true mechanical clock.

Sotheby's

Dutch Rococo ormolu-mounted red and gilt japanned musical clock, circa 1740, with matching later bracket, 24 1/4" high x 14 1/4" wide x 9 1/4" deep. **$12,500**

Sotheby's

George I part-ebonized burr maple longcase clock, Richard Pack, London, circa 1720, arched dial fitted with subsidiary dial in arch flanked by foliate-engraved spandrels, silvered chapter ring surmounted by 31-day dial and centered by subsidiary seconds dial above two winding holes and oval reserve signed "Rich. Pack / London"; five pillar two-train bell-striking movement with anchor escapement, domed top with three gilt ball-form finials above arched blind-fret-carved cornice, glazed door flanked by Doric columns with brass capitals and socles, molded neck above rectangular case centered by cupboard door with glass oculus, raised on plinth, 8' 3 1/2" high x 20 1/4" wide x 10 1/2" deep, dial is 12". **$21,250**

Sotheby's

Louis XVI ormolu mantel clock, circa 1775, dial signed "Lis Musson A Paris," 14 1/4" high x 12 1/2" wide x 4 1/2" deep. **$5,625**

Skinner, Inc., www.skinnerinc.com

French Neoclassical mantel clock, Paris, white marble, black slate, and ormolu case with gilt bezel, hands, and bas-relief panel of cherubs with goat below convex Arabic dial with outer calendar ring marked 1-31, silk thread suspension, eight-day, spring-powered, time and count-wheel strike movement, spool feet, 13" high. **$1,920**

Sotheby's

▶ *Louis XIV ormolu cartel clock attributed to André-Charles Boulle, circa 1710, dial signed "Jean Baptiste Baillon," movement signed "J. Bte. Baillon," 25 3/4" high x 10 1/2" wide.* **$75,000**

Skinner, Inc., www.skinnerinc.com

Miniature silver and enameled desk clock, probably Switzerland, circa 1920, turquoise enameled case with ribbed pagoda top capped by basket of flowers, silvered face with Arabic numerals and hinged engine-turned back opening to 15-jewel damascened nickel, lever-escapement, rear-wind movement, 2 1/4" high. **$960**

Skinner, Inc., www.skinnerinc.com

Gilt classical urn-form clock by Lepaute, Paris, circa 1825, fire gilt case with swan neck handles, ornate cast bezel, 3" porcelain Roman numeral dial marked "Lepaute a Paris," Breguet-style hands, eight-day, time and count-wheel strike, spring powered movement with silk thread suspension, brass and convex glass rear dust cover, ormolu decorated raised plinth, bun feet, 13" high. **$1,845**

Skinner, Inc., www.skinnerinc.com

Father Time statue clock, France, circa 1880, eight-day, spring-powered, time and count-wheel strike movement, 3 1/2" black dial with applied brass Roman numerals, serpent hands, ouroboros bezel, brass crescent moon pendulum bob, carried by patinated brass statue of winged, bearded man with scythe, black slate plinth, 16" high. **$2,214**

Skinner, Inc., www.skinnerinc.com

Simon Willard rocking ship tall clock, Roxbury, circa 1810, mahogany case with fret top, brass, stop-fluted, freestanding columns flanking 12" painted iron Roman numeral dial inscribed Simon Willard, floral spandrels and painted arch with American coastal scene, rocking ship automaton and ship in background, both flying American flags, inlaid rectangular waist door flanked by brass stop fluted quarter columns, inlaid base and tall bracket feet, eight-day, time and hour strike movement with two tin-cased weights, period pendulum and key, 91" high. **$31,200**

Skinner, Inc., www.skinnerinc.com

Ornately carved oak tall clock, Elliott, London, circa 1890, arched hood with egg-and-dart molding above fabric-backed sound frets, floral carved columns flanking composite brass Arabic numeral dial, subsidiary dials for tune selection and chime/silent, moon's age in arch, arched waist door with ribbon and floral design, ogee bracket feet, eight-day, quarter-chiming movement on eight bells or four gongs, pendulum and three brass cased weights, 93 1/2" high. **$5,100**

Skinner, Inc., www.skinnerinc.com

French white marble and ormolu annular dial clock, circa 1800, bronze standing cherub with gilt quiver and outstretched arm points to time on two porcelain annular dial rings showing hours with Roman numerals and minutes with Arabic, white and variegated gray marble plinth with military trophies, classical ormolu friezes on all sides, inset foliate designs along base, fluted bun feet support marble urn with leafage ormolu mounts, intertwined serpents and removable lid opens to eight-day, time and count-wheel strike, spring-powered movement with silvered platform escapement, 29" high. **$18,000**

Japanese Shaku Dokei clock, early 19th century, traditional case with glazed hood, trunk with 13 movable brass characters terminating in key drawer, pierced and engraved front plate decorated with central circle and floral vines, weight-driven movement, verge escapement with front mounted short pendulum, weight with bow and arrow pointer, wooden display stand, 12 1/2" high including stand. **$5,400**

Ephraim Willard rocking ship tall clock, Boston, circa 1800, mahogany case with inlaid scroll-top hood and vase-shape classical brass finials, applied handles, brass stop-fluted freestanding columns flanking 13" painted iron Roman numeral dial inscribed "Warranted for Mr. James Gardner, E. Willard, Boston," with painted rocking American ship automaton in arch and gilt scroll spandrels, rectangular waist door with line and marquetry inlays flanked by brass stop fluted quarter columns and marquetry plinths, base with line and fan inlay on French feet, eight-day time, hour striking movement with iron weights and seconds beating pendulum, 95" high. **$42,000**

Ormolu skeleton clock, circa 1830, dial signed Berthold Hger. Du Roi, 14" high x 9 1/4" wide x 3 3/4" deep. **$17,500**

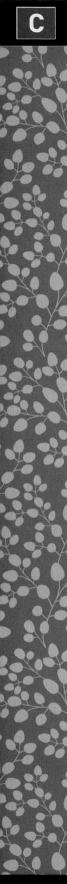

Sotheby's

Rare directoire ormolu and patinated bronze "Bon Savage" mantel clock, circa 1795, dial signed "Piel À Paris," 21 1/2" high x 16 3/4" wide x 5 3/4 " deep. **$62,500**

Skinner, Inc., www.skinnerinc.com

Bigelow, Kennard & Co. mahogany nine tubular bell chime clock, London, circa 1890, flat-top case with dentil and scrolled molding, fluted columns with carved capitols flanking tombstone upper door, composite brass dial with Arabic numerals marked Bigelow Kennard & Co., subsidiary dials tune selection and chime silent, glazed waist door, eight-day quarter-chiming movement on nine tubular bells, marked "J.J.E. Made in England," pendulum and three brass cased weights, 92" high. **$2,160**

Skinner, Inc., www.skinnerinc.com

Champlevé clock and barometer set, France, circa 1880, both dials in cream porcelain with blue markings, time dial with Arabic numerals, champlevé frieze, base and dial surrounds, bull's-eye glass over top-mounted compass and platform escapement, eight-day, time-only movement, aneroid barometer and thermometer, 5 1/2" high x 6 1/2" wide x 2 3/4" deep. **$2,160**

Sotheby's

George III Revival inlaid mahogany, satinwood, harewood, and faux tortoiseshell table timepiece, circa 1890, circular white enamel dial with Arabic numerals and surmounted by brass finial raised on concave form neck centered by oval reserve continuing to demi-lune top with four brass finials above four fluted columns, Tuscan capitals raised on conforming stepped base inlaid with radiating checkerboard tiles, movement numbered 25373 and initialed I F, 18 1/2" high. **$5,000**

Sotheby's

George III painted and inlaid satinwood balloon-shaped bracket clock by James Upjohn, case attributed to Thomas Brownley, decoration to John Bromley, circa 1795-1800, figured satinwood and tulip wood cross-banded ebony and boxwood strung veneered case painted en grisaille with musical trophy, sides with ribbon-tied swags of oak leaves and vine leaves, egg-and-tongue, pearl beading, stiff leaves and patera ornament, urn-form finial, white-enameled dial signed "Upjohn / Bond Street / London," foliate and flower-engraved brass back-plate to movement signed James, reverse door with open fret panel, 26" high. **$37,000**

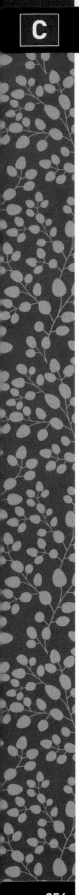

Heritage Auctions

Empire-style green marble, patinated and gilt bronze figural mantle clock with Cupid and Psyche, early 20th century, 30 1/2" x 19 1/2" x 8". **$9,375**

Heritage Auctions

French empire-style lyre-form marble and gilt bronze mounted mantle clock, circa 1900, circular dial with Arabic numerals within marble lyre-form case, gilt bronze mounts of ribbon-tied floral garland throughout, marks to mechanism: 6183, 02, 77, 20" high. **$3,750**

Heritage Auctions

French empire-style marble and gilt bronze mounted figural mantle clock, 20th century, marks to mechanism: TIFFANY & CO, A1 (encircled), 16 1/2" high. **$1,625**

Sotheby's

Louis XIV-style ormolu-mounted brass and tortoiseshell-inlaid bracket clock, late 19th century, signed "E. Gübelin Lucerne," 48" high x 17" wide x 8 1/2" deep. **$5,000**

Heritage Auctions

French champlevé enamel and gilt bronze glazed columnar mantle clock, late 19th century, bronze dial, enamel Arabic numerals, glass swing door to front and reverse, winged seated figural finial, champlevé decoration throughout, marks: MADE IN FRANCE, 1774, 7 (on works), 21" high. **$1,250**

Heritage Auctions

◀ *KPM porcelain and gilt metal temple-form clock, circa 1890, with allegorical panels depicting four seasons to sides, porcelain cupola to top decorated with allegorical depictions of three muses, gilt finial to each corner and top, supported by four cobalt columns with gilt metal mounts on four gilt feet; marks to porcelain: (underglaze blue scepter) D; marks to mechanism: R.B. BREVETE, S.G.D.G., (bee), 14 1/8" high.* **$1,125**

Coca-Cola Collectibles

By Allan Petretti

O rganized Coca-Cola collecting began in the early 1970s. The advertising art of The Coca-Cola Co., which used to be thought of as a simple area of collecting, has reached a whole new level of appreciation. Because of their artistic quality, these images deserve to be considered true Americana.

Coca-Cola art is more than bottles and trays, more than calendars and signage, more than trinkets, giveaways, and displays. It incorporates all the best that America has to offer. The Coca-Cola Co., since its conception in 1886, has taken advertising to a whole new level. So much so that it has been studied and dissected by scholars as to why it has proved to be so successful for more than 120 years.

Can soda pop advertising be considered true art? Without a doubt! The very best artists in America were an integral part of that honorary place in art history. Renowned artists like Rockwell, Sundbloom, Elvgren, and Wyeth helped take a quality product and advance it to the status of an American icon and all that exemplifies the very best about America.

This beautiful advertising directly reflects the history of our country: its styles and fashion, patriotism, family life, the best of times, and the worst of times. Everything this country has gone through since 1886 can be seen in these wonderful images.

Allan Petretti

For more information on Coca-Cola collectibles, see Petretti's *Coca-Cola Collectibles Price Guide*, 12th edition, by Allan Petretti.

ALLAN PETRETTI is one of the world's top authorities on Coca-Cola memorabilia. He conducts seminars for Coca-Cola collector groups and has been interviewed by the *Wall Street Journal, USA Today, London Times,* and *New York Times,* and has appeared on many television shows, including "History Detectives."

James D. Julia, Inc.

Wood display sign, circa 1940s, birch veneer plywood with embossed tin appliqués with original hanging chain, reverse marked "Designed & Manufactured by Kay Displays, Inc., 230 Park Avenue, New York City," very good condition, 39" wide x 11" high. **$1,777**

Mosby & Co. Auctions

Buddy Lee doll, hard plastic body in complete original outfit with hat, minor soiling to clothing, minor age wear, 14" high. The Buddy Lee doll began as a promotional mascot for Lee Jeans between 1920 and 1962; in addition to the Coca-Cola version, there was a railroad worker, gas station attendant, and cowboy Buddy Lee. **$510**

Mosby & Co. Auctions

▲ *Game set, circa 1940s, both decks of playing cards new in box, correct dominoes and checkers, instructions, and four unused score pads, missing shaker cup for dice, some edge wear, scuffing and split corner to box, 11 3/4" high x 10 3/4" wide.* **$275**

Victorian Casino Antiques

▶ *Red countertop porthole clock on swivel base, "Drink Coca Cola 5 [cent symbol], Delicious, Refreshing," 15" diameter x 17" high.* **$200**

▶ *Sprite boy tin sign, circular with embossed edge and mounting/hanging holes and rope, circa 1947, 12 3/4" diameter.* **$325**

◀ *Serving tray, 1903, lithograph of Hilda Clark holding glass of Coca-Cola, minor scratching to center and light, typical age crazing, 18 1/2" high x 15 1/4" wide. Clark was the first woman to be featured on a Coca-Cola serving tray in 1895 and maintained her status as the familiar face of Coca-Cola until 1903.* **$6,000**

▲ *Two-sided porcelain sign, circa 1938, produced by Tennessee Enamel Manufacturing Co., one small surface flake to lower right corner and two small chips to lower center on one side.* **$2,400**

Neon clock by Neon Products Inc., Lima, Ohio, fine working condition, 18 1/4" high x 18 1/4" wide x 6 3/4" deep. **$4,000**

Victorian Casino Antiques

Drink Coca Cola die-cut sports cars cardboard festoon sign featuring cars from various countries with man and woman in center, "Pause...Refresh," circa 1958, 66" high x 23" wide. **$1,000**

Morphy Auctions

Prototype window display, circa 1920s to 1930s, framed under conservation glass, Rip Van Winkle with original artwork on eight different cutout pieces, watercolor or gouache on light cardboard, miniscule to no wear, near mint-plus condition, 23" x 32" framed. This display never became a production item and, as a result, is the only known example. **$7,800**

Mosby & Co. Auctions

Smith Miller truck, die-cast aluminum and wood, 1940s, includes original crates, minor surface wear, 14" long x 7 1/2" high. **$475**

Serious Toyz Auctions

Rare battery-operated dispenser bank, LineMar (Marx), Japan, 1950s, lithographed tin with plastic glasses, tool in clip inside top of lid, includes box, mint/unused condition, 10"; fill top reservoir with Coke, insert a penny, and it dispenses a mini glassful. **$862**

Showtime Auction Service

▲ *Rare rotation light-up sign showing Sprite boy, late 1940s, excellent working condition, 18" diameter.* **$2,000-$4,000**

Victorian Casino Auctions

▲ *Vintage "Refresh, Drink Coca-Cola" advertisement sign in gold-painted Art Deco Coca-Cola wood and metal frame, with bowling girl with bottle of Cok, copyright 1946 The Coca-Cola Co., lithograph produced in United States by Niagara Lith. Co., 35" x 56".* **$850**

Serious Toyz Auctions

Coca-Cola Route Truck, 1950s, Sanyo, Japan, battery-operated tin truck in original box, scarce, 12 1/2". **$453**

Victorian Casino Auctions

"Drink Coca-Cola" child's pedal car with matching trailer with cooler, Gearbox Pedal Car Co., Cedar Rapids, Iowa, "refresh yourself" yellow and red motif, excellent condition. **$200-$800**

Victorian Casino Auctions

▼ *"Drink Coca Cola" embossed self-framed tin advertisement sign, "Take home a carton," bottle six-pack, Robertson-Dualife 1-42, 18" x 54".* **$650**

Victorian Casino Auctions

▲ *"Happy Holidays" light-up Christmas floor/lawn display with Coca-Cola bottle, snow, and thermometer, 36" high.* **$90**

Victorian Casino Auctions

▶ *Tabletop pretzel dish by The Brunhoff Mfg. Co., metal with three Coca-Cola bottles on edges, marked "Made In USA 1935."* **$250**

James D. Julia, Inc.

▲ *Vending machine spinner sign, circa 1950s, originally placed atop Coca-Cola vending machines and held in place with four rubber suction feet, near excellent condition, 12 1/2" high.* **$2,073**

Morphy Auctions

▶ *Chewing gum Dutch boy die-cut, strong color, clean break line at neck, light soiling, small spots, and mild stains, rarely seen on market, 29" high x 22" wide.* **$47,000**

James D. Julia, Inc.

1908 paper sign, rare, fashionably attired woman in crimson outfit with bottle of Coca-Cola in soda fountain setting, professional restoration to areas of paper-loss at top corners, very good-plus condition, image 14" x 21 3/4" high. **$6,900**

James D. Julia, Inc.

Die-cut floor-standing easel-back display with woman in summer attire relaxing in oversized wicker chair with bottle of Coke, 1920s, good to very good condition, professional restoration to creases with color touch up, light soiling, 25 1/4" wide x 35 1/4" high. **$11,850**

Coin-Operated Devices

Coin-operated devices fall into three main categories: amusement or arcade games, trade stimulators, and vending machines.

Vending machines have been around longer than any other kind of coin-op, and the 1880s witnessed the invention of many varieties. Gambling devices and amusement machines soon followed suit. The industry swelled during the 1890s and early 1900s but slowed during World War I. It rebounded in the 1920s and 1930s, which is considered the "Golden Age" of coin-ops.

Coin-ops reflect the prevailing art form of the era in which they were produced. Early machines exhibit designs ranging from Victorian to Art Nouveau and Art Deco, while later devices manufactured from 1940 on feature modernism.

For more information on coin-operated devices, visit the website of the Coin Operated Collectors Association at http://coinopclub.org.

Victorian Casino Antiques

Mills Novelty Puritan Bell countertop three-reel trade stimulator, circa 1926, restored with keys. **$885**

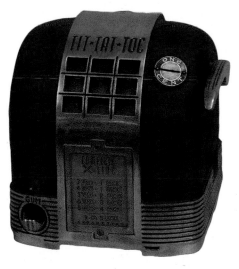

Victorian Casino Antiques

Daval Mfg. 1¢ Tit-Tat-Toe three-reel countertop cigarette trade stimulator with gumball vendor, circa 1936, good restored condition with key. **$900**

Victorian Casino Antiques

◀ *Mills Industries 25¢ Hightop Deluxe slot machine with jackpot, circa 1948, with key.* **$1,610**

Victorian Casino Antiques

▼ *Groetchen Tool Ginger 1¢ countertop three-reel cigarette trade stimulator, circa 1937, with keys.* **$633**

Victorian Casino Antiques

▶ *Red cast iron countertop Whiting's Sculptoscope stereo viewer arcade machine with stereo cards inside, drum-form round base version, circa early 1900s, with keys.* **$720**

Morphy Auctions

Master 1¢/5¢ vending machine, five turns for a nickel and one turn for a penny, original condition, box and keys present, excellent condition, 16" high. **$408**

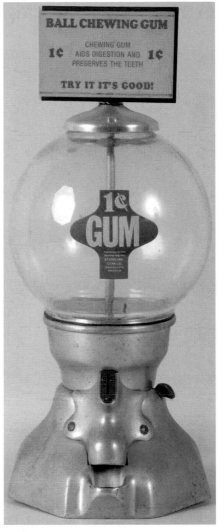

Morphy Auctions

Standard Gum Co. 1¢ aluminum gumball dispenser, original condition with marquee, working condition, padlock but no key, wall mounting bracket, very good condition, 17 1/2" high. **$336**

Morphy Auctions

Reel Poker 1¢/25¢ coin-op trade stimulator with gumball dispenser, back door with lock and key, pump for spinning action needs adjustment, unrestored, very good original condition, 9 1/2" wide. **$348**

Victorian Casino Antiques

◄ *Mills Novelty 5¢ Black Cherry halftop slot machine with jackpot, circa 1945, with key.* **$1,320**

Victorian Casino Antiques

▲ *The Lark 1¢ countertop five-reel poker trade stimulator with gumball vendor, "Your Fortune," circa 1931, with key.* **$345**

Victorian Casino Antiques

◄ *W.L. Kline Co. countertop diamond penny-drop cigar trade stimulator, "You Always Get One, and Sometimes More," "We Smoke the Trophy Cigar," Star Advertiser Pat. 1897, wood and glass with mirrored back.* **$1,120**

Victorian Casino Antiques

▲ *O.D. Jennings & Co. 1¢ Little Duke jackpot slot machine, three-wheel, circa 1932.* **$1,725**

Victorian Casino Antiques

▲ *O.D. Jennings & Co. 5¢ Automatic O.K. Counter Vender Dutch Boy Mints of Quality slot machine with oak slot machine stand, front mint vendor with Vens mints, with key, circa 1925.* **$1,180**

Victorian Casino Antiques

▶ *Early cast iron gambling wheel countertop match dispenser featuring picture of woman inside brass numbered ship's wheel with metal ball inside.* **$1,232**

James D. Julia, Inc.

Cast iron shoe shine machine, circa 1920s-1930s, restored, often found in high-end restaurants or hotels and used by male patrons; after a penny is inserted the front door opens to expose brushing mechanism, at which time a man would place his shoe in line with the brush; porcelain plate on either side reads PRESERVE YOUR SHINE 1¢ KEEPS THEM CLEAN BLACK OR TAN SAVES TIME AND MONEY DOES NOT PUT ON DRESSING, 39" high x 16" wide x 12" deep. **$770**

Victorian Casino Antiques

Coin-Op Exhibit Supply Mauser "Dale" gun shooting gallery floor arcade machine with owl and target, "Shoot This World Famous 15 Shot Automatic Mauser Pistol" wooden marquee, good condition with some minor blemishes/paint chips, circa 1947, with keys. **$805**

Victorian Casino Antiques

Prophecy of the Pharaoh $1 crystal ball fortune teller floor arcade game by American Sammy Corp., Elk Grove, Illinois; one of two known, possibly from Disneyland, with keys. **$2,400**

Jumping Jack 1¢/5¢ trade stimulator with dice, original unrestored condition, one crack in front viewing glass and side viewing glass, currently not functioning, good condition, 11 1/4" long. **$324**

Theater lobby candy vending machine, 1920-1930s, restored, Art Deco-styled wooden cabinet with nickel-plated trim, veneered wood grain, string inlay, acid etched/reverse decorated glass inset panels, glass viewing windows to peruse 10 different choices of candy, 75" high x 57" wide x 18" deep. **$17,775**

Esmeralda fortune teller machine, restored, with original Edison cylinders in working order, one of only a handful known to exist and possibly one of only three with original Edison cylinders made for machine, circa 1920s-1930s, Esmeralda waves her right hand over tarot cards while bowing her head and verbally reading fortune, heard using set of accompanying earphones, 75" high x 27" wide x 20" deep. **$43,845**

James D. Julia, Inc.

Haunted Churchyard model, believed to be produced in the 1950s by Kraft Co., often found in arcades; English model depicts church and adjacent graveyard with village drunkard sitting atop grave; when machine is activated, a series of comical encounters begin, including a tomb that opens to reveal an ominous figure, rising stone and appearance of skeleton, ghost popping up from behind stone, and grave upon which drunkard sits opens and skeleton rises from inside; church is constructed of aluminum castings; lacks keys for front door, 70" high x 25" wide x 18" deep. **$6,221**

James D. Julia, Inc.

Climbing Fireman arcade, 1920s, two players race their firemen to top of ladder at third story window of typical English dwelling, first player to reach top gets his coin back, bell rings, and firemen descend to prepare for another run up ladders; machine encased in oak cabinet with cast iron legs, only electrical component is bulb inside to illuminate building façade, machine is complete other than operation to return penny to winning player, some signs of minor repair to rear panel, 72" high x 25" wide x 17" deep. **$9,480**

James D. Julia, Inc.

◄ *Mills Electricity is Life shock machine, restored, upper portion of case features large papier maché plaque with various embossed male figures, circular section with details related to corresponding shock levels, such as, "These points indicate healthy heart" or "Increased voltage benefit system," as operator engages handles the voltage increases, indicated by a Mills owl rising in number and intensity measuring tolerance for pain, iron plate embossed with image of Ben Franklin holding a kite with Colonial buildings in background and lightning bolts striking kit, 78" high x 28" wide x 25" deep.* **$13,035**

Victorian Casino Antiques

▶ *Pace Royal Comet Club 5¢ bell console slot machine, circa 1937, restored, works with key.* **$5,100**

Comics

By Barry Sandoval

Back in 1993, Sotheby's auctioned a copy of Fantastic Four #1 (1961) that was said to be the finest copy known to exist. It sold for $27,600, which at the time was considered an unheard-of price for a 1960s comic. Last year, Heritage Auctions sold that same copy for $203,000 … and it's not even the finest known copy anymore.

It used to be that only comics from the 1930s or 1940s could be worth thousands of dollars. Now, truly high-grade copies of comics from the Silver Age (1956-1969 by most people's reckoning) can sell for four, five, or even six figures. Note I said truly high-grade. Long gone are the days when a near mint condition copy was only worth triple the price of a good condition copy. Now near mint is more like 10-20 times good, and sometimes it's as much as a factor of 1,000.

A trend of the last couple of years has been that the "key" issues have separated even further from the pack, value-wise. Note that not every key is a "#1" issue – if you have Amazing Fantasy #15, Tales of Suspense #39, and Journey into Mystery #83, you've got the first appearances of Spider-Man, Iron Man, and Thor. (Beware of reprints and replica editions, however.)

Barry Sandoval

The most expensive comics of all remain the Golden Age (1938-1949) first appearances, like Superman's 1938 debut in Action Comics #1, several copies of which have sold for $1 million or more. However, not every single comic from the old days is going up in value. Take western-themed comics. Values are actually going down in this genre as the generation that grew up watching westerns is at the age where they're looking to sell, and there are more sellers than potential buyers.

Comics from the 1970s and later, while increasing in value, rarely garner anywhere near the same value as 1960s issues, primarily because in the 1970s comics were increasingly seen as a potentially valuable collectible. People took better care of them, and in many cases hoarded multiple copies.

What about 1980s favorites like The Dark Knight Returns and Watchmen? Here the demand is high, but the supply is really high. These series were heavily hyped at the time and were done by well-known creators, so copies were socked away in great quantities. We've come across more than one dealer who has 20-30 mint copies of every single 1980s comic socked away in a warehouse, waiting for the day when they're worth selling.

I should mention one surprise hit of the last couple of years. When Image Comics published The Walking Dead #1 in 2003, it had a low print run and made no particular splash in the comics world. Once AMC made it into a television series, however, it was a whole different story. High-grade copies of #1 have been fetching $1,000 and up lately.

If you've bought comics at an auction house or on eBay, you might have seen some in CGC

BARRY SANDOVAL is Director of Operations for Comics and Comic Art, Heritage Auctions. In addition to managing Heritage's Comics division, which sells some $20 million worth of comics and original comic art each year, Sandoval is a noted comic book evaluator and serves as an advisor to the *Overstreet Comic Book Price Guide*.

holders. Certified Guaranty Co., or CGC, is a third-party grading service that grades a comic book on a scale from 0.5 to 10. These numbers correspond with traditional descriptive grades of good, very fine, near mint and mint, with the higher numbers indicating a better grade. Once graded, CGC encapsulates the comic book in plastic. The grade remains valid as long as the plastic holder is not broken open. CGC has been a boon to the hobby, allowing people to buy comics with more confidence and with the subjectivity of grading taken out of the equation. Unless extremely rare, it's usually only high-grade comics that are worth certifying.

One aspect of collecting that has absolutely exploded in the last 20 years has been original comic art, and not just art for the vintage stuff. In fact, the most expensive piece Heritage Auctions has ever sold was from 1990: Todd McFarlane's cover art for Amazing Spider-Man #328, which sold for more than $650,000. It's not unusual for a page that was bought for $20 in the 1980s to be worth $5,000 now.

If you want to get into collecting original comic art, McFarlane would not be the place to start unless you've got a really fat wallet. I suggest picking a current comic artist you like who isn't yet a major "name." Chances are his originals will be a lot more affordable. Another idea is to collect the original art for comic strips. You can find originals for as little as $20, as long as you're not expecting a Peanuts or a Prince Valiant. Heritage Auctions (HA.com) maintains a free online archive of every piece of art they've sold and it is an excellent research tool.

As expensive as both comic books and comic art can be at the high-end of the spectrum, in many ways this is a buyer's market. In the old days you might search for years to find a given issue of a comic; now you can often search eBay and see 10 different copies for sale. Also, comic conventions seem to be thriving in almost every major city – and while the people in crazy costumes get all the publicity, you can also find plenty of vintage comic dealers at these shows. From that point of view, it's a great time to be a comic collector.

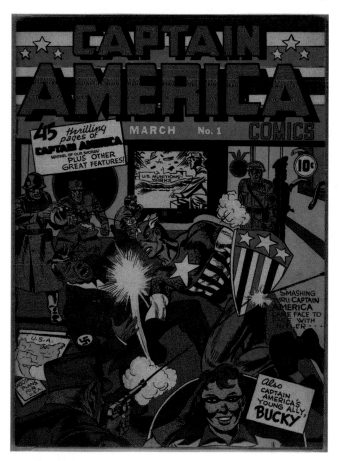

Captain America Comics #1 (1941), CGC-rated 9.0 (very fine/near mint).
$96,686

Batman: The Dark Knight Returns #1 (1986), CGC-graded 9.6 (near mint+). **$143**

The Avengers #4 (1964), CGC-graded 9.6 (near mint). **$31,070**

The Brave and the Bold #29 (1960), CGC-graded 8.0 (very fine). **$5,975**

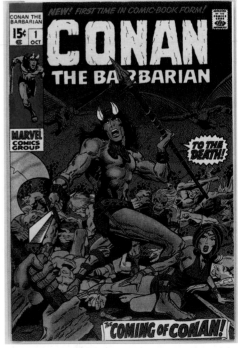

Conan the Barbarian #1 (1970), CGC-graded 9.8 (near mint/mint), Empire Comics Collection. **$3,884**

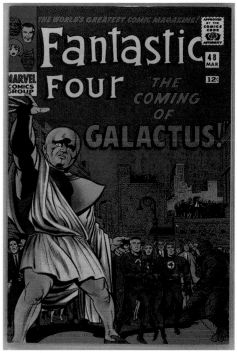

The Amazing Spider-Man #50 (1967), CGC-graded 9.8 (near mint/mint). **$26,290**

Fantastic Four #48 (1966), CGC-graded 9.8 (near mint/mint). **$13,145**

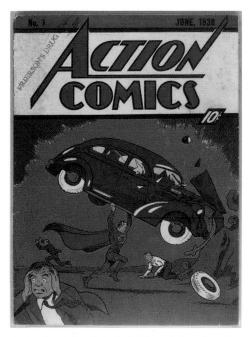

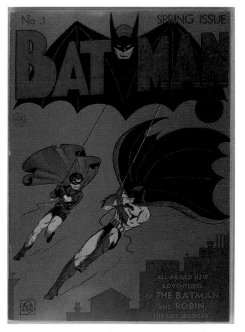

Action Comics #1 (1938), CGC-graded 3.0 (good/very good), Billy Wright Collection. **$298,750**

Batman #1 (1940), CGC-graded 8.5 (very fine+), Billy Wright Collection. **$274,850**

Superman vs. the Amazing Spider-Man #1 (1976), very fine/near mint. **$180**

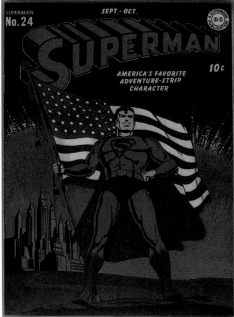

Superman #24 (1943), CGC-graded 9.4 (near mint). **$41,825**

Wolverine (Limited Series) #1 (1982), CGC-graded 10 (mint). **$15,535**

Tales of Suspense #59 (1964), CGC-graded 9.4 (near mint). **$1,912**

Flash Comics #1 (1940), CGC-rated 9.6 (near mint). **$273,125**

Four Color #9 (1942), CGC-graded 8.5 (very fine+). **$7,768**

Green Hornet Comics #1 (1940), CGC-graded 8.5 (very fine). **$14,375**

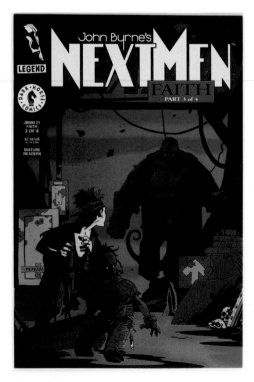

John Byrne's Next Men #21 (1993), second appearance of Hellboy, CGC-graded 9.6 (near mint). **$62**

The Incredible Hulk #1 (1962), CGC-graded 9.2 (near mint). **$125,475**

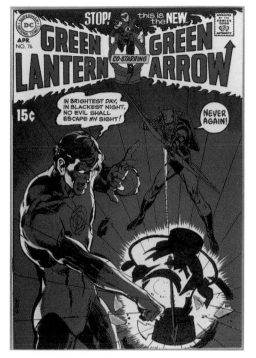

Green Lantern #76 (1970), CGC-rated 9.8 (near mint/mint). **$37,343**

Justice League of America #28 (1964), CGC-graded 9.6 (near mint). **$1,610**

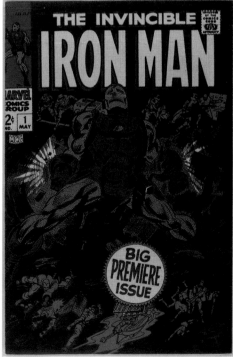

Journey into Mystery #83 (1962), the introduction of Thor, CGC-graded 9.0 (very fine/near mint). **$13,225**

Iron Man #1 (1968), CGC-graded 9.8 (near mint/mint). **$7,468**

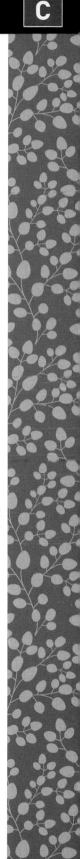

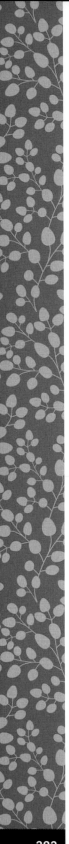

Mystery in Space #90 (1964) CGC-graded 9.6 (near mint). **$1,150**

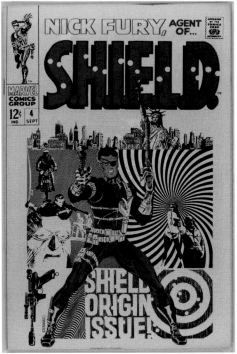

Nick Fury, Agent of S.H.I.E.L.D. #4 (1968), CGC-graded 9.8 (near mint/mint). **$1,135**

The Savage She-Hulk #1 (1980), CGC-graded 9.8 (near mint/mint). **$131**

Marvel Feature #1 Red Sonja (1975), CGC-graded 9.8 (near mint/mint). **$430**

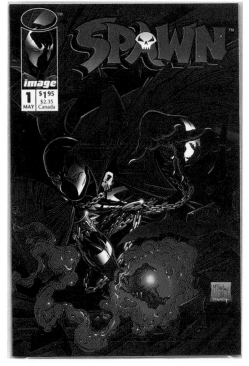

Spawn #1 (1992), CGC-graded 9.8 (near mint/mint). **$42**

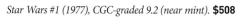

Star Wars #1 (1977), CGC-graded 9.2 (near mint). **$508**

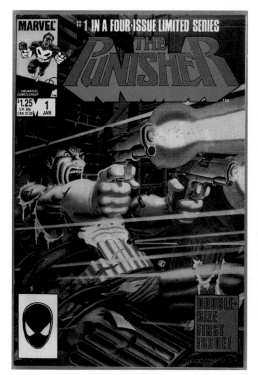

The Punisher #1 (1986), CGC-graded 9.8 (near mint/mint). **$286**

The Silver Surfer #1 (1968), CGC-graded 9.8 (near mint/mint). **$11,950**

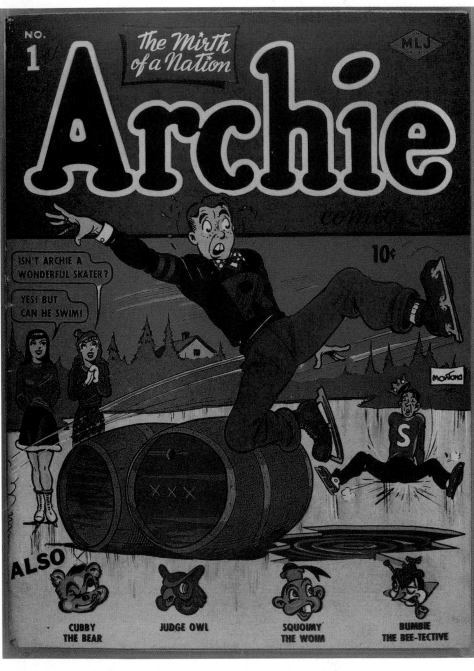

Archie Comics #1 (1942), CGC-graded 8.5 (very fine+). **$167,300**

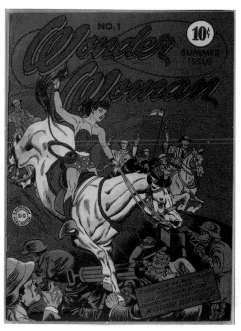

Wonder Woman #1 (1942), CGC-graded 8.5
(very fine+). **$53,775**

X-Men #3 (1964), CGC-graded 9.8
(near mint/mint). **$16,730**

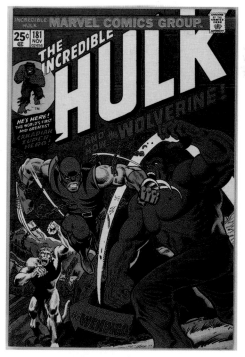

Watchmen #1 (1986), CGC-graded 9.8
(near mint/mint). **$478**

The Incredible Hulk #181 (1974), CGC-graded 9.8
(near mint/mint). **$9,560**

Cookie Jars

ookie jars, colorful and often whimsical, are popular with collectors. They were made by almost every manufacturer in all types of materials. Figural character cookie jars are the most popular.

Cookie jars often were redesigned to reflect newer tastes. Hence, the same jar may be found in several different variations, and these variations can affect the price.

Many cookie-jar shapes were manufactured by more than one company and, as a result, can be found with different marks. This often happened because of mergers. Molds also were traded and sold among companies.

Some cookie jars by American Bisque were enhanced with flashers—a plastic piece, technically known as a lenticular image, that changes when the item is moved back and forth.

For more information on cookie jars, see *Warman's Cookie Jars Identification and Price Guide* by Mark F. Moran.

Victorian Casino Antiques

▶ *American Bisque Herman & Katnip with A.B. Co. paper label under lid, marked "Herman & Katnip – USA," not stamped on bottom, very good condition with some crazing, rarest of all American Bisque jars, only six known to exist.* **$1,560**

Victorian Casino Antiques

▼ *Brush Pottery Formal Pig, marked "W7 USA" on bottom, Winton designed, black coat version, good condition.* **$108**

Victorian Casino Antiques

▲ American Bisque Cow Jumped Over the Moon flasher, marked "806 USA" on bottom, A.B. Co. Cookies "Hand-Painted" label on lid, light blue sky and light brown cow, sun's facial expression changes, small chip on right side of cow's head; considered hardest to find and most beautiful flasher jar. **$109**

Victorian Casino Antiques

▲ Warner Bros. Champ Kangaroo, sculpted and designed by Don Winton for DeForest, yellow sweater version, unmarked, some crazing, very rare. **$780**

Victorian Casino Antiques

▶ Brush Pottery Pink Elephant with Monkey finial, marked "Brush USA" on bottom, good condition, very rare, only 10-12 made. **$1,020**

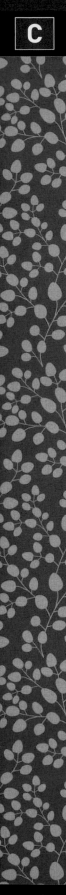

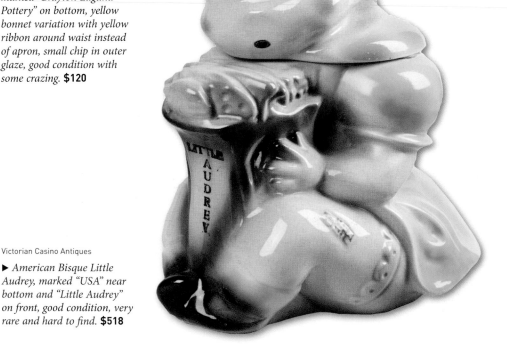

Victorian Casino Antiques

◀ *National Potteries Corp. Spaceship, marked "NAPCO 1961 Bedford Ohio K5324" on bottom with NAPCO Ceramics paper label, blue variation, "COOKIES OUT OF THIS WORLD!" on front, small hairline crack in back.* **$210**

Victorian Casino Antiques

▲ *Brayton Laguna Matilda, marked "Brayton Laguna Pottery" on bottom, yellow bonnet variation with yellow ribbon around waist instead of apron, small chip in outer glaze, good condition with some crazing.* **$120**

Victorian Casino Antiques

▶ *American Bisque Little Audrey, marked "USA" near bottom and "Little Audrey" on front, good condition, very rare and hard to find.* **$518**

Victorian Casino Antiques

► *McCoy Pottery Multicolor Leprechaun,
unmarked, limited production, no red on
cheeks/ears, good condition, exceptionally
rare.* **$720**

Victorian Casino Antiques

▼ *McCoy Pottery Red Leprechaun, No.
169, unmarked, limited production, never
appeared in McCoy catalogs, excellent
condition, rare.* **$540**

Victorian Casino Antiques

► *Sinclair Oil Green
Dinosaur advertising
jar, marked "USA
1943" on bottom, good
condition, very rare.*
$1,800

Victorian Casino Antiques

▶ *American Bisque Olive Oyl with removable plastic flower in hat, marked "USA" near bottom, thin-neck version was the prototype for Olive Oyl cookie jars, good condition with minor crazing, very rare.* **$960**

Victorian Casino Antiques

▲ *American Bisque Popeye with real corncob pipe, marked "USA" near bottom, raised star on collar, thin-neck version, which was the prototype for Popeye cookie jars, good condition, very rare.* **$173**

Victorian Casino Antiques

▶ *American Bisque Olive Oyl, marked "USA" near bottom, excellent condition with some crazing on nose, very rare, possibly a prototype.* **$480**

Victorian Casino Antiques

Brush Pottery Laughing Hippo, marked "W27 Brush USA" on bottom, Winton designed, circa 1961, Hippo with monkey on its back, good condition with minor crazing. **$180**

Victorian Casino Antiques

◄ *American Bisque Casper, marked "Harvey Publications Inc. USA" on back and "Casper" on front, some crazing, good condition.* **$210**

Victorian Casino Antiques

Brush Pottery Elephant with Ice Cream Cone, marked "W8 USA" on bottom, Winton designed, circa early 1950s, pink jacket with yellow bow variation, small hairline crack on cheek. **$120**

Victorian Casino Antiques

▲ *Walt Disney Productions Mary Poppins, marked "Copyright MCMLXIV Walt Disney Productions" on bottom, "Mary Poppins IT'S A JOLLY HOLIDAY" on front, 3" hairline crack on front of skirt, hard to find jar.* **$300**

Victorian Casino Antiques

▲ *Walter Lantz Woody Woodpecker head, marked "1967 Walter Lantz All Rights Reserved. A Registered Trademark of and Licensed By Walter Lantz Productions Inc." on bottom and "Woody Woodpecker" on back, sold on Home Shopping channel, good condition with minor scuff mark.* **$270**

Victorian Casino Antiques

▶ *Pearl China Cooky chef, marked with gold stamp "Pearl China Co. Hand Decorated 22 Kt. Gold USA - 639" on bottom, gold detailing, good condition.* **$84**

Victorian Casino Antiques

▲ *Pearl China Mammy, marked with gold stamp "Pearl China Co. Hand Decorated 22 Kt. Gold USA" on bottom, gold Mammy lettering on front, good condition.* **$96**

Folk Art

Folk art generally refers to items that originated among the common people of a region and usually reflect their traditional culture, especially regarding everyday or festive items. Unlike fine art, folk art is primarily utilitarian and decorative rather than purely aesthetic.

Exactly what constitutes the genre is a question that continues to be vigorously debated among collectors, dealers, museum curators, and scholars. Some want to confine folk art to non-academic, handmade objects. Others are willing to include manufactured material.

Folk art can range from crude drawings by children to academically trained artists' paintings of "common" people and scenery. It encompasses items made from a variety of materials, from wood and metal to cloth and paper.

The accepted timetable for folk art runs from its earliest origins up to the mid-20th century.

Pook & Pook, Inc.

▲ *David Y. Ellinger (American, 1913-2003), oil on velvet theorem of bowl of fruit, signed lower left, 14" x 18 1/2". Provenance: Pete and Sally Riffle, Dayton, Ohio.* **$889**

Pook & Pook, Inc.

▲ *Carved and painted pine countertop cigar store figure of Naval officer, 28" high.* **$577**

Pook & Pook, Inc.

◄ *Victorian string work valentine, late 19th century, in mahogany shadow box frame, 8 3/4" x 8 3/4".* **$182**

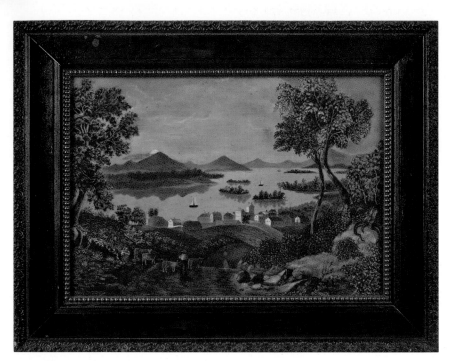

Pook & Pook, Inc.

American sandpaper drawing, 19th century, probably of Lake George, 14" x 20". **$851**

Pook & Pook, Inc.

American colored sandpaper drawing, 19th century, with train and bridge, 18" x 22". **$474**

Pook & Pook, Inc.

▲ Abraham Huth (Southeastern Pennsylvania, active 1807-1830), watercolor and ink on paper taufschein, done for Johannes Becktolf, 1829, with central rectangular panel with yellow, red, and green border enclosing script, surmounted by yellow, red, and green starburst flanked by birds and flowering vines, above yellow and green lawn with house and trees, 13" x 16". **$21,330**

Pook & Pook, Inc.

▲ English or American silk on linen sampler, dated 1827, wrought by Jean Hamilton, central verse above open field of various floral stems and potted flowers, over Georgian mansion with green lawn flanked by stylized trees, stylized floral border, 18" x 16". **$2,607**

Pook & Pook, Inc.

◄ Cast iron star windmill weight, circa 1900, 15" high x 15" wide. **$889**

Pook & Pook, Inc.

Henry Young (Southeastern Pennsylvania, active 1817-1861), watercolor and ink on paper certificate of birth and baptism, done for Michael Wagnor, 1856, Snyder County, son of Solomon and Sarah Wagnor, upper script flanked by blue, red, and yellow stars, over figures of husband and wife with candlestand between them and vase on top, wife wearing blue dress with lace collar and husband wearing yellow pants and holding bouquet, 10 1/4" x 7 3/4". **$17,775**

Pook & Pook, Inc.

▼ *Pennsylvania silk on linen sampler, circa 1832, wrought by Susan S. Harris, 16 1/2" x 17 1/2".* **$1,659**

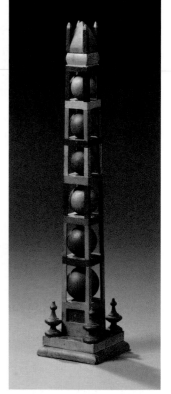

Skinner, Inc.; www.skinnerinc.com

▶ *Carved and polychrome painted obelisk whimsy, America, 19th century, spire-top obelisk with six cages ascending in size toward base, each containing conformingly sized sphere, on square base with turned spires on corners, painted in red, white, green, blue, and yellow, 18" high, base 3 3/4" wide.* **$6,000**

Pook & Pook, Inc.

Pennsylvania carved pine bag stamp, inscribed John Shott, 9 3/4" x 11 1/2". **$3,888**

Pook & Pook, Inc.

Pastel portrait of woman, circa 1830, 16" x 13". **$444**

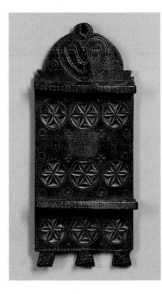

Skinner, Inc.; www.skinnerinc.com

Brown-painted carved wooden spoon rack, possibly Bergen County, New Jersey, 1767, with chip-carved heart on arched crest above nine floral medallions and two slotted tiers for eight spoons flanking indistinctly inscribed label, incised "1767" on reverse, loss, age cracks, 22 1/2" high x 9 1/4" wide. **$3,600**

Skinner, Inc.; www.skinnerinc.com

Painted chip-carved tramp art mirror, America, early 20th century, shaped frame with conforming notched and stepped geometric wood segments, painted red, green, and gold, losses, 26 1/2" x 18 1/2". **$1,680**

Carved Worcester Turnpike mile marker sign post, circa 1810, weathered tombstone-shaped gray slate post with finely chiseled inscription "To Boston Line 27 Ms / 1810 / To Worceste[r] 10 Ms," mounted on cement slab, signpost 28" high x 14 3/4" wide x 3" deep, 35" high x 21" wide x 12 1/2" deep overall. **$9,600**

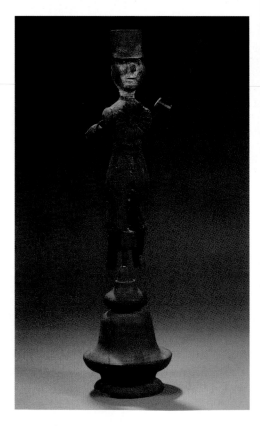

Still life with watermelon, oil on canvas, American School, 19th century, unsigned, puncture to background upper left, several drips, scattered retouch, 22 1/4" x 32", unframed. **$1,140**

▲ *Carved polychrome painted religious panel, probably Continental, 18th century, relief-carved wood panel depicting Christ amidst heavens with sun, moon, and stars in cloud of glory over earth with sea and animal figures, craquelure with scattered paint losses, period painted molded wood frame with pegged and rosehead nail joinery, 15 1/2 x 10".* **$840**

◄ *Painted carved wood and tin figural whirligig, late 19th century, carved wooden figure with tin shako cap, pressed brass blossom applied to chest, blue glass bead eyes, tin paddle arms, applied canvas trousers, painted dark red, white, and black, mounted on urned baluster-turned post, losses, 25 1/8" high.* **$2,460**

Skinner, Inc.; www.skinnerinc.com

▲ Large tramp art cabinet, Samuel Annino (Sicilian/American, born circa 1887), probably Massachusetts, 1917, mirrored gallery and shelf supported by square columns on projecting cabinet with cupboard doors opening to two shelves, on deeply cutout skirt centering drop with incised carving "SA/1917," and cutout sides, 61 3/4" high x 39 1/2" wide x 18 1/2" deep. **$2,400**

Skinner, Inc.; www.skinnerinc.com

▶ Hooked table runner with floral design, America, 19th century, oblong runner hooked with wool and cotton fabric segments, sisal and wool yarns, ornamented with raised and shirred blossoms and buds down center surrounded by scroll borders, leaves in corners, edged with cotton binding, imperfections, 15 1/2" x 75". **$1,680**

Skinner, Inc.; www.skinnerinc.com

◀ Figural hooked rug with two roosters, America, late 19th/early 20th century, roosters flanking tree or bush, on variegated black background with linear tan border, composed of multicolored wool, cotton, and silk fabric segments, 23" x 37 1/4". **$7,200**

Pook & Pook, Inc.

John Orne Johnson Frost (American, 1852-1928), oil on paperboard, New England coastal scene, 48 1/4" x 28 1/2". **$30,810**

Pook & Pook, Inc.

Carved and painted owl on perch, circa 1900, 19 1/2" high. **$652**

Pook & Pook, Inc.

▲ *Elgin Woodmanse cast iron rooster windmill weight, circa 1900, 15 3/4" high x 16 3/4" long.* **$948**

Pook & Pook, Inc.

◄ *New York painted shoe trade sign, 19th century, inscribed W. H. Vandy Shoe Shop, 25 1/2" high x 22 1/4" wide.* **$3,318**

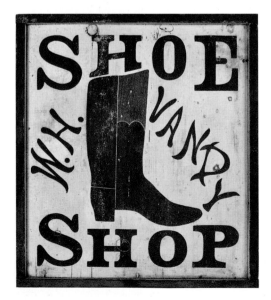

Pook & Pook, Inc.

Pair of Prior Hamblin School oil on board folk portraits, circa 1840, of husband and wife, 16" x 12". **$4,266**

Skinner, Inc.; www.skinnerinc.com

▲ *Carved and painted wood parrot on branch, America, late 19th/early 20th century, polychrome painted parrot with incised feather and eye details, 14 3/4" high, total 12" wide.* **$1,080**

Skinner, Inc.; www.skinnerinc.com

▶ *Pine whimsy, America, carved in two sections from single piece of wood topped with loop suspending caged ball and bear figure, three chain links, caged rabbit figure with bun terminal, dark brown stained surface, minor repair, 20 1/4" high x 1 3/4" diameter.* **$840**

Pook & Pook, Inc.

▲ *Lehigh County, Pennsylvania painted dower chest, inscribed "Salame Gaumerrin 1809," two hearts on lid repeat on panel, centering six-pointed star over two stippled drawers, end panels with three color philphlots, ogee bracket feet, 30 1/4" high x 47 3/4" wide x 22 1/4" deep.* **$22,515**

Pook & Pook, Inc.

▶ *Henry Young (Southeastern Pennsylvania, active 1817-1861), watercolor and ink on paper fraktur for Elizabeth and Peter Fluck, 1821, Northumberland County, upper script flanked by red and blue stars over profile of husband and wife with candlestand between them and wine decanter on top, wife wearing red dress with flowers and holding her husband's hand, husband wearing blue coat and holding wine glass, 11" x 7 1/2".* **$6,518**

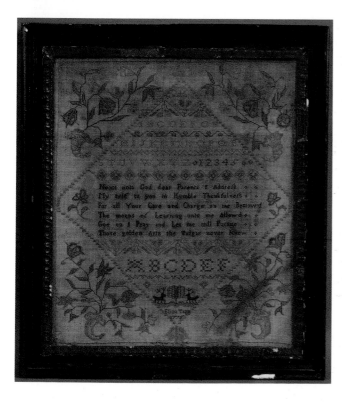

Pook & Pook, Inc.

▲ *Francis Charles Portzline (Southeastern Pennsylvania, active 1800-1855), watercolor and ink on paper taufschein done for Johannes Buffard, 1819, Manheim Township, Schuylkill County, with central heart enclosing script, flanked by red birds perched in tulip trees and typical calligraphy designs, all in green, yellow, and red, signed lower right Francis Portzline, 8" x 11 1/2".* **$4,266**

Skinner, Inc.; www.skinnerinc.com

◀ *Framed schoolgirl sampler, England, late 18th century, with alphabet and poem within diamond cartouche framed by cornucopia filled with flowers, signed "Eliza Tagg/1775," sight size 13" x 11 1/2".* **$1,080**

Pook & Pook, Inc.

Berks County, Pennsylvania watercolor and ink on paper taufschein done for Gertraut Frichbaum, 1769, with central script surmounted by green bordered heart enclosing script, flanked by flowering vines arising from hearts, all within sawtooth border, 8" x 12 1/2". Provenance: Lester Zettle. **$8,295**

Pook & Pook, Inc.

Pook & Pook, Inc.

Carved mahogany cornucopia watch hutch, early 19th century, 8 1/2" high. **$1,541**

New England silk embroidered memorial, inscribed "Deacon Jon. Friend obt. February 25 1785 Aged 67," 14 1/4" x 11 1/2". **$1,304**

FURNITURE

Furniture Styles
American

Style: Pilgrim Century
Dating: 1620-1700
Major Wood(s): Oak

General Characteristics:
Case pieces: rectilinear low-relief carved panels; blocky and bulbous turnings; splint-spindle trim
Seating pieces: shallow carved panels; spindle turnings

Style: William and Mary
Dating: 1685-1720
Major Wood(s): Maple and walnut

General Characteristics:
Case pieces: paint decorated chests on ball feet; chests on frames; chests with two-part construction; trumpet-turned legs; slant-front desks
Seating pieces: molded, carved crest rails; banister backs; cane, rush (leather) seats; baluster, ball and block turnings; ball and Spanish feet

Style: Queen Anne
Dating: 1720-50
Major Wood(s): Walnut

General Characteristics:
Case pieces: mathematical proportions of elements; use of the cyma or S-curve broken-arch pediments; arched panels, shell carving, star inlay; blocked fronts; cabriole legs and pad feet
Seating pieces: molded yoke-shaped crest rails; solid vase-shaped splats; rush or upholstered seats; cabriole legs; baluster, ring, ball and block-turned stretchers; pad and slipper feet

Style: Chippendale
Dating: 1750-85
Major Wood(s): Mahogany and walnut

General Characteristics:
Case pieces: relief-carved broken-arch pediments; foliate, scroll, shell, fretwork carving; straight, bow or serpentine fronts; carved cabriole legs; claw and ball, bracket or ogee feet
Seating pieces: carved, shaped crest rails with out-turned ears; pierced, shaped splats; ladder (ribbon) backs; upholstered seats; scrolled arms; carved cabriole legs or straight (Marlboro) legs; claw and ball feet

Style: Federal (Hepplewhite)
Dating: 1785-1800
Major Wood(s): Mahogany
and light inlays

General Characteristics:
Case pieces: more delicate
rectilinear forms; inlay with
eagle and classical motifs;
bow, serpentine or tambour fronts; reeded quarter columns at
sides; flared bracket feet
Seating pieces: shield backs; upholstered seats; tapered
square legs

Style: Federal (Sheraton)
Dating: 1800-1820
Major Wood(s): Mahogany and mahogany
veneer and maple

General Characteristics:
Case pieces: architectural pediments; acanthus
carving; outset (cookie or ovolu) corners and
reeded columns; paneled sides; tapered, turned,
reeded or spiral-turned legs; bow or tambour
fronts, mirrors on dressing tables
Seating pieces: rectangular or square backs;
slender carved banisters; tapered, turned or
reeded legs

Style: Classical (American Empire)
Dating: 1815-1850
Major Wood(s): Mahogany and
mahogany veneer and rosewood

General Characteristics:
Case pieces: increasingly heavy
proportions; pillar and scroll
construction; lyre, eagle, Greco-
Roman and Egyptian motifs; marble
tops; projecting top drawer; large ball
feet, tapered fluted feet or hairy paw feet; brass,
ormolu decoration
Seating pieces: high-relief carving; curved backs; out-scrolled
arms; ring turnings; sabre legs, curule (scrolled-S) legs; brass-
capped feet, casters

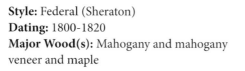

Style: Victorian –
Early Victorian
Dating: 1840-1850
Major Wood(s): Mahogany
veneer, black walnut
and rosewood

General Characteristics:
Case pieces: Pieces tend to
carry over the Classical style
with the beginnings of the
Rococo substyle, especially in
seating pieces.

Style: Victorian – Gothic Revival
Dating: 1840-1890
Major Wood(s): Black walnut,
mahogany and rosewood

General Characteristics:
Case pieces: architectural
motifs; triangular arched
pediments; arched panels;
marble tops; paneled or
molded drawer fronts; cluster
columns; bracket feet, block
feet or plinth bases
Seating pieces: tall backs;
pierced arabesque backs with
trefoils or quatrefoils; spool
turning; drop pendants

Style: Victorian – Rococo (Louis XV)
Dating: 1845-1870
Major Wood(s): Black walnut, mahogany and rosewood

General Characteristics:
Case pieces: arched carved pediments; high-relief carving, S- and C-scrolls, floral, fruit motifs, busts and cartouches; mirror panels; carved slender cabriole legs; scroll feet; bedroom suites (bed, dresser, commode)
Seating pieces: high-relief carved crest rails; balloon-shaped backs; urn-shaped splats; upholstery (tufting); demi-cabriole legs; laminated, pierced and carved construction (Belter and Meeks); parlor suites (sets of chairs, love seats, sofas)

Style: Victorian – Renaissance Revival
Dating: 1860-1885
Major Wood(s): Black walnut, burl veneer, painted and grained pine

General Characteristics:
Case pieces: rectilinear arched pediments; arched panels, burl veneer; applied moldings; bracket feet, block feet, plinth bases; medium and high-relief carving, floral and fruit, cartouches, masks and animal heads; cyma-curve brackets; Wooton patent desks
Seating pieces: oval or rectangular backs with floral or figural cresting; upholstery outlined with brass tacks; padded armrests; tapered turned front legs, flared square rear legs

Style: Victorian – Louis XVI
Dating: 1865-1875
Major Wood(s): Black walnut and ebonized maple

General Characteristics:
Case pieces: gilt decoration, marquetry, inlay; egg and dart carving; tapered turned legs, fluted
Seating pieces: molded, slightly arched crest rails; keystone-shaped backs; circular seats; fluted tapered legs

Style: Victorian – Eastlake
Dating: 1870-1895
Major Wood(s): Black walnut, burl veneer, cherry and oak

General Characteristics:
Case pieces: flat cornices; stile and rail construction; burl veneer panels; low-relief geometric and floral machine carving; incised horizontal lines
Seating pieces: rectilinear; spindles; tapered, turned legs, trumpet-shaped legs

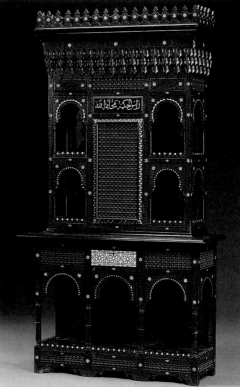

Style: Victorian Jacobean and Turkish Revival
Dating: 1870-1890
Major Wood(s): Black walnut and maple

General Characteristics:
Case pieces: A revival of some heavy 17th century forms, most commonly in dining room pieces
Seating pieces: Turkish Revival style features: oversized, low forms; overstuffed upholstery; padded arms; short baluster, vase-turned legs; ottomans, circular sofas
Jacobean Revival style features: heavy bold carving spool and spiral turnings

Style: Victorian – Aesthetic Movement
Dating: 1880-1900
Major Wood(s): Painted hardwoods, black walnut, ebonized finishes

General Characteristics:
Case pieces: rectilinear forms; bamboo turnings, spaced ball turnings; incised stylized geometric and floral designs, sometimes highlighted with gilt
Seating pieces: bamboo turning; rectangular backs; patented folding chairs

Style: Art Nouveau
Dating: 1895-1918
Major Wood(s): Ebonized hardwoods, fruitwoods

General Characteristics:
Case pieces: curvilinear shapes; floral marquetry; whiplash curves
Seating pieces: elongated forms; relief-carved floral decoration; spindle backs, pierced floral backs; cabriole legs

Style: Turn-of-the-Century (Early 20th Century)
Dating: 1895-1910
Major Wood(s): Golden (quarter-sawn) oak, mahogany hardwood stained to resemble mahogany

General Characteristics:
Case pieces: rectilinear and bulky forms; applied scroll carving or machine-pressed designs; some Colonial and Classical Revival detailing
Seating pieces: heavy framing or high spindle-trimmed backs; applied carved or machine-pressed back designs; heavy scrolled or slender turned legs; often feature some Colonial Revival or Classical Revival detailing such as claw and ball feet

Style: Mission (Arts and Crafts movement)
Dating: 1900-1915
Major Wood(s): Oak

General Characteristics:
Case pieces: rectilinear through-tenon construction; copper decoration, hand-hammered hardware; square legs
Seating pieces: rectangular splats; medial and side stretchers; exposed pegs; corbel supports

---

Style: Colonial Revival
Dating: 1890-1930
Major Wood(s): Oak, walnut and walnut veneer, mahogany veneer

General Characteristics:
Case pieces: forms generally following designs of the 17th, 18th and early 19th centuries; details for the styles such as William and Mary, Federal, Queen Anne, Chippendale or early Classical were used but often in a simplified or stylized form; mass-production in the early 20th century flooded the market with pieces that often mixed and matched design details and used a great deal of thin veneering to dress up designs; dining room and bedroom suites especially popular
Seating pieces: designs generally followed early period designs with some mixing of design elements

Style: Art Deco
Dating: 1925-1940
Major Wood(s): Bleached woods, exotic woods, steel and chrome

General Characteristics:
Case pieces: heavy geometric forms
Seating pieces: streamlined, attenuated geometric forms; overstuffed upholstery

---

Style: Modernist or Mid-Century
Dating: 1945-1970
Major Wood(s): Plywood, hardwood or metal frames

General Characteristics: Modernistic designers such as the Eames, Vladimir Kagan, George Nelson and Isamu Noguchi lead the way in post-War design. Carrying on the tradition of Modernist

designers of the 1920s and 1930s, they focused on designs for the machine age, which could be mass-produced for the popular market. By the late 1950s many of their pieces were used in commercial office spaces and schools as well as in private homes.
Case pieces: streamlined or curvilinear abstract designs with simple detailing; plain round or flattened legs and arms commonly used; mixed materials including wood, plywood, metal, glass and molded plastics
Seating pieces: streamlined and abstract curvilinear designs generally using newer materials such as plywood or simple

hardwood framing; Fabric and synthetics such as vinyl were widely used for upholstery with finer fabrics and real leather featured on more expensive pieces; seating made of molded plastic shells on metal frames and legs used on many mass-produced designs

Style: Danish Modern
Dating: 1950-1970
Major Wood(s): Teak

General Characteristics:
Case and Seating pieces: This variation of Modernistic post-war design originated in Scandinavia, hence the name; designs were simple and restrained with case pieces often having simple boxy forms with short rounded tapering legs; seating pieces have a simple teak framework with lines coordinating with case pieces; vinyl or natural fabric were most often used for upholstery; in the United States dining room suites were the most popular use for this style although some bedroom suites and general seating pieces were available

English

Style: Jacobean
Dating: Mid-17th century
Major Wood(s): Oak, walnut

General Characteristics:
Case pieces: low-relief carving, geometrics and florals; panel, rail and stile construction; applied split balusters
Seating pieces: rectangular backs; carved and pierced crests; spiral turnings ball feet

Style: William and Mary
Dating: 1689-1702
Major Wood(s): Walnut, burl walnut veneer

General Characteristics:
Case pieces: marquetry, veneering; shaped aprons; 6-8 trumpet-form legs; curved flat stretchers
Seating pieces: carved, pierced crests; tall caned backs and seats; trumpet-form legs; Spanish feet

Style: Queen Anne
Dating: 1702-1714
Major Wood(s): Walnut, mahogany, veneers

General Characteristics:
Case pieces: cyma curves; broken arch pediments and finials; bracket feet
Seating pieces: carved crest rails; high, rounded backs; solid vase-shaped splats; cabriole legs; pad feet

Style: George I
Dating: 1714-1727
Major Wood(s): Walnut, mahogany, veneer and yew wood

General Characteristics:
Case pieces: broken arch pediments; gilt decoration, japanning; bracket feet
Seating pieces: curvilinear forms; yoke-shaped crests; shaped solid splats; shell carving; upholstered seats; carved cabriole legs; claw and ball feet, pad feet

Style: George II
Dating: 1727-1760
Major Wood(s): Mahogany

General Characteristics:
Case pieces: broken arch pediments; relief-carved foliate, scroll and shell carving; carved cabriole legs; claw and ball feet, bracket feet, ogee bracket feet
Seating pieces: carved, shaped crest rails, out-turned ears; pierced shaped splats; ladder (ribbon) backs; upholstered seats; scrolled arms; carved cabriole legs or straight (Marlboro) legs; claw and ball feet

Style: George III
Dating: 1760-1820
Major Wood(s): Mahogany, veneer, satinwood

General Characteristics:
Case pieces: rectilinear forms; parcel gilt decoration; inlaid ovals, circles, banding or marquetry; carved columns, urns; tambour fronts or bow fronts; plinth bases
Seating pieces:
shield backs; upholstered seats; tapered square legs, square legs

Style: Regency
Dating: 1811-1820
Major Wood(s): Mahogany, mahogany veneer, satinwood and rosewood

General Characteristics:
Case pieces: Greco-Roman and Egyptian motifs; inlay, ormolu mounts; marble tops; round columns, pilasters; mirrored backs; scroll feet
Seating pieces: straight backs, latticework; caned seats; sabre legs, tapered turned legs, flared turned legs; parcel gilt, ebonizing

Style: George IV
Dating: 1820-1830
Major Wood(s): Mahogany, mahogany veneer and rosewood

General Characteristics:
Continuation of Regency designs

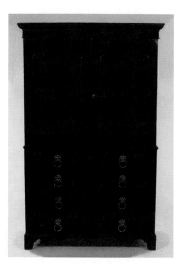

Style: William IV
Dating: 1830-1837
Major Wood(s): Mahogany, mahogany veneer

General Characteristics:
Case pieces: rectilinear; brass mounts, grillwork; carved moldings; plinth bases
Seating pieces: rectangular backs; carved straight crest rails; acanthus, animal carving; carved cabriole legs; paw feet

Style: Victorian
Dating: 1837-1901
Major Wood(s): Black walnut, mahogany, veneers & rosewood

General Characteristics:
Case pieces: applied floral carving; surmounting mirrors, drawers, candle shelves; marble tops
Seating pieces: high-relief carved crest rails; floral & fruit carving; balloon backs, oval backs; upholstered seats, backs; spool, spiral turnings; cabriole legs, fluted tapered legs; scrolled feet

Style: Edwardian
Dating: 1901-1910
Major Wood(s): Mahogany, mahogany veneer, and satinwood
General Characteristics: Neo-Classical motifs and revivals of earlier 18th century and early 19th century styles

Antique Furniture

Skinner, Inc.; www.skinnerinc.com

Federal inlaid birch bowfront bureau, northern New England, circa 1810, cockbeaded drawers centering wavy birch inlaid ovals bordered by diamond stringing and mitered panels, all within crossbanded borders, inlaid base with slightly flaring French feet, old replaced brasses marked "PATENT," refinished, minor imperfections, 39" high, case 38 1/2" wide, 19 3/4" deep. **$28,290**

Skinner, Inc.; www.skinnerinc.com

Federal carved and wavy birch inlaid mahogany chest of drawers, Portsmouth, New Hampshire, circa 1810-1820, case of cockbeaded drawers and elliptic front with flanking quarter-engaged, ring-turned, reeded posts ending in vase- and ring-turned legs, replaced brass pulls, old refinish, minor imperfections, 37 1/2" high, 43 3/4" wide, 21 1/2" deep. **$9,600**

Pook & Pook, Inc.

Pennsylvania painted poplar dower chest, circa 1800, decorated with large panels of potted tulips, birds, and cats on stippled ochre ground, inscribed on underside of lid Philip Zerbe in German script, probably eastern Lebanon County, 27 1/2" high x 48 1/4" wide. **$14,220**

Rago Arts and Auction Center

Grueby Gustav Stickley, rare early Yeddo plant stand with 10" tile (no. 11), Eastwood, New York, circa 1900, unmarked, 24" x 15" square. **$18,750**

Pook & Pook, Inc.

Berks County, Pennsylvania pine hanging corner cupboard, circa 1790, double raised panel door and scalloped two-tier drop, inscribed on inside of door, From Eshelman family, Oley Valley PA, 55 1/2" high x 27 1/2" wide. **$52,140**

Pook & Pook, Inc.

Diminutive Pennsylvania walnut hanging cupboard, circa 1770, molded cornice overhanging raised panel door, open shelf with scrolled sides, retaining old red painted surface, 26" high x 17 1/4" wide x 12 1/2" deep. **$35,550**

Pook & Pook, Inc.

Benjamin Goodwin, Lancaster, Pennsylvania, Chippendale walnut desk and bookcase, late 18th century, 93 1/2" high x 48" wide x 24 1/2" deep. **$45,030**

Pook & Pook, Inc.

Chester County, Queen Anne walnut secretary desk, dated 1744, possibly made by Joel Bailey for Isaac and Ann Marshall in the year of their wedding, molded cornice over raised tombstone panel door flanked by recessed panels, above fall front enclosing fitted interior with prospect door inlaid IM 1744, over two short and two long drawers and fishtail apron supported by bracket feet, 75" high x 35" wide. **$33,180**

Pook & Pook, Inc.

▲ *Pair of Delaware Valley Chippendale walnut dining chairs, circa 1770, each with four carved shells and ball and claw feet.* **$37,920**

Pook & Pook, Inc.

◄ *Southeastern Pennsylvania Queen Anne walnut chest on frame, circa 1780, with five short and four long drawers, resting on base with scalloped apron and trifid feet, 70" high x 37 1/2" wide.* **$10,073**

Rago Arts and Auction Center

L. & J.G. Stickley triple door bookcase, Fayetteville, New York, circa 1916, branded "The Work of...," 55" x 72 1/2" x 12". **$11,250**

Pook & Pook, Inc.

Lancaster County, Pennsylvania painted pine one-piece corner cupboard, circa 1790, ivory door and rattail hinges, old blue/green painted surface, 87" high x 40" wide. **$10,073**

Pook & Pook, Inc.

Irish Chippendale George III mahogany six-legged dropleaf table, carved knees and ball and claw feet, 28" high x 18 1/2" wide x 71 1/2" deep. **$8,888**

Rago Arts and Auction Center

Gustav Stickley five-legged dining table, Eastwood, New York, circa 1904, large red decal, 30 1/4" x 48" with two 12" leaves. **$8,750**

Pook & Pook, Inc.

Hussey family Massachusetts Chippendale carved and figured mahogany desk and bookcase, circa 1770, probably Newburyport, original finial and cast brass hardware, 92" high x 40" wide x 22 1/2" deep. **$37,920**

Pook & Pook, Inc.

◀ *New England Queen Anne cherry high chest, circa 1770, fan-carved drawers, 77 1/4" high x 39 1/2" wide.* **$8,888**

Rago Arts and Auction Center

▼ *L. & J.G. Stickley triple-door bookcase, Fayetteville, New York, 1912-1916, unmarked, 55" x 72" x 12".* **$8,750**

Modern Furniture

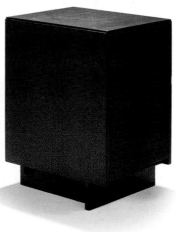

Rago Arts and Auction Center

Pair of three-drawer bedside tables, New Hope, Pennsylvania, before 1954, walnut, unmarked, designed by George Nakashima, manufactured by Nakashima Studios, 25 1/2" x 15 1/2" x 19". Provenance: Letter of authentication from Mira Nakashima. **$12,500**

Rago Arts and Auction Center

Custom bench with drawers, New Hope, Pennsylvania, 1962, Persian walnut, walnut, designed by George Nakashima, manufactured by Nakashima Studios, signed with client's name, 16 1/2" x 108" x 22". Provenance: Copy of original drawing, order card, and evaluation from Mira Nakashima. **$22,500**

▲ *Walnut double dresser, New Hope, Pennsylvania, 1959, designed by George Nakashima, manufactured by Nakashima Studios, signed with client name, 31 3/4" x 60" x 20".* **$18,750**

▶ *Two-tiered table, Paoli, Pennsylvania, 1956, walnut, hickory, designed by Wharton Esherick (1887-1970), signed WE 1956, 27 3/4" x 27 1/2" x 16".* **$31,250**

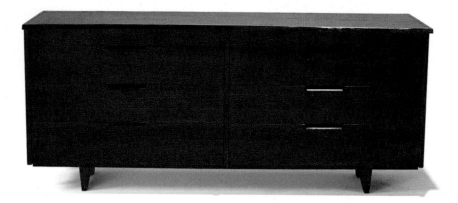

Rago Arts and Auction Center

Double dresser, New Hope, Pennsylvania, 1967-1968, Persian walnut, walnut, unmarked, designed by George Nakashima, manufactured by Nakashima Studios, 32" x 72" x 23 1/2". **$20,000**

Rago Arts and Auction Center

Pair of Conoid chairs, New Hope, Pennsylvania, 1969, walnut, hickory, designed by George Nakashima, manufactured by Nakashima Studios, signed with client's name, 35 1/2" x 20" x 21 1/2". **$13,750**

Rago Arts and Auction Center

▲ *Pair of club chairs, United States, 1960s, oak, distressed leather, unmarked, designed by James Mont, manufactured by James Mont Design, 30" x 32" x 42 1/2".* **$12,500**

Rago Arts and Auction Center

◄ *Etruscan dining table, New York, 1960s, etched and patinated bronze, pewter, designed by Philip and Kelvin LaVerne, etched signature, on casters, 28 1/2" x 40" diameter.* **$17,500**

Rago Arts and Auction Center

▼ *Hanging wall case, New Hope, Pennsylvania, 1962, walnut, pandanus cloth, designed by George Nakashima, manufactured by Nakashima Studios, signed with client's name, 14 1/4" x 50" x 14". Provenance: Copy of original drawing, order card, and evaluation from Mira Nakashima.* **$11,250**

Rago Arts and Auction Center

Custom dining table with allegorical scene, New York, 1960s, etched, patinated and polychromed bronze, pewter, designed by Philip and Kelvin LaVerne, raised signature, 31" x 60" square. **$35,000**

Rago Arts and Auction Center

Occasional table, New Hope, Pennsylvania, 1960s, gilt iron and wood, cleft slate, unmarked, designed by Paul Evans, manufactured by Paul Evans Studio, 21 3/4" x 28" diameter. **$16,250**

Rago Arts and Auction Center

Looped side table, New Hope, Pennsylvania, 1960s, gilt iron and wood, cleft slate, unmarked, designed by Paul Evans, manufactured by Paul Evans Studio, 15" x 18" diameter. **$15,000**

Rago Arts and Auction Center

Skyline coffee table, New Hope, Pennsylvania, 1970, welded and polychromed steel, bronze, composite, glass, welded signature and date, designed by Paul Evans, manufactured by Paul Evans Studio, 16" x 42" square. **$13,750**

Rago Arts and Auction Center

Cityscape credenza, United States, 1970s, patinated and chromed steel, signed, designed by Paul Evans, manufactured by Directional, 32" x 72" x 18". **$17,500**

Rago Arts and Auction Center

▼ *Six-drawer dresser, United States, 1950s, lacquered wood, brass, designed by Tommi Parzinger, manufactured by Parzinger Originals, unmarked, 32" x 85 1/2" x 18 1/2".* **$15,000**

Rago Arts and Auction Center

Grasshopper lounge chair, Denmark, 1960s, chrome-plated steel, leather, canvas, unmarked, Preben Fabricius, Jorgen Kastholm, Alfred Kill, 32 1/2" x 28 1/4" x 57". **$13,750**

Rago Arts and Auction Center

Chieftain chair, Denmark, 1949, teak, leather, leatherette, branded, cabinetmaker Niels Vodder, Copenhagen, designed by Finn Juhl, 37" x 40 1/2" x 35". **$27,500**

Rago Arts and Auction Center

▲ *Pair of lounge chairs (NV 45), Denmark, 1940s, teak, wool, leather, one branded, by cabinetmaker Niels Vodder, Copenhagen, Denmark, designed by Finn Juhl, 32 3/4" x 27 1/2" x 30".* **$22,500**

Rago Arts and Auction Center

▶ *Bellevue chair, France, 1950s, enameled plywood, enameled steel, chromed steel, unmarked, designed by Andre Bloc, 32 1/2" x 16" x 19".* **$11,875**

Rago Arts and Auction Center

Wing lounge chair (no. 503), United States, 1970s, sculpted walnut, wool, unmarked, designed by Vladimir Kagan, manufactured by Vladimir Kagan Designs, Inc., 42" x 31" x 33". **$10,000**

Rago Arts and Auction Center

▲ *Pair of two-drawer side tables (no. 464-393), United States, 1940s, lacquered cork, mahogany, brass, branded and stenciled, designed by Paul Frankl, manufactured by Johnson Furniture Co., 24 1/4" x 24" x 19".* **$10,000**

Rago Arts and Auction Center

◄ *Station wagon desk, United States, 1940s, painted cork, stained and lacquered mahogany, brass, branded, designed by Paul Frankl, manufactured by Johnson Furniture Co., 28" x 60 1/4" x 27".* **$10,000**

Rago Arts and Auction Center

Woven-front cabinet, Berne, Indiana, 1950s, bleached mahogany, brass, brass label, designed by Edward Wormley, manufactured by Dunbar, 38" x 61 1/2" x 18 1/4". **$10,000**

Rago Arts and Auction Center

*Console table, New Hope,
Pennsylvania, 1960s, sculpted
walnut, inlaid marble, holly,
unmarked, designed by Phil
Powell, 28" x 80 3/4" x 20 1/2".*
$15,000

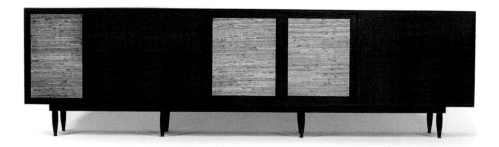

Rago Arts and Auction Center

*Long cabinet, New Hope,
Pennsylvania, circa 1959, walnut,
cherry, woven grass cloth,
unmarked, designed by Phil
Powell, 33" x 21" x 114".* **$11,250**

Rago Arts and Auction Center

▲ *Deep relief cabinet, United States, 1960s, welded and polychromed steel, patinated bronze, cleft slate, polychromed wood, unmarked, designed by Paul Evans, manufactured by Directional, 31" x 96" x 20 1/2".* **$56,250**

Rago Arts and Auction Center

▲ *Custom coffee table, New Hope, Pennsylvania, 1960s, torch-cut, welded, and polychromed steel, gilt wood, cleft slate, unmarked, designed by Paul Evans, manufactured by Paul Evans Studio, 14 1/4" x 96" x 24".* **$11,250**

Rago Arts and Auction Center

◄ *Sculptured metal two-door cabinet, United States, 1968, bronze, composite, painted wood, cleft slate, designed by Paul Evans, manufactured by Directional, signed and dated, 17 1/2" x 50" x 17".* **$10,000**

GLASS

American Brilliant Cut Glass

Cut glass is made by grinding decorations into glass by means of abrasive-carrying metal or stone wheels. An ancient craft, it was revived in 1600 by Bohemians and spread through Europe to Great Britain and America.

American cut glass came of age at the Centennial Exposition in 1876 and the World Columbian Exposition in 1893. America's most significant output of high-quality glass occurred from 1880 to 1917, a period now known as the Brilliant Period. Glass from this period is the most eagerly sought by collectors.

Woody Auction

Six wine glasses, cranberry cut to clear, Hob Diamond pattern by Dorflinger, colored foot, 4 3/4". **$944**

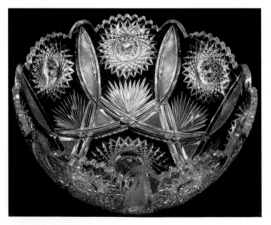

Woody Auction

Single-piece punch bowl, Dauntless pattern by Bergen, extra clear blank, 7" x 14". **$236**

Woody Auction

Signed Tuthill round shallow tray, Vintage pattern, 12". **$1,888**

Woody Auction

Six wine glasses, Hobstar, Crosscut Diamond, Strawberry Diamond, and Star motif, modified Apple Core stem, 4 1/2" high. **$207**

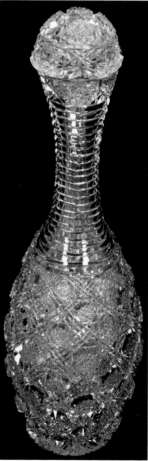

Woody Auction

Signed Libbey centerpiece compote, Hobstar, Cane, Vesica, and Notched Fan motifs, rare canoe-shaped design, pattern #202 by Libbey, superior blank, 7" x 12 1/2". **$2,596**

Woody Auction

Rare bowling pin decanter, rare Trellis pattern, with exact pattern cut stopper, step cut neck, ray base, 15 3/4". **$1,888**

Woody Auction

Oval tray, Genoa pattern by Clark, 14 3/4" x 10 1/2". **$266**

Woody Auction

Rare tall champagne pitcher, Hobstar, Chain of Hobstar, Fan & Vertical Ray motif, embossed sterling spout with elaborate monogram, triple notched handle, Primrose pattern by Straus, 17" high. **$2,006**

Woody Auction

Tall pitcher, sharply cut Hobstar with Strawberry Diamond and Prism Fields, pattern cut handle, Hobstar base, clear blank, Genoa pattern by Clark, 11 1/4". **$1,770**

Woody Auction

◄ *Single-piece punch bowl, Hobstar, Strawberry Diamond, Hob Diamond and Fan motifs, 5/8" blank, 7" x 14".* **$472**

Woody Auction

Compote, Hobstar, Strawberry Diamond and Fan motif, notched teardrop stem, Hobstar base, 9" x 8 3/4". **$89**

Woody Auction

Rolled rim two-part punch bowl, Triple Mitre Trellis pattern with matching ladle marked J.D. Bergen, excellent condition, top and base have 1/2" difference of movement, clear blank, 14" x 10". **$108**

Woody Auction

Blown mold bowl, Hobstar, Strawberry Diamond and Interlocking Vesica motif, 4" x 11". **$590**

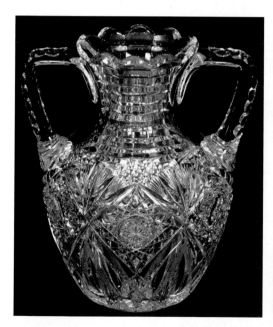

Woody Auction

Signed Egginton two-handled vase, Marquis pattern, 9 1/2". **$649**

Woody Auction

▶ *Pair of corset-shaped vases, Brunswick pattern by Hawkes, one vase with outside rim chip, 13 3/4" high.* **$266**

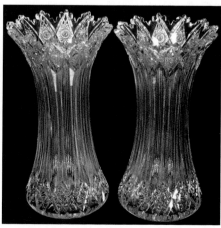

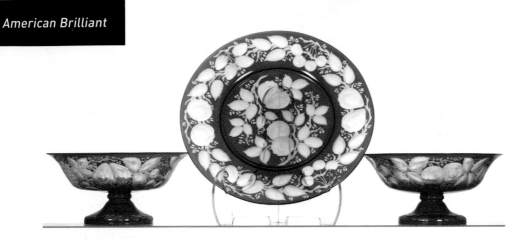

Woody Auction

▲ Three-piece serving set, amber cut to clear, 14 3/4" round tray with pair of 5 1/4" x 10 3/4" pedestal compotes, engraved multi-fruit branch décor, attributed to Pairpoint. **$826**

Woody Auction

◄ Single-piece punch bowl, Hobstar, Strawberry Diamond, Cane and Star motifs, 1/2" thick blank, 7" x 16". **$767**

Woody Auction

Round tray, Hobstar, Strawberry Diamond and Nail Head Diamond motif, heavy blank, well cut, 13 1/2". **$1,416**

Woody Auction

Sugar shaker, prism cut body, sterling top, 5 1/4" high. **$89**

Woody Auction

Pair of candlestick holders, blue cut to clear, Flute and Festoons pattern, 10 3/4". **$590**

Woody Auction

Pedestal vase, cranberry cut to clear, Hobstar, Cane & Fan motif, Hobstar foot, 9" high. **$1,888**

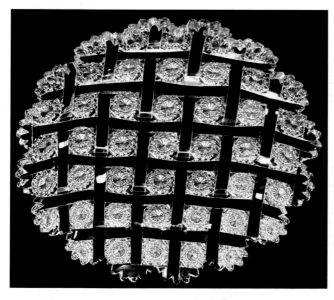

Woody Auction

Signed Hawkes round tray, Lattice and Rosette pattern (also known as Willow pattern), perfect condition, 10". **$5,900**

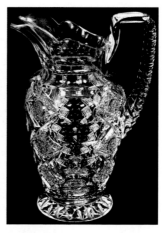

Woody Auction

Footed water pitcher, Queens pattern by Hawkes, triple notch handle, Hobstar base, fine quality, 10 1/2". **$2,124**

Woody Auction

Compote, green cut to clear, Cane, Cross Cut Diamond, Star and Fan motif, green and white lattice ribbon twist stem, 8" x 6 3/4". **$590**

Woody Auction

Rare round tray, Alhambra pattern by Meriden, one tooth with slight angle polish, 12". **$2,714**

Woody Auction

Eight wine glasses, cranberry cut to clear, Russian pattern with star cut buttons, 4 1/2" high. **$1,534**

Woody Auction

Square vase, complete Harvard pattern, 16" high. **$1,003**

Woody Auction

Four apple green wine glasses, Russian pattern, clear diamond cut stem with rayed base, 4 5/8" high.
$1,888

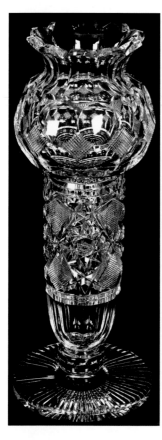

Woody Auction

Signed Hawkes tulip-shaped vase, Franklin pattern, No. 236, 12" high. **$295**

Woody Auction

Six wine glasses, cranberry cut to clear, unique Cane, Vesica and Hobstar motif, St. Louis Diamond apple core stem, 5 1/4" high.
$1,180

▶ *Rare two-handled, double-spout decanter, Harvard pattern by Libbey and shape #302, pattern cut handles, stopper and base, includes two 3 1/2" Double Teardrop stem cordial glasses, finest quality, decanter 10".* **$5,015**

Woody Auction

▲ *Wine glass, green cut to clear, engraved Floral and Rococo design, pattern cut base, attributed to Dorflinger, 5 1/2" high.* **$295**

Woody Auction

Signed Hawkes round tray, Holland pattern, blank is thinner near edge on one quarter of tray, 14 1/2". **$1,416**

Art Glass

Art glass is artistic novelty glassware created for decorative purposes. Types of art glass include leaded glass, molded glass, blown glass, and sandblasted glass. Tiffany, Lalique, and Steuben are some of the best-known makers of art glass. Daum Nancy, Baccarat, Gallé, Moser, Mt. Washington, Fenton, and Quezal are a few others.

James D. Julia, Inc.

◄ *Austrian fan vase, iridescent orange shading to gold with green highlights, slightly ruffled top, ground pontil, unsigned, very good to excellent condition, 12" high x 11 1/2" wide.* **$790**

James D. Julia, Inc.

▼ *Large Moser decorated center bowl, pink shading to white glass with applied amber heavily ruffled edge, enameled decoration of acorns, leaves, and branches with dragonflies, butterflies, and insects; interior of bowl has enameled moth in center and is surrounded by green, gold, and brown leaves; 19 applied acorns to interior and exterior, unsigned but numbered 854, remnants of paper label still visible; very good to excellent condition, 16" diameter x 8 3/4" high.* **$10,073**

James D. Julia, Inc.

Loetz octopus vase, Federzeichnung pattern, reminiscent of double gourd with long collared neck, octopus design trimmed with ornate gold pattern, finished with enameled floral design in light blue and orange, signed "Patent" with 9159 on underside, very good condition with wear to gold, 11 1/2" high. **$5,333**

James D. Julia, Inc.

Mt. Washington Royal Flemish vase decorated with snow geese in flight against large sunburst with surrounding panels of blue and teal separated by raised gold gilding and stars, collar decorated with gold gilded stylized flowers and leaves surrounding three winged griffins set against amethyst background, back of vase decorated with gilded stars and two additional geese in flight, very good to excellent condition, unsigned, 14 1/4" high. **$4,859**

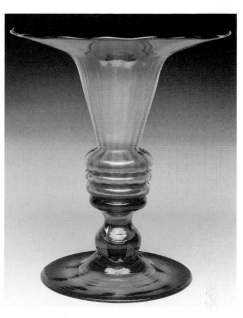

James D. Julia, Inc.

▲ *Alexandrite pedestal-form trumpet vase, gently ribbed, purple flared rim receding to topaz and ending in blue foot, very good to excellent condition, 5" high.* **$2,103**

James D. Julia, Inc.

▲ *Webb green overlay acid-carved vase, floral design encircling cylindrical neck with two acid-carved butterflies hovering over flowers, bulbous foot of vase decorated with round facet cuts through to clear, underside of vase is star cut, unsigned, very good condition with one nick to edge of one round facet and some slight roughness at lip, 13 1/2" high.* **$948**

James D. Julia, Inc.

▲ *Mt. Washington lava glass vase with matte black finish and colored glass shards in green, blue, purple, red and teal, very good to excellent condition, 3 1/2" high.* **$1,067**

Pook & Pook, Inc.

◄ *Muller Fres cameo glass vase, 7" high.* **$385**

Skinner, Inc.; www.skinnerinc.com

Pair of cranberry-colored Bohemian glass vases on stands, 19th century, each with cut stiff leaf rim and gilded trim and foliage, raised oval cartouches polychrome-enameled with figures of women in landscapes, 15" high. **$5,228**

James D. Julia, Inc.

Moser mercury glass pokal, clear glass with mercury lining, decorated with enameled stylized flowers and leaves with two center cartouches with gilded paintings of castles, applied rigaree around top and bottom as well as lid, applied snail-like cabochons on foot and lid, applied cabochons and rigaree are all gilded, very good condition with some wear to mercury, one small flake on outside lip of pokal, 20 1/2" high. **$8,295**

James D. Julia, Inc.

Moser footed bowl decorated with stylized leaves and berries, supported by four applied gilded leaf-shaped feet that continue high onto bowl's side, top of each foot enameled with insects, inside edge of bowl enameled with insects and berries, very good to excellent condition with some minor wear to gilding, unsigned, 9" long x 4 1/2" high. **$4,148**

James D. Julia, Inc.

Gallé French cameo vase, decoration of amber dragonfly and lily pads over frosted and blue background, signed Gallé in cameo relief on side of vase, very good to excellent condition, 22 1/2" high. **$10,665**

James D. Julia, Inc.

Moser enameled vase, cranberry glass with white enameled decoration of cupids surrounded by gold enamel scrolls, four applied snail feet with gold enamel, very good to excellent condition with minor wear to gold enamel, unsigned, 8" high. **$1,659**

James D. Julia, Inc.

Mt. Joye pansy vase, clear glass shading to opalescent at top, enameled on front with pansies and green leaves and stems, unsigned, very good to excellent condition, 13 1/2" high. **$948**

James D. Julia, Inc.

Webb cameo glass vase decorated with center wheel-carved long-billed bird resting on branch surrounded by leaves, flowers, and fruit, foliage decoration extends around full body of vase with back of vase decorated by two large wheel-carved flowers, grass and leaves at bottom are wheel-carved and extend around to bottom of foot, lip of vase is encircled by bamboo branch, carving is all set against frosted blue background, unsigned, very good to excellent condition, 5" high. **$8,888**

James D. Julia, Inc.

Moser enameled vase, smoke-colored glass with applied blue crystal rigaree to edge of vase and wishbone decoration around top, enameled decoration of bird flying over garden of flower blossoms, pods, leaves and branches, polished pontil, unsigned but numbered 3, very good to excellent condition, 11 1/2" high. **$1,422**

James D. Julia, Inc.

▶ *Webb (Woodall Team) cameo vase carved in Oriental pattern on light celadon green glass as part of "Chinese" series, design includes roses with stems and leaves surrounding entire body of vase with additional Oriental patterns weaving through roses and adorning neck and lip, unsigned, very good to excellent condition with one nick to rose petal on shoulder of vase, 8 3/4" high x 6" wide.* **$18,960**

James D. Julia, Inc.

◀ *Webb carved and applied vase, cameo carved clear glass flowers surrounding vase against acid-carved background, decorated with applied oval cabochons with colored glass inclusions and wheel carved decorations, decorated with random padded light blue wheel-carved flowers, unsigned, very good to excellent condition, 7" high.* **$18,368**

◀ *Loetz cytisus silver overlay vase with blue iridescent body shading to pastel yellow at lip and platinum iridescent oil spot decoration, finished with silver overlay framing four pinched sides, very good to excellent condition, 4 1/2" high.* **$2,607**

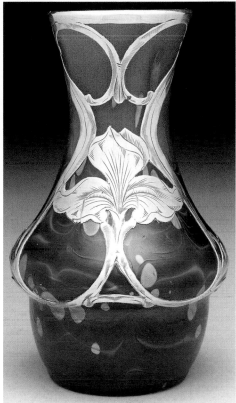

▲ *Loetz art glass vase, bulbous form shouldered with short neck and flared rim, decoration of wave pattern in blues, purples, and platinum on background of purple with copper iridescent finish, signed Loetz Austria, carved flower to underside of vase, very good to excellent condition, 7" high.* **$2,552**

▲ *Loetz cytisus silver overlay vase, dark blue iridescent body shading to translucent salmon color at top, light blue iridescent random oil spots, finished with silver overlay of iris front and back, very good to excellent condition, 6" high.* **$4,740**

▶ *Stevens & Williams Pompeian Swirl peach and coral bowl, ruffled rim with light blue interior, very good to excellent condition, 3 1/2" high x 7 1/2" wide.* **$1,185**

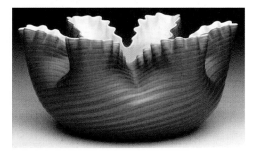

James D. Julia, Inc.

Frederick Carder presentation vase, baluster form with vertical coloration of blue and deep purple with soft green cased lining decorated with Art Nouveau silver overlay pattern of flowers, stems, and leaves, further overlaid with cartouche inscribed, "To my dear friend John Northwood 1st as a token of appreciation and esteem from Frederick C. Carder," vase also stamped Sterling twice on either side of bottom rim, very good to excellent condition with one silver overlay stem missing, believed to have been done at the factory, 13" high. **$13,035**

James D. Julia, Inc.

Gallé French cameo aquatic vase, underwater scene of seaweed cameo and intaglio carved in several layers, decoration set against shades of green, also has trapped bubbles in the making, part of decoration depicting bubbles produced by seaweed, silver and gold mica throughout, lower third of vase fire-polished, elaborate Gallé signature to side of vase, very good to excellent condition, 7 3/4" high. **$4,148**

Bonhams

Art Nouveau silver overlaid emerald glass vase, circa 1900, Black, Starr & Frost, stamped PATENTED G3384 and BLACK, STAR & FROST, 12 1/4" high. **$812**

James D. Julia, Inc.

Steuben Tyrian vase, bulbous shaped, multi-shaded blue ground with platinum heart and vine decoration, rolled rim, signed on underside Tyrian, very good condition with minor mineral deposits to interior and minor scratches to underside consistent with age, 5 1/2" high x 8" diameter. **$9,480**

James D. Julia, Inc.

▶ *Gallé vase with purple marquetry iris flowers with yellow and red centers set against mottled yellow and white background, wheel-carved flowers in background encircling entire vase, signed on side with engraved signature Gallé, very good to excellent condition, 8" high.* **$21,330**

James D. Julia, Inc.

▲ *Alexandrite cabinet vase, bulbous form with quadrefoil rim, amethyst to topaz, diamond quilt decoration, very good to excellent condition, 2 1/2" high.* **$1,126**

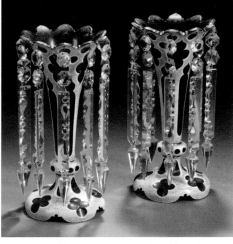

Skinner, Inc.; www.skinnerinc.com

Two pairs of similar Bohemian overlay glass tulip-form vases, 19th century, white cut to cranberry, each with scrolled gilding and stylized floral and foliate designs, two are 11 1/2" high, other two 13 1/2" high. **$1,560**

Skinner, Inc.; www.skinnerinc.com

Pair of Bohemian overlay glass girandoles, 19th century, white cut to cranberry with gilded trim and scrolled background, stylized foliate form panels, with prism pendants, 11 1/2" high. **$1,320**

James D. Julia, Inc.

Monumental Durand King Tut green vase, classic Egyptian form vase with bulbous bottom, elongated neck and flared rim, decorated with platinum King Tut pattern overall, gold interior, signed on underside Durand 1974-18, very good to excellent condition with chip out of polished pontil and two open bubbles on side, 18" high. **$2,430**

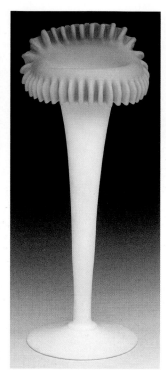

James D. Julia, Inc.

Mt. Washington Peach Blow jack-in-the-pulpit vase, shading from pink to pale blue with crimped top and matte finish, very good to excellent condition, 13" high. **$1,659**

James D. Julia, Inc.

Schneider ewer with base layer of yellow and purple powdered glass with design of Art Deco strawberry tree fruits with foliage, design acid etched and enameled, orange is applied glass, finished with applied glass purple handle, signed Schneider in script to side of ewer, very good to excellent condition, 12" high. **$4,148**

James D. Julia, Inc.

Gallé French cameo perfume bottle in black and frost depicting butterflies and moths, wheel-carved insects set against martele or "hammered" background glass, finished with original black and frost stopper also of martele glass, signed on underside Emile Galle Nancy, very good to excellent condition, 4" high. **$20,738**

James D. Julia, Inc.

Argy-Rousseau Pate de Verre vase titled "The Garden of Hesperides" (sometimes called the "Apple Picker"), red-orange maidens picking yellow fruit, background of yellow, peach, and frost in upper half, yellows, oranges, and browns to lower geometric portion; signed G. ARGY-ROUSSEAU on side, marked "France" on bottom, very good to excellent condition, 9" high. **$18,960**

James D. Julia, Inc.

▲ *Gallé French cameo vase, wheel-carved iris in purple and green set against mottled green, blue, and purple ground with internal bubble decoration, accented with white and purple vertical ribbing, finished with circular pedestal foot in complimentary colors, signed on side with engraved elaborate Gallé, very good to excellent condition, 6 1/2" high.* **$9,480**

Skinner, Inc.; www.skinnerinc.com

◄ *Pair of Bohemian enameled glass vases, 19th century, cylindrical shape with polychrome flowers, foliage, and butterflies, gilded trim, 17" high.* **$300**

Daum Nancy

Daum Nancy fine glass, much of it cameo, was made by Auguste and Antonin Daum, who founded a factory in 1875 in Nancy, France. Most of their cameo and enameled glass was made from the 1890s into the early 20th century.

Cameo glass is made by carving into multiple layers of colored glass to create a design in relief. It is at least as old as the Romans.

James D. Julia, Inc.

▶ *French cameo tumbler-shaped vase decorated with burgundy enameled flowers with gold highlights and green leaves and stems, bottom portion decorated with Art Nouveau acid cutback pattern, mottled ground of orange shading to purple, signed in cameo "Daum Nancy" with Cross of Lorraine on side of vase, very good to excellent condition, 4 3/4" high.* **$1,481**

James D. Julia, Inc.

▼ *Cameo and enamel bowl with cameo flowers, stems, and leaves enameled in green with flowers and buds in purple, clear foot internally decorated with mottled orange, brown, and white, background of sides of bowl are acid textured, signed on side in cameo "Daum Nancy" with Cross of Lorraine, very good to excellent condition, 3" high.* **$2,074**

James D. Julia, Inc.

▲ *French cameo and enamel vase with floral pattern in purple with green leaves and brown stems set against yellow and green molten ground, signed "Daum Nancy" with Cross of Lorraine on side of vase, very good to excellent condition, 9" high.* **$2,963**

James D. Julia, Inc.

◄ *Salt set with four salts with cameo flowers against acid-textured background with gilded details on flowers, each salt set in silver-footed base with French hallmarks, four gilded silver salt spoons, set housed in original fitted presentation box marked on inside lid "Aubert Rue de Siam Brest," each salt signed on underside of glass "Daum Nancy" with Cross of Lorraine; very good to excellent condition with some wear and split to leatherette covering on top of presentation box; salts 2" wide x 1 1/2" high, box 8 1/2" x 9 1/4".* **$4,444**

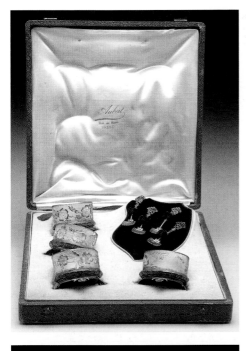

James D. Julia, Inc.

▲ *Tumbler vase with purple enamel and cameo violets atop green cameo and enameled stems, leaves set against internally decorated background of mottled white shading to mottled purple at foot, signed on side in cameo "Daum Nancy France" with Cross of Lorraine, very good to excellent condition, 4 1/2" high.* **$1,481**

James D. Julia, Inc.

▲ *French cameo vase with ground of striated pink, yellow, and purple with allover daisy floral pattern in yellow and brown with green foliage, earthen-toned footed pedestal, signed on side "Daum Nancy France" with Cross of Lorraine, very good to excellent condition, 13 1/2" high.* **$4,253**

James D. Julia, Inc.

◄ *Rectangular winter scene vase decorated with cameo trees on all four sides with enameled tree bark and snow on trees and covering ground, yellow shading to orange background, signed on underside in black enamel "Daum Nancy" with Cross of Lorraine, very good to excellent condition, 7 1/4" high.* **$7,110**

James D. Julia, Inc.

Monumental size cameo and enamel vase with yellow mottled ground receding to deep purple at foot with overall decoration of flowers with bumblebees, gold gilt Art Nouveau pattern at foot, signed "Daum Nancy" with Cross of Lorraine on underside of foot, very good to excellent condition, 21" high. **$11,850**

James D. Julia, Inc.

Wheel-carved poppy vase with acid-carved stems and leaves leading to four padded and wheel-carved red poppy flowers, cameo decoration set against mottled brick red background shading to light blue, background finished in martelé carving, signed on underside with etched signature "Daum Nancy" with Cross of Lorraine, very good to excellent condition, 11 1/2" high. **$14,220**

James D. Julia, Inc.

◄ *Applied glass covered jar, rare, one green-gold applied cabochon, one green applied insect, and one red applied leaf on body with acid etched maple leaves, lid has applied and wheel-carved handle with red applied insect on top, signed on underside with remnants of engraved and gilded "Daum Nancy" with Cross of Lorraine, very good to excellent condition, 4 1/2" high.* **$2,844**

James D. Julia, Inc.

Bleeding heart vase decorated with cameo and enamel bleeding heart flowers, stems, and leaves on front and back, back of vase shows bleeding hearts as buds, front shows them in full bloom; stems, leaves, and flowers enameled and highlighted with gilding, cameo work set against mottled blue background shading to cream, background finished with acid texture; signed on underside with etched signature "Daum Nancy" and Cross of Lorraine, very good to excellent condition, 16" high. **$10,073**

James D. Julia, Inc.

Blackbird vase, quadrefoil-shaped, light blue to gray background decorated with blackbirds and deciduous trees, enameled in gray and black, some blackbirds in flight while others rest in trees, signed "Daum Nancy" to underside of vase, very good to excellent condition, 2 3/4" high. **$5,036**

James D. Julia, Inc.

Enameled and cameo vase depicting Dutch winter scene with village, windmills, and church with snow-covered ground and deciduous trees, background mottled in orange and blue representing skyline, cameo decoration cut against added acid-textured clear glass background, mottled orange and blue internal decoration cased on interior, signed "Daum Nancy" with Cross of Lorraine on side of vase, very good to excellent condition, 3 3/4" high. **$3,259**

James D. Julia, Inc.

▼ Cameo and applied glass jar with layered autumnal-colored cameo oak leaves and background, decorated with applied acorns and insect, one oak leaf decorated with faceted cabochon with foil backing, matching lid with carved and applied insect, signed on underside with incised signature "Daum Nancy" with Cross of Lorraine, very good to excellent condition, 4" square x 4 1/2" high. **$3,555**

James D. Julia, Inc.

Large French cameo lamp with domical-shaped shade decorated in earthen hues with pattern of grape clusters and vines on mottled yellow and peach ground, shade supported by three-armed base with same grape cluster and leaf decoration and background coloration, signed in cameo on shade "Daum Nancy" with Cross of Lorraine, signed in cameo "DN" with Cross of Lorraine on base, very good to excellent condition with single socket replaced and painted, shade 15" diameter, lamp 24" high. **$5,333**

James D. Julia, Inc.

Quadrefoil-shaped bowl with violets in various stages of bloom in purple with green stems and foliage set against purple and white frosted ground, signed "Daum Nancy" with Cross of Lorraine on side of bowl, very good to excellent condition, 3" high x 8" diameter. **$4,740**

James D. Julia, Inc.

Martelé vase decorated with amber cameo flowers, dark green stems and leaves, set against shaded brown to amber to clear background with hand-carved martelé finish, base signed on underside with gold engraved signature "Daum Nancy" with Cross of Lorraine, very good to excellent condition, 7 1/2" high. **$3,259**

James D. Julia, Inc.

French cameo tray of vitrified glass depicting grapes with leaves in purple, green, russet, and brown on molten ground of green, purple, and frost, scalloped border, signed "Daum Nancy" with Cross of Lorraine in cameo, very good to excellent condition, 8 1/4" diameter. **$948**

James D. Julia, Inc.

French cameo vase with fiery mottled background in yellow, orange, and red with green, floral, and foliage design, signed in cameo "Daum Nancy" with Cross of Lorraine, very good to excellent condition with rubbing at top of upper rim, 14 1/2" high. **$1,154**

James D. Julia, Inc.

French cameo and enameled vase depicting Aesop's Fables' "The Fox & The Crow" in black on frosted to green ground with gold gilt foliage and gold gilt to upper and lower rims, signed on underside "Daum Nancy" with Cross of Lorraine, minor wear to gold gilt, otherwise very good to excellent condition, 8" high. **$1,659**

James D. Julia, Inc.

▲ *Cameo and enamel vase, large bulbous form with mottled ground ranging from blue to sapphire to green, floral enamel decoration with blue blossoms and green foliage, martelé at foot, signed on underside with carved "Daum Nancy" with Cross of Lorraine, very good to excellent condition, 17 3/4" high.* **$5,036**

James D. Julia, Inc.

◄ *Covered jar with enameled thistle pattern in gold, red, and black set on frosted ground, signed "Daum Nancy" with Cross of Lorraine on bottom of jar, very good condition with some wear to gold mostly to underside of jar, 1 1/2" x 3 1/4".* **$1,481**

James D. Julia, Inc.

French cameo lamp, stylized flowers in Art Deco pattern in peach and chartreuse set against frosted ground, mushroom-shaped shade supported by three arms and base finished with single socket, signed on shade and base "Daum Nancy" with Cross of Lorraine, very good to excellent condition, shade 9" across with 3 3/4" fitter, lamp 18 1/2" high. **$5,333**

Mark Mussio, Humler & Nolan

Martelé vase with life-size flower heads and buds and thick lengthy stems alternating with ovate foliage over "hammered" surface, hand-carved flowers in orange with green leaves amid clouds, base bears signature of "Daum Nancy" engraved beneath, excellent original condition, 11 7/8" high. **$4,900**

James D. Julia, Inc.

Covered powder jar with violets, green leaves, and stems on frosted ground receding to mottled orange, lid marked "DN" with Cross of Lorraine, jar marked "Daum Nancy" with Cross of Lorraine, very good to excellent condition, 2" high x 3 1/2" diameter. **$2,370**

James D. Julia, Inc.

▲ *Cameo and enameled covered jar with thistle design against internally decorated background of pink shading to yellow and frost, thistle flowers enameled in blue, matching lid with large central thistle flower with blue enamel and radiating stylized leaves trimmed in gold gilt, signed on underside in gold "Daum Nancy" with Cross of Lorraine, very good to excellent condition, 2" high x 3" diameter.* **$2,252**

James D. Julia, Inc.

▲ *French cameo wheel-carved vase with olive green acid cutback leaves and stems against mottled yellow and cream background, long thorned rose stems lead to two wheel-carved roses and buds in pink, lower backside decorated with acid-cut butterfly, foot with three heart-shaped cameo panels with rose in center of each, engraved "Daum Nancy France" on side of foot, very good to excellent condition, 18" high.* **$6,518**

James D. Julia, Inc.

Cameo and enameled footed vase decorated with cameo violets enameled in purple with gilded outline of stylized leaves around foot, finished with three applied blue glass loop feet, signed on underside with engraved signature "Daum Nancy," very good to excellent condition, 4 5/8" diameter x 4" high. **$9,480**

James D. Julia, Inc.

Winter scene trefoil-shaped rose bowl decorated with deciduous snow-tipped trees and snow-covered ground with orange and yellow background representing sunset, signed "Daum Nancy" with Cross of Lorraine on underside of vase, very good to excellent condition, 2 3/4". **$2,963**

Depression Glass

By Ellen T. Schroy

Depression glass is the name of colorful glassware collectors generally associated with mass-produced glassware found in pink, yellow, crystal, or green in the years surrounding the Great Depression in America.

The housewives of the Depression-era were able to enjoy the wonderful colors offered in this new inexpensive glass dinnerware because they received pieces of their favorite patterns packed in boxes of soap, or as premiums given at "dish night" at the local movie theater. Merchandisers, such as Sears & Roebuck and F. W. Woolworth., enticed young brides with the colorful wares that they could afford even when economic times were harsh.

Because of advancements in glassware technology, Depression-era patterns were mass-produced and could be purchased for a fraction of what cut glass or lead crystal cost. As one manufacturer found a pattern that was pleasing to the buying public, other companies soon followed with their adaptation of a similar design. Patterns included several design motifs, such as florals, geometrics, and even patterns that looked back to Early American patterns like Sandwich glass.

Ellen T. Schroy

As America emerged from the Great Depression and life became more leisure-oriented again, new glassware patterns were created to reflect the new tastes of this generation. More elegant shapes and forms were designed, leading to what is sometimes called "Elegant Glass." Today's collectors often include these more elegant patterns when they talk about Depression-era glassware.

Depression-era glassware is one of the best-researched collecting areas available to the American marketplace. This is due in large part to the careful research of several people, including Hazel Marie Weatherman, Gene Florence, Barbara Mauzy, Carl F. Luckey, and Kent Washburn. Their books are held in high regard by researchers and collectors today.

Regarding values for Depression glass, rarity does not always equate to a high dollar amount. Some more readily found items command lofty prices because of high demand or other factors, not because they are necessarily rare. As collectors' tastes range from the simple patterns to the more elaborate patterns, so does the ability of their budget to invest in inexpensive patterns to multi-hundreds of dollars per form patterns.

The Depression-era glassware researchers have many accurate sources, including company records, catalogs, magazine advertisements, oral and written histories from sales staff, factory workers, etc.

American Pioneer, green ice bucket, **$80.**

For more information on Depression glass, see *Warman's Depression Glass Identification and Price Guide, 6th Edition,* or *Warman's Depression Glass Field Guide, 5th Edition,* both by Ellen T. Schroy.

ELLEN T. SCHROY, one of the leading experts in her field, is the author of *Warman's Depression Glass Identification and Price Guide* and *Warman's Depression Glass Field Guide.* Her books are the definitive references for Depression glass collectors.

Anniversary, pink wall pocket, **$90.**

Bowknot, green footed tumbler, **$25.**

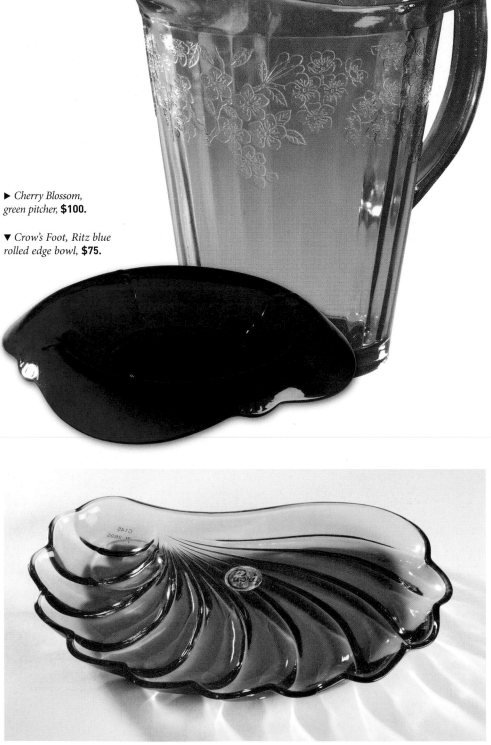

▶ *Cherry Blossom, green pitcher,* **$100.**

▼ *Crow's Foot, Ritz blue rolled edge bowl,* **$75.**

Capri, azure blue fan-shaped snack plate, **$10.**

Doric and Pansy, ultramarine salt and pepper shakers, **$650 pr.**

English Hobnail, pink bowl with hexagonal foot, two handles, **$75.**

Flower Garden With Butterflies, crystal powder jar, **$85.**

Fairfax, amber footed candy dish, **$45.**

Jubilee, yellow plate, 14" diameter, three legs, **$210.**

Madrid, amber pitcher, **$450.**

Lincoln Inn, red sherbet, **$20.**

Mayfair Open Rose, ice blue candy dish, **$200.**

Miss America, pink candy jar, **$165.**

Moondrops, cobalt blue butter dish, **$350.**

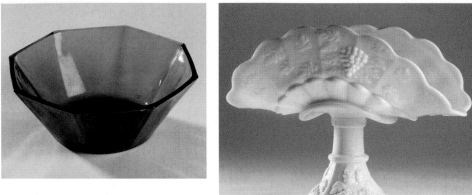

▲ *Moroccan Amethyst, round bowl,* **$18.**

▶ *Paneled Grape, white banana stand,* **$130.**

Peacock & Wild Rose, green elliptical vase, **$350.**

Pyramid, yellow ice bucket, **$225.**

▲ *Rock Crystal, amber vase,* **$80.**

◄ *Radiance, red decanter, No. 26 blank, silver overalay decoration,* **$225.**

Romanesque, green and amber candlesticks, **$13.75 ea.**

▲ *Royal Lace, cobalt blue creamer,* **$50**, *and sugar,* **$155.**

◄ *Sandwich, Hocking, desert gold cookie jar,* **$50.**

▼ *Sunflower, green trivet,* **$325.**

Tulip, blue, oblong bowl, **$100.**

Fenton Art Glass

T he Fenton Art Glass Co. was founded in 1905 by Frank L. Fenton and his brother, John W., in Martins Ferry, Ohio. They initially sold hand-painted glass made by other manufacturers, but it wasn't long before they decided to produce their own glass. The new Fenton factory in Williamstown, W.V., opened on Jan. 2, 1907. From that point on, the company expanded by developing unusual colors and continued to decorate glassware in innovative ways.

Two more brothers, James and Robert, joined the firm. But despite the company's initial success, John W. left to establish the Millersburg Glass Co. of Millersburg, Ohio, in 1909. The first months of the new operation were devoted to the production of crystal glass only. Later iridized glass was called "Radium Glass." After only two years, Millersburg filed for bankruptcy.

Fenton's iridescent glass had a metallic luster over a colored, pressed pattern, and was sold in dime stores. It was only after the sales of this glass decreased and it was sold in bulk as carnival prizes that it came to be known as carnival glass.

Fenton became the top producer of carnival glass, with more than 150 patterns. The quality of the glass, and its popularity with the public, enabled the new company to be profitable through the late 1920s. As interest in carnival subsided, Fenton moved on to stretch glass and opalescent patterns. A

◄ *Marigold carnival glass covered sugar and creamer in Leaf Tiers.* **$200**

▼ *Mongolian Green pieces, mid-1930s. From left: flared vase, 5 1/2" high.* **$70+**
"Flip" vase, 6 1/4" high. **$85+**
Cupped and lobed bowl, 4 1/4" high. **$55+**

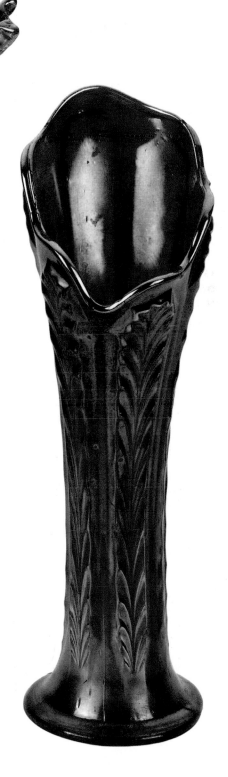

▲ *Sapphire carnival glass vase in Knotted Beads.* **$450**

▶ *Green carnival glass vase in Plume Panels, 12" high.* **$190**

line of colorful blown glass (called "off-hand" by Fenton) was also produced in the mid-1920s.

During the Great Depression, Fenton survived by producing functional colored glass tableware and other household items, including water sets, table sets, bowls, mugs, plates, perfume bottles and vases.

Restrictions on European imports during World War II ushered in the arrival of Fenton's opaque colored glass, and the lines of "Crest" pieces soon followed.

In the 1950s, production continued to diversify with a focus on milk glass, particularly in Hobnail patterns.

In the third quarter of Fenton's history, the company returned to themes that had proved popular to preceding generations, and began adding special lines, such as the Bicentennial series.

Innovations included the line of Colonial colors that debuted in 1963, including amber, blue, green, orange and ruby. Based on a special order for an Ohio museum, Fenton in 1969 revisited its early success with "Original Formula Carnival Glass." Fenton also started marking its glass in the molds for the first time.

The star of the 1970s was the yellow and blushing pink creation known as Burmese, which remains popular today. This was followed closely by a menagerie of animals, birds, and children.

In 1975, Robert Barber was hired by Fenton to begin an artist-in-residence program, producing a limited line of art-glass vases in a return to the off-hand, blown-glass creations of the mid-1920s.

Shopping at home via television was a recent phenomenon in the late 1980s when the "Birthstone Bears" became the first Fenton product to appear on

◄ *Amberina finger bowl in Hobnail, made for L.G. Wright Glass Co., 1970s, 3" high.* **$15+**

Tangerine stretch-glass dolphin-handle comport in Diamond Optic and pair of Tangerine stretch-glass candleholders in Diamond Optic, late 1920s. Comport, 5" high. **$100+** *Candleholders, 3" high.* **$100+ pair**

QVC (established in 1986 by Joseph Segel, founder of The Franklin Mint).

In the latter part of the century, Fenton established a website, www.fentonartglass.com, as a user-friendly online experience where collectors could learn about catalog and gift shop sales, upcoming events and the history of the company.

In August 2007, Fenton discontinued all but a few of its more popular lines, and in 2011 ceased production entirely.

For more information on Fenton Art Glass, see *Warman's Fenton Glass Identification and Price Guide,* 2nd edition, by Mark F. Moran.

◄ *Blue Opalescent covered jug and tumbler in Rib Optic with cobalt handles, part of a lemonade set that would have included six tumblers, 1920s; jug, 10" high; tumbler, 5" high.* **$700+ for complete set**

▲ *Celeste Blue bud vase, 1920s, 11 1/2" high.* **$55+**

◄ *Two candlesticks with Black (Ebony) bases, 1920s: blue, 8" high; Grecian Gold, 10" high.* **$120+ each**

Blue Overlay shakers in Floral Sprig, made for L.G. Wright, 1940s, 3 1/2" high. **$75+ pair**

▲ *Gold Crest hat basket with gold handle, mid-1940s, 6 1/2" high.* **$50+**

▲ *Aqua Crest large basket, 1940s, 14 1/2" wide, 13" high.* **$500+**

▲ *Blue Opalescent hanging shade in Coin Dot, early 1960s, 13" high.* **$250+**

▶ *Early milk glass flared vase in Basket Weave with Open Edge, circa 1933, 4" high.* **$35+**

◄ *French Opalescent petite epergne in Hobnail (horn sits in shallow ring rather than hole), with original label, early 1950s, 4 1/2" high.* **$90**

▲ *French Opalescent "pancake" lamp in Coin Spot, early 1930s, 10" high.* **$325+**

▲ *Green Transparent comport in Ribbed Holly Sprig, early 1920s, 4" high.* **$20+**

◄ *Honeysuckle Opalescent lamp in Coin Dot, late 1940s, 16" high.* **$250+**

Jade Green pieces in Wide Rib, early 1930s.
Left: creamer and sugar, each 3 3/4" high. **$80+ pair**
Center and right: jug with crimped ice lip, 7 1/2" high, and tumbler, 4 1/4" high. **$125+ pair**

◄ *Silver Jamestown flared, footed vase with irregular crimp, late 1950s, 13" high.* **$145+**

▼ *Ivy Overlay vase, 1950s, 8" high.* **$90+**

◄ *Two pairs of New World shakers in Cranberry Opalescent and Green Opalescent Rib Optic, 1950s, sold in pairs of two sizes, 4" high and 5" high.*
Cranberry. **$175 pair**
Green, rare. **$300 pair**

Amethyst carnival glass turned-up punch bowl in Wreath of Roses, base, six cups, Vintage interior. **$650**

▲ *Ruby jug and tumbler in Georgian, part of lemonade set that would have included six tumblers, 1930s; jug, 7 1/2" high; tumbler, 4" high.* **$150+ for complete set**

▲ *Ruby candle vase, 1930s, 7" high.* **$80+**

▲ *Topaz Opalescent creamer and sugar in Hobnail, early 1940s, each 2" high.* **$50 pair**

▶ *Wild Rose cased-glass covered jar, made for L.G. Wright, 1940s, 6 1/2" high.* **$325+**

Nymph Ruby console set including figurine in flower frog, flared petal bowl, ebony base and footed candleholders, early 1930s; nymph, frog, bowl and stand, 9" high; candleholders, 4 1/2" diameter. **$225+ for set**

Venetian Red flared and scalloped vase, mid-1920s, 5 1/2" high. **$75+**

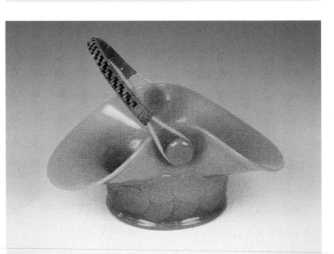

▶ *Chinese Yellow basket in Big Cookies, with rattan handle, 1930s, 11" wide.* **$200+**

◀ *Mongolian Green macaroon jar in Ribbon Band, mid-1930s, 6 1/4" high.* **$225+**

Ruby slipper ashtray in Daisy and Button, late 1930s, found in many other colors, 6" long. **$25**

Blue carnival glass water pitcher and six tumblers in Orange Tree Orchard. **$750**

▲ Peach Crest double-crimped vases with Charleton decoration, 1940s, each 8" high. **$100+ each**

▲ Silver Crest melon-form perfume bottle with Charleton decoration by Abels, Wasserberg of New York, mid-1940s, 7" high. **$85**

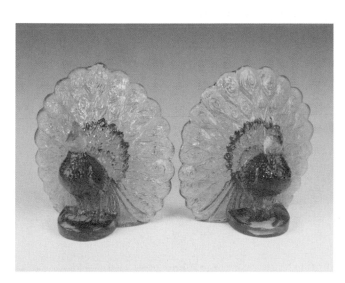

◄ Rose peacock-form bookends, 1935, each 6" high. **$500+ pair**

Lalique

René Jules Lalique was born on April 6,1860, in the village of Ay, in the Champagne region of France. In 1862, his family moved to the suburbs of Paris.

In 1872, Lalique began attending College Turgot where he began studying drawing with Justin-Marie Lequien. After the death of his father in 1876, Lalique began working as an apprentice to Louis Aucoc, who was a prominent jeweler and goldsmith in Paris.

Lalique moved to London in 1878 to continue his studies. He spent two years attending Sydenham College, developing his graphic design skills. He returned to Paris in 1880 and worked as an illustrator of jewelry, creating designs for Cartier, among others. In 1884, Lalique's drawings were displayed at the National Exhibition of Industrial Arts, organized at the Louvre.

At the end of 1885, Lalique took over Jules Destapes' jewelry workshop. Lalique's design began to incorporate translucent enamels, semiprecious stones, ivory, and hard stones. In 1889, at the Universal Exhibition in Paris, the jewelry firms of Vever and Boucheron included collaborative works by Lalique in their displays.

In the early 1890s, Lalique began to incorporate glass into his jewelry, and in 1893 he took part in a competition organized by the Union Centrale des Arts Decoratifs to design a drinking vessel. He won second prize.

Lalique opened his first Paris retail shop in 1905, near the perfume business of François Coty. Coty commissioned Lalique to design his perfume labels in 1907, and he also created his first perfume bottles for Coty.

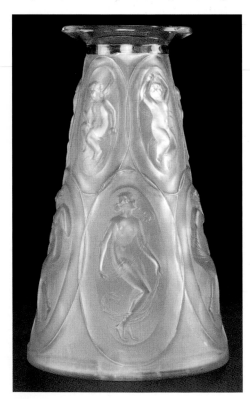

In the first decade of the 20th century, Lalique continued to experiment with glass manufacturing techniques, and mounted his first show devoted entirely to glass in 1911.

During World War I, Lalique's first factory was forced to close, but the construction of a new factory was soon begun in Wingen-sur-Moder, in the Alsace region. It was completed in 1921, and still produces Lalique crystal today.

In 1925, Lalique designed the first "car mascot" (hood ornament) for Citroën, the French automobile company. For the next six years, Lalique would design 29 models for companies such as Bentley, Bugatti, Delage, Hispano-Suiza, Rolls Royce, and Voisin.

Heritage Auctions

◄ *Camees vase, circa 1923, clear and frosted tapering vase with everted rim, marks: R. LALIQUE, FRANCE, N0 891 (engraved), 9 3/4" high.* **$1,188**

Lalique's second boutique opened in 1931, and this location continues to serve as the main Lalique showroom today.

René Lalique died on May 5, 1945, at the age of 85. His son, Marc, took over the business at that time, and when Marc died in 1977, his daughter, Marie-Claude Lalique Dedouvre, assumed control of the company. She sold her interest in the firm and retired in 1994.

For more information on Lalique, see *Warman's Lalique Identification and Price Guide* by Mark F. Moran.

Heritage Auctions

Frosted Charmilles vase, circa 1924, ovoid-form with frosted molded leaves, marks: R. LALIQUE (molded), 14" high. **$2,250**

James D. Julia, Inc.

Poissons pattern vase, allover pressed design of swimming fish, blue glass with iridescent finish, signed on underside in block letters R. Lalique, very good to excellent condition with hole drilled in bottom center, 9" high. **$4,860**

James D. Julia, Inc.

Amethyst glass buckle, three sections with stag in center and curling fern bows encircling stag and adorning two outside panels, housed in brass backing with matching fern-type design in repose, original satin-covered and lined box marked on interior of lid "Lalique Place Vendome 24 Paris," very good to excellent condition, 4 1/4" long. **$8,888**

Heritage Auctions

▶ *Opalescent Oleron vase, circa 1927, globular-form vase with body of frosted glass with molded fish, marks: R. Lalique, France, No 1010 (engraved), 5 1/2" high.* **$938**

Heritage Auctions

▲ *Perdrix plateau tray, post-1945, rectangular-form with frosted partridges against foliage to verso, marks: Lalique, France (engraved), 1" x 18" x 12".* **$2,500**

James D. Julia, Inc.

▲ *Ronces lamp base covered with pattern of intertwining thorny stems in green glass with gray patination, glass supported by stepped metal base with Greek key pattern, upper hardware has acanthus leaves and is finished with single socket, very good to excellent condition with wear to hardware commensurate with age, overall 21" high.* **$1,422**

Pook & Pook, Inc.

▲ *Twelve clear and frosted wine glasses in Angel pattern, 8" high.*
$1,007

Heritage Auctions

Opalescent Monnaie du Pape vase, circa 1914, ovoid vase with stylized foliate decoration, marks: R. LALIQUE (molded), 9" high.
$3,250

James D. Julia, Inc.

◄ *Druids pattern opalescent vase with raised opalescent berries surrounding top three quarters of vase, impressed stems covering background, signed on underside with raised block letters R. Lalique and etched "France," very good to excellent condition, 7" high.* **$1,422**

Heritage Auctions

▼ *Perruches vase, circa 1919, clear glass with green patina, marks: R. LALIQUE (molded), 10 1/2" high.* **$6,875**

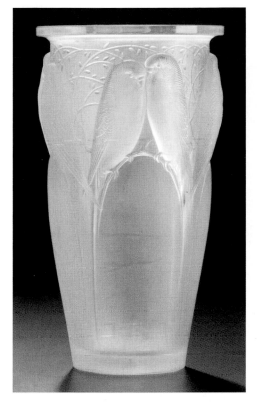

Opalescent Suzanne statuette, circa 1925, frosted glass modeled as female nude holding drapery with outstretched arms, marks: R. LALIQUE (molded), 9" high x 7 1/4" wide. **$10,000**

Opalescent Ceylan vase, circa 1924, baluster-form vase with blue patina, marks: R. LALIQUE, FRANCE (stenciled), 9" high. **$8,125**

Vitesse automobile mascot, circa 1928, modeled as female nude in forward motion with arms raised, marks: R. LALIQUE, FRANCE (molded), 7 1/4" high. **$8,750**

▲ *Six figurines vase, circa 1912, clear with frosted figural panels, marks: R. Lalique (engraved), 8" high x 5 1/2" diameter.* **$2,375**

Pook & Pook, Inc.

Luxembourg frosted glass bowl, signed on base, 8 1/4" high. **$2,252**

Heritage Auctions

Clear and frosted Epis vase, circa 1931, tapering vase with vertical fluting, marks: R. LALIQUE, FRANCE (stenciled), 6 1/2" high. **$688**

Mark Mussio, Humler & Nolan

Nonnettes low bowl with three pairs of opalescent lovebirds beneath, mold marked R. Lalique France on bottom, small factory bubbles, otherwise excellent condition, 2 1/4" x 8 1/2" diameter. **$425**

Mark Mussio,
Humler & Nolan

▲ *Opalescent Avallon vase with birds
perched in branches feasting on cherries,
engraved R. Lalique France in block letters
along with shape number 986 on bottom,
excellent condition, 5 3/4" high.* **$1,500**

Mark Mussio, Humler & Nolan

▲ *Escargot vase, opalescent centrifugal
pattern casting champagne color and
overall pale tint of blue gray, engraved
R. Lalique France in script with
number 937 beneath base, tiny nick to
one side and half-inch chip on end of
oval base, 8 1/4" high.* **$2,000**

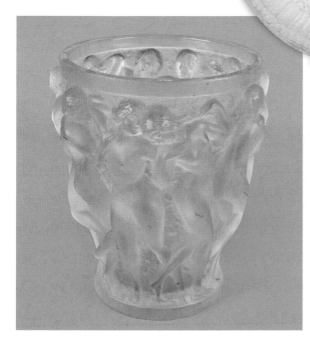

Pook & Pook, Inc.

*Bacchantes clear and frosted glass vase,
signed on base, 9 1/2" high.* **$2,252**

Elite Decorative Arts

Floral Marguerites bowl, script signature to bottom, 2 1/4" high x 13 1/2" diameter. Provenance: From the estate of Count and Countess Claes-Eric de Lewenhaupt of Sweden. **$605**

Elite Decorative Arts

Sculpture of two satin finish doves sharing a resting place, titled Ariane, etched signature to side of base, 8 1/4" high, total weight 2944 grams. Provenance: From the estate of Count and Countess Claes-Eric de Lewenhaupt of Sweden. **$424**

Elite Decorative Arts

*Relief frosted crystal Femmes Antiques, 20th century, etched "FRANK C. T. 1895 * 11-6 1965," script mark to bottom, 9 5/8" high, total weight 1903 grams. Provenance: From the estate of Count and Countess Claes-Eric de Lewenhaupt of Sweden.* **$1,331**

Quezal

T he Quezal Art Glass Decorating Co., named for the quetzal – a bird with brilliantly colored feathers found in tropical regions of the Americas – was organized in 1901 in Brooklyn, New York, by Martin Bach and Thomas Johnson, two disgruntled Tiffany workers. They soon hired Percy Britton and William Wiedebine, two more former Tiffany employees.

The first products, unmarked, were exact Tiffany imitations. Quezal pieces differ from Tiffany pieces in that they are more defined and the decorations are more visible and brighter. No new techniques were developed by Quezal.

Johnson left in 1905. T. Conrad Vahlsing, Bach's son-in-law, joined the firm in 1918, but left with Paul Frank in 1920 to form Lustre Art Glass Co., which in turn copied Quezal pieces. Martin Bach died in 1924, and by 1925, Quezal had ceased operations.

The "Quezal" trademark was first used in 1902 and placed on the base of vases and bowls and the rims of shades. The acid-etched or engraved letters vary in size and may be found in amber, black, or gold. A printed label that includes an illustration of a quetzal was used briefly in 1907.

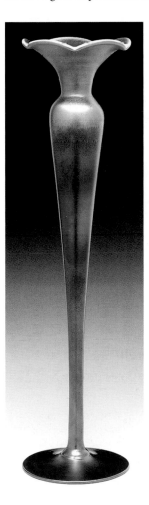

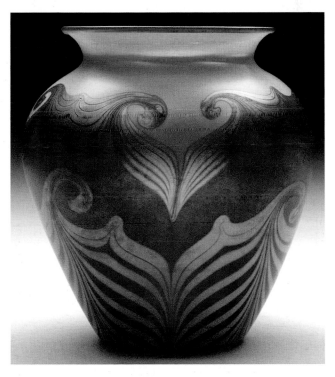

James D. Julia, Inc.

◄ *Rare lily vase decorated in blue with iridescent finish in green, yellow, and purple on exterior, gold interior, signed Quezal on underside, very good to excellent condition, 11" high.* **$1,580**

James D. Julia, Inc.

▲ *Bulbous vase with flared lip in green with platinum hooked feather design trimmed in gold, finished at top in ivory iridescent ground, signed Quezal, very good to excellent condition with wear on bottom consistent with age, 6" high.* **$1,541**

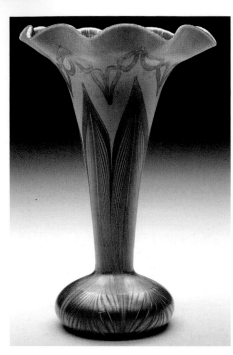

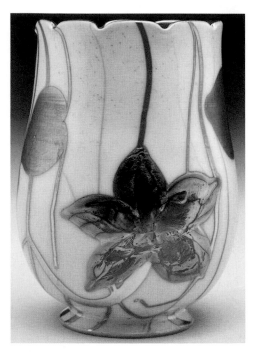

James D. Julia, Inc.

Ruffled trumpet vase with bulbous bottom, decorated with green pulled feathers with gold trim and rare ribbon effect at top, interior has gold iridescent finish and is stretched, unsigned, very good to excellent condition, 9" high. **$972**

James D. Julia, Inc.

Green tulip shade decorated with three large iridescent purple flowers and iridescent gold hearts and vines on opal ground, gold lined, signed with early engraved signature, one of four matching shades, very good to excellent condition, 5" high with 2 1/4" fitter. **$3,259**

James D. Julia, Inc.

Large shade with ivory ground, decorated with gold pulled feather design with green border, interior finished with ivory opalescent ground, signed Quezal on fitter rim, very good to excellent condition, 18" diameter x 3 1/4" fitter. **$1,718**

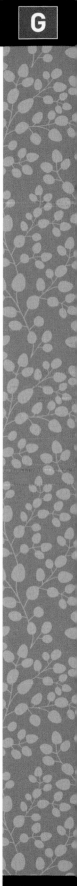

James D. Julia, Inc.

▲ Large shade with hooked feather decoration in iridescent gold and blue over cream background, interior white lining, unsigned, several chips to fitter edge, otherwise very good to excellent condition, 4 1/4" fitter x 11 3/4" high. **$1,659**

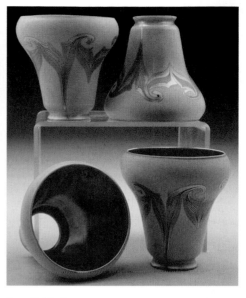

James D. Julia, Inc.

▲ Four bell-shaped shades decorated with blue opposing hooked feathers with gold trim on ivory ground, each signed Quezal in fitter, very good to excellent condition, one has chip at fitter, all with minute roughness at fitter, each shade: 2 1/4" fitter x 5 1/4" high. **$1,422**

James D. Julia, Inc.

▶ Trumpet vase decorated on exterior with full green pulled feather pattern with gold feather pattern at stretched ruffled top, signed Quezal V, very good to excellent condition with wear to interior gold, 7" high. **$1,541**

James D. Julia, Inc.

◄ *Large form, flared rim gold vase with iridescent finish in purple, green and blue, signed Quezal on underside, very good to excellent condition, 10" high.* **$326**

James D. Julia, Inc.

▶ *Bulbous form vase with circular foot and flared rim in green, decorated with hooked feather and fishnet pattern in platinum with gold pulled feather design at neck, signed Quezal E599, very good to excellent condition, 8 1/4" high.* **$6,814**

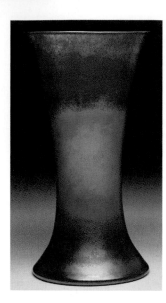

James D. Julia, Inc.

▶ *Jack-in-the-pulpit vase, diminutive size with stretched gold face, decorated with green pulled feather design, back of face is ivory color with green pulled feather design and platinum iridescent border, signed Quezal 875 on underside, very good to excellent condition, 9" high.* **$4,148**

James D. Julia, Inc.

▼ *Large decorated trumpet-shaped shade, deeply scalloped with purple hooked feather design with green border and platinum iridescent finish, signed Quezal, very good to excellent condition, 2 1/4" fitter x 6 3/4" high.* **$1,778**

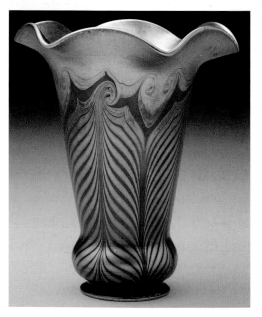

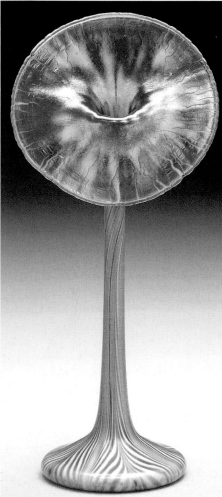

Tiffany Glass

Tiffany & Co. was founded by Charles Lewis Tiffany (1812-1902) and Teddy Young in New York City in 1837 as a "stationery and fancy goods emporium." The store initially sold a wide variety of stationery items, and operated as Tiffany, Young and Ellis in lower Manhattan. The name was shortened to Tiffany & Co. in 1853, and the firm's emphasis on jewelry was established.

The first Tiffany catalog, known as the "Blue Book," was published in 1845. It is still being published today.

In 1862 Tiffany & Co. supplied the Union Army with swords, flags and surgical implements.

Charles' son, Louis Comfort Tiffany (1848-1933) was an American artist and designer who worked in the decorative arts and is best known for his work in stained glass. Louis established Tiffany Glass Co. in 1885, and in 1902 it became known as the Tiffany Studios. America's outstanding glass designer of the Art Nouveau period produced glass from the last quarter of the 19th century until the early 1930s. Tiffany revived early techniques and devised many new ones.

More information on Tiffany is located in the "Lighting" section.

Michaan's Auctions

▶ *Tiffany Studios turtle back tile clock, iridescent blue, green, and purple turtle back tiles set in bronze, case unsigned, enamel dial signed Tiffany & Co., 13" high.* **$76,700**

James D. Julia, Inc.

◀ *Pine needle picture frame, large rectangular-shaped frame decorated with bronze pattern of pine needles backed by green glass with blue striations, frame finished with two rows of bronze beading, bronze work finished with brownish red patina finish with touches of green, signed Tiffany Studios New York 916, very good to excellent condition, 12" x 14 1/2" outside, 8" x 10" inside.* **$4,313**

Michaan's Auctions

▲ *Tiffany Studios Alamander chandelier depicting blossoms against background of mottled confetti glass, shade impressed Tiffany Studios, New York, 28 1/4" diameter.* **$212,400**

Michaan's Auctions

▼ *Tiffany Studios inkstand, lobed vessel decorated with intaglio-carved pink and green peonies, mount and cover with swagged bands of green glass beads intersected by cabochon carnelians with Mexican fire opal on top, cameo Favrile glass with jeweled and enameled silver cover and mount, 1907, glass inscribed L.C. Tiffany-Favrile T4820, 3 1/2" high, 5 1/2" diameter.* **$59,000**

Michaan's Auctions

▲ *Tiffany Studios Apple Blossom window depicting apple tree in full bloom with limbs covered in flowers, cloud-streaked sky, and body of water, panel with metal tag impressed Tiffany Studios New York, circa 1915, 50" high x 20 1/2" wide, 60 1/4" high x 30 1/2" wide with museum frame.* **$118,000**

Michaan's Auctions

◀ *Tiffany Studios scent bottle-on-stand, inscribed mark Ex. identifies piece as one displayed at an international exhibition, glass with plique-a-jour and champleve enameled gold mount, collar and cover impressed TIFFANY & CO. and 18K (twice), bottle inscribed L.C.T 9270, stand inscribed Louis C. Tiffany Ex., impressed TIFFANY & CO., circa 1900-1905, Art Nouveau foliate mount suggests it was designed specifically for display in Paris, 7 1/16" high on stand, bottle 6 15/16" long.* **$70,800**

Michaan's Auctions

▲ *Tiffany Studios pair of claw foot andirons, gilt-bronze surmounted with Favrile glass turtleback tiles, unsigned, 23 1/2" high.* **$82,600**

Michaan's Auctions

◀ *Tiffany Studios Aquamarine vase, inscribed L.C. Tiffany-Favrile 5202G, 9 7/8" high.* **$65,000**

Introduced around 1911-1912, Aquamarine glass was the last major technique publicized by Tiffany Studios. Compositions of aquatic plants and other marine life were fashioned out of small colored glass canes that the glassblower pulled into required forms with a metal hook not unlike a crochet needle. At various stages in the process, the composition was encased in layers of clear or tinted glass gathered on a blow pipe from a crystal pot. The result provided the viewer with the impression of looking into a fishbowl or pond; better examples provided a sense of motion within the water. The effect is illusionary as the decoration is far smaller than it appears, the thick outer mass of glass acting as a magnifying lens. In addition to flora, aquamarine glassware includes fish, algae, sea anemones, jellyfish and mollusks, in many instances presented within a complete ecological environment.

Michaan's Auctions

▶ *Tiffany Studios Rambling Rose table lamp mounted on rare bronze base that features green Favrile glass blown into openings in bronze from just above lower section up to light cluster, shade unsigned, base impressed TIFFANY STUDIOS NEW YORK 25873, with Tiffany Glass and Decorating Co. logo, 25" high, shade 16" diameter.* **$141,600**

Michaan's Auctions

Tiffany Studios flowerform vase, inscribed o2417, 14 1/8" high. **$64,900**

Michaan's Auctions

◀ *Tiffany Studios reactive glass paperweight vase, inscribed 18 A-Coll. L.C.Tiffany-Favrile, 5 3/8" high.* **$64,900**

"Reactive" is a term broadly used to describe the change in color that occurs both when a single color of glass is refired and when differently colored batches of glass are fired together; in both instances, the chemical reaction that takes place can generate dramatic new chromatic effects. Whereas such changes can be anticipated and therefore controlled to a certain degree, the firing temperature and mix of metallic oxides often provide "accidents" that in many instances result in startling optical effects that may be hard to replicate. Many of these happy mistakes were routinely set aside for analysis and further experimentation. Some, as in this example, were reserved for Tiffany's own collection.

▼ *Tiffany Studios cameo flowerform vase, inscribed L.C.T. W6778, 14 1/8" high.* **$64,900**

▲ *Tiffany Studios Magnolia landscape window depicting flowering magnolia tree in foreground of landscape with a river meandering down from a mountainous pass to a lake, setting sun behind mountains sending rays of light up into the sky, effect achieved by selective acid etching on rear layers of glass, unsigned, circa 1912, 44 1/4" high x 30 1/4" wide, 55" high x 40" wide with frame.* **$177,000**

▶ *Tiffany Studios flowerform vase with broad, undulating mouth, 14 3/8" high.* **$236,000**

Michaan's Auctions

◄ *Tiffany Studios Exposition scent bottle-on-stand, glass, gold mount set with amethysts, stand inscribed Paris Exposition 1900 Louis C. Tiffany 14K, and impressed TIFFANY & CO 8415, circa 1900, 7 1/4" high.* **$76,700**

James D. Julia, Inc.

▲ *Blotter ends decorated in nautical theme showing seahorses, shells, and sailing vessels all on gold doré finish, signed Tiffany Studios New York 1841, very good to excellent condition, 2 1/4" x 12".* **$863**

Michaan's Auctions

▶ *Tiffany Studios millefiore paperweight vase, several superimposed layers of decoration within a thick outer wall of glass, inscribed Louis C. Tiffany P2386, 11 3/4" high.* **$76,700**

The millefiore technique (literally, "thousand flowers") has existed since at least the second century B.C. In it, cross-sections of the desired motif, usually a flowerhead, are sliced off a long glass rod that carries the pattern through its entire length. These tiny glass segments are applied to the object at hand, which is then reheated to fuse the millefiori into its surface.

Michaan's Auctions

◄ *Tiffany Studios Daffodil table lamp, Favrile glass blown through bronze, shade of confetti glass as background to blossoms, impressed TIFFANY STUDIOS NEW YORK 1449, base is bronze with blown glass, impressed TIFFANY STUDIOS NEW YORK and 28621, with Tiffany Glass and Decorating Co. logo, 21" high, shade 16" diameter.* **$129,800**

James D. Julia, Inc.

▼ *Handkerchief box, etched metal design of pine needles atop caramel striated glass, box finished with double rows of beading and four bun feet, signed Tiffany Studios New York 824, very good to excellent condition with minor wear, 2 1/2" high x 8" wide x 8" long.* **$1,208**

Halloween Collectibles

By Mark B. Ledenbach

As a collector of vintage Halloween memorabilia for 25 years, I find the evolution of the imagery for this fun hobby endlessly fascinating.

Halloween became quite the event in the first decade of the last century, mainly through the exchange of festive postcards. Those cards, with the art drawn by such luminaries as Winsch and Clapsaddle, typically accented the agricultural roots of Halloween, then branched out into the more whimsical realm of witches, black cats, blazing jack-o'-lanterns, bats, cavorting devils and the like.

Mark B. Ledenbach

As Halloween became an event to be celebrated with parties – primarily given by and for adults through the 1920s – the imagery began to change. From about 1909 through 1913, manufacturers of party supplies like Dennison of Framingham, Massachusetts, simply offered an array of seasonally decorated crepe papers from which the host would fashion decorations and party favors. The imagery from this period tends to be more subdued and somewhat pedestrian. However, as the manufacturers became more entranced by the business possibilities of offering finished goods for sale, the lines of available products exploded into a dazzling array of seals, silhouettes, tally cards, place cards, invitations, diecuts, aprons, and costumes. To keep up with the seemingly endless kinds of products to be sold to adults, the imagery became more complex, scary, and perhaps sometimes chilling.

The most innovative purveyor of such complex Halloween imagery was the Beistle Co. of Shippensburg, Pennsylvania. They provided nut cups, die-cuts, lanterns, games, table decorations, and other small paper decorations that are especially coveted by collectors today. The firm's design sensibilities are easily recognized today for their ingenuity in extending Halloween imagery beyond what was offered previously by other manufacturers. Examples of this would be Beistle's 1930-1931 identical dual-sided lantern and 1923 fairy clock.

Imagery through about 1940 tends to be more adult-focused. However, as trick-or-treating become more of an entrenched feature of Halloween celebrations, the target market segment for parties ceased to be adults and moved inexorably toward juveniles. The impact on Halloween imagery was profound. Out were the more complex and scary images of devils, witches and black cats, to be replaced by less threatening, less interesting, and less memorable imagery of apple-cheeked witches, grinning, plump devils and friendly black cats. The air of implied menace, so evocative of early Halloween imagery, had been replaced by a sugar-high-inducing cuteness that any retailer could carry without censure.

MARK B. LEDENBACH is the author of *Vintage Halloween Collectibles: An Identification and Price Guide,* 2nd edition published by Krause Publications. His website is www.HalloweenCollector.com.

Through the present day, cuteness has been dethroned by goriness. One can shop at any mass retailer and find diecuts of skulls with worms wriggling through eye sockets, costumes complete with wretch-inducing masks trumpeting various deformities or tortures, and other horrors meant to shock and perhaps dismay. The sense of subtlety and artistry so apparent in the majority of decorations made prior to 1940 is nowhere in evidence today.

As with many hobbies, certain sub-categories have done better than others. Hotter categories are embossed German die-cuts; U.S. die-cuts, especially those made by Dennison and Gibson; Beistle paper products; boxed seals, silhouettes and cut-outs from Dennison; tin tambourines; and German candy containers and figurals as well as Halloween-themed games. Colder categories include tin noisemakers, U.S. pulp, and hard plastic.

Collecting vintage Halloween memorabilia became a red-hot hobby complete with sky-rocketing prices and always scarce supply in the early 1990s. Even with all of the economic cycles since and the rise of more efficient supply channels like eBay, prices continue to climb for nearly all genres of near-mint condition or better items. For example, embossed German die-cuts sold then for between $30-$75. Today many examples bring $100-$400, with the rarest items like a winged bat devil and a large fireplace screen topping $2,250. Even ephemera like a 1932 Beistle grandfather clock mechanical invitation bring astronomical prices. One recently sold for over $1,700.

As referenced above, not all categories have benefited. The garish hard plastic made in such huge quantities during the 1950s used to command head-scratching prices of $40-$1,000. Today prices have decreased to about half of the market's height given more collector awareness of the ubiquity of these items.

Unlike Christmas items, Halloween decorations were purchased with the intention of using them once, then tossing them out after the event with no sentiment. This is the primary supply driver behind the rapid escalation of prices today. The primary demand driver is the large number of new collectors entering this fun field as each Halloween season comes around.

As with all hobbies wherein the values have risen tremendously, reproductions and fantasy pieces are a problem. Consult other collectors and buy the right references before plunking down cash. Get in the habit of asking a lot of questions. Don't be shy!

Jack-o'-lantern with raccoon eyes, Germany, 1920s, 7 1/4" x 7", heavily embossed. **$165**

Fairy honeycomb band hat, United States, Beistle, printed name, 1923, 6" x 11 1/2" long. **$250**

"Sacred Be Ye Fire O Halloween," mechanical, United States, 1910-1917, non-embossed with easel for use as table decoration, 9 3/4" x 7 1/4". **$475**

Fan with differing imagery on each side and black honeycomb center, United States, Beistle, no mark, pre-1920s, 8 1/2" x 2 3/4". **$425**

Black cat centerpiece, United States, Gibson Art Co., Cincinnati, Ohio, late 1920s, each side is different, detached sides are often mistakenly sold as individual die-cuts, 6 1/4" x 3 3/4". **$200**

Box of six assorted face-on-leaf seals, United States, Dennison, first appeared in its 1924 Bogie Book, 3 3/4" x 2 1/4", sold with stock number H684. **$250**

Composition witch candy container, bottom plug, Germany, early 1920s, 4 3/4" high. **$300**

Place card with flip-out base, United States, Beistle, diamond mark, 1930-1931, marked with patent number 1616568, lightly embossed (unusual for Beistle place card), 3" x 4" x 4". **$100**

Nut cup, Gibson Art Co., Cincinnati, Ohio, 1920s, 1 3/4" x 1 3/4" x 3". **$35**

Winged ghost table decoration, United States, Beistle, no mark, 1925-1931, 11 1/2" x 20". **$375**

Softcover Bogie Book, United States, Dennison, 1921, 7 3/4" x 5 1/4", 32 numbered pages. **$200**

Full-bodied cardboard witch centerpiece, United States, Beistle, no mark, mid-1950s, 24" x 13 1/2" wide. This superbly detailed item was made for no more than two seasons. Because of a flawed design, the piece would generally bend and then rip at the waist. Therefore, these typically have tape or some other sort of repair at this juncture. The art is interesting in that the witch is anything but a crone, whereas her cat looks quite fearsome. This is a definite transitional piece away from the more challenging earlier designs toward the typically more banal ones seen later. **$275**

Green-faced broomed witch, United States, Beistle, no mark, late 1950s, 21" x 9", non-embossed.
$300

Porcelain children's lidded teapot, Germany, 1913-1932, 4" x 5". **$600**

Bux – The Hallowe'en Owl, United States, Beistle, HE Luhrs mark, 1940s, patent number 1593646, 9" x 14". **$165**

Tin clicker, Germany,
1930s, 3 3/4" high. **$65**

Candle table decoration,
United States, Dennison,
late 1920s, note cat face
in the flames, candle's
expression, cats along
base skew to give effect of
rounded base, 6 1/4" x
5 3/4" wide. **$185**

Box of 25 boy and spook seals, #H636, United States,
Dennison, 1922-1924, 1 1/2" x 2 1/2. **$140**

Place card with running mice along bottom
border, United States, Whitney Co. of Worcester,
Massachusetts, 1920s, 4 1/4" x 3". **$85**

Hallowe'en Decorations box for German die-cuts,
Germany, 1920s, 8 3/4" x 1 3/4" x 9 1/2". **$350**

Handbags

By Noah Fleisher

The market for vintage, high-end luxury accessories is one of the hottest markets in the world right now and, even more important, it's brought an entirely new and non-traditional clientele to the world of high-end collectible auctions.

Matt Rubinger, who heads the Luxury Accessories category for Heritage Auctions, is the foremost authority on handbags, has been in the business since he was 13 years old, and is largely responsible for driving this upswing in attention to the market. He has been profiled by the Associated Press, *The Wall Street Journal* and *The Washington Post,* among others.

"Collectibles and collecting have traditionally been male-dominated pursuits," Rubinger said. "No one in the business was looking at these very high quality pieces of enduring *haute couture* as having value beyond being arm candy. This assumption effectively dismissed half the potential population of collectors, that is, women."

Via his work with innovative websites like Portero.com and Moda Operandi, and for the last three years running his department at Heritage, Rubinger has more than succeeded in establishing his category's brand. He's focused the attention of all collectors, men and women, on the category as an important and viable investment-grade tangible and drawn international mainstream

Noah Fleisher

attention at the same time via huge sales, including the highest price ever paid at auction for a handbag, in December 2011, when he sold an Hermès Diamond Birkin for more than $203,000.

"That was the moment when the luxury accessories market really matured," said Rubinger. "A price realized like that legitimized the pursuit in the broader public imagination. Suddenly, what savvy women have known for years – that a great handbag is an investment as well as a collectible and a fashion statement – was recognized by the

Heritage Auctions

◀ *Mark Cross 1970s shiny black alligator four-piece trunk set with beige leather and red velvet interior, pristine condition; piece 1, 30" wide x 18" high x 9" deep; piece 2, 26" wide x 16" high x 8" deep; piece 3, 20" wide x 14" high x 8" deep; piece 4, 13" wide x 9" high x 8.5" deep.* **$28,680**

NOAH FLEISHER received his Bachelor of Fine Arts degree from New York University and brings more than a decade of newspaper, magazine, book, antiques and art experience to his position as Public Relations Director of Heritage Auctions, one of the country's foremost auction houses. He is the former editor of *Antique Trader, New England Antiques Journal* and *Northeast Antiques Journal,* is the author of *Warman's Modern Furniture,* and has been a longtime contributor to *Warman's Antiques and Collectibles.*

Heritage Auctions

▲ *Valentino burgundy velvet, pearl and crystal evening bag, excellent condition, 9.5" wide x 5" high x 1" deep.* **$400**

Heritage Auctions

▲ *Prada brown leather bag with top handles and padlock, very good condition, 14" wide x 10" high x 5" deep.* **$325**

Heritage Auctions

▶ *Vintage Bottega Veneta blue and red medium woven leather hobo bag, excellent condition, 18" wide x 12" high.* **$688**

Heritage Auctions

▼ *Gucci beige leather Monogram shoulder bag with gold heart detail, excellent condition, 9" wide x 5" high x 1.5" deep.* **$325**

rest of the collecting world, the men, many of whom were married to these women. Now, when we have an auction and a collector is considering their options on a $50,000 handbag, their husband is right there with them discussing the possibility."

It's an exciting thing to see a market being born and to be conscious of the fact that you are seeing, right in front of you, the birth of a powerhouse. For Rubinger, however, it's not a surprise. He just does the math and looks at the market objectively.

"You can walk into a high-end retail outlet and buy a bag for a few hundred or a few thousand dollars and it loses a good deal of value the minute you walk out of the store, and it will never get that value back," he said. "However, if you spend, say, $20,000 on an Hermès bag, or $5,000 on a Louis Vuitton, that bag will hold its value five, 10 and 20 years later and, in many cases, will have risen and will return a significant amount on that initial investment."

Handbags are not graded like coins, cards or comics – though do not be surprised if this happens in the future – though there are criteria they are judged on:

Pristine – The piece is in perfect condition and appears to have never been used. It is in as-new condition.

Excellent – The piece is in nearly perfect condition, with only very slight signs of use.

Very good – The piece has been used but well cared for with no major flaws or wear.

Good – The piece has been used and shows wear. It is in as-is condition.

Fair – The piece exhibits condition issues that may or may not be repairable, but is still wearable as purchased.

Heritage Auctions

▶ *Gucci solid 18k yellow gold and diamond minaudiere evening bag with interchangeable multicolor tassels, excellent condition, 6.5" wide x 4" high x 2" deep, designed by Aldo Gucci, son of the founder of Gucci, and contains 577 grams of 18k gold (not including mirror) and 12.84 cts of diamonds.* **$40,000**

Heritage Auctions

▶ *Chanel shiny black crocodile Medium Double Flap Bag with gold hardware, very good condition, 9" wide x 5.5" high x 2" deep.* **$4,688**

Now, unless you are a veteran buyer in the market and a true aficionado of the form, these criteria will not mean a tremendous amount to the untrained eye. They are, nonetheless, the standard by which the objects are measured, and the main reason that neophyte handbag collectors needs to educate themselves, studying auction records and sales on business websites and, perhaps most importantly, consulting experts like Rubinger.

"It's not difficult to look at a handbag and assess its beauty and style relative to its intended purpose," said Rubinger, "but unless you know what is good, and what is not good, it's very easy to overpay for something that does not warrant it."

As with anything of great value, there's a significant market in fakes. Handbags are no exception, as evidenced by the sheer number of fake Hermès, Chanel, and Vuitton bags you buy on the street in Chinatown. Move up the ladder of fakes a rung or two and you have very well-crafted fakes that can be sold in stores, online or even by fly-by-night "dealers" who will not be there the next time you call.

Experts like Rubinger have the institutional knowledge and the expertise writ hard in their DNA and can spot a fake across the room. If you are interested in the market and want to get into it, then it is imperative that you do your homework and talk to an expert, like Rubinger, who will be more than happy to share his expertise with you, regardless of your price point.

"This is an emerging market and there are tremendous opportunities for collectors of all levels and all ages," said Rubinger. "Know what you want, know where to find it, and go after the very best examples you can afford, whether it's $100 or $100,000."

The good news is that there are great examples available in those price ranges, and everywhere in between. All they are waiting for are the right stylish collectors.

Heritage Auctions

◄ *Hermès Extraordinary Collection 35cm diamond, Shiny Black porosus crocodile Birkin Bag with 18k white gold hardware, excellent condition, 14" wide x 10" high x 7" deep.* **$122,500**

Heritage Auctions

Hermès 35cm Shiny Gris Elephant porosus crocodile Birkin Bag with palladium hardware, pristine condition, 14" wide x 10" high x 7" deep. **$86,500**

Heritage Auctions

Hermès rare 30cm Shiny Violet porosus crocodile Birkin Bag with palladium hardware, excellent to pristine condition, 12" wide x 8" high x 6" deep. **$74,500**

Heritage Auctions

Hermès rare 35cm Matte Pink 5P alligator Birkin Bag with palladium hardware, pristine condition, 14" wide x 10" high x 7" deep. This bag is one of the rarest and most sought-after bags in the world; produced once or twice per year, this color is known as bubblegum pink. **$104,500**

Heritage Auctions

Hermès 35cm Matte Brighton Blue porosus crocodile Birkin Bag with palladium hardware, pristine condition, 14" wide x 11" high x 7" deep. **$113,525**

Heritage Auctions

Hermès 42cm Bordeaux Shiny porosus crocodile JPG Birkin Bag with palladium hardware, excellent condition, 16.5" wide x 8" high x 8" deep. **$43,750**

Heritage Auctions

Hermès 30cm Shiny Graphite nilo crocodile Birkin Bag with palladium hardware, excellent condition, 12" wide x 8.5" high x 6" deep. **$71,700**

Heritage Auctions

▲ *Hermès 40cm Matte Bleu de Malte alligator Birkin Bag with palladium hardware, 16" x 11" x 8", pristine condition.* **$71,700**

Heritage Auctions

▶ *Hermès Extraordinary Collection 18cm Diamond Blue Jean porosus crocodile double-gusset Constance Bag with 18k white gold hardware, excellent condition, 7" wide x 6" high x 2" deep.* **$50,000**

Heritage Auctions

Hermès 35cm Shiny Braise Red porosus crocodile Birkin Bag with palladium hardware, pristine condition, 14" wide x 10" high x 7" deep. **$95,600**

Heritage Auctions

Hermès rare 30cm Matte White Himalayan crocodile Birkin Bag with palladium hardware, pristine condition, 12" wide x 8" high x 6" deep. **$89,500**

Heritage Auctions

Hermès rare 35cm shearling Kelly Bag with palladium hardware, pristine condition, 14" wide x 9.5" high x 5" deep, one of the most sought-after by experienced Hermès collectors. **$32,500**

Heritage Auctions

Hermès limited edition 36cm Barenia leather and wicker picnic Kelly Bag with palladium hardware, pristine condition, 14" wide x 10" high x 5" deep. **$25,000**

Hermès 35cm Blue Roi Ostrich Birkin Bag with palladium hardware, excellent condition, 14" wide x 10" high x 7" deep. **$30,000**

Hermès limited edition Bleu Sapphir Gulliver leather Quelle Idole Mini Kelly Bag, very good to excellent condition, 6" wide x 5" high x 3" deep. **$10,313**

▼ *Hermès Shiny Indigo nilo crocodile Kelly Cut Clutch with palladium hardware, very good condition, 12" wide x 5" high x 1" deep.* **$16,250**

▲ *Hermès Exceptional Collection Shiny Rouge H porosus crocodile 30cm Birkin Bag with solid 18k white gold and diamond hardware, pristine condition, 12" wide x 8" high x 6" deep.* **$203,150**

▶ *Hermès 35cm Shiny Rouge H porosus crocodile Birkin Bag with palladium hardware, pristine condition, 14" wide x 10" high x 7" deep.* **$59,000**

Heritage Auctions

◄ *Hermès 35cm Rouge Vif Buffalo Leather Trim Bag with gold hardware, very good to excellent condition, 13.5" wide x 10" high x 3" deep.* **$2,000**

Heritage Auctions

▼ *Hermès natural Barenia leather Evelyne Messenger Bag, very good to good condition, 12.75" wide x 12.5" high x 3" deep.* **$1,313**

Heritage Auctions

▲ *Hermès one-of-a-kind silk Runway bag with gold hardware, excellent condition, 7" wide x 8" high x 4" deep, handcrafted.* **$8,125**

Heritage Auctions

◄ *Chanel limited edition matte black crocodile Paris-Biarritz oversize travel bag, pristine condition, 22" wide x 13" high x 7" deep.* **$17,500**

Heritage Auctions

▼ *Chanel shiny black crocodile classic 12" double flap bag with gold hardware, pristine condition, 12" wide x 8" high x 3.5" deep.* **$14,340**

Heritage Auctions

▲ *Chanel rare black matte crocodile oversize Paris-Baritz tote bag, pristine condition, 15" wide x 12" high x 5" deep.* **$11,950**

Heritage Auctions

▲ *Chanel lambskin leather Flap Bag with gold hardware, very good condition, 7" wide x 5" high x 2" deep.* **$1,313**

Heritage Auctions

◄ *Chanel Red Caviar Leather Everyday Tote Bag with contrast stitching, 13" wide x 11" high x 5" deep.* **$2,000**

Heritage Auctions

◄ *Chanel Natural Lizard Jumbo Double Flap Bag with gunmetal hardware, pristine condition, 12" wide x 8" high x 5" deep; the Flap Bag has been a best seller since its introduction by Coco Chanel in February 1955.* **$7,500**

Heritage Auctions

► *Gucci 1960s special order Bordeaux Crocodile Heritage Logo Weekender Bag, 17.5" x 13" x 9", excellent condition.* **$7,768**

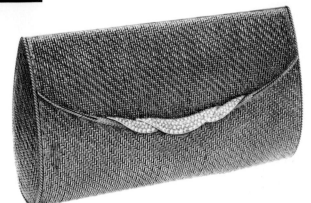

Heritage Auctions

◀ *Van Cleef & Arpels 18k yellow gold and diamond basket weave evening bag, excellent condition, 6.5" wide x 4" high x 1" deep, gold hard case with single flap opening and diamond design in Art Deco-style casing sits at tip of flap.* **$27,500**

Heritage Auctions

▲ *Louis Vuitton Damier canvas oversize wardrobe trunk with burnt orange Alcantara interior, pristine condition, 43" wide x 25.5" high x 21.5" deep.* **$13,750**

Heritage Auctions

▶ *Louis Vuitton rare Vison Monogramme mink and black alligator Le Fabuleux Bag, 2004 Les Extraordinaires Collection, 14" x 9" x 5"; flagship piece of the 2004 Fall/Winter Les Extraordinaires Show Collection; only five were released in the United States and sold out before they reached the boutiques.* **$8,963**

Heritage Auctions

Judith Leiber full bead silver, purple, gray, and green Arabian Karma Camel minaudiere, pristine condition, 5" wide x 4.5" high x 3" deep. **$6,573**

Heritage Auctions

Judith Leiber rare Tomato full bead minaudiere evening bag. **$4,183**

Heritage Auctions

Judith Leiber full bead pink and gold crystal Cupcake minaudiere evening bag, excellent condition, 3" wide x 4.5" high x 3" deep. After establishing her own brand in 1963, Leiber began crafting ingenious shapes beaded with Austrian crystals. Her minaudieres are now featured in the permanent collections of The Metropolitan Museum of Art in New York, The Victoria and Albert Museum in London, and The Houston Museum of Fine Arts. **$4,688**

Heritage Auctions

▲ *Bulgari 18k yellow gold melone minaudiere evening bag with 1.21ct round diamond clasp, excellent condition, 6.5" wide x 4" high x 2" deep, created in the 1960s, possibly one of only three made.* **$22,000**

Heritage Auctions

▲ *Judith Leiber full bead Pink Piglet crystal minaudiere evening bag, excellent condition, 4" wide x 4" high x 3" deep.* **$2,000**

Heritage Auctions

▶ *Judith Leiber half bead gold crystal minaudiere evening bag, excellent condition, 6" wide x 8" high x 1.5" deep.* **$688**

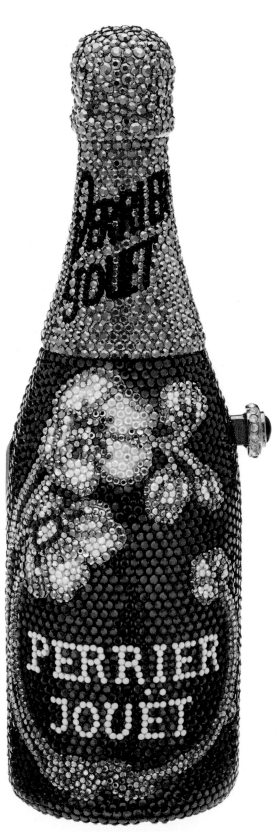

Heritage Auctions

Kathrine Baumann full bead Special Perrier Jouet Champagne Bottle minaudere, 7" x 3" x 2", excellent condition. **$6,573**

Heritage Auctions

▲ *Bottega Veneta black Intrecciato Napa leather Medium Weekend Bag, excellent condition, 19" length x 11" high x 10" deep.* **$1,313**

Heritage Auctions

▲ *Marc Jacobs rare deep red matte crocodile Runway limited edition clutch, excellent condition, 11.5" wide x 8" high x 2.5" deep.* **$1,250**

Heritage Auctions

▲ *Carlos Falchi black python clutch handbag with silver chain, in new condition, 12.25" long x 6" high x 1" wide, approximate strap drop 14".* **$400**

Heritage Auctions

▶ *Kieselstein-Cord shiny black crocodile large trophy bag with gold crocodile hardware, excellent to pristine condition, 12" wide x 10" high x 4" deep.* **$13,125**

JEWELRY

Jewelry

J ewelry has been a part of every culture throughout time. It is often reflective of times, as well as social and aesthetic movements, with each piece telling its own story through hidden clues that, when interpreted, will help solve mysteries surrounding them. Jewelry is generally divided into periods and styles. Each period may have several styles, with some of same styles and types of jewelry being made in both precious and non-precious materials. Additionally, there are recurring style revivals, which are interpretations of an earlier period. For example, Egyptian Revival that took place in early and late 1800s, and then again in 1920s.

For more information on jewelry, see *Warman's Jewelry 5th Edition* by Christie Romero.

Jewelry Styles

Georgian diamond brooch set throughout with old pear and old mine-cut diamonds, approximately 9 carats, silver-topped gold mount, 1 3/4" x 1 5/8". **$5,925**

Georgian, 1760-1837. Fine jewelry from this period is quite desirable, but few good-quality pieces have found their way to auction in recent years. Sadly, much jewelry from this period has been lost.

Victorian, 1837-1901. Queen Victoria of England ascended the throne in 1837 and remained queen until her death in 1901. The Victorian period is a long and prolific one; abundant with many styles of jewelry. It warrants being divided into three sub-periods: Early or Romantic period dating from 1837-1860; Mid or Grand period dating from 1860-1880; and Late or Aesthetic period dating from 1880-1901.

Sentiment and romance were significant factors in Victorian jewelry. Often, jewelry and clothing represented love and affection, with symbolic motifs such as hearts, crosses, hands, flowers, anchors, doves, crowns, knots, stars, thistles, wheat, garlands, horseshoes and moons. The materials of the time were also abundant and varied. They included silver, gold, diamonds, onyx, glass, cameo, paste, carnelian, agate, coral, amber, garnet, emeralds, opals, pearls, peridot (a green gemstone), rubies, sapphires, marcasites, cut steel, enameling, tortoise shell, topaz, turquoise, bog oak, ivory, jet, hair, gutta percha and vulcanite.

Sentiments of love were often expressed in miniatures.

Sometimes they were representative of deceased loved ones, but often the miniatures were of the living. Occasionally, the miniatures depicted landscapes, cherubs or religious themes.

Hair jewelry was a popular expression of love and sentiment. The hair of a loved one was placed in a special compartment in a brooch or a locket, or used to form a picture under a glass compartment. Later in the mid-19th century, pieces of jewelry were made completely of woven hair. Individual strands of hair would be woven together to create necklaces, watch chains, brooches, earrings and rings.

In 1861, Queen Victoria's husband, Prince Albert, died. The queen went into mourning for the rest of her life, and she required that the royal court wear black. This atmosphere spread to the populace and created a demand for mourning jewelry.

Mourning jewelry is typically black. When it first came into fashion, it was made from jet, fossilized wood. By 1850, there were dozens of English workshops making jet brooches, lockets, bracelets and necklaces. As the supply of jet dwindled, other materials were used such as vulcanite, gutta percha, bog oak and French jet.

By the 1880s, the somber mourning jewelry was losing popularity. Fashions had changed and the clothing

Heritage Auctions

▲ *Late Victorian diamond, emerald, ruby, cultured pearl and gold pierced brooch, one mine-cut diamond, 7.15 x 5.30 mm and approximately 0.75 carat, one pear-shaped diamond, 6.20 x 4 mm and approximately 0.45 carat, European-, mine- and rose-cut diamonds, approximately 7.55 carats, pear- and oval-shaped emeralds, approximately 4.40 carats, cushion- and rectangular-shaped rubies, approximately 2.10 carats, pearls, 4.70 x 5 mm, set in 18k gold, pinstem and "C" catch, gross weight 31.40 grams, 2" x 2 5/8".* **$4,780**

Edwardian ring, demantoid garnet, diamond, platinum and gold, square-shaped demantoid garnets set in 18k gold, approximately 1.80 carats, European- and single-cut diamonds set in platinum, approximately 0.85 carat, gross weight 6.40 grams, size 7 (sizeable). **$3,250**

Arts & Crafts sapphire and diamond pendant, Archibald Knox, Liberty & Co., set with cushion-cut sapphire, approximately 10 x 8.80 x 5.35 mm, approximately 4.25 carats, and rose-cut diamonds, suspending cushion-cut sapphire drop, platinum-topped gold mount, suspended from platinum chain, in original Liberty & Co. fitted box, pendant is 1 1/2" long, chain 15 1/2" long. **$6,000**

was simpler and had an air of delicacy. The Industrial Revolution, which had begun in the early part of the century, was now in full swing and machine-manufactured jewelry was affordable to the working class.

Edwardian, 1890-1920. The Edwardian period takes its name England's King Edward VII. Though he ascended the throne in 1901, he and his wife, Alexandria of Denmark, exerted influence over the period before and after his ascension. The 1890s was known as La Belle Epoque. This was a time known for ostentation and extravagance. As the years passed, jewelry became simpler and smaller. Instead of wearing one large brooch, women were often found wearing several small lapel pins.

In the early 1900s, platinum, diamonds and pearls were prevalent in the jewelry of the wealthy, while paste was being used by the masses to imitate the real thing. The styles were reminiscent of the neo-classical and rococo motifs. The jewelry was lacy and ornate, feminine and delicate.

Arts & Crafts, 1890-1920. The Arts & Crafts movement was focused on artisans and craftsmanship. There was a simplification of form where the material was secondary to the design. Guilds of artisans banded together. Some jewelry was mass-produced, but the most highly prized examples of this period are handmade and signed by their makers. The pieces were simple and at times abstract. They could be hammered, patinated and acid etched. Common materials were brass, bronze, copper, silver, blister pearls, freshwater pearls, turquoise, agate, opals, moonstones, coral, horn, ivory, base metals, amber, cabachon-cut garnets and amethysts.

Art Nouveau, 1895-1910. In 1895, Samuel Bing opened a shop called "Maison de l'Art Nouveau" at 22 Rue de Provence in Paris. Art Nouveau designs in the jewelry were characterized by a sensuality that took on the forms of the female figure, butterflies, dragonflies, peacocks, snakes, wasps, swans, bats, orchids, irises and other exotic flowers. The lines used whiplash curves to create a

Sotheby's

▲ *Art Nouveau hair comb, gold, tortoiseshell, opal and enamel, Georges Fouquet, France, circa 1905-1908, carved tortoiseshell comb of Egyptian inspiration with lotus and papyrus motifs, set with opal cabochons, black and green enamel, signed G. Fouquet, numbered 4680, with signed box.* **$22,500**

feeling of lushness and opulence.

1920s-1930s. Costume jewelry began its steady ascent to popularity in the 1920s. Since it was relatively inexpensive to produce, there was mass production. The sizes and designs of the jewelry varied. Often, it was worn a few times, disposed of and then replaced with a new piece. It was thought of as expendable, a cheap throwaway to dress up an outfit. Costume jewelry became so popular that it was sold in both the upscale stores and the "five and dime" store.

During the 1920s, fashions were often accompanied by jewelry that drew on the Art Deco movement, which got its beginning in Paris at the "Exposition Internationale des Arts Décoratifs et Industriels Modernes" held in 1925. The idea behind this movement was that form follows function. The style was characterized by simple, straight, clean lines, stylized motifs and geometric shapes. Favored materials included chrome, rhodium, pot metal, glass, rhinestones, Bakelite and celluloid.

One designer who played an important role was Coco Chanel. Though previously reserved for evening wear, Chanel wore costume jewelry during the day, making it fashionable for millions of other women to do so, too.

Bonhams

▲ *Art Deco diamond and synthetic emerald brooch/pendant, circa 1925, 2.20 carats, mounted in platinum, 2 3/8" long.* **$3,500**

Bonhams

Pair of retro ruby and 18 karat gold earclips, Cartier, circa 1945, signed Cartier, no. 1597/2332, accompanied by signed box, total oval-shaped ruby cabochon weight 1.75 carats, 9/16" diameter (14 karat gold findings).
$1,625

With the 1930s came the Depression and the advent of World War II. Perhaps in response to the gloom, designers began using enameling and brightly colored rhinestones to create whimsical birds, flowers, circus animals, bows, dogs and just about every other figural form imaginable.

Retro Modern, 1939-1950. Other jewelry designs of the 1940s were big and bold. Retro Modern had a more substantial feel to it and designers began using larger stones to enhance the dramatic pieces. The jewelry was stylized and exaggerated. Common motifs included flowing scrolls, bows, ribbons, birds, animals, snakes, flowers and knots.

Sterling silver now became the metal of choice, often dipped in a gold wash known as vermeil.

Designers often incorporated patriotic themes of American flags, the V-sign, Uncle Sam's hat, airplanes, anchors and eagles.

Post-War Modern, 1945-1965. This was a movement that emphasized the artistic approach to jewelry making. It is also referred to as Mid-Century Modern. This approach was occurring at a time when the Beat Generation was prevalent. These avant-garde designers created jewelry that was handcrafted to illustrate the artist's own concepts and ideas. The materials often used were sterling, gold, copper, brass, enamel, cabochons, wood, quartz and amber.

1950s-1960s. The 1950s saw the rise of jewelry that was made purely of rhinestones: necklaces, bracelets, earrings and pins.

The focus of the early 1960s was on clean lines: pillbox hats and A-line dresses with short jackets were a mainstay for the conservative woman. The large, bold rhinestone pieces were no longer the must-have accessory. They were now replaced with smaller, more delicate gold-tone metal and faux pearls with only a hint of rhinestones.

At the other end of the spectrum was psychedelic-colored clothing, Nehru jackets, thigh-high miniskirts and go-go boots. These clothes were accessorized with beads, large metal pendants and occasionally big, bold rhinestones. By the late 1960s, there was a movement back to mother nature and the "hippie" look was born. Ethnic clothing, tie dye, long skirts, fringe and jeans were the prevalent style and the rhinestone had, for the most part, been left behind.

Late Georgian

1760-1837

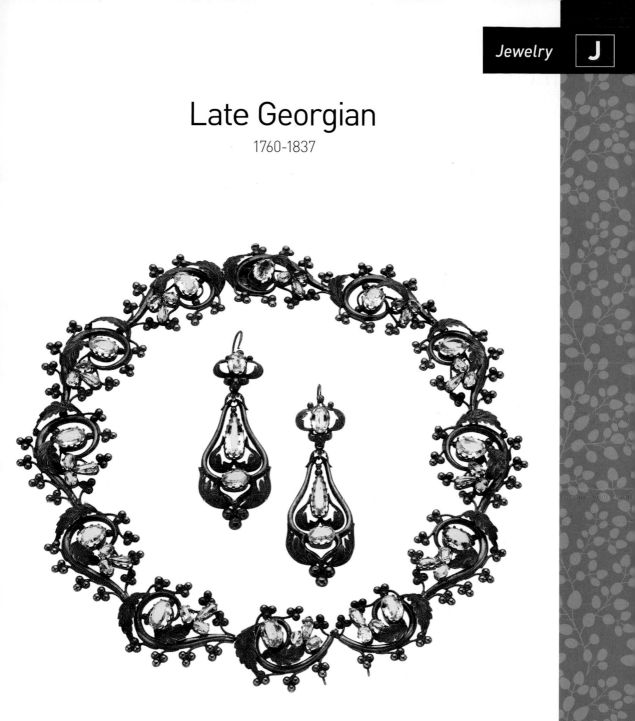

Heritage Auctions

Pink topaz and gold jewelry suite, French; demi parure includes necklace with oval and pear-shaped pink topaz, approximately 34.40 carats, set in textured 15k gold, with pendant wires and clasp; matching earrings made for pierced ears, detachable drops with oval and pear-shaped pink topaz, approximately 11.10 carats, set in 15k gold ear wires; French hallmarks; necklace 18" x 1 1/4", earrings with drop, 2 7/8" x 7/8", without drop, 3/4" x 5/8". **$7,170**

Aquamarine and gold jewelry suite, Czechoslovakia; demi parure includes necklace with oval aquamarine, approximately 45.15 carats, set in 18k gold, stationed on swagged chain; detachable earrings designed for pierced ears, with oval and pear-shaped aquamarines, approximately 11.05 carats, set in textured 18k gold, ear wires; Czechoslovakian hallmarks; original fitted box; centerpiece 1 5/8" x 7/8", necklace 15" long, earrings with drop, 2 1/2" x 3/4", without drop, 5/8" x 1/2". **$5,078**

Diamond and silver-topped gold pendant-brooch, European-, mine- and rose-cut diamonds, approximately 7.35 carats, set in silver-topped 14k gold, pendant wire, removable pinstem and catch on reverse, 1 1/8" x 1 3/8". **$4,780**

Victorian
1837-1901

Late Victorian enamel, ruby, diamond and gold snake bracelet, round-shaped rubies, approximately 3.50 carats, rose-cut diamonds, approximately 0.50 carat, green enamel applied on 18k gold, articulated gold tongue, 83.37 grams, 6 1/2" x 3/4". **$7,187**

Late Victorian diamond, ruby, cultured pearl and gold brooch, mine-cut diamonds, approximately 2.75 carats, rose-cut diamonds, approximately 0.25 carat, oval-shaped rubies, approximately 3.40 carats, seed pearls and pearls ranging in size from 1.20 x 1.40 mm to 7.25 x 7.35 mm, set in 18k gold, pinstem and catch on reverse; approximately 3 carats, 13.70 grams; 2 1/8" x 1 5/8". **$3,750**

▲ *Pair of early Victorian micromosaic bracelets, Castellani, circa 1860, each designed as series of square links set with eau de nil and silver colored tesserae with letters spelling AMOR/ROMA, within rope work borders, to foxtail chain connections, each signed with interlaced Cs, can be joined together and worn as necklace, approximately 7" long.* **$27,098**

▶ *Mid-Victorian hardstone cameo, cultured pearl, diamond and gold brooch, French, round-shaped hardstone cameo, 21 x 21 mm, cultured pearls, 3.20 x 3.50 mm, natural-cut diamonds, set in 18k gold, pinstem and "C" catch, French hallmarks, 9.20 grams, 1 1/4" x 1 1/4".* **$1,135**

◀ *Mid-Victorian gold and micromosaic brooch, circa 1870, circular mosaic of seated woman in peasant costume holding basket of grapes, elaborate frame of gold wire and beadwork with mosaics of doves, floral sprigs and leaves, reverse with glazed compartment, some tesserae missing.* **$3,600**

Mid-Victorian hardstone cameo gold pendant-brooch, oval-shaped banded onyx cameo, 50 x 34 mm, depicting lady's profile in high relief, set in 14k gold frame, bail, pinstem and catch on reverse, 41.10 grams, 2 1/2" x 1 3/4". **$896**

▲ *Early Victorian Vacheron & Constantin diamond, enamel and gold hunting case pocket watch with accompanying brooch, fob and key, circa 1850. Victorian gold mourning brooch with applied black and white enamel accents supports watch, key and fob. Case: 38 mm, hinged, circular 18k yellow gold with smooth edge and decorated case front and back, black champleve enamel, rose-cut diamonds; No. 83139 dial: white enamel with black Roman numerals, gilt "moon" hour and minute hands. Movement: 31 mm, gilt, 13 jewels, detached lever, keywind and set, No. 83139, signed Vacheron & Constantin on center bridge, lateral bridge escapement; signed and numbered Vacheron & Constantin in Geneve. E. E. Rodgers on cuvette, triple signed Vacheron & Constantin on dial, movement and dustcover.* **$3,107**

Mid-Victorian onyx cameo, half-pearl, pearl and gold pendant-brooch, oval-shaped and banded, depicting lady's profile, resting within 18k yellow gold frame, freshwater pearls with half-pearl accents, bail hook, pinstem and hinged "C" clasp on reverse, 29.30 grams, 2 7/8" x 1 3/4". **$1,852**

Heritage Auctions

◄ *Late Victorian diamond, sapphire, ruby, enamel and gold hinged bangle, European-cut diamond, 7.70 x 7.50 x 4 mm and approximately 1.50 carats, oval-shaped sapphire, 9.20 x 7.60 x 4.60 mm and approximately 2.70 carats, cushion-shaped ruby, 7 x 6.50 x 3.50 mm and approximately 1.45 carats, round-shaped sapphire, approximately 0.65 carat, European-cut diamond, approximately 0.45 carat, European-cut diamonds, approximately 3.90 carats, set in 18k white gold, blue enamel applied on 18k yellow gold; total diamond weight approximately 5.85 carats, 46.70 grams, 6 3/4" x 1 1/2".* **$10,755**

Heritage Auctions

◄ *Late Victorian diamond, enamel and silver-topped gold corset brooch, rose-cut diamonds, approximately 0.90 carat set in silver, blue and white enamel applied on 18k gold, pinstem and catch on reverse, 17.40 grams, 1 1/4" x 1 1/2".* **$5,078**

Heritage Auctions

◄ *Late Victorian sapphire, diamond and silver-topped gold earrings designed for pierced ears, oval-shaped sapphires, approximately 10.70 carats, European-cut diamonds, approximately 3.70 carats, set in silver-topped gold, leverbacks, 11.63 grams, 1 5/8" x 3/4".* **$3,883**

Heritage Auctions

Late Victorian diamond, enamel and gold earrings, French, designed for pierced ears, mine- and rose-cut diamonds, approximately 4.90 carats, black enamel applied on 18k gold, French hallmarks, 16.80 grams, 2" x 1". **$4,481**

Heritage Auctions

Late Victorian diamond and gold starburst pendant-brooch, European-cut diamond, 9.80 x 9.70 x 4.60 mm and approximately 2.60 carats, European-cut diamonds, approximately 15 carats, set in 14k gold retractable pendant bail, removable screw-set pinstem and catch on reverse; total diamond weight approximately 17.60 carats, 22.15 grams, 2" x 2". **$16,730**

Heritage Auctions

Late Victorian amethyst, diamond and silver-topped gold necklace, Netherlands, oval and cushion-shaped amethysts, approximately 89.35 carats, European-cut diamonds, approximately 17.25 carats set in silver-topped 14k gold, 84.30 grams, 15" long, centerpiece 3 1/2" x 2". **$27,485**

Heritage Auctions

◄ *Mid-Victorian Etruscan Revival gold jewelry suite: earrings designed for pierced ears with matching convertible pendant-brooch, two locket compartments on reverse, all in 14k yellow gold, gross weight 45 grams; earrings 2" x 1 3/4", pendant-brooch 2 13/16" x 1 15/16".* **$2,390**

Heritage Auctions

▼ *Late Victorian diamond and gold heart-shaped pendant, pear-shaped rose-cut diamond, 12 x 8.90 mm and approximately 1.10 carats, rose-cut diamonds, approximately 3.95 carats set in textured 14k gold, total diamond weight approximately 5.05 carats, 13.20 grams, 1 1/2" x 1 1/8".* **$2,600**

Heritage Auctions

▼ *Mid-Victorian gold suite: mesh choker necklace in 14k gold and matching 14k gold mesh pin, black enamel, pinstem and catch on reverse, 74.40 grams; necklace 13" x 1"; pin 3" x 7/8".* **$2,629**

Arts & Crafts
1890-1920

▲ *Arts & Crafts moonstone, sapphire and diamond necklace, Louis Comfort Tiffany, circa 1915, designed as cabochon moonstone within twisted rope work frame with circular-cut sapphires and diamonds, three row fancy link chain and clasp similarly set, signed Tiffany & Co., approximately 18 1/2" long.* **$25,103**

▶ *Arts & Crafts pendant-brooch, 18k gold, plique à jour enamel and opal, René Lalique, circa 1903-1904, designed as two facing dragonflies applied with white, blue, teal and pale blue plique à jour enamel wings and enamel bodies, set in center with oval cabochon opal, white opal spindleberries and white enameled stems, signed Lalique, pin fitting missing.* **$170,500**

▲ *Arts & Crafts 18k gold, moss agate, and carnelian bracelet, Margaret Rogers, Boston, bezel-set moss agate tablets spaced by carnelian disks with foliate accents, signed MR, 6 5/8".* **$4,740**

◀ *Arts & Crafts 18k gold and diamond bangle, bezel-set overall with old European- and old mine-cut diamonds, approximately 3.10 carats, foliate motifs and scrolling tendrils, interior circumference 7 1/2".* **$7,703**

Heritage Auctions

▲ *Arts & Crafts brooch, Tiffany & Co., circa 1907, moonstone, Montana sapphire, plique à jour enamel and platinum, faceted cushion-shaped moonstone, 9.36 x 8.08 4.61 mm and approximately 2 carats, round-shaped Montana sapphires, approximately 0.20 carat, opalescent plique à jour enamel, set in platinum, marked Tiffany & Co., likely designed by or under direction of L.C. Tiffany, 1 13/16" x 1/2".* **$3,750**

Skinner, Inc., www.skinnerinc.com

Arts & Crafts 14k gold, sapphire and diamond ring, attributed to Edward Oakes, bezel-set with circular-cut sapphire, approximately 6.20 x 3.65 mm, old European-cut diamond, approximately 0.60 carat, circular-cut sapphire, floral and foliate motifs, conforming shoulders with old mine-cut diamond accents, unsigned, size 5 3/4. **$5,629**

Skinner, Inc., www.skinnerinc.com

Arts & Crafts 18k gold, sapphire and freshwater pearl necklace, Margaret Rogers, Boston, designed as circular pendant bezel-set with sapphire, approximately 10 x 8.90 mm, framed by circular-cut sapphires, shaped pearls and wire scrolls, suspended from chain of navette-form links each set with bezel-set sapphires and pearls, signed MR, pendant 1 5/8" diameter, chain 16 1/4" long. **$10,665**

Skinner, Inc., www.skinnerinc.com

Arts & Crafts zircon and cultured pearl suite, attributed to Edward Oakes, brooch designed as branch of leaves with clusters of bezel-set zircons and cultured pearls, earrings en suite, unsigned, brooch 2 1/2" and earrings 1". **$2,370**

Sotheby's

▲ *Arts & Crafts emerald and diamond necklace, circa 1905, swag, floral and ribbon design, set with pear- and cushion-shaped emeralds, cushion-shaped circular-cut and rose diamonds, fine chain back, approximately 14" long.* **$31,710**

Skinner, Inc., www.skinnerinc.com

▶ *Arts & Crafts 18k gold and diamond necklace, Edward Oakes, central triangular element with bezel-set old mine-cut diamonds and elaborate foliate motifs, suspended from conforming old mine-cut diamond and floret links, ending in chain, unsigned, 17" long.* **$8,591**

Skinner, Inc., www.skinnerinc.com

Arts & Crafts 14k gold and faience scarab necklace, F.G. Hale, designed as bezel-set faience scarab among lotus blossom motifs, suspended from baton- and ball-link chain, signed, pendant 1 3/4", chain 16 1/4" long. **$5,036**

Skinner, Inc., www.skinnerinc.com

Arts & Crafts 14k gold and serpentine necklace, set with shaped and oval cabochons, cabochon sapphire accent, quatrefoil motifs centering blue stones, seed pearls, ear studs en suite, 13 3/4" long, 2 7/8" drop. **$4,622**

Art Nouveau

1895-1910

Art Nouveau diamond, emerald, ruby and gold bracelet, Lebolt & Co., European-cut diamonds, approximately 0.85 carat, oval-shaped emerald cabochon, approximately 0.70 carat, square-shaped emeralds, approximately 0.20 carat, round-shaped rubies, set in 18k gold, maker's mark for LeBolt & Co., 36.38 grams, 6 3/4" x 3/4". **$5,937**

Art Nouveau brooch, demantoid garnet, diamond, plique à jour enamel, and silver-topped gold, round-shaped demantoid garnets, approximately 2.30 carats, European- and single-cut diamonds, approximately 0.90 carat, green plique à jour enamel, set in silver-topped gold, pinstem and catch, 13.55 grams, 3" x 2 1/8". **$4,687**

Sotheby's

▶ *Art Nouveau gold, diamond, enamel and pearl pendant-necklace, attributed to Louis Aucoc, France, circa 1900, depicting Birth of Venus with bust supported on diamond-set starfish, white diamond star allusion to Venus as white star in night sky, framed by openwork floral motif with peach and yellowish-green enamel, supporting pearl drop, approximately 7.9 x 6.8 mm, gold link chain with small plaques of similar design to pendant, set throughout with old European-cut, single-cut and rose-cut diamonds, approximately 1.50 carats, unsigned, French assay mark, 22" long, fitted box signed Tiffany & Cie.* **$37,500**

Skinner, Inc., www.skinnerinc.com

▼ *Art Nouveau plique à jour enamel, ruby and diamond necklace, shaped plique à jour enamel plaques set with cabochon and circular-cut rubies, old European- and rose-cut diamonds, platinum-topped 18k gold mount, 14k white gold filigree chain, Continental hallmark, 20 3/8" long.* **$8,888**

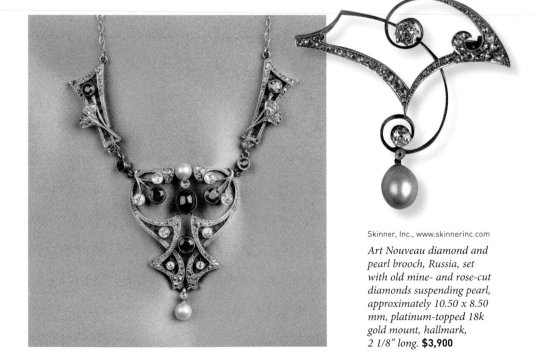

Skinner, Inc., www.skinnerinc.com

Art Nouveau diamond and pearl brooch, Russia, set with old mine- and rose-cut diamonds suspending pearl, approximately 10.50 x 8.50 mm, platinum-topped 18k gold mount, hallmark, 2 1/8" long. **$3,900**

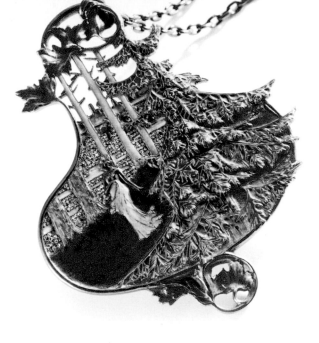

Sotheby's

Art Nouveau gold, diamond and enamel landscape pendant and chain, René Lalique, circa 1898-1900, pendant designed as partially clad woman in forested landscape against sky of diamonds, leafy flourishes above and below, blue and pale green enamel accents and small rose-cut diamonds, back of pendant finished in pale bluish-green enamel, signed Lalique, oval gold link chain, three diamonds missing, 18 1/2" long. **$326,500**

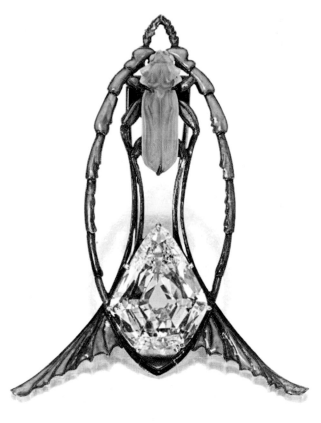

Sotheby's

Art Nouveau pendant, gold, platinum, opal, diamond and plique à jour enamel, Paul Robin, France, circa 1900, large pendant applied with plique à jour enamel depicting pink trees, mountains and clouds framed by gold branches, pine cones and needles, top set with old mine- and old European-cut diamonds, approximately 1.75 carats, set with modified cushion-shaped opal, approximately 4.5 by 4.0 cm, pendant set with drop-shaped opal, approximately 4.5 by 2.3 cm, maker's mark, French assay mark. **$92,500**

Sotheby's

Art Nouveau gold, diamond, enamel and glass brooch, Lalique, circa 1900, stylized insect decorated with scarab beetle of pale blue opalescent glass above calf's-head-cut diamond, approximately 15.3 by 18.3 by 5.1 mm, within modified navette-shaped frame with fin terminals applied with opalescent blue enamel, signed Lalique. **$217,000**

Sotheby's

Art Nouveau pendant-brooch, gold, pearl, diamond and enamel, France, circa 1900, designed as bare-breasted maiden with arms outstretched in form of American dancer Loïe Fuller, peach, cream and pale green enamel, star at top set with old European-cut diamond, set at bottom with two old mine-cut diamonds, supporting pearl drop, approximately 8.4 by 7.6 mm, indistinct maker's mark, French assay mark. **$18,750**

© Christie's Images Ltd. 2009

Pendant La Bretonne, Art Nouveau enamel and multi-gem piece, sculpted gold female bust in profile, calibré-cut opal costume, bonnet extending to form scrolling frame, single old European rose-cut diamond trim, carved amethyst sleeve against openwork green and yellow enamel floral background suspending drop-shaped amethyst cabochon from detachable rose-cut diamond foliate hoop, mounted in gold, circa 1900, showing traditional motif of young French Breton woman in new style, signed Vever for Henri Vever, Paris. **$400,000-$600,000**

Sotheby's

Rare Art Nouveau corsage ornament, enamel, gold, emerald and diamond, Fédor Anatolevitch Lorie, circa 1900, designed as hybrid dragonfly, helmeted female head set with two cabochon sapphires to winged torso, lilac plique à jour enamel wings with circular-cut diamonds and cabochon emeralds to tapering articulated body, suspended by arms from pair of pink enamel and gem-set stag beetles, mounted in 14k yellow gold. **$234,579**

Skinner, Inc., www.skinnerinc.com

Art Nouveau 14k gold, enamel, and seed pearl suite, Krementz & Co., pin and earrings, maker's mark, pin 2", earrings 1". **$1,225**

Skinner, Inc., www.skinnerinc.com

Art Nouveau 18k gold and enamel ring, Wiese, France, depicting winged Nike with scroll motifs, maker's mark and guarantee stamps, signed, size 9 1/2. **$6,518**

Skinner, Inc., www.skinnerinc.com

▼ *Art Nouveau 18k gold and plique à jour enamel gem-set pendant, L. Gautrait, France, designed as maiden with plique à jour enamel tresses wearing diamond and rose-cut diamond diadem, opal accents, diamond and pearl drop, suspended from fancy link chain, pendant signed L. Gautrait, chain with partial maker's mark for Leon Gariod, guarantee stamps, 2" x 2 1/2"; chain 20" long.* **$21,600**

Heritage Auctions

▲ *Art Nouveau necklace, diamond, freshwater pearl, plique à jour enamel and 18k gold, rose-cut diamond, freshwater pearl, 66.30 grams, pendant 2 1/8" x 1 1/8", chain 54" long.* **$4,481**

Edwardian

1890-1920

Heritage Auctions

◄ *Edwardian diamond, platinum-topped gold bracelet, European-cut diamonds, approximately 2.25 carats, rose-cut diamonds, set in platinum-topped gold, 20.20 grams, 7 1/8" x 1/2".* **$4,687**

Doyle New York

▲ *Edwardian platinum, sapphire and diamond ring, circa 1915, pierced platinum mount centering one cushion-shaped sapphire, approximately 2 carats, flanked by two old European-cut diamonds, approximately 2 carats, numerous small single-cut diamonds, hinged shank, size 8 1/4.* **$21,250**

Heritage Auctions

▲ *Edwardian diamond and platinum articulated brooch, European-cut diamonds, approximately 1.70 carats, rose-cut diamonds, approximately 0.70 carat, set in platinum, attached to white metal frame, pinstem and catch, total diamond weight approximately 2.40 carats, 12.34 grams, 2 1/4" x 1 5/8".* **$3,750**

▲ *Edwardian diamond and platinum brooch, European-cut diamonds, approximately 2.25 carats, set in platinum, 7 grams, 3/4" x 2".* **$1,375**

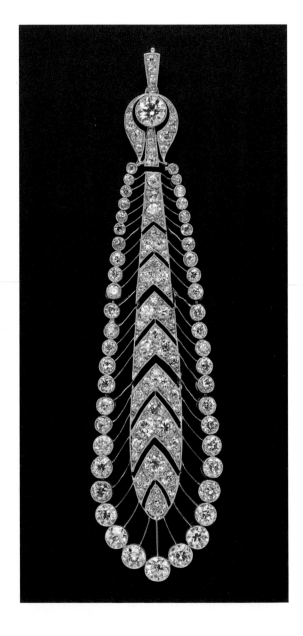

▶ *Edwardian platinum and diamond pendant, Tiffany & Co., old European-cut diamonds on knife-edge bars, approximate total weight 7.75 carats, millegrain accents, signed, 3 3/4" long.* **$18,000**

Heritage Auctions

◄ *Edwardian brooch, circa 1910, diamond and platinum-topped gold, European-cut diamonds, approximately 2 carats, rose-cut diamonds, set in pierced platinum-topped 18k yellow gold, total diamond weight approximately 3 carats, 8.80 grams, 2" x 7/8".* **$2,629**

Heritage Auctions

▲ *Edwardian diamond, platinum and gold brooch, European-cut diamond, 6.92 x 6.85 x 4.71 mm and approximately 1.35 carats, European-cut diamonds, approximately 1.30 carats, set in platinum, 14k gold pinstem and catch, total diamond weight 2.65 carats, 8.50 grams, 2 5/8" x 1/2".* **$4,062**

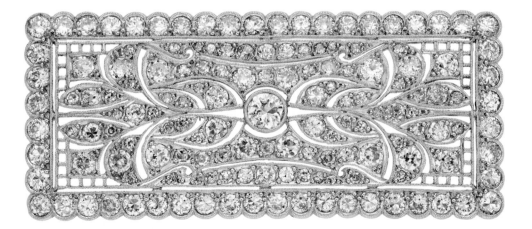

Heritage Auctions

▲ *Edwardian diamond and platinum-topped gold brooch, centering European-cut diamond, 5.20 x 5.40 x 2.90 mm and approximately 0.50 carat, European-cut diamonds, approximately 9.20 carats, single-cut diamonds, approximately 0.80 carat, set in platinum-topped 18k gold, pinstem and catch, total diamond weight approximately 10.50 carats, 24.80 grams, 2 5/8" x 1 1/8".* **$5,312**

Heritage Auctions

▶ *Edwardian sautoir, diamond, seed pearl, enamel, platinum and gold, French, woven seed pearl necklace has openwork platinum sections, European- and rose-cut diamonds, detachable pendant, European- and rose-cut diamonds, seed pearl tassel with rose-cut diamond and enameled platinum cap, French hallmarks, total diamond weight approximately 4.20 carats, 62.50 grams, necklace 27" long, pendant 4" x 1 1/2", combined dimensions: 31" x 1 1/2".* **$15,000**

Skinner, Inc., www.skinnerinc.com

▶ *Edwardian demantoid garnet and diamond snake brooch set with circular-cut demantoid garnets framed by old mine-cut diamonds, cushion-cut ruby head, platinum-topped 18k gold mount, 2 1/4" long.* **$8,100**

Doyle New York

▲ *Edwardian platinum, diamond and plique à jour enamel swallow brooch, circa 1915, pierced plaque centering diamond-set swallow atop plique à jour enamel ocean scene with blue sky, clouds outlined in platinum, framed by pierced florets set with diamonds, edged by black onyx, approximately 13.8 dwt.* **$18,750**

Sotheby's

▲ *Edwardian set of necklace,
bracelet and pair of earrings,
Tiffany & Co., designed by Louis
Comfort Tiffany, circa 1910, formed
of sculpted gold links of foliate and
scroll design, set with variety of
colored stones, including sapphires
in multiple hues, blue and purple
spinel, pink tourmaline, amethyst
and zircon, in round, cushion and
various fancy shapes, necklace
18 1/2" long, bracelet 6 7/8",
earrings with later-added backs,
signed Tiffany & Co.* **$121,000**

Sotheby's

▶ *Edwardian platinum and blue
diamond ring, Tiffany & Co.,
circa 1900, modified marquise-
shaped blue diamond, 3.54 carats,
mounting set with old European-
cut and single-cut diamonds,
approximately .35 carat, partial
signature "T" for Tiffany & Co.,
two diamonds missing, size 3 1/2,
fitted box signed Tiffany & Co.*
$2,434,500

Doyle New York

▲ *Edwardian platinum and diamond brooch, circa 1915, stylized flower with filigree decoration set with five old European-cut diamonds, approximately 4.50 carats, and 56 old European-cut diamonds, approximately 4.85 carats, approximately 30.3 grams.* **$11,875**

Heritage Auctions

▶ *Edwardian sapphire, diamond, gold and platinum necklace, cushion-shaped sapphire, 16.78 x 11.24 x 3.01 mm and 7.34 carats, four European-cut diamonds, 6 x 6 x 3.30 mm, 7 x 7 x 4.10 mm, 5.10 x 5.40 x 3.10 mm and 5 x 5.40 x 3.10 mm and approximately 0.75, 1.25, 0.50 and 0.50 carats, respectively, European- and single-cut diamonds, approximately 2.85 carats, set in platinum, 14k white gold pinstem and catch on reverse, detachable platinum chain with rose-cut diamond accents, total diamond weight approximately 5.85 carats, 23.10 grams, pendant-brooch 2" x 1 1/2", chain 16" long.* **$9,560**

Lamps & Lighting

By Martin Willis

A fine lamp provides both illumination as well as a decorative focal point for a room. This dual-purpose trend had its origins in the mid-to-late 1800s with American lighting. As with most game-changing style movements, timing was key in this evolution.

Arguably, the vanguard name of decorative lighting was Louis Comfort Tiffany (1848-1933) of New York City. Urban homes became electrified on a wide scale near the end of the 19th century; it was then that Tiffany was becoming recognized as a designer as well as a commercial success.

Tiffany's first stained glass shade for an electric lamp was designed by Clara Driscoll around 1895. Since their introduction over a century ago, Tiffany's shades have always had a unique, glowing quality to them due to their masterful designs and chemically compounded stained glass colors. Today, Tiffany Studios lamps remain collector's favorites. Rare and unusual designs – including the Hanging Head Dragonfly, Peony, Apple Blossom, and Wisteria patterns – generate the most interest and dollars; outstanding examples have commanded up to $2 million. More common items such as Acorn, Tulip, or Favrile art glass shade lamps have experienced falling prices relative to a decade ago.

Martin Willis

Tiffany's commercial success catalyzed the creation of many new stained glass lamp companies. Contemporaries included Duffner & Kimberly, Suess, Chicago Mosaic, and Wilkinson. See *Mosaic Shades II* by Paul Crist, for more information.

There were several other companies in the United States making fine glass lamps at the turn of last century. These included Handel, from Meriden, Connecticut, and Pairpoint, from New Bedford, Massachusetts. Handel was known primarily for its reverse painted shades. Fine examples of the company's landscape, aquarium, and other unusual motifs have garnered prices up to $85,000. Pairpoint opened in 1880 and soon merged with Mt. Washington Glass of Boston. They created reverse painted shades as well, the most popular being their "Puffy"

MARTIN WILLIS is the Director of the Decorative Arts at James D. Julia, Inc., one of the nation's premier auction galleries. Formerly of New Hampshire, Willis comes from a family of auctioneers: His father, Morgan Willis, developed and ran the Seaboard Auction Gallery in Eliot, Maine, which Martin eventually took over. He has 40 years of experience in the antique auction business from companies in Maine, New Hampshire, Massachusetts, Colorado and California. He spent six years with Clars Auction Gallery of Oakland, California, as senior appraiser, cataloger and auctioneer, handling the estate of TV mogul Merv Griffin as well as talk show host Tom Snyder. In 2009, Martin launched Antique Auction Forum, a biweekly podcast on the art and antiques trade with followers across North America and throughout the world.

shade. Prices for Pairpoint lamps start around $1,000 and peak about $25,000 for top examples.

Perhaps the most notable European glass lamp manufacturer from the late 19th century was Daum, founded by Jean Daum in France in 1878. The company is still in business today, manufacturing crystal art glass. Daum's lamps were made of cameo glass, produced through a proprietary technique of using acid to cut through layers of fused glass. This creates dramatic color reliefs. During the heyday, 1895-1914, Daum produced beautiful cameo glass lamp bases and shades. Today, early examples can be purchased starting at $1,000. Exceptional pieces may garner up to $80,000.

It is important to note that when it comes to vintage lamps, reproductions and fakes dominate the secondary market. If a price seems too good to be true, it probably is. It is imperative to buy from a reputable dealer or an auction house that will stand behind an item's authenticity. If a piece has the word "style" as part of its description, i.e., a "Tiffany style" lamp, this indicates that it is either a reproduction or that the seller is uncertain of its origins. Always ask plenty of questions before investing in a fine art lamp.

As always, anything is worth whatever someone will pay, and there are often good buys available – even from top manufacturers. With the exception of the very rarest examples, enthusiasts should be able to find and afford a nice authentic vintage lamp to admire and enjoy.

Rago Arts & Auction Center

Rare Handel table lamp, Meriden, Connecticut, circa 1910, shade with stylized leaves and buds, obverse and reverse painted acid-etched glass, patinated metal, three sockets, shade marked U.S. Patent No. 979664 and HANDEL 5468, base stamped Handel, 22" x 15". **$12,500**

James D. Julia, Inc.

Pair of Durand lamps with amber glass bodies, faceted stems and bases, topped with gold iridescent tulip shades with vertically ribbed bodies and flaring ruffled lips, very good to excellent condition, 20" high. **$830**

Skinner, Inc.; www.skinnerinc.com

Figural alabaster lamp, Italy, early 20th century in two parts, carved as woman kneeling to pick flowers above fountain with two birds, based incised "Italy," 12 3/4" long. **$984**

Skinner, Inc.; www.skinnerinc.com

Figural alabaster lamp, Italy, early 20th century, with green shade and stem mounted to base with carved female dancer, incised "Prof. G. Bessi Italy," 34 1/4" high overall. **$923**

Skinner, Inc.; www.skinnerinc.com

▶ *Pair of parcel-gilt bronze lamp bases, Continental, 19th century, each cast as putto with dark brown/black patina, holding either lit torch or bow and arrow, seated atop fluted column, on square base with flames to corners and pendant garlands, on four toupie feet, 20" high to top of putto heads.* **$1,920**

Rago Arts & Auction Center

Handel table lamp, Meriden, Connecticut, 1910s, chipped-glass shade obverse and reverse painted with palm trees, bronze base, three sockets, shade stamped Handel Lamps patent no. and HANDEL 6310 F. U., base stamped Handel, 24" x 15". **$3,125**

Rago Arts & Auction Center

Roycroft Helmet shade table lamp, East Aurora, New York, 1920s, wood-grain pattern, hammered copper, mica, single socket, orb and cross mark, 13 1/2" x 7" diameter. **$2,125**

Rago Arts & Auction Center

Dirk van Erp early trumpet lamp with vented cap, San Francisco, 1911-1915, hammered copper, mica, single socket, closed box windmill stamp, 19 1/2" x 16" diameter. **$10,625**

Rago Arts & Auction Center

Rare Pittsburgh table lamp with lighting base, circa 1915, decorated with Native American at river's edge, obverse-painted milk glass, patinated metal, two sockets, unmarked, 21 1/2" x 16". **$5,938**

Rago Arts & Auction Center

Daum cameo glass ceiling fixture, Nancy, France, 1900s, glass, iron, single socket, marked Daum Nancy, bowl 7" x 16", 31" tall total. **$6,250**

James D. Julia, Inc.

Mt. Washington Royal Flemish Garden of Allah lamp, Royal Flemish decoration of camels, pyramids, palm trees, and Arabs on shade and lamp base, russet, brown and gold, shade has collar with enameled decoration of gold scrolls and frosted beads, original metal hardware with embossed Grecian figures of Socrates, Cicero and others, original clear chimney, metal burner signed "The Daylight C.&K," very good to excellent condition, shade 10" diameter, lamp 22" high. **$12,443**

James D. Julia, Inc.

Morgan table lamp with hand-painted pansies and fully leaded shade, J. Morgan & Sons of New York, tuck-under style shade with irregular border, obverse painted, enameled decoration on irregular-shaped panels of glass, flowers in purple, blue, mauve, orange, and yellow, textured and striated panels of glass used in flowers, smaller green panels of glass represent foliage, green to white ground; three-socket single-stem base with applied metal tendrils ending in leaves with circular foot; very good to excellent condition with minor hairlines commensurate with age, small areas of solder work to shade; shade 18" diameter, 23" high overall. **$20,738**

James D. Julia, Inc.

▲ *Satin glass fairy lamp, ball-shaped dome with raspberry-colored mother-of-pearl herringbone decoration, enameled with two robins resting on branch, shade rests on herringbone mother-of-pearl pink shading to white base with gold branches and leaves, very good condition with one nick to bottom edge of shade.* **$770**

James D. Julia, Inc.

▶ *Durand threaded art glass lamp base, yellow ground decorated with white pulled feather pattern with green border and applied glass threading, set in ornate metal foot, single socket, glass is very good to excellent condition with several areas of thread loss, 12" high overall.* **$365**

James D. Julia, Inc.

Quezal lamp base, gold hooked feather design with green iridescent outline against cream background, shoulder and neck finished in bright gold iridescence with pink, blue, and green highlights, very good to excellent condition, glass portion 13 1/2" high, 26" high overall. **$711**

James D. Julia, Inc.

Moe Bridges scenic table lamp with reverse-painted shade of white birch trees on shoreline with blue water, shrubbery, and blue sky, two-armed base with paw feet, shade signed "Moe Bridges Co 186"; shade in very good to excellent condition, base has been polished; shade 18" diameter, lamp 23" high. **$2,726**

James D. Julia, Inc.

Cleveland pattern fairy lamp, domed shade with light green, frosted, and cream vertical ribs, shade has acid stamped markings "RD 50725 Trademark Fairy," rests in clear pressed glass base marked "S. Clarkes Patent Trademark Fairy," very good to excellent condition with some minor roughness to bottom edge of shade, 4 3/4" high. **$474**

James D. Julia, Inc.

Austrian art glass desk lamp, brass gooseneck base with ribbon design at shade holder, Art Nouveau leaf pattern to stepped foot of base, which supports flared-out art glass shade attributed to Loetz with oil spot decoration ending in deep blue pattern, very good to excellent condition with minor wear to base commensurate with age, shade 4 1/2" high x 2 1/4" fitter, base 13" high. **$1,422**

Mark Mussio, Humler & Nolan

Rookwood Arts & Crafts-style lamp with hand-carved thistle by Rose Fechheimer, circa 1905, heavy form with original electrical fittings done in two-tone mat finish, marks include mostly obscured company logo, date and shape number, artist's initials carved inside base, pale green shade is appropriate but not original; excellent original condition; ceramic portion 15 3/4" high. **$2,800**

James D. Julia, Inc.

Rare Duffner & Kimberly leaded orchid table lamp, shade with four heavily textured or mottled central panels in orange, red, and yellow, background foliage in green with blue and purple striated background, panels set in rows of geometric glass in blue, green, and purple; Art Nouveau style base with vertical ribbing to central shaft and large saucer foot, four sockets and pierced top cap with finial, signed on underside DKC (Duffner Kimberly Co); shade in very good to excellent condition with a few tight hairlines, base in very good to excellent condition with finial appearing to be old replacement; shade 16" diameter, 24" high overall. **$11,850**

James D. Julia, Inc.

Duffner & Kimberly leaded table lamp, large geometric panels of spring green glass as backdrop for Art Nouveau floral pattern in orange, yellow, and cream with foliage in green and blue, shade supported by four-socket ornate base with four acorn pulls, pierced heart top cap and finial; shade in very good to excellent condition with a few tight hairlines, finish to base enhanced; shade 19" diameter, lamp 22" high. **$4,740**

James D. Julia, Inc.

▶ *Pairpoint Puffy rose bouquet table lamp, blown glass shade with roses in burgundy and white against variegated green ground of leaves and stems, tree trunk base in high relief with patina finish of gold and green, two pull chains and sockets; shade signed "The Pairpoint Corp" and "Patent Applied For," base signed "Pairpoint Mfg. Co," "P" in diamond and "3001"; very good to excellent condition; shade 10" diameter, lamp 19 1/2" high.* **$10,935**

James D. Julia, Inc.

Blue satin fairy lamp with ruffled base of blue shading to white, matching shade has melon ribbed body with cased white interior and applied clear frosted ruffled lip, very good to excellent condition, 5 1/4" high. **$415**

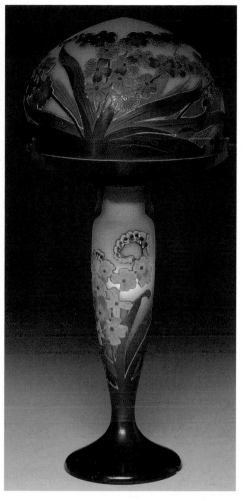

James D. Julia, Inc.

Gallé French cameo boudoir lamp with creamy ground and purple and blue floral and foliage pattern overall, layer of chartreuse green glass behind pattern, shade supported by three-armed base with cast iron supports and single socket in identical pattern, signed "Gallé" in cameo to shade and base, very good to excellent condition with base having slight rub to finish, 14" high. **$7,703**

James D. Julia, Inc.

◄ *Fairy lamp epergne with clear crystal inverted saucer foot supporting plantlike brass stem that houses two vases and leads upwards to fairy lamp, vases of clear blown glass with single band of applied rigaree, fairy lamp has clear shade topped by original silk shade with wooden bead dangles, shade marked on inside metal fitter "Cricklite," very good to excellent condition with minor staining to shade, 17" high.* **$1,126**

James D. Julia, Inc.

▶ *Pairpoint owl table lamp, rarest and most desirable of all Pairpoint lamps made and only eighth example known to exist. Exaggerated, blown out, molded owl shade, white feathers with light brown, yellow, and gray highlights, brown and gold eyes and beak, border decorated with green foliage, pine needles, and tree limbs; owl-shaped metal base with original patina and glass eyes, single socket, and original shade ring; shade signed on outside edge in gold "Pat. Applied For"; shade in very good condition with small chip and 2" sliver to inside rim, base in very good to excellent condition; shade 12" diameter with 10" fitter, 20 1/2" high overall.* **$77,025**

James D. Julia, Inc.

◀ *Austrian table lamp with peach ground, green lines, and blue oil spots on kerosene-style shade, detailed Art Nouveau base with flower foot and three-dimensional lizard with tail going up center shaft in green and gold, base with clear font with decorative metal top, single socket and shade support; very good to excellent condition; shade 10" diameter, lamp 29" high.* **$6,518**

James D. Julia, Inc.

Pairpoint Puffy apple tree table lamp with background of green leaves with bluish highlights and pink and white apple blossoms surrounding orange and yellow apples, three bumblebees on one side and two butterflies on other side, tree trunk base with four-arm spider and double socket cluster with desirable patina finish; shade signed "The Pairpoint Corp" on interior and exterior, base signed on underside "Pairpoint Mfg. Co." with "P" inside diamond and "3091"; very good to excellent condition; shade 14" diameter, lamp 21" high. **$23,700**

James D. Julia, Inc.

Handel Hawaiian sunset table lamp with nine bent panels of glass with overlay of palm trees and Hawaiian foliage, each panel ends with irregular border of glass in light green and white with green paint on exterior in overlay border design; large "elephant's foot" base with three sockets, three acorn pulls, flattened style cap and finial, desirable brown finish; shade signed "Handel" on applied tag to inside shade, base impressed "Handel" on underside of foot; very good to excellent condition; shade 24" diameter, lamp 27" high. **$4,740**

James D. Julia, Inc.

◄ *Dirk van Erp table lamp with conical shade of hammered copper with four mica panels in copper, gold and silver coloration, bulbous base of hammered copper with four arms and single socket, copper straps on shade are riveted on outside of copper cone at top, base has signature van Erp windmill with closed box and is signed "Dirk van Erp"; very good to excellent condition with wear to copper finish on shade and base; shade 15" diameter, lamp 16" high.* **$8,295**

James D. Julia, Inc.

Moe Bridges boudoir lamp with reverse-painted shade of sunset over lake with trees and foliage, two-arm Grecian-style base with green highlights and stamped "Moe Bridges Co. Milwaukee"; very good to excellent condition; shade 8" diameter, lamp 12" high. **$681**

James D. Julia, Inc.

▲ *Tiffany prism student lamp with artichoke foot and adjustable single arm that supports shade consisting of 12 Tiffany amber glass prisms, brown patina with green highlights, base signed "Tiffany Studios New York 10914"; very good to excellent condition; 26" high.* **$11,258**

James D. Julia, Inc.

◄ *Handel leaded table lamp, large shade with stylized overlapping leaf leaded design and striated green glass with red glass border band, large Handel base with pattern on foot matching shade, five gooseneck sockets and original openwork cap, shade unsigned, base signed on underside with raised block letters "Handel"; shade in very good condition with one tight hairline in large panels and a few tight hairlines in border panels, base in very good to excellent condition with replaced sockets; shade 25 1/2" diameter, lamp 30" high.* **$4,740**

James D. Julia, Inc.

Porcelli Studios leaded lamp with band of varying flowers in orange, pink, red, and purple with variegated green background, geometric rows at top and bottom in blue and green, three-socket base with pierced top cap, signed "Joseph Porcelli"; very good to excellent condition, patina is flaking from one socket arm on base, one turn switch is broken; shade 22" diameter, lamp 26" high. **$11,850**

Skinner, Inc.; www.skinnerinc.com

Pair of silvered bronze figural lamp bases, Continental, late 19th century, each cast as a couple with arms clasped together, mounted on marble base, signed to bronzed "Duchoiselle," one clearly dated "1856," other with illegible date, bronze figure to 11" high. **$960**

James D. Julia, Inc.

Austrian Art Nouveau lamp with bronze base with organic lines and maiden's head on front, single arching arm supports shade ring, mushroom shade with amber mottled decoration against light yellow background; very good to excellent condition; shade 10" diameter, lamp 18" high. **$2,844**

Skinner, Inc.; www.skinnerinc.com

Pair of bronze cobra lamps, late 19th/ early 20th century, each with coiled body on octagonal bronze base, electrified, unsigned, 12" high. **$2,760**

Skinner, Inc.; www.skinnerinc.com

Pair of Bohemian overlay glass girandoles, 19th century, each white cut to green with gilt trim and polychrome enameled flowers, cut prism pendants, 12 1/2" high. **$2,040**

Skinner, Inc.; www.skinnerinc.com

Figural alabaster table lamp, Paris, early 20th century, carved as dramatic woman in flowing dress beneath domed and tasseled shade, reverse incised "Lenell, Paris" on onyx base, electrified, 21 3/4" high overall. **$960**

Skinner, Inc.; www.skinnerinc.com

◄ *Cold-painted bronze and metal lamp, Austria, early 20th century, faint impressed Bergman mark, modeled as cottage with minstrel at one side, doors opening to reveal cobbler at work, 11 3/8" high.* **$3,120**

Pair of gilt-bronze four-light wall sconces, late 19th century, each with four scrolling foliate arms with rocaille-style sconces and wall mount decorated with putto among flowers, 15" high x 14 1/2" wide x 12" deep. **$1,080**

James D. Julia, Inc.

Pairpoint Puffy grape table lamp, blown out shade depicting clusters of grapes and leaves in purple against green with yellow, brown, and purple leaves, rare and important base depicting clusters of grapes in relief with two sockets and acorn pull chains, finished with square foot with grape leaves in relief; shade signed "The Pairpoint Corp" and stamped "Pat Applied For," base signed on underside "Pairpoint Mfg Co," "P" in diamond and "3089"; very good to excellent condition; shade 12" diameter, lamp 19 1/2" high. **$13,365**

James D. Julia, Inc.

Tiffany Studios prism table lamp with large bronze top supporting gold glass prisms with peach, green and purple, three-armed bronze decorated Tiffany single-socket base, green-brown patina finish, very good to excellent condition, 19" high. **$13,628**

Maps & Globes

Throughout the ages, pictorial maps have been used to show the industries of a city, the attractions of a tourist town, the history of a region or its holy shrines. Ancient artifacts suggest that pictorial mapping has been around since recorded history began. "Here be dragons" is a mapping phrase used to denote dangerous or unexplored territories, in imitation of the medieval practice of putting sea serpents and other mythological creatures in blank areas of maps.

Swann Auction Galleries

▲ *Hugo Allard, "Novi Belgii Novaeqve Angliae nec non partes Virginiae," Amsterdam, circa 1662.* **$5,040**

Heritage Auctions

▶ *George III terrestrial globe, J & W Cary, London, circa 1815, globe with ring listing months and constellations, set in satinwood tripod base with ebonized details supporting compass, marks: Cary's New Terrestrial Globe; good condition with some water spots, cracking and losses to veneer, losses to ring that in parts has been in-painted, globe does not sit center on ring, cracking of veneer at top axis of globe, 46" high x 29" diameter.* **$21,250**

Pook & Pook, Inc.

▲ *Ink and watercolor map of North America, mid-19th century, 22" x 18".*
$830

Heritage Auctions

▶ *Merchant Shippers terrestrial globe with compass, George Philip & Son, Ltd., London, circa 1900, set on cabriole legs supporting compass shelf at base and at top globe set within ring labeling months and constellations, marks: Philips 18" Merchant Shippers Globe; good condition with some water spotting, 44" high.* **$4,375**

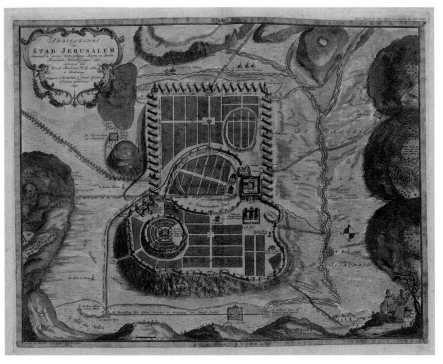

Swann Auction Galleries

Willem Albert Bachiene, untitled composite atlas with 12 hand-colored maps of Holy Land interest, Gorinchem, 1748-1750. **$3,600**

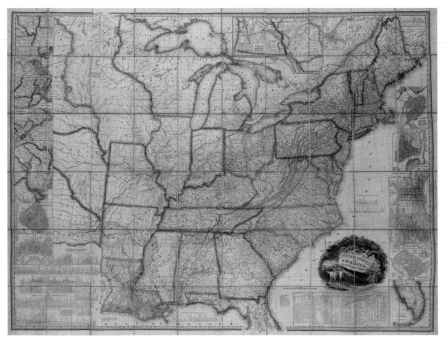

Swann Auction Galleries

Henry Schenck Tanner, "United States of America," Philadelphia, 1829. **$8,400**

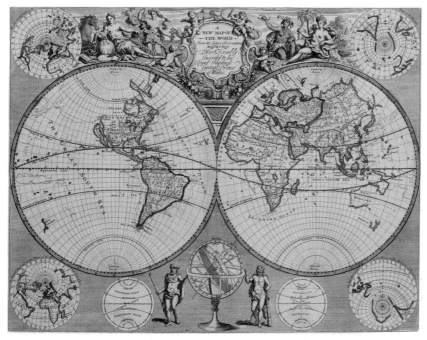

Swann Auction Galleries

John Senex, "A New Map of the World," London, 1721. **$1,968**

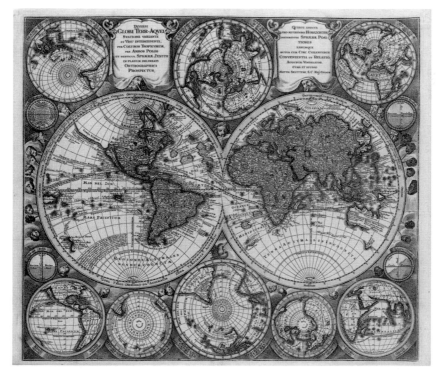

Swann Auction Galleries

Matthaeus Seutter, "Diversi Globi Terr-Aquei," Augsburg, circa 1730. **$2,640**

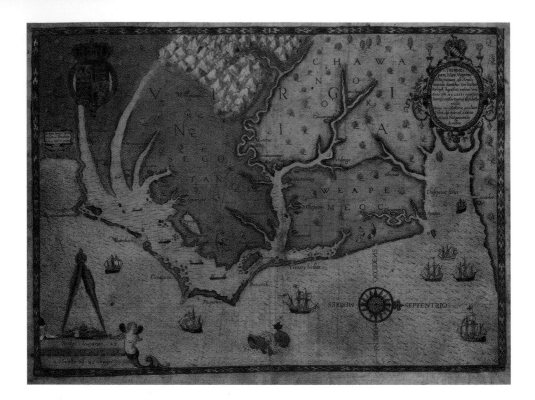

▲ *Theodore de Bry, "Americae pars, nunc Virginia," Frankfurt, 1590.* **$8,400**

Miniature ivory terrestrial globe, Great Britain, 19th century. **$2,640**

▲ *Jean Baptiste Bourguignon d'Anville, "Amérique Septentrionale," Paris, 1746.* **$1,200**

Swann Auction Galleries

Thomas Kitchin, "Map of the United States in North America," London, 1783. **$1,020**

Swann Auction Galleries

John Senex, "A Map of Louisiana and of the River Mississipi," London, 1721. **$2,280**

Heritage Auctions

▶ *Victorian terrestrial globe and compass in mahogany stand, W. & A.K. Johnston, Edinburgh, Scotland and London, circa 1891, brass mount within calendar and zodiac outer rim, mounted on mahogany tripod base with incurved legs centering compass, marks: 18 INCH, TERRESTRIAL GLOBE, BY W. & A.K. JOHNSTON, Geographer, Engravers & Printers, TO THE QUEEN, 1891, EDINBURGH & LONDON; significant yellowing to globe surface, rubbing, water and sun damage to rim separating at joints, 41" high x 23" diameter.* **$5,000**

Swann Auction Galleries

Ranzan Takai, "Great Annotated Dictionary of Edo," Kyoto, 1861. **$510**

Swann Auction Galleries

Edward Wells, "A New Map of the most Considerable Plantations of the English in America," London, 1700. **$900**

Swann Auction Galleries

Frederick de Wit, "Nova Totius Terrarum Orbis Tabula," Amsterdam, 1670 or later. **$5,520**

Swann Auction Galleries

Emanuel Bowen, "A New and Accurate Map of New Jersey, Pensilvania, New York and New England," London, circa 1747. **$1,440**

Swann Auction Galleries

Lucas Jansz Waghenaer, "The Sea Coastes of England," London, 1588. **$1,080**

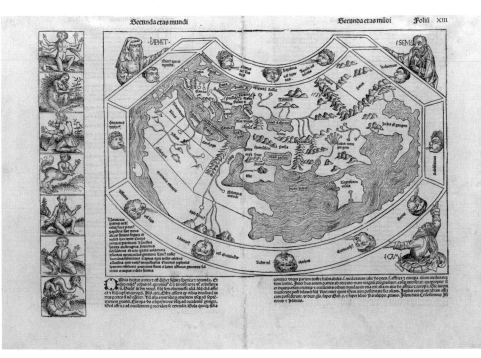

Swann Auction Galleries

Hartmann Schedel, "Secunda etas mundi," Nuremberg, 1493. **$7,200**

Maritime Art & Artifacts

By Martin Willis

For extended periods, sometimes even years, a sailor could be at sea on a whaling expedition. But little of that time was spent doing actual whaling work. Often months would pass between sightings. Sailors had hours of idle time, and some filled that time creating trinkets and art.

Sailors' artwork includes scrimshawed whale's teeth and bone; fancy rope knot work; wood and ivory carvings, such as whimsies, cane heads, pie crimpers, pipe tampers, and fids (made for splicing rope); and more. There were valentines made with seashells, swifts (yarn winders), corset busks, and many more interesting and beautiful pieces.

The art of scrimshaw began in the early 1800s and is still practiced today. A scrimshaw artist is called a scrimshander. Starting with a raw tooth, in its natural state with ridges, a scrimshander would spend hours polishing it to a smooth surface. He would then begin his design using a sharp needle and India ink. Most of the time black ink was used, but sometimes other colors were also used, mostly red.

Martin Willis

I have been lucky enough to see some fabulous whale's tooth scrimshaw work. In the 1980s I spent several days with collector Barbara Johnson in Princeton, New Jersey. Her entire collection was a premier selection of some of the finest pieces known, considered the foremost in the world.

Scrimshaw can tell a story, often with a design of the captured whale on the verso side. The work may be valued as primitive or folk art. In general, most collectors want extensive detail and a great subject, including beautiful maidens, couples, portraits, whaling ships, American eagles and political designs, whaling scenes, and home ports or ports visited. Sometimes a tooth is completely covered with art telling intricate stories, some with named places and dates. Surprisingly, most scrimshaw work is not signed by the scrimshander.

An original period scrimshaw tooth is very desirable and can sell from several hundred dollars to $50,000. In rare cases a few have sold for as much as $100,000, including one called Susan's Tooth from the whaling ship "Susan," by scrimshander Frederick Myrick.

However, the record goes to the scrimshander known only as "The Pagoda Artist." An

MARTIN WILLIS is the Director of the Decorative Arts at James D. Julia, Inc., one of the nation's premier auction galleries. Formerly of New Hampshire, Willis comes from a family of auctioneers: His father, Morgan Willis, developed and ran the Seaboard Auction Gallery in Eliot, Maine, which Martin eventually took over. He has 40 years of experience in the antique auction business from companies in Maine, New Hampshire, Massachusetts, Colorado and California. He spent six years with Clars Auction Gallery of Oakland, California, as senior appraiser, cataloger and auctioneer, handling the estate of TV mogul Merv Griffin as well as talk show host Tom Snyder. In 2009, Martin launched Antique Auction Forum, a biweekly podcast on the art and antiques trade with followers across North America and throughout the world.

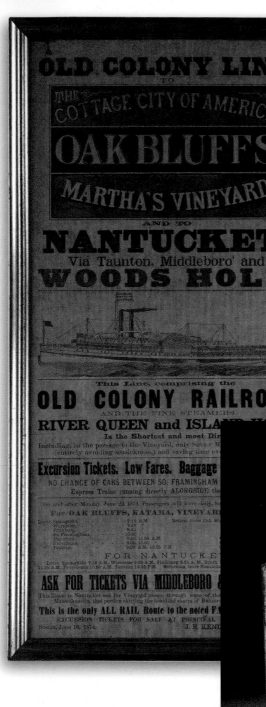

Swann Auction Galleries

Old Colony Line to the Cottage City of America / Oak Bluffs / Martha's Vineyard / and to / Nantucket, 1874. **$1,920**

Skinner, Inc.; www.skinnerinc.com

Painted nautical traverse board, divided into two parts with top section having 32 compass points for recording direction sailed, eight copper pegs attached to center with string, bottom section for recording speed, four rows of holes, columns representing certain speed, four pegs attached with string, 17 1/2" high. **$7,200**

Skinner, Inc.; www.skinnerinc.com

Scrimshaw carved and decorated bone jagging wheel, faceted carved handle with engraved motifs including foreshortened ships, whales, hearts, stars, leaves, and flowers, 4 3/4" long. **$450**

Coeur d'Alene Art Auction

Paul Grimm (1891-1974), "Sailboat Liberty," oil on canvasboard, signed lower left, 9" x 12". **$2,340**

unsigned and attributed tooth sold several years ago in Portsmouth, New Hampshire, for $303,000.

Before purchasing a vintage scrimshawed tooth, seek an expert's opinion. An old tooth should have a mellow patina, and the ink should be somewhat faded. Resin fakes can fool a novice, and antique whale's teeth can be recently scrimshawed. The ink is usually very dark on these pieces.

Whale's teeth are hollow on the underside, unless cut. Later teeth usually look very white. Sometimes people confuse walrus or elephant ivory with whale ivory. Walrus tusks are scrimshawed as well but are worth a fraction of the value of whale's teeth.

Collecting scrimshaw fell out of favor for many years until President John F. Kennedy was elected. He was an avid collector, and this spawned a renewed interest in the hobby. Today there are many collectors all around the world.

Fine examples of scrimshaw are exhibited at the New Bedford Whaling Museum (www.whalingmuseum.org) and the Peabody Essex Museum (www.pem.org) in Salem, Massachusetts.

Coeur d'Alene Art Auction

Edgar Payne (1882-1947), "Brittany Boats" (circa 1923), oil on canvas, signed lower right, 25" x 30".
$70,200

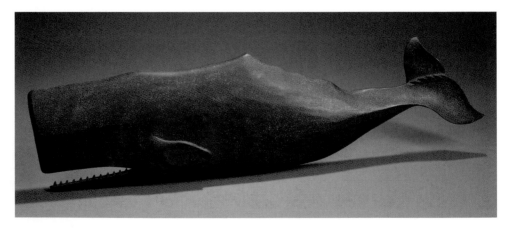

Skinner, Inc.; www.skinnerinc.com

Large carved and painted wooden sperm whale plaque, Clark G. Voorhees, Jr. (1911-1980), Old Lyme, Connecticut, and Weston, Vermont, third quarter 20th century, signed with impressed artist's initials "CV" and "C. VOORHEES" on reverse, 9 1/2" high x 35 1/4" long. **$13,200**

Bonhams

*Edgar Payne (1883-1947), "Brittany Boats," oil on canvas, signed "Edgar Payne" lower left, 28" x 34",
32 1/2" x 38 1/2" overall.* **$35,000**

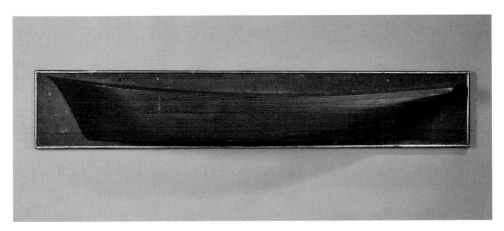

Skinner, Inc.; www.skinnerinc.com

*Large half-hull ship model, probably Maine, early 20th century, shaped laminated contrasting wood segments, mounted
on dark green-painted panel with applied gilt molding, back of panel with penciled inscriptions "1904 Washburn
Bros. / Thomaston / 170 feet," likely referring to Washburn Brothers Shipyard in Thomaston, Maine, minor joinery
separations, 11 3/4" x 66".* **$3,900**

Skinner, Inc.; www.skinnerinc.com

Sailor's brass-bound leather-covered camphorwood sea trunk, China, early 19th century, rectangular trunk, lid centered with engraved pewter plaque with "Peleg Simmons / New Bedford," sides covered with black leather studded with brass tack borders, brass swing handles on sides, minor imperfections, 13" high x 31 1/4" wide x 16" deep. Provenance: Peleg Simmons was born in Tiverton, Rhode Island, in 1804. At the age of 19 he went on a whaling voyage out of New Bedford, Massachusetts from June 18, 1822 to April 27, 1823 on the ship George & Martha, and at age 21 from June 2, 1827 to July 7, 1828 on the ship Galeta. The New Bedford city directory later lists him as a laborer and a fisherman. He died, unmarried, on Nov. 13, 1871, at the age of 67. **$600**

Skinner, Inc.; www.skinnerinc.com

Scrimshaw whale's tooth depicting ship of the line flying American flag flanked by floral borders, heightened with red, green, and blue, with initials "LS" near base, 3 3/8" wide x 6 1/2" long. **$2,040**

Bonhams

Thomas Arnold McGlynn (American, 1878-1966), "Fishermen's Wharf, San Francisco," oil on canvas, signed "Thos. A. McGlynn" lower left, 19 1/4" x 21", 23 1/2" x 25 1/2" overall. **$5,250**

Skinner, Inc.; www.skinnerinc.com

Schooner diorama, America, late 19th/early 20th century, painted wooden half-hull three-masted schooner flying American flag, sailing with two small steam vessels, lighthouse and cottage in foreground, painted putty sea and background, mounted in deep gilt-gesso and molded wood frame, 25" x 42 1/2" overall. **$840**

Skinner, Inc.; www.skinnerinc.com

◀ Engraved whalebone busk, 19th century, with five engraved motifs heightened with red and green sealing wax, eagle with banner inscribed "E PLURIBUS UNUM," wreath centered with monogram "AEL," spray of flowers, another wreath centered with inscription "Tho' Lost to Sight / to Memory Dear," and urn of flowers, 14 3/8" x 1 1/2". **$3,120**

Skinner, Inc.; www.skinnerinc.com

Sea captain's writing box, America, late 19th century, rectangular bird's-eye maple box with hinged lid, brass swing handles, side drawer with compartments, interior with velvet-covered writing surface, storage cavities, and compartments for ink and writing utensils, shrinkage cracks on lid, 8" high x 22" wide x 10 5/8" deep. Provenance: This box reportedly belonged to Captain Samuel P. Smith of Edgartown, Massachusetts, according to inscriptions on an envelope with a clipping of a small news article about the captain. **$475**

Bonhams

Armin Hansen (American, 1886-1957), "Men of Dogger Bank," oil on board, signed "Armin Hansen" lower left, signed and titled " 'Men of Dogger Bank" / Armin Hansen" on reverse, 10" x 12", 15 1/2" x 17 1/2" overall. **$25,000**

Albertus van Beest (Dutch/American, 1820-1860), "Rowing Ashore," ink and watercolor en grisaille on paper, signed and dated "Albertus Van Beest/1850" lower left, pale mat burn, several fox marks or small stains, sight size 12 7/8" x 19 7/8". **$1,920**

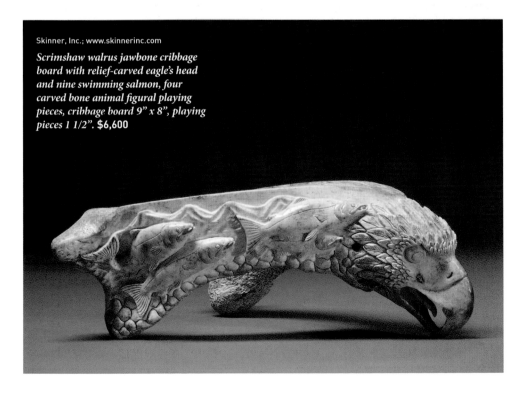

Scrimshaw walrus jawbone cribbage board with relief-carved eagle's head and nine swimming salmon, four carved bone animal figural playing pieces, cribbage board 9" x 8", playing pieces 1 1/2". **$6,600**

Skinner, Inc.; www.skinnerinc.com

Sailor-made inlaid pine trinket box, late 19th century, rectangular black-painted box with hinged lid, center of lid with inlaid pewter sperm whale figure flanked by ivory heart and diamond-shaped plaques, sides with hearts and front with diamond-shaped escutcheon, interior with small mirror affixed to lid, 2 7/8" high x 8" wide x 5 5/8" deep. **$1,440**

Coeur d'Alene Art Auction

David James (1853-1904), "Evening, Cornish Coast" (1891), oil on canvas, signed and dated lower right, 30" x 50". **$10,530**

Bonhams

Armin Hansen (American, 1886-1957), "Ebb Tide," oil on board, signed "Armin Hansen N. A." lower left, signed and titled " 'Ebb Tide' / By / Armin Hansen / Monterey – Cal" on reverse, 10 1/4" x 14", 15 3/4" x 19 3/4" overall. **$15,000**

Skinner, Inc.;
www.skinnerinc.com

Scrimshaw "ABC" box, 19th century, small turned cylindrical box with threaded closure, cover with engraved flowers heightened with red sealing wax and engraved "ABC," box contains 13 bone disks inscribed with letters of alphabet, minor crack, 1 1/8" high. **$600**

Bonhams

Thomas Kinkade (American, 1958-2012), "Skagway in 1898," oil on canvas stretched over board, signed and dated with artist's device "T. Kinkade / © 1988 / John 3:16" lower right, 30" x 48", 41 1/2" x 59 1/2" overall. **$31,250**

Provenance: This work is accompanied by a letter written by the consignor. In it, he writes that after vacationing with Kinkade on the consignor's yacht in Southeast Alaska, the artist asked if he would like to commission a work on the Klondike Goldrush, an interest both men shared. The consignor writes that he agreed, and "I charted a plane to fly [Kinkade and his wife] to Skagway to photograph the town and the terrain. Later I provided Thomas historical photographs of some of the famous ships that came to Skagway during the gold rush. This is the genesis of his painting 'Skagway 1898.'"

Skinner, Inc.; www.skinnerinc.com

T.S. & J.D. Negus two-day marine chronometer and display case, No. 1458, New York, circa 1860, 3 3/4" silvered Roman numeral dial marked with maker's name, location and number as above, subsidiary seconds and up/down indicator dials, gold hour, minute, and indicator hands, blued seconds, two-day chain fusee movement with split bimetallic two-arm balance and blued steel helical hairspring, brass and clear acrylic case on wooden base, 6 1/2" high. **$1,169**

Skinner, Inc.; www.skinnerinc.com

Morris Tobias binnacle timepiece, No. 123, London, circa 1795, with fusee movement signed "Morris. Tobias, No. 123, London," foliate-pierced balance bridge engraved "Patent Morris Tobias, London," slow/fast regulation, 4 1/2" enamel dial, No. 122, with brass hands, inner Roman numeral chapter ring and two outer sets of Arabic numerals for time and bells of watch, lacquered-brass bowl on pivots, dovetailed mahogany case with aperture in lid, 7 1/2" wide. **$4,800**

Bonhams

▲ *Model of Canadian two-masted fishing and racing schooner, Bluenose, Eugène Leclerc (Canadian 1885-1968), mid-20th century, inscribed Bluenose and E. Leclerc, fitted within clear acrylic case and wall mounted wood shelf, model 39" long, shelf 47 1/2" long.* **$563**

Pook & Pook, Inc.

◄ *Relief carved and painted plaque of sailing ship, circa 1900, 20 3/4" x 34 1/2".* **$5,451**

T.S. & J.D. Negus two-day break circuit chronometer, No. 1254, New York, circa 1860, 4" silvered 24-hour silvered Arabic numeral dial marked with maker's name and serial number as above, up/down indicator and seconds dial, gold hour, minute, and indicator hands, blued second hand, screw fit bezel marked U.S. Navy, two-day chain fusee movement with maintaining power, two-arm split, bimetallic balance and helical hairspring mounted in gimbaled brass bowl, brass-bound, three-tiered rosewood box with printed instructions inside lid, inset mother-of-pearl plaque marked BREAK CIRCUIT, two wire connection terminals and tipsey key, boxed 7 3/4" high. **$4,200**

"Peoples Line, Steamer Drew," color lithograph, New York, circa 1867. **$330**

Skinner, Inc.; www.skinnerinc.com

Heath & Co. sextant, London, model Hezzanith with pierced frame, quick release index arm, inset silvered scale calibrated 0-130, vernier knob calibrated 0-55 for fine adjustment, sun shades, horizon mirror, fitted mahogany box with tag reading "Bell" Pattern, Mark III, Sextant; 7" high, with set of binoculars and additional eyepieces. **$540**

Skinner, Inc.; www.skinnerinc.com

J.M. Kleman hanging crown or telltale compass, Amsterdam, circa 1790, 6" fleur-de-lis dry map suspended on central pin, scale divided in four quadrants, cast brass ornamentation in shape of crown surrounds compass dome, gimbaled suspension, 6 3/4" overall diameter. **$5,000-$7,000**

Bonhams

William Garthwaite (British, 1821-1899), "The Wreck of an Indiaman," oil on canvas, signed and dated "W. Garthwaite 1851" lower left, signed, titled and dated "Wreck of an Indiaman. / W Garthwaite – 1851" on reverse, 12" x 17". **$1,000**

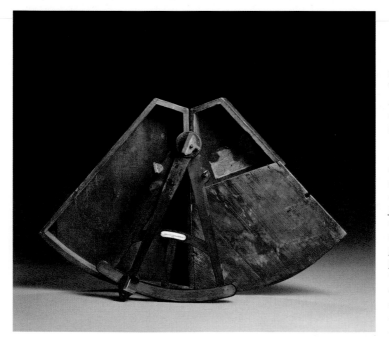

Skinner, Inc.;
www.skinnerinc.com

Mahogany and boxwood octant, circa 1782, bone plaque engraved "Captain John Ashton 1782," boxwood arc with carved center grid and divided 0-90 in both directions, two small fleur-de-lis markings, index arm with ivory-edge reader, sighting pinnula, horizon mirror, pine fitted keystone box with label on inside stating in part, "Gedney King, No. 10 North Row Boston," octant 15", box 18 3/4" long. **$3,900**

Movie Posters

By Noah Fleisher

There is magic in old movie posters; the best directly channel the era from which they came. The totality of movie poster art, the oldest and rarest going back more than a century, taken as a whole, is no less than a complete graphic survey of the evolution of graphic design and taste in Western culture.

The broad appeal of movie posters stems from that nostalgia and from the fact that so many pieces can be had at very fair prices. This makes it an attractive place for younger collectors, many of whom don't even realize they are starting on the incredible journey that collecting can be. Most are simply looking to fill space on a wall or give a gift, and they fill it with art from a movie they loved when they were kids, or one that meant something to them at a specific point in their lives.

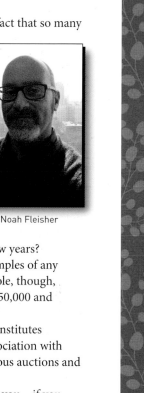

"There's a natural evolution with many of them," said Grey Smith, director of movie posters at Heritage Auctions. "As they progress in their lives, they tend to progress as collectors, trading up as they go. When it's all said and done, you see accomplished, broad-based collections."

Movie posters can rightly be called a gateway collectible for that very reason. Very few true collectors just collect one thing and, for more than a few, the first taste comes in the form of movie posters.

Noah Fleisher

So where, exactly, is the top of the market and how has it fared in the last few years?

"As always, Universal horror is the top of the market," said Smith. "Top examples of any great film – the older the better – will always bring respectable prices. As a whole, though, the market is off from five and 10 years ago when top posters were bringing $250,000 and $350,000, but it's been steady at the bottom of the high end and in the middle."

What does this mean to today's collectors? It means that a cooled market constitutes incredible opportunity to the trained eye. The untrained eye can benefit by association with reputable dealers and auction houses, by keeping a steady eye on prices in various auctions and on eBay, and by learning what they like, where to get it and when to buy.

Any dealer or auction house worth its salt is going to spend some time with you – if you want – at whatever level you are collecting, to help you figure out what you can get within your budget. From $100 to $1,000 and up into five and six figures, there are relative bargains to be had right now and, to go back to the top of this discussion, the artwork just can't be beat.

"Ultimately, I would tell anyone looking to buy a movie poster to buy it because they like it," said Smith, echoing the first rule of the business across all categories. "It's all about individual taste. Never get into something for the money because you'll be disappointed."

Besides buying online or from auction houses – at least a few of which, like Heritage, have

NOAH FLEISHER received his Bachelor of Fine Arts degree from New York University and brings more than a decade of newspaper, magazine, book, antiques and art experience to his position as Public Relations Director of Heritage Auctions, one of the country's foremost auction houses. He is the former editor of *Antique Trader*, *New England Antiques Journal* and *Northeast Antiques Journal*, is the author of *Warman's Modern Furniture*, and has been a longtime contributor to *Warman's Antiques and Collectibles*.

Heritage Auctions

"Moon Over Miami" (20th Century Fox, 1941), one sheet, Style B: Don Ameche and Betty Grable joined forces for their second film together in this romantic musical; airbrushed borders and touchup to folds, very fine condition on linen, 27" x 41". **$15,535**

*"Flash Gordon Conquers the Universe,"
Universal, 1940, stock one sheet: Buster
Crabbe as Alex Raymond's legendary
spaceman and Carol Hughes as Dale
Arden; linen trimmed up to edge of
poster; prior to restoration, pinholes
and tiny chips off each corner, slight
paper loss at middle center point and
in top of "v" of Universe, airbrushing in
yellow of title to correct for paper loss,
fine/very fine condition on linen,
27" x 41".* **$8,365**

weekly offerings online to
complement its larger thrice
yearly events – good posters
can be found, for the intrepid
explorer, in country auctions,
flea markets and antiques
shows across the country.

The movies are universal
and every town had a movie
house. The result is that
posters were distributed
everywhere and, while not
meant for display purposes in
the long-term, many found second
lives as insulation in walls or as a single layer in a thick, glued board of movie posters, as
theater owners would wallpaper the posters over each other from week to week. The erudite
eye can pick out the corners of one of these constructs, or can recognize the quality of paper
and the neat folds of a quietly stashed one-sheet. The result can often be a treasure, financially
and artistically.

Two aspects of movie poster collecting that get much attention and much misinformation
are restorations versus forgeries and fakes.

Every collector should be wary of fakes and forgeries: If it seems too good to be true, ask
questions and consult reputable sources. There are always unscrupulous people looking to take
advantage of the unsuspecting. A pro will know, based on a variety of factors, whether you
have a once-in-a-lifetime find or if you're looking at a clever reprint.

This should never be confused, however, with respectable restoration. Older posters often
come with the damage of age – they were not printed on the highest quality paper, as they were
not meant to be lasting mementos. Movies played for a few weeks and were replaced, as were
the posters. If a poster is linen-backed or framed, there has likely been restoration work on it,
and a good dealer or auctioneer will be very up front about this.

"Oftentimes a poster would not have been saved had it not been for quality restoration,"
said Smith. "Good restoration work is respectful of the original and will enhance the value
of a piece, not hurt it. A fake is a fake, no matter what, and should never be portrayed as an
original. Educate yourself, check your sources and you should do just fine."

Heritage Auctions

"Ocean's 11" (Warner Brothers, 1960), door panel, set of six: starring Frank Sinatra, Peter Lawford, Sammy Davis, Jr., Dean Martin, Joey Bishop, and Angie Dickinson; panels dedicated to Martin, Davis, Lawford, Sinatra, Dickinson, and rarely seen cast panel showcasing image similar to insert; prior to restoration, each panel had trim in lower border that was restored, Dickinson panel with some chipping in upper right corner, pinholes in upper corners, and airbrush work near upper border, Davis panel with some airbrush work along upper edge, cast panel with pinholes in upper corners, borders airbrushed, fine+ condition on linen, 20" x 60". **$21,510**

Heritage Auctions

"The Public Enemy" (Warner Brothers, 1931), window card: James Cagney's portrayal of big city gangster, co-starring Jean Harlow, film chronicled rise and fall of Cagney's character during Prohibition; restoration to approximately 2" at top of imprint area, chip and small tear in left and lower borders, airbrush work to white background, fine+ condition, 14" x 22". **$11,353**

Heritage Auctions

"Marihuana" (Roadshow Attractions, 1936), one sheet: cult classic about evils of smoking marijuana though artwork leads one to believe film is about heroin usage, posters were low budget and rare; borders airbrushed, minor color touch-up to fold lines, fine/very fine condition on linen, 27" x 41". **$6,573**

Heritage Auctions

"The 3 Stooges in Cash and Carry" (Columbia, 1937), title lobby card: The 3 Stooges' 25th short for Columbia; pinhole in each upper corner, wear to top border and rounded corners, fine+ condition, 11" x 14". **$10,158**

Heritage Auctions

"The 3 Stooges in Hoi Polloi" (Columbia, 1935), title lobby card: classic short based on premise of George Bernard Shaw's "Pygmalion"; restored to address chip from upper left and right corner within border, replaced paper in lower left corner, airbrush work in lower right corner, fine+ condition, 11" x 14". **$10,158**

Heritage Auctions

"The Adventures of Robin Hood" (Warner Brothers, 1938), six sheet: all-star cast with Errol Flynn as Robin Hood, Olivia de Havilland as Maid Marian, Basil Rathbone as Sir Guy of Gisbourne, Claude Rains as Prince John; duel between Flynn and Rathbone depicted on rare six sheet, possibly only known example to survive; pinholes in corners, minor edge tears extended into artwork, small chips along folds, small hole in middle of title, four censor stamps, professional restoration, fine/very fine condition on linen, 81" x 81".
$41,825

Heritage Auctions

"The 3 Stooges in I'll Never Heil Again" (Columbia, 1941), one sheet: short with The 3 Stooges taking on dictators of the world, sequel to "You Nazty Spy"; rare, prior to restoration there were two small chips on left border and small amount of surface paper loss on back, touchup to folds, very fine- condition on linen, 27" x 41". **$7,768**

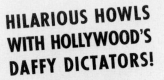

HILARIOUS HOWLS WITH HOLLYWOOD'S DAFFY DICTATORS!

THE 3 STOOGES
CURLY · LARRY · MOE
I'LL NEVER HEIL AGAIN

Produced and Directed by JULES WHITE

A COLUMBIA SHORT-SUBJECT PRESENTATION

THEY'RE OFF··· THEIR NUTS

PLAYING THE PONIES

Heritage Auctions

"The 3 Stooges in Playing the Ponies" (Columbia, 1937), one sheet: The 3 Stooges trade their restaurant for a broken-down racehorse named Thunderbolt; prior to restoration missing paper at top right corner extending into "S" in Stooges, small tears in bottom border, pinholes in background, touchup to folds and borders, fine/very fine condition on linen, 27" x 41". **$26,290**

Heritage Auctions

"Attack of the 50 Foot Woman" (Allied Artists, 1958), one sheet by artist Reynold Brown: jealous wife Allison Hayes is scratched by an alien, grows to enormous proportions, and goes on destructive rampage; professional restoration to small hole in left border, tiny hole in right border, some bleedthrough in background from writing on verso, touchup work to folds, linen backing trimmed to borders, fine+ condition on linen, 27" x 41". **$10,158**

Movie Posters

Heritage Auctions

"The Wizard of Oz" (MGM, 1939), half sheet, Style A, and partial pressbook (28 pages plus covers, 16" x 18"): poster with portraits of film's leading characters, inset of Dorothy, Tin Man, and Scarecrow on Yellow Brick Road, Dorothy in Oz with Glinda the Good Witch; touchup to folds, color enhancement within image due to fading, airbrush work to borders to address small chips; with Exploitation Section from original release pressbook, front and back covers filled with color renderings of characters, interior pages contain promotional pieces and posters, including sheet music, 20" x 60" cut-outs, six cut-out hangers, valances, banners, flags, 40" x 60" displays, seven-foot Telescopic Streamer Display, and instructions for "Back to School with the Wizard of Oz" campaign; book was folded once in half horizontally, small tear with tape on each page, writing in upper right of front cover; very good/fine condition on paper, 22" x 28". $71,700

"The 3 Stooges in Mutts to You" (Columbia, 1938), one sheet: Professional dog washers Larry, Curly, and Moe take home abandoned baby found on their doorstep, directed by silent screen comedian Charley Chase, co-starring Bess Flowers, Lane Chandler, and Vernon Dent; prior to restoration, pinhole in each corner, two small tears near lower left corner, touchup work to folds, very fine condition on linen, 27" x 41". **$28,680**

▶ *"The Thin Man" (MGM, 1934), one sheet, Style C: mystery starring William Powell and Myrna Loy, husband-and-wife sleuths, based on best-selling novel by Dashiell Hammett; possible only copy of Style C, excellent condition prior to professional restoration to small chip in center crossfold, 2" tear in background behind Powell's head, touchup to folds, very fine-condition on linen, 27" x 41".* **$35,850**

"The War of the Worlds" (Paramount, 1953), six sheet: H.G. Wells' Martian invasion tale featuring groundbreaking special effects by George Pal, starring Gene Barry, Ann Robinson, and Les Tremayne; poster showcases massive three-fingered alien appendage extending to snatch human couple; prior to restoration, crossfold separation with minor chipping, chips in upper horizontal fold, small chip to left of alien claw, vertical tear in title, touchup work to folds, post-restoration stain on lower verso, fine+ condition on linen, 79" x 80.5". Provenance: From the collection of Bruce Willis. **$7,170**

Heritage Auctions

"2001: A Space Odyssey" (MGM, 1969), one sheet, Psychedelic Eye style: cited as one of the greatest science fiction films ever made with special effects at film's end; film's 70 mm prints were re-launched in New York City in 1969 and two posters were created, using tagline, "The Ultimate Trip," featuring Starchild on one and Psychedelic Eye with Starchild at center on other; rarest of all "2001: A Space Odyssey" one sheets; with original New York Transit Authority shipping label, rolled, very fine+ condition, 27" x 41". **$14,340**

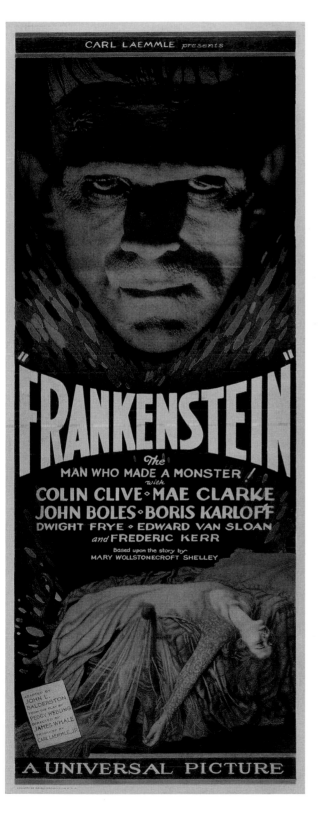

Heritage Auctions

"Frankenstein" (Universal, 1931), insert: only confirmed insert poster for this international horror sensation directed by James Whale and starring Boris Karloff; borders trimmed to edge of art, slight trim into upper yellow band on top edge, borders replaced, small chip from upper left corner replaced, some small tears, never folded, slight horizontal crease through Dwight Frye and Edward Van Sloan's credits, some color touchup to stress lines in lower blue band by Universal's credit, minor color correction to monster's portrait, rolled, fine+ condition, 14" x 36". **$262,900**

"Citizen Kane" (RKO, 1941), one sheet, Style A: Orson Welles stars as Charles Foster Kane in one of the finest pictures ever made; minor touchup to folds, restored small hole at bottom and small chip in bottom horizontal fold, dust shadow on left border and on edge of right border, small tear in cast list on right side, small nicks in left and right borders and top left corner, very fine-condition on linen, 27" x 41". **$38,838**

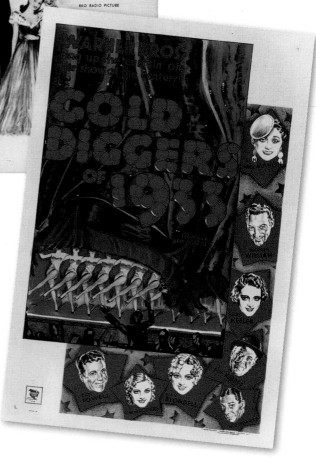

"Gold Diggers of 1933" (Warner Brothers, 1933), one sheet, Style B: film adapted from 1919 Broadway play by Avery Hopwood, in which a young man from a wealthy family (Dick Powell) bankrolls a struggling Broadway show and finds true love; poster features artwork of Powell, Ginger Rogers, Joan Blondell, Ruby Keeler, and Guy Kibbee, never used, slight fold wear, very fine+ condition on linen, 27" x 41". **$31,070**

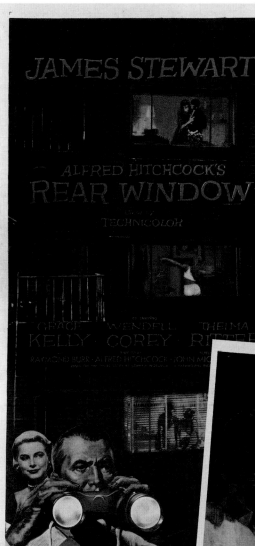

Heritage Auctions

"Rear Window" (Paramount, 1954), three sheet: Alfred Hitchcock film starring James Stewart as wheelchair-bound photographer who believes he has witnessed a murder while spying on fellow apartment inhabitants, co-starring Grace Kelly; prior to restoration it had pinholes in borders with a few in background, tear in left border, two tears near title, slight paper loss in lower right corner, two holes in lower border, touch-up work, borders airbrushed, very fine- condition on linen, 41" x 80". **$8,365**

Heritage Auctions

"The Adventures of Sherlock Holmes" (20th Century Fox, 1939), one sheet: starring Basil Rathbone as Sherlock Holmes against arch rival Professor Moriarty, who is set to steal the Crown Jewels, co-starring Ida Lupino and George Zucco as Moriarty; unrestored copy with pinholes in corners, very fine+ condition, 27" x 41". **$10,755**

Heritage Auctions

"Dr. Jekyll and Mr. Hyde" (Paramount, 1931), jumbo lobby card: based on novel written by Robert Louis Stevenson as an allegory on evils of drinking, starring Fredric March, poster depicts Mr. Hyde, who charges police who have come to arrest him; card with conservation to two chips in upper edge and two chips in right edge, few minor crimps within image area, very fine- condition, 14" x 17". **$20,315**

Heritage Auctions

"Dr. Jekyll and Mr. Hyde" (Paramount, 1931), jumbo lobby card: Mr. Hyde (Fredric March) drinks elixir that will convert him back to Dr. Jekyll; three corners with some minor creases supported on verso of card, minor crimps within image, light large crease from center of top edge running through March's raised arm, professional conservation, very fine condition, 14" x 17". **$19,120**

Heritage Auctions

"Sunset Boulevard" (Paramount, 1950), one sheet, Style A: film noir gem concerns a writer (William Holden), who plays confidant and companion to aging silent film actress (Gloria Swanson) in order to further his career; minor chips in edges of poster and tiny tears, slight color touchup to center points and to tiny tears along fold lines and pinholes in corners, damage to lower right corner, professionally restored, linen backing trimmed almost to edge of poster, fine+ condition on linen, 27" x 41". **$20,913**

Music Memorabilia

By Susan Sliwicki

These days, it's almost unthinkable to see your favorite band perform in concert or at a music festival without taking at least a little bit of the show home with you, be it a T-shirt, a trucker's cap or even a tour jacket.

But the items we take for granted that we will see these days in artists' online shops and on their merchandise tables at concerts weren't always a given. Concert T-shirts didn't start popping up until the 1960s, and even then, the focus was less on making a buck from fans than providing shirts for crew members, record label officials and venue employees. Savvy bands and managers soon caught on that fans would gladly shell out a few bucks for a tangible link to their favorite acts, and the merch business was born.

When it comes to concert T-shirts, buyers tend to fall in one of two main camps, says Jacques van Gool, owner of Backstage Auctions, a Houston-based auction house that specializes in music memorabilia consigned by artists and industry insiders.

"You've got one big group that buys them purely as a collectible, and as soon as they get the shirt, they put it in a plastic bag and preserve it together with the other T-shirts they have," van Gool said. "And you have the people that buy them to wear them, as a simple fashion statement."

Backstage Auctions

Grateful Dead 1978 tour original concert T-shirt. **$79**

Van Gool falls in the second camp, with baseball-style T-shirts being a personal favorite. Concert tees often serve as a conversation starter, he said.

"I just love them for their design," he said. "I think concert shirts are great, and they're meant to be worn."

Of course, wearing your band loyalty on your sleeve, so to speak,

---

SUSAN SLIWICKI'S favorite childhood memories are of hours spent hanging out with her oldest brother, who let her listen to his collection of albums, including Pink Floyd's "Dark Side of the Moon" and Deep Purple's "Machine Head," in exchange for her silence as long as the record was still spinning on the turntable. A journalist by trade, Sliwicki brought her two greatest passions — words and music — together when she joined *Goldmine* magazine in 2007 and became its editor in 2011.

can be tough to do if you've got your heart set on an original-era T-shirt from the '60s and '70s. First, such items were made in limited quantities, if at all. Second, enough time has passed that the selection, availability, and quality of the ones that remain are at a premium. And third, the ones that did survive in good condition tend to surface in very select sizes.

"On the crew, you're hardly ever going to find somebody in a size small. For the most part, these were manual laborers who were big, beefy, burly guys, who at minimum needed a large or an extra large," he said. "And all the shirts from the 1970s and '80s, they are by definition smaller than today's shirts, because people were smaller 20, 30, 40 years ago. A shirt that is labeled large in the 1970s is comparable to a small today."

The news about size and availability gets worse if you've got your heart set on snagging a vintage tour jacket.

Backstage Auctions

Led Zeppelin 1977 Oakland Stadium BGP promoter warmup jacket. **$785**

"Any jacket from the '70s or '80s is either a crew jacket or a record company promotional item," van Gool said. "Either the band wanted to do something nice for [its] crew and gave them all a jacket at the start of a tour, or the record company wanted to promote the release of a new album and made X number of jackets that [it] sent out to mostly radio stations or distribution companies. They were always made in very small quantities, literally from a couple dozen to a few hundred, at the most."

Although it's common to find jackets amid the apparel choices these days, they weren't routinely available for fans to purchase until the 1990s. Of course, just because something is available doesn't mean it's friendly to the average budget. Last winter, van Gool spotted a leather jacket offered at a Rush concert for $750.

"For a collector, there's a big difference between an official merchandise jacket, because those were made in much larger quantities and are much easier to get your hands on, than, say, the crew jackets or the promo jackets from the '70s and '80s – crew jackets, in particular, because very few were made, and most of them actually were worn," van Gool said. "Those jackets were not built to last. A lot of them just got completely torn and thrown away, or they got so dirty and stained they got thrown away, too. Those tour jackets are definitely a more unusual find."

If the thought of dropping more than $500 on a vintage shirt or jacket gives you sticker shock, consider another avenue of wearable concert memorabilia: the backstage pass.

The phrase "backstage pass" today tends to bring to mind the image of a laminated card on a lanyard – a format that is both durable and prestigious because it typically identifies the wearer as someone with access to the artist. But stick-on passes, also known as silk passes, have their own appeal because they were used for a specific date or venue, which can put them in demand if they were from an artist's final performance, or if something historic happened during that event.

"In the '70s, they all looked so different, and it could be that you had almost what looked like a business card with something written on it," van Gool said. "In some cases, they even used buttons as backstage passes."

Although there's no official scale when it comes to grading concert and promotional apparel, the concept is much the same as it is with vinyl records, right down to the belief that you'll never see a truly flawless example that deserves a grade of mint condition.

"If you've got a shirt that is spotless, stainless, no damage of any kind, then that usually is or should be graded excellent. Most shirts are probably graded anywhere between good and very good. When you've got a shirt that's 30 to 40 years old, there's going to be a flaw," van Gool said. "When a shirt comes off the press, it doesn't get sealed or anything, so there's a lot of human hands touching it, and it's always going to be exposed to some degree of the elements."

Common flaws include tiny holes, small food or beverage stains, sweat stains, or another type of wear.

"But shirts severely stained, that have the arms cut off, and shirts where people would cut the neck out or make a V-cut in the neck, anything along those lines should be graded fair or poor," he said.

Unless, of course, that cut shirt was worn by a rock star, such as one worn by Van Halen frontman David Lee Roth that Backstage offered at auction.

"We had photos of him wearing the shirt, and he was known for cutting not only the sleeves off, but cutting a sizeable portion of the flank off the shirt, and cut[ting] the neck out. Essentially, it was a rag, just hanging off his neck," van Gool said. "If you or I would've done it, the value would've dropped to 25 cents. Since he did it, it ended up selling for $600 or $700."

Just because a shirt is in well-loved, fragile condition doesn't mean it lacks value.

"There are shirts, especially from the late '60s and all the way into the '70s, that are so exceptionally rare that you want to have that shirt regardless of condition," he said.

While condition is a factor in value, rarity plays into things, too. Determining an item's rarity comes down to where, when, and how it was offered.

At the bottom of the value pyramid are the mass-produced, official merchandise shirts offered for sale at concerts, and, in the case of today's acts, in online stores. But if an artist prints up a shirt exclusive to one particular venue and offers that shirt only at the event, its rarity increases.

"In the '70s, people didn't buy merchandise at a concert. It may have been there, but it was a new thing to buy a shirt or program," van Gool said. "As a result, concert shirts from the '70s obviously should be a lot more valuable than shirts from the '80s, which are in turn more valuable than those from the '90s, and so on."

Next up in value: promotional shirts that were made by record companies from the 1970s into the 1990s.

"Record companies spent a lot of money on promotional shirts, and they were made in varying quantities, but some shirts were made a lot more than others," he said.

For instance, a variety of promo shirts were made for Bruce Springsteen's "Born in the U.S.A." album and tour. As a result, those shirts are more readily available than others. But those promo shirts still are scarcer than the concert T-shirts from that same album and era, he said.

At the top of the rarity heap are promoter shirts, which were around mostly in the 1970s and 1980s and typically handed out to people working for the promotional company, at the venue, or, on occasion, to the band. Multiple factors make promo T-shirts incredibly desirable among collectors, he said.

"They were never made for commercial purposes, so they only made 50 or 100 of those shirts," van Gool said. "And second, they're great because the design is unique to the promoter, and the promoter kind of had free rein to decide how fancy or not fancy to make their shirts. Third, they're unique, because typically on the back of the shirts, it would print a couple of dates from that tour."

More than 100 such rare shirts from Bill Graham Presents events in the 1970s were featured in Backstage's 2013 Vintage Concert Swag Auction, including a Led Zeppelin jacket from 1977, a couple of Pink Floyd shirts from 1977, and various Rolling Stones shirts from concerts and events in the 1970s.

Although color doesn't define or explain a shirt's rarity, it can offer some visual cues as to the era in which the shirt was made.

"In our experience, people were more frivolous with colors in the '70s than they were in the '80s and on. In fact, shirts past the '70s have become quite boring; they're either black or white, and black is starting to win that battle," van Gool said. "In the '70s, you had orange and green and blue, and I'm talking about lime green and traffic-light orange, colors that would make your cheeks smack, they're so in your face. That is a little bit of spillover from the late '60s, where colors were so much more a part of everything, including music memorabilia."

FAQs about Vintage Artist Apparel

Maybe you've taken the plunge and purchased a tour jacket at auction. Perhaps you're debating whether that vintage shirt you've been eyeing on eBay is the real deal. Either way, you probably have a few questions, and Jacques van Gool of Backstage Auctions is ready to help with answers to some of the most common topics related to vintage concert and artist apparel.

Question: What's the best way to care for and enjoy vintage T-shirts? Is the fabric fragile? Should you ever wash them, let alone wear them?

Answer: In my experience, the cotton quality from the '70s and the early '80s is much better than what it is today. I have seen 30-, 40-year-old shirts, used, that are in better condition than shirts that are 10 years old. In general, the quality of shirts was a lot better then than it is today. You can wash them or dry them. There's no special care required.

Question: What factors should I consider if I want to archive a shirt?

Answer: The two most important ones: climate controlled and dry. As long as your fabric is not exposed to extreme temperatures, and more importantly is not exposed to moisture, be that humidity or anything else, you should be OK. Whether you fold them, whether you hang them, whether you bag them, whether you frame them — all are OK.

Although, if you intend on displaying the shirt, another rule comes into play: as long as it's away from natural light. Shirts do fade with exposure to light, especially sunlight. If you do frame it, hang it on a wall that doesn't get exposure [to] sunlight or a lamp shining right at the shirt; this may cause discoloration.

I have seen people who have all their shirts hanging in their closet. Some hang with a plastic cover over them, others have them folded and in a closet. Other people put them in bags, and that's also to keep the dust out.

Question: How can bidders be sure they're getting an authentic concert, venue, or tour T-shirt vs. a reproduction or a fake?

Answer: It kind of differs from shirt to shirt. Obviously, there're a lot of shirts that have been reproduced. The three big differences between an authentic shirt and reproduction shirt:

First, the dimensions of the reproduced shirt are different. In 99 out of 100 cases, those shirts are going to be bigger, because nobody reproduces a 1970s shirt in 1970s dimensions because they're too small for today's people.

Second, the tags. And that's a hard one, because you would have to know the original manufacturer and those tags, but that information is most likely out there. There are obviously a lot of tags used today by companies that didn't exist in the '70s or '80s. It's very easy when you see a label or a tag to say, "Hold on here, that's not a '70s or '80s tag." The other thing in the last 10 years, most of the shirts that are being made are being made tagless. Up to the '90s, every shirt came with a tag.

The last one, and this may sound a little weird: Use your nose. Aged fabric is very much the same as aged paper. You can smell the difference.

Of course that's hard to do online. If you buy a shirt online and you're not entirely convinced that this is an authentic shirt, at least resort to the first two: dimensions and research about the tag.

Jacques van Gool and his wife, Kelli van Gool, own Backstage Auctions. The business celebrated its 10th anniversary in the fall of 2013. For more information, visit www.backstageauctions.com.

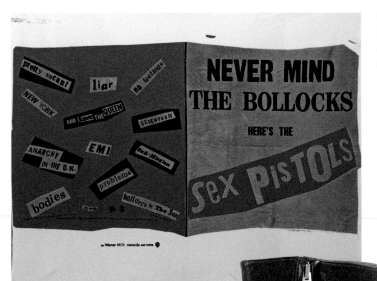

Backstage Auctions

Sex Pistols, 1977, "Never Mind the Bollocks," rare promo banner. **$2,596**

Bonhams

George Harrison's "Beatle Boots," black leather, calf-length with zip fastening, each inscribed inside in blue and red ballpoint ink, "Mr George 2062," left sole indistinctly stamped "8," circa 1964. Provenance: The Harrison Family Collection. **$99,054**

Bonhams

John Lennon's first car, 1965 Ferrari 330GT 2+2. When word spread in February 1965 that Lennon passed his driving test, numerous car dealers brought a variety of luxury vehicles to his Kenwood home in Weybridge, Surrey. After inspecting the cars, Lennon chose this right-hand drive Ferrari 330GT 2+2 coupe. **$581,358**

Bonhams

Brown leather and snakeskin jacket custom-made for The Who bassist John Entwistle in early 1970s by Skin Room, Ealing, West London; matching lining, two button-down breast pockets, seven buttons to front. **$8,490**

Christie's

Complete set of handwritten lyrics, in Jim Morrison's hand, for The Doors' song "L.A. Woman," 1971, 33 lines written in blue felt pen on three sheets of yellow legal paper, with top left corner initialed J.M./Doors. Provenance: The Personal Collection of Danny Sugarman; The Collection of Red Ronnie. **$95,411**

Christie's

Fuzz Face guitar effects pedal owned by Jimi Hendrix, circa 1969-1970, spherical metal pedal with two manual contacts and one foot contact, 7" diameter. Provenance: The Collection of Red Ronnie. **$9,638**

Heritage Auctions

Buddy Holly's personally owned and worn black silk, short-sleeved, jacket-style shirt, New Roma, size XL, 17-17 1/2, with "BH" hand-written on it, excellent condition. Provenance: Originally from Maria Elena Holly's personal collection. **$3,125**

Heritage Auctions

Brown velvet and gold silk brocade gypsy-style vest with decorative stitching, several pockets and tiny mirror appliques, owned and worn by Jimi Hendrix, who gave vest to his attorney, Stevens Weiss; fine condition with signs of wear and some cigarette burns. Provenance: From the Stevens Weiss Archive. **$30,000**

Christie's

Beatles autographed sheet music for "Please Please Me," 1963, printed by Dick James Music Limited, signed on cover in blue ballpoint pen by Paul McCartney, Ringo Starr, John Lennon, and George Harrison, 10 3/4" x 8 1/2". The signatures were believed to have been acquired at The Cavern Club in Liverpool, England, circa 1963. **$32,768**

Hake's Americana & Collectibles

Beatles Giant Bobbing Head store display figure set by Car Mascots, Inc., 14" to 15" tall, produced in limited quantities and available only to retailers for use as store display models, each with Beatle's facsimile signature decal on front of base, underside with ink stamp "©1964 Car Mascots Inc.," all four have complete "Made in Japan Car Mascot Inc. Los Angeles 28 Calif. USA" labels of 1 1/8" diameter, some scattered professional restoration. **$11,006**

Heritage Auctions

Circular poster promoting The Doors, The UFO and The Peanut Butter Conspiracy's April 21-23, 1967, performances at The Kaleidoscope at Ciro, 8443 Sunset Strip; purple and red-hued psychedelic image of Jim Morrison in profile, with Ray Manzarek, Robby Krieger, and John Densmore surrounding him, very good condition, 18.5" diameter. **$11,875**

Heritage Auctions

Concert poster for Big Brother and the Holding Co. with Janis Joplin (Baba Love Co., 1968) for group's April 19, 1968, performance at Selland Arena in Fresno, California, Mint Tattoo listed as opening act, Moby Grape listed as coming attraction; very good-plus condition, approximately 17" x 24.5". **$7,500**

Heritage Auctions

Michael Jackson white cotton V-neck, short-sleeved T-shirt, circa 2000s, inscribed in black felt-tip pen, designer tag reads "Ragno/Sport," similar tag sewn on left-side bottom hem, handwritten message reads "Burn All Tabloids I Love You So Much Michael Jackson." **$20,000**

Julien's Auctions

Gray and black suit jacket made for Elvis Presley by Sy Devore, gray slubbed fabric, single button, black satin lining, collar and cuffs, Sy Devore label on interior, interior pocket label reads, "Name Elvis Presley/Date 5-10-60 No. 8238," with letter of authenticity. **$34,375**

Julien's Auctions

Pair of Elvis Presley's stage-worn, cap-toe black and white Florsheim leather shoes gifted to Elvis' fan club president, Gary Pepper, inscribed on sole of left shoe, "To Gary Thanks for everything your friend Elvis Presley," with letter of authenticity. **$46,875**

Julien's Auctions

Eltro-Voice RE16 microphone owned and studio-used by Elvis Presley, engraved "Elvis" on stem, stamped with serial number 8552; microphone used during part of Elvis' final recording session in January/February 1976 and in 1972 MGM film "Elvis on Tour," while recording "Separate Ways"; 8" x 2", with two letters of authenticity. **$11,520**

Julien's Auctions

Frank Sinatra's custom house-shaped mailbox with "F. Sinatra" stenciled on both sides, moveable weathervane steeple, fitted with electrical wiring so name could be illuminated, 15" x 19" x 9". **$3,520**

Julien's Auctions

Brown velvet jacket with long coattails and pants worn by Liberace in photo on cover for "Impossible Dream" album, gold-toned beads and faux pearl inlays, white cotton tuxedo bib with lace ruffles, brown velvet bow and gold-toned rope thread entwined with faux pearl and iridescent stone pieces, two Cuna labels, one reads, "Name: Liberace Date: 3/69"; with copy of "Impossible Dream" album. **$12,800**

Jacket, T-shirt, and jeans worn onstage by Slash during Super Bowl XLV halftime show appearance with Fergie of The Black-Eyed Peas, D2D black cotton V-necked T-shirt; size large Chrome Hearts jacket with satin lining, metal rosettes, swords, and belt buckle; size 30 black Logan Riese denim jeans with leather decorations. **$15,000**

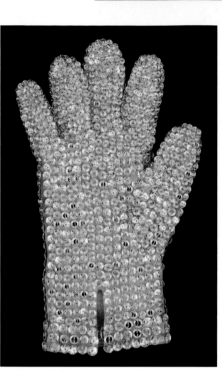

Sequined glove worn onstage by Michael Jackson during 1984 Jacksons' Victory tour; at end of concert in Dallas, Jackson gave glove to terminally ill child; glove shows signs of wear and traces of Jackson's makeup on inside. **$37,023**

Elvis Presley's stage-worn diamond and 14-karat gold nugget ring, 16 round brilliant-cut diamonds and three emerald-cut diamonds totaling 8.05 carats; Presley gifted ring to Lloyd Perry, fan in audience at 1975 concert in Asheville, North Carolina; with letter of provenance, newspaper articles, and photographs. **$57,068**

Gotta Have Rock and Roll

John Lennon-signed Record Plant Studios sticker in good condition, framed, 10" x 11"; with video documentary produced by NBC. After Lennon broke a guitar string while recording at The Record Plant in New York on Dec. 7, 1980, engineer Thom Panunzio rounded up an extra guitar string from musician Willie Nile, who also was at the studio. The next evening, Dec. 8, Penunzio asked Lennon for an autograph for his friend, Karl; the Beatle signed, "To Karl, who strung me along! Thanks John Lennon 1980," along with a self-portrait caricature, on the sticker before leaving the studio to go home to The Dakota. He was fatally shot that night. **$60,000**

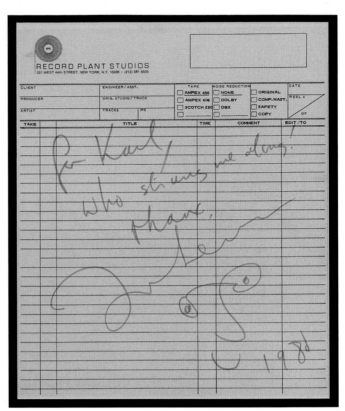

Gotta Have Rock and Roll

Black leather motorcycle jacket worn onstage by Bruce Springsteen during European leg of 1984-1985 "Born in the USA" tour, very good condition, from private collection of longtime associate of Springsteen's, with letter of provenance and photograph of Springsteen wearing jacket. **$11,400**

Gotta Have Rock and Roll

Original Polaroid photograph of Jimi Hendrix, signed by guitarist in black felt-tip marker, 3 1/2" square. **$10,365**

Sotheby's

Beethoven-autographed manuscript of exercises and drafts of composition for piano, two pages, Vienna, after 1800. Beethoven signed this sheet music, which belonged to Frederic Chopin, with autograph dedication signed by collector Aloys Fuchs in red ink: "Dem Herrn Fr. Chopin von seinem Verehrer und Freund Wien im Juni [1]831 Aloys Fuchs"; well preserved, a few tears, 8.6" x 12.2". **$331,040**

Gotta Have Rock and Roll

Original cardboard poster for The Beatles' Aug. 14, 1966, concert at Cleveland Stadium, good condition, some creasing, staining and wear, 1/4" tear at top edge, 14 1/2" x 20"; only four of these posters are known to have survived. **$23,582**

Sotheby's

Limited edition framed Cibachrome print titled "Keith Haring, New York" by Annie Leibovitz, signed and numbered 26/40 in ink in margin, taken in 1986, two years before artist was diagnosed with AIDS, 9 1/2" x 11 1/2". Haring's art was featured on picture sleeves and record albums; he died in 1990. **$40,624**

Musical Instruments

Musical instruments—devices designed to make musical sounds—fall into four basic categories: string, wind, brass, and percussion. Their visual beauty, history, technology, acoustic ability, and investment potential appeal to many people.

Collectors of musical instruments may focus on an individual instrument or family of instruments, on instruments from a particular geographic region, or on a specific manufacturer.

Antique instruments that pre-date the 20th century can be valuable because of their craftsmanship and historical significance. The violin, also called the fiddle, is one of the most popular antique instruments. It is the smallest, highest-pitched member of the violin family, which includes the viola, cello and double bass. Antique violins are often viewed as investments because of their likelihood to increase in value.

Instruments owned or played by famous musicians, such as Johnny Cash, Elvis Presley, and Jimi Hendrix, or played at well-known concerts such as Woodstock, are also highly desirable. In this segment of the hobby the most popular instrument is the guitar, which has ancient roots and is used in a wide variety of musical styles. It typically has six strings, but four-, seven-, eight-, 10-, 11-, 12-, 13- and 18-string guitars also exist. The size and shape of the neck and the base also vary. There are two main types of guitars: electric and acoustic.

For more information on other music-related collectibles, please see the "Music Memorabilia" and "Records" sections.

Sotheby's

Gilt-bronze mounted kingwood and end-cut marquetry art-case grand piano a queue with art case designed by Joseph-Émmanuel Zwiener, Hamburg, serial no. 108641, bronze mounts attributed to designs by Léon Messagé or Otto Rohloff; Steinway musical instrument with serial no. 15410 made in 1911, hinged, serpentine, gilt-bronze molded top decorated on border with marquetry foliate and flowering garland, case with gilt-bronze mounts, including musical trophy centered by violin to back and each side with two identical cartouches, 40 1/2" high x 68" wide x 94" long. **$422,500**

Rare "Dehua" flute, Xiao, 17th/18th century, molded in form of hollow bamboo stalk, pierced with five apertures to top, one to reverse and two to sides, mouthpiece formed by short, V-shaped cut, two-character inscription reading "feng ming" (the phoenix sings), 23 7/8". **$290,562**

Neil Young and The Squires, 1964, original handmade drumhead. **$2,513**

ZZ Top circa 1980s fully signed, 14" Ludwig drumhead. **$472**

Korn, 2006 lineup, signed Squier guitar. **$236**

Christie's

George III satinwood, cross-banded, mahogany, square piano, circa 1775, probably by Joseph Merlin, spans four octaves, with ivory (natural) and ebony (accidental) key covers, bi-chord throughout; two stop levers — one lifts dampers and other engages harp stop, hinged case lid encloses removable inner baffle with circular sound hole, on folding square legs, cartouche on fascia shows traces of inscription, reverse of fascia has later pencil inscription "Joseph Merlin 1770 to 1774," 29 3/4" high x 19" wide x 43" deep. **$8,468**

Backstage Auctions

Anthrax guitarist Scott Ian's tour-used and signed Randall V2 amplifier. **$400**

Backstage Auctions

Mudvayne's Matt McDonough concert-used and signed 15" cymbal. **$100**

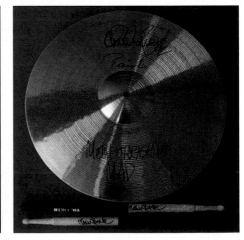

Backstage Auctions

Anthrax drummer Charlie Benante's concert-used and signed 15" cymbal from European leg of band's "Big Four" tour. **$250**

Bonhams

Flamenco guitar attributed to Conde Brothers, Madrid, labeled Conde Hermanos, Constructores, Calle Santiago Maganto, 4, Pozuelo de Alarcon, Madrid, (Espana); spruce table with inlaid colored wood decoration around sound hole, rosewood back and ribs, pale marginal inlay decoration, mechanical turners and rollers, minor use and wear, in case, back 19 7/16" long. **$2,826**

Backstage Auctions

Soundgarden guitarist Chris Cornell's 6129-T silver Jet Gretsch guitar. **$7,750**

Sotheby's

Upright studio piano with 58 keys from La Belle Aurore in movie "Casablanca" (Warner Bros., 1942), serial no. 253333, inscribed with maker's mark: Richardson's Inc., Los Angeles, with FNP11990 in marker; circa 1942, finished in viridian green with ivory trompe l'oeil craquelure interior panels. **$602,500**

▶ *Silvered Selmer Mark VI tenor saxophone, 1955, with padded silvered keys, engraved floral design, in case, with soprano saxophone branded Couesnon & Co, in case.* **$7,672**

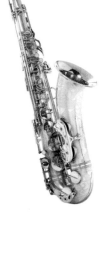

Brass ophicleide by Charles Joseph Sax, circa 1825, nine brass padded keys, use wear and restoration, fitted case. **$2,019**

Viola by Walter Mayson, Manchester, England, 1879, labeled "Deus Adsit Obsit Mundus," Gualterus Maysonus, Fecit Manrunii, A.D. 1879, signed internally, minor use and wear, in case, back 16" long. **$3,230**

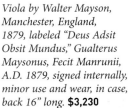

English harp-lute (dital-harp) attributed to A. Barry, London, circa 1815, seven stave back with open sound hole, table margins decorated with mythic flora and fauna, for 11 strings with pitch varying keys, use, wear and neglect, 34 1/20" long overall. **$1,817**

Selmer balanced action brass tenor saxophone, 1954, serial no. 56574, very good condition, original finish with minor corrosion, nicks and scratches, one small dent each at thumb rest and in bow, with original hard case. **$7,500**

Heritage Auctions

Early 1960 Gibson Les Paul Standard sunburst solid-body electric guitar, serial no. 0 1494, good condition, original except for tuners, which were replaced, original tuners in case but have shrunken buttons, pots date to 50th week of 1959, caps correct but unusual for era, all solder joints undisturbed, finish is original but appears buffed, treble side binding thinned and broken at 11th fret, most likely from buffing process, original hard case included. **$134,500**

Heritage Auctions

Restored 1941 Martin D-45 natural acoustic guitar, serial no. 78882, good condition, top removed to repair bracing and bridge plate issues, all interior patches and repair neat and clean, bridge replaced and is correct size, finish shadow around bridge from previous oversized bridge, pickguard replaced with what appears to be period-correct size and shape, 6" splint in top, repaired cracks in Brazilian back and sides, tuners are newer, open-gear Grovers, original hard case included. **$110,500**

Heritage Auctions

Rare cherry-finish 1959 Gibson ES-335 semi-hollow body electric guitar, serial no. A31602, good condition, correct style reproduction tuners and replaced nut, original finish faded to orange-red with moderate checking, considerable wear to original frets, electronics working but need cleaning, hard case included. **$35,000**

Heritage Auctions

◄ *Pearl Jam drummer Dave Abbruzzese's personally owned and stage-played bass drum and signed cymbal, very good condition, black and white finish with chrome hardware, stickers on head, including cannabis leaf, cymbal autographed and inscribed "Its my Saber[?]" by Abbruzzese, two white replacement rim rings for drum, one with slight warp.* **$1,875**

Bonhams

▲ *English concertina by Charles Wheatstone, 36 nickel keys, six fold blackbellows, two metal fret-cut endplates of floral design, leather straps and bone thumb rests, wooden hand rests inscribed Linota, use and wear, fitted leather case, 6 1/4" diameter.* **$4,442**

Heritage Auctions

◄ *Steve Marriott's 1957 Gibson Les Paul Custom black solid-body electric guitar, serial no. 7-8756, good condition, well-used by Small Faces and Humble Pie guitarist/vocalist; re-necked following a break while touring in Texas in 1969; middle pickup replaced with tortoise cover, original middle PAF pickup in case, original tail piece, ABR-1 bridge, switch tip, poker chip and knobs, original Grover screw holes under finish on headstock, Schaller-style tuners currently installed, replaced neck has no dot in "I" of Gibson, corresponding with 1969 re-neck, non-original bone nut, both remaining pickups are PAF and all three have stickers, frets are original to replaced neck and show moderate wear, several replaced plate and pickup ring screws, several replacement parts included in case, with photo of Marriott playing guitar with Humble Pie, includes Humble Pie road case.* **$31,250**

Heritage Auctions

Circa 1980s Fender Balboa acoustic electric guitar signed by 166 musicians and celebrities, seldom-seen model from Fender's California Series, acoustic body with single Venetian-style cutaway, Stratocaster-style neck, "six on a side" headstock (serial no. 5727001). Instrument originally owned by Canadian music enthusiast Charlie "Pride" Fraser, who gave it to Judy McKenzie, shortly before his death from cancer. McKenzie and Gary Hunter raised money by traveling North America to get guitar signed by entertainers and then auctioning it to benefit The Canadian Cancer Society. Signatures include John Rich and Big Kenny Alphine of Big and Rich, Cowboy Troy, Loretta Lynn, Dolly Parton, Reba McEntire, Toby Keith, George Strait, Randy Travis, Martina McBride, Wanda Jackson, Kris Kristofferson, Merle Haggard, Kix Brooks and Ronnie Dunn of Brooks & Dunn, Charley Pride, Randy Bachman and Fred Turner of Bachman-Turner Overdrive, Willie Nelson, Alan Jackson, Hank Williams, Jr., George Jones, Taylor Swift, Lyle Lovett, Charlie Daniels, Mel Tillis, David Allan Coe, Dwight Yoakam, Roy Clark, Chubby Checker, B.B. King, Bobby Vinton, Lady Antebellum's Hillary Scott, Dave Haywood and Charles Kelley, Charlie Sheen, Brett Michaels, Peter Noone of Herman's Hermits, and Jay Leno; includes hardshell case, Durham Furniture cherry display cabinet, and scrapbook. **$22,500**

Heritage Auctions

Italian-made 1960s Vox Country-Western acoustic guitar owned and used by Phil "Fang" Volk of Paul Revere and The Raiders, spruce top, maple sides and back, rosewood fingerboard with eight white-dot inlays, black headstock and plastic pickguard reading "Vox," black fleur-de-lis design around sound hole, serial number 211405, cracking evident on varnish, case included, 41" long, consigned directly by Volk, who used guitar in studio and on set of TV show "Where The Action Is!" with Dick Clark. **$1,563**

Heritage Auctions

Stan Kesler's owned and signed 1956 Fender Precision solid-body electric bass guitar, serial no. 13241, sunburst finish with white pickguard, single pickup, thumb rest, and two rotary controls, signed in silver ink with "Stan Kesler 1957" on front, and "I Forgot to Remember to Forget 1955 Stan Kesler," a reference to one of five songs Kesler wrote that Elvis Presley recorded, on back of body. Kesler was a songwriter, engineer and studio musician for Sam Phillips' Sun Records label. **$9,375**

Heritage Auctions

Rare 1996 Jackson Roswell Rhoads aluminum solid-body electric guitar, serial no. RSW054, all-original custom shop guitar, aircraft aluminum body and headstock, Tom Holmes humbucker, all electronics original and in working order, original hard case, some paperwork included. **$4,063**

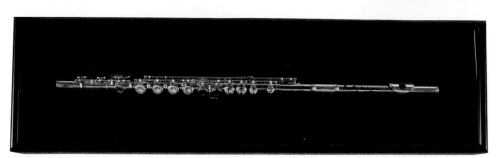

Heritage Auctions

Gemeinhardt Model 2SP silver-plated concert flute, serial no. J40384, signed by Jethro Tull flutist and vocalist Ian Anderson, professionally framed in shadow-box display, excellent condition, 32" x 9" x 2 1/2". **$1,063**

Heritage Auctions

Rare 1920 Gibson Harp sunburst acoustic guitar, serial no. 55510, very good, playable condition, straight neck, no body cracks, non-original six string tuners, original finish, dirty and scratched with normal play wear, with original hard case. **$6,250**

Heritage Auctions

Arctic White 1991 Gibson EDS-1275 solid body, double-necked electric guitar signed by Robert Plant and Jimmy Page of Led Zeppelin, serial no. 90161411, excellent condition, minimal wear with minor finish scratches, all electronics original and in good working order, signed by Plant and Page, with original hard case. **$10,000**

Heritage Auctions

Gibson J-200 custom black 12-string acoustic guitar, 1960, special ordered by David Guard of The Kingston Trio, serial no. A34487, originally featured sunburst finish (back remains that way), top, sides and neck refinished in mid-1960s, original hard case with slip cover, very good condition. **$12,500**

Heritage Auctions

Bach Stradivarius Model 42 brass trombone, 1993, no. 107738 in very good condition, light wear, minor dents, scratches and rust spots to connector area, slide moves with ease, with original hard case. **$813**

Skinner, Inc., www.skinnerinc.com

Two balalaikas, one three-string labeled "COBOT, NO. 256" and the other six-string labeled "6P.70K," both with beech backs, pine tops and walnut inlays, very good playing condition. **$125**

Heritage Auctions

Fender Bassman tweed guitar amplifier, 1958, serial no. BM02715, good condition, transformers correct but some caps replaced on main turret board, tubes non-original Mesas, power supply caps replaced with Sprague Blues, speakers and pots all date to 1959 but label date code is HD, indicating April 1958, date stamp on chassis is IJ, indicating October 1959. Provenance: From the Collection of Lee Herrington. **$5,938**

Skinner, Inc., www.skinnerinc.com

Kohler & Campbell Arts & Crafts oak upright piano with bench. Provenance: Penny Marshall Collection. **$500**

Heritage Auctions

Fender Custom Shop 1996 John Lodge Edition RB Classic precision bass, no. 9 of 20, excellent unplayed condition, made by Fender's Rich Briere with bassist John Lodge, based on 1962 P-Bass that Lodge used during his early days with The Moody Blues, ash body, satin maple neck with Lodge's facsimile signature on headstock, white pickguard signed in black felt-tip pen by Moody Blues' band members John Lodge, Graeme Edge, Ray Thomas, and Justin Hayward, with original hard case and manufacturer's "case candy." **$2,250**

Heritage Auctions

J.R. Stewart Le Domino black soprano ukulele, late 1920s, good condition, all original, chipping to original finish, tuners need to be replaced, bridge reglued for proper playability, with original soft case. **$625**

Heritage Auctions

Dobro sunburst resonator guitar, circa 1941, fair condition, no serial or model number, elongated fret board on round neck, binding repairs to back and sides at butt area, with non-original hard case. **$1,188**

Heritage Auctions

Gibson Mastertone tenor banjo, no hole tone ring indicates 1927 model, fair condition, broken binding and missing screws, loose neck, nicks and scratches to finish, missing nut, dent in flange, pitting and discoloration to metal parts, with hard case. **$4,000**

Julien's Auctions

Custom hand-carved mahogany-body DBZ guitar, serial no. F09090397, with image of late rocker Ronnie James Dio, Dio logo, and "Ronnie James Dio 1942-2010" and "In Loving Memory of Ronnie James Dio" inscribed into mahogany body. **$2,560**

Skinner, Inc., www.skinnerinc.com

Replica of modern Stroh violin. **$175**

Skinner, Inc., www.skinnerinc.com

Violin labeled Joannes Baptista Zanoli with case and bow, repaired top and neck, open A-peg crack, back 353 mm long. **$2,400**

Skinner, Inc., www.skinnerinc.com

Gibson Mandolin Style A 1, No. 13110, one-piece back, ebony fingerboard with pearl eyes, missing strings, scratched on back, binding on side of fingerboard coming unglued, with leather case, back 13 7/8". **$900**

Hammond organ, serial no. 497886, from Elvis Presley's Graceland bedroom. Presley gave the organ to his dentist and friend Dr. Lester Hoffman in February 1977, accompanied by signed letter of authenticity, 37" x 43 1/2" x 24". **$35,200**

Banjo stamped "The Luscomb Banjo Patented Aug. 28, 1888" with Washington Street address in Boston, mother-of-pearl inlaid fretboard, case, 35" x 12 1/4". **$600**

Child's cello labeled "Antonius Stradivarius," not set up, damage to edges and corners, missing saddle, open seams throughout, flecks and scratches, top of rib separated from neck, back 27 1/4" long. **$950**

1913 Gibson style O guitar, serial no. 141018, owned by singer-songwriter Delaney Bramlett of Delaney & Bonnie, refinished, binding replaced. Provenance: From the estate of Delaney Bramlett. **$10,240**

Skinner, Inc., www.skinnerinc.com

Assorted saxophone mouthpieces, including semi-vintage Selmer Jazz Metal Alto, D; older Otto Link Tenor Tone Edge; and Rico Baritone B7 (plastic). **$275**

Julien's Auctions

Don Wilson's 1967 Fender Jazzmaster electric guitar, serial no. 163145, owned and used by The Ventures' rhythm guitarist, all original with two pickups, two tone switches, factory Jazzmaster tailpiece and sunburst, stamped "Demo" above plate and on body below plate, originally a gift from Fender, significant play wear on body, with sticker-covered original hardshell case and 34 photos. **$75,000**

Julien's Auctions

Conway Twitty's stage- and studio-played 1957 Gretsch 6130 Roundup guitar in hand-tooled leather case that reads "Conway Twitty" across front body and signed by leather artist; guitar has cowboy-scene belt buckle-style tailpiece, 23 frets with "humptop" inlays, original four Gretsch G arrow knobs, and horseshoe under Gretsch logo on headstock, original replaced with gold-colored guard; includes certificate of authenticity and 45 RPM single of Twitty's "It's Only Make Believe." **$23,750**

Julien's Auctions

Marshall 4x12 slant speaker cabinet, serial no. 11898, owned by Jimi Hendrix, speakers are Celestion 25-watt greenbacks dated 1968, tears to grill cloth and vinyl covering on cabinet, plaque on back reads "Made In England," accompanied by letter of authenticity, 30" x 29" x 14". **$23,750**

Gotta Have Rock and Roll

Bruce Springsteen's stage-used key of A harmonica played by The Boss when performing "The River" during his 1984-1985 "Born in the USA" tour, with detailed letter of provenance. **$1,735**

Julien's Auctions

2006 PRS Santana model prototype guitar used in studio by guitarist Carlos Santana, serial no. 6107107, "Prototype #4" written on back of headstock, maple glow, maple top, two humbuckers, single-coil pickup in middle position, original hardshell case, certificate of authenticity signed by Santana, photo of him with guitar. **$23,750**

Julien's Auctions

Early production, 1928, all-wood National Triolian guitar with floral decal on back, no serial number, guitar has National Del Vecchio light-gauge cone and newer biscuit bridge, original cone and biscuit bridge included. **$3,840**

Julien's Auctions

Richie Sambora-owned and -signed Gibson 1275 Jimmy Page reissue double-neck guitar, serial no. Jimmy Page 082-2007, one of 250 replicating Page's original Gibson EDS-1275 model, with original hardshell case and Gibson Custom Shop certificate signed by Page. **$12,800**

Julien's Auctions

Fender XII Lake Placid 12-string electric guitar used by Elvis Presley in 1967 United Artists film "Clambake," serial no. 177898, with copy of film. Provenance: From the estate of Lance LeGault. **$35,200**

Julien's Auctions

Red lacquered Baldwin baby grand piano signed in black marker on bench and fallboard by Rolling Stones' singer Mick Jagger, Eastern white spruce soundboard, hard rock maple spruce bridge, Baldwin/Renner action, individually balanced spruce keys, piano 5' 2" long x 4' 9 5/8" wide x 3' 3" tall, bench 17 1/2" x 35" x 14 1/2". **$12,160**

North American Indian Artifacts

By Russell E. Lewis

Our interest in Native American material cultural artifacts has been long-lived, as was the Indian's interest in many of our material cultural items from an early period.

During recent years, it has become commonplace to have major sales of these artifacts by at least four major auction houses, in addition to the private trading, local auctions, and Internet sales of these items.

Anthropologists have written millions of words on American Indian cultures and societies and have standardized various regions of the country when discussing these cultures.

We have been fascinated with the material culture of Native Americans from the beginning of our contact with their societies. The majority of these valuable items are in repositories of museums, universities, and colleges, but many items that were traded to private citizens are now being sold to collectors of Native American material culture.

Native American artifacts are now acquired by collectors in the same fashion as any material cultural item. Individuals interested in antiques and collectibles find items at farm auction sales (an especially good place for farm family collections to be dispersed), yard sales, estate sales, specialized auctions, and from private collectors trading or selling items.

Native American artifacts are much more difficult to locate for a variety of reasons, including the following: scarcity of items; legal protection of items being traded; more vigorous collecting of artifacts by numerous international, national, state, regional, and local museums and historical societies; frailties of the items themselves, as most were made of organic materials; and a more limited distribution network through legitimate secondary sales.

However, it is still possible to find some types of Native American items through the traditional sources of online auctions, auction houses in local communities, antique stores and malls, flea markets, trading meetings, estate sales, and similar venues. The most likely items to find in the above ways would be items made of stone, chert, flint, obsidian, and copper. Most

organic materials will not have survived the rigors of a marketplace unless they were recently released from some estate or collection and their value was unknown to the previous owner.

For more information on Native American collectibles, see *Warman's North American Indian Artifacts Identification and Price Guide* by Russell E. Lewis.

Skinner, Inc.; www.skinnerinc.com

Eskimo polychrome carved wooden mask, circa late 19th/early 20th century, depicting female face with pierced crescent-shaped eyes and mouth, traces of black, blue, white, and red pigments, pierced in four places at edge for attachment, wood loss, 8 3/4" high. **$10,800**

RUSSELL E. LEWIS is a university professor, anthropologist, collector and author of several books, including *Warman's North American Indian Artifacts Identification and Price Guide.*

Skinner, Inc.; www.skinnerinc.com

Ute or Jicarilla Apache beaded hide boy's shirt, circa last quarter 19th century, fringed tab-cut bottom and fringed cuffs, long triangular bibs with quilled and beaded rosette on one side and two beaded rosettes with brass shoe button centers on opposite, beaded shoulder and sleeve strips with multicolored geometric designs on white background, bead loss, 25" long. **$22,800**

Skinner, Inc.; www.skinnerinc.com

Yancton Sioux beaded buffalo hide blanket strip, circa 1870, multicolored geometric designs on light green background, minor bead loss, mounted on custom panel, 63" long, 6" wide, roundel 8" diameter. **$15,600**

Skinner, Inc.; www.skinnerinc.com

Plains Cree beaded buffalo hide man's moccasins, circa last quarter 19th century, multicolored geometric and cross designs on yellow and pumpkin background, horse track designs at heels, blue trade cloth tongues and trim, remnant red trade cloth, 10" long. **$6,600**

Skinner, Inc.; www.skinnerinc.com

Woodlands carved wooden bowl, circa 19th century, round form with gently curved sides and single pierced projection, dark rich patina, 3 1/4" high, 13 1/2" diameter. **$8,400**

Skinner, Inc.; www.skinnerinc.com

Anasazi polychrome pottery bowl, painted on inside with black and white stepped scroll design, 4" high, 9" diameter. **$2,091**

Skinner, Inc.; www.skinnerinc.com

Pair of Southern Arapaho beaded hide man's moccasins, circa last quarter 19th century, hide stained yellow and red, long heel fringe and fringe off vamp, partially beaded with multicolored geometric designs, 11" long excluding fringe. **$5,535**

Skinner, Inc.; www.skinnerinc.com

Northern Arapaho beaded hide woman's dress, circa 1870s, fringed at sleeve ends and bottom, rectangular yoke beaded with multicolored geometric designs on blue background, minor bead loss, tears in hide, 53" long, 42" wide. **$27,600**

Skinner, Inc.; www.skinnerinc.com

Pair of Cheyenne woman's high-top moccasins, circa 1880s, stained with yellow ochre and beaded with multicolored geometric designs on white background, German silver buttons down side, custom stand, 15 1/2" high, moccasins 9 1/2" long. **$6,600**

Skinner, Inc.; www.skinnerinc.com

Apache pictorial basketry olla, woven in diamond latticework pattern with rows of human figures, animals, and geometric devices, stitch loss, damage to bottom, 24" high, 21 1/2" diameter. **$12,300**

Skinner, Inc.; www.skinnerinc.com

Cheyenne beaded hide pipebag, circa 1870s, classic bar design with unusual fringed drop from opening, traces of yellow pigment, 22 1/2" long, including fringe. **$6,000**

Skinner, Inc.; www.skinnerinc.com

Cheyenne beaded hide knife sheath, circa 1870s, rawhide liner covered with soft hide and beaded on one side with multicolored geometric designs, quill-wrapped fringe off top, row of tin cone and wool danglers, includes commercial knife, 10 1/4" high. **$4,500**

Skinner, Inc.; www.skinnerinc.com

Cheyenne painted hide dance shield, circa last quarter 19th century, on wooden hoop, painted with central red and green spiderweb design on yellow ochre field, 12 1/2" diameter. **$2,091**

Rago Arts and Auction Center

Anasazi pottery, five bowls and pitcher with polychrome decoration, southwestern United States, circa 1100 AD, tallest 6". **$2,125**

Skinner, Inc.; www.skinnerinc.com

Two beaded hide peyote pouches, possibly Comanche, circa late 19th century, one with twisted fringe and small German silver buttons, other with bifurcated flap and partially beaded fringe, 10" long, including fringe. **$7,800**

Skinner, Inc.; www.skinnerinc.com

Crow beaded parfleche knife sheath, circa 1880, classic Crow design painted on one side, blue trade cloth and beadwork down one side, custom stand, 13" high without fringe. **$7,200**

Skinner, Inc.; www.skinnerinc.com

Crow beaded hide and cloth mirror bag, circa late 19th century, beaded on both sides with classic Crow geometric designs, strap with trade cloth panels and beaded detail, fringe strung with large yellow and brass beads, 20" long, including fringe, 5 1/2" wide. **$18,000**

Skinner, Inc.; www.skinnerinc.com

Crow beaded buffalo hide rifle scabbard, circa 1870s, fringed at mouth, long twisted fringe from barrel, red trade cloth insets and beaded with classic Crow geometric designs and pony beaded edging, traces of red pigment, some damage to trade cloth, twisted fringe restored, 52" long. **$21,600**

Lakota beaded hide possible bag, circa 1870s, buffalo hide, beaded on front, sides, and flap with multicolored geometric designs on light blue background with tin cone and red horse hair danglers, slight stiffness to hide in areas, 24" x 11 1/2". **$16,800**

Kiowa beaded commercial leather strike-a-lite pouch, circa last quarter 19th century, beaded front and back with multicolored geometric designs, tin cone dangler, small German silver button, twisted fringe with German silver and cowrie shell attachments, includes forged striker, tin cone loss, 15 1/2" long, including drops. **$7,800**

Hawaiian necklace, Lei Niho Palaoa, circa first quarter 19th century, with hook-shaped ivory pendant suspended from multi-strand plaited human hair necklace, 3 3/4" long. **$7,800**

Skinner, Inc.; www.skinnerinc.com

Pair of Jicarilla Apache beaded hide man's leggings, circa 1870s, with yellow and green pigments, perforated tabs at top, fringe at sides and cuffs, beaded strips with multicolored geometric designs, period repairs, some water stains, includes custom wall mounts, 38" long. **$3,480**

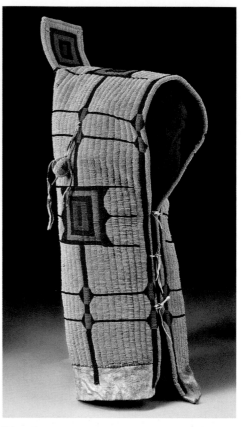

Skinner, Inc.; www.skinnerinc.com

Lakota beaded hide cradle, circa 1870s, buffalo hide form with canvas strip up back, beaded with classic box and border design on blue background, beaded tab at top from recycled painted parfleche, beaded ball with quill-wrapped fringe hangs from one side, 24" high. **$33,600**

Skinner, Inc.; www.skinnerinc.com

Kiowa beaded commercial leather dispatch case, circa 1880s, beaded on front with bold multicolored concentric design, geometric lane on flap and two lanes at lower back, German silver button and tweezers, hide fringe from bottom, 12" long, including fringe. **$10,800**

Skinner, Inc.; www.skinnerinc.com

Kiowa beaded hide man's moccasins, circa 1870s, partially beaded with multicolored geometric designs, row of tin cones off vamp, hide painted red, yellow, and blue, heel fringe restored, blue pigment on cuffs touched up, 11" long, excluding fringe. **$13,200**

Skinner, Inc.; www.skinnerinc.com

Pair of Lakota beaded hide moccasins, circa late 19th century, multicolored hexagon and cross devices on white background and translucent red "buffalo tracks," minor bead loss, 10" long. **$1,169**

Skinner, Inc.; www.skinnerinc.com

Lakota beaded and quilled hide possible bag, circa last quarter 19th century, multicolored beaded box-and-border design on flap and ends, front with multicolored quilled design, red cloth tufts, quill-wrapped drops, detailed with tin cone and red horse hair danglers, 22" x 14". **$3,120**

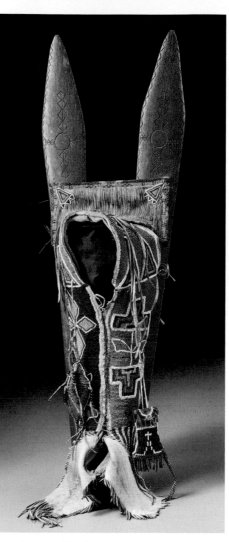

Skinner, Inc.; www.skinnerinc.com

Kiowa beaded hide cradle, circa last quarter 19th century, with canvas liner, cradle beaded with classic Kiowa geometric and abstract floral designs on three different background colors, miniature strike-a-lite pouch hanging from one side and umbilical fetish from other, mounted on wood slat frame with incised symbolic designs and traces of red, blue, and yellow pigments, includes otter hide drop with six beaded bear paws and two tie-on beaded strips added by Joseph Rivera, minor bead loss, slats 24 1/2" long. **$57,000**

Skinner, Inc.; www.skinnerinc.com

Lakota beaded hide possible bag, circa late 19th century, beaded on flap, sides, and front with classic multicolored geometric designs, tin cone and red horse hair danglers, 22" x 14 1/2". **$2,952**

Skinner, Inc.; www.skinnerinc.com

Rare Lakota pictorial beaded pipebag, circa last quarter 19th century, antelope and elk beaded on each side, row of brass tacks below beaded panel and remnant quill-wrapped fringe, hide very stiff and brittle, bead and quill loss, 25" long. **$4,500**

Skinner, Inc.; www.skinnerinc.com

Lakota pictorial beaded buffalo hide cradle, circa 1880s, with cloth lining and muslin drop from bottom, beaded with four downward-facing mounted warriors wearing war bonnets and carrying society staffs or coup sticks, with multicolored crosses, beaded rawhide tab with bugle beads and brass hawk bells in fringe, cradle edge with cloth bundles, remnant ribbon and brass shoe button decoration, 25" high. **$78,000**

Skinner, Inc.; www.skinnerinc.com

Navajo classic child's blanket, striped background overlaid with concentric stepped cross design, tightly woven in indigo, raveled cochineal-dyed reds, light green, and light gray-blue, stains, 49" x 31". **$16,800**

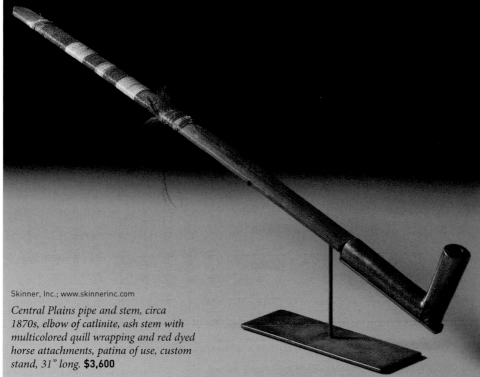

Skinner, Inc.; www.skinnerinc.com

Central Plains pipe and stem, circa 1870s, elbow of catlinite, ash stem with multicolored quill wrapping and red dyed horse attachments, patina of use, custom stand, 31" long. **$3,600**

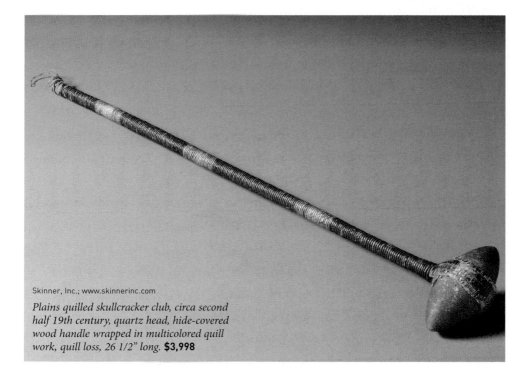

Skinner, Inc.; www.skinnerinc.com

Plains quilled skullcracker club, circa second half 19th century, quartz head, hide-covered wood handle wrapped in multicolored quill work, quill loss, 26 1/2" long. **$3,998**

Skinner, Inc.; www.skinnerinc.com

Three Plains horn spoons and lead-inlaid straight pipe, circa 19th century, two larger mountain sheep horn spoons, one with perforated and notched finial, buffalo horn spoon with bird head finial, brass tack eyes, quill-wrapped neck, tapered wood pipe with twisted lead inlay, to 14 1/4" long. **$2,583**

Skinner, Inc.; www.skinnerinc.com

Lakota beaded commercial leather strike-a-lite pouch, circa last quarter 19th century, beaded on front with multicolored geometric designs, large German silver button, twisted fringe, tin cone danglers, 13" long, including drops. **$2,460**

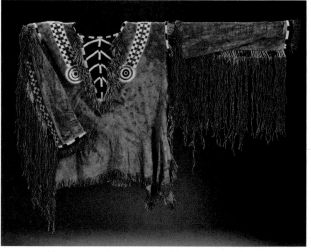

Skinner, Inc.; www.skinnerinc.com

Skinner, Inc.; www.skinnerinc.com

Plateau beaded hide flat bag, circa late 19th century, beaded on one side with central American eagle framed by multicolored floral designs, hide strap, includes Plexiglas box, 12 1/2" x 10 1/2". **$1,599**

Rare Plains pony, seed bead, and quilled hide shirt, circa mid-19th century, body of shirt fringed at edges and with sides open to underarm with remnant yellow ochre overall, cloth-wrapped neck opening with white pony bead decoration, cloth-lined fringed tabs covered in red trade cloth and pony trader blue, white, white center red, and translucent dark red pony beads; initials "E.B." (Eugene Burr) under front flap, sleeves with red trade cloth insets, short fringe at cuffs, pony bead decoration, around shoulder and down each sleeve is long fringe decorated at top with white and indigo blue-wrapped quillwork and large pony trader blue pony beads, sleeves and shoulders decorated with directly applied loom-beaded strips with multicolored geometric designs done in seed beads; shoulder strips terminating with rosettes done in "spiderweb" overlay technique, traces of red pigment on inside of cuffs, thread-sewn throughout, 29" long. **$144,000**

Skinner, Inc.; www.skinnerinc.com

*Plains catlinite pipebowl and wood stem, circa last quarter
19th century, T-bowl with convex profile and relief-carved
detail, ash stem with ribbed decoration, file branding, traces
of red pigment, 22 1/2" long.* **$1,200**

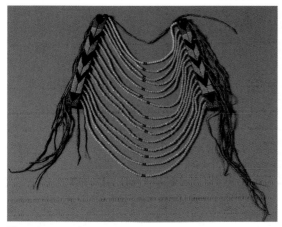

Skinner, Inc.; www.skinnerinc.com

*Northern Plains beaded commercial leather and hide loop
necklace, circa late 19th century, multicolored chevron design
and strands of large light blue beads, fringe down both sides,
beaded strips 7 3/4" long.* **$1,920**

Skinner, Inc.; www.skinnerinc.com

*Zuni polychrome pottery olla, circa 1880s, with series of rain
bird motifs with fine line detail, detailed scroll patterns below
rim, 10 1/2" high, 13 1/2" diameter.* **$10,800**

Skinner, Inc.; www.skinnerinc.com

*Plateau beaded cloth and hide cradle, circa
late 19th century, hide covered wood with
dark blue trade cloth panel decorated with
bilateral floral design using multicolored
faceted seed beads, large trade beaded fringe
and brass tack details, 37" high.* **$2,880**

Skinner, Inc.; www.skinnerinc.com

Yokuts pictorial lidded basket, circa 1920, decorated with rattlesnake design and three human figures, 5 1/2" high, 6 1/2" diameter. **$4,305**

Rago Arts and Auction Center

Zia pottery olla, stylized bird, foliate and geometric designs with ruffled rim, early 20th century, 10 1/4" x 11". **$5,313**

Skinner, Inc.; www.skinnerinc.com

Large Zuni polychrome storage jar, four-color ovoid form decorated with three large birds, flowering plants, abstract feather devices, scalloped band from rim, 16 1/4" high, 15" diameter. **$24,000**

Skinner, Inc.; www.skinnerinc.com

Northwest Coast carved wood adze, 19th century, with forged iron blade, one end of handle in form of stylized animal in profile, dark patina, 8 3/4" long. **$4,200**

Perfume Bottles

By Kyle Husfloen

A lthough the human sense of smell isn't nearly as acute as that of many other mammals, we have long been affected by the odors in the world around us. Science has shown that scents or smells can directly affect our mood or behavior.

No one knows for certain when humans first rubbed themselves with some plant or herb to improve their appeal to other humans, usually of the opposite sex. However, it is clear that the use of unguents and scented materials was widely practiced as far back as Ancient Egypt.

Some of the first objects made of glass, in fact, were small cast vials used for storing such mixtures. By the age of the Roman Empire, scented waters and other mixtures were even more important and were widely available in small glass flasks or bottles. Since that time glass has been the material of choice for storing scented concoctions, and during the past 200 years some of the most exquisite glass objects produced were designed for that purpose.

It wasn't until around the middle of the 19th century that specialized bottles and vials were produced to hold commercially manufactured scents. Some aromatic mixtures were worn on special occasions, while many others were splashed on to help mask body odor. For centuries it had been common practice for "sophisticated" people to carry on their person a scented pouch or similar accoutrement, since daily bathing was unheard of and laundering methods were primitive.

Commercially produced and brand name perfumes and colognes have really only been common since the late 19th and early 20th centuries. The French started the ball rolling during the first half of the 19th century when D'Orsay and Guerlain began producing special scents. The first American entrepreneur to step into this field was Richard Hudnut, whose firm was established in 1880. During the second half of the 19th century most scents carried simple labels and were sold in fairly generic glass bottles. Only in the early 20th century did parfumeurs introduce specially designed labels and bottles to hold their most popular perfumes. Coty, founded in 1904, was one of the first to do this, and they turned to Rene Lalique for a special bottle design around 1908. Other French firms, such as Bourjois (1903), Caron (1903), and D'Orsay (1904) were soon following this trend.

The rules of value for perfume bottles are the same as for any other kind of glass—rarity, condition, age, and quality of glass.

The record price for perfume bottle at auction is something over $200,000, and those little sample bottles of scent that we used to get for free at perfume counters in the 1960s can now bring as much as $300 or $400.

For more information on perfume bottles, see *Antique Trader Perfume Bottles Price Guide* by Kyle Husfloen.

Heritage Auctions

◄ *Chinese carved soapstone and rose quartz perfume bottle, etched figural and landscape decoration, 19th century, 3 1/4" high.* **$163**

KYLE HUSFLOEN, Southern California representative for Kaminski Auctions, is a well-respected expert on antiques and collectibles. He was with Antique Trader publications for more than 30 years.

Heritage Auctions

Dutch rock crystal and gold perfume bottle, 18k gold hinged lid with floral decoration, maker unknown, Netherlands, circa 1865, marks: left facing lion head, 4 1/2" high. **$625**

Heritage Auctions

Three Murano glass perfume bottles with stoppers, 20th century, tallest one 11 3/8" high. **$531**

Skinner, Inc., www.skinnerinc.com

Wedgwood black jasper dip perfume bottle, England, 19th century, applied white classical figure in relief to either side, unmarked, 4 1/4" high. **$300**

Heritage Auctions

Two Lalique glass L'air Du Temps Pattern perfume bottles, 20th century, created for Nina Ricci, marks: Lalique®, NINA RICCI FRANCE, larger bottle 7 3/4" high, smaller bottle 6" high. **$688**

Skinner, Inc., www.skinnerinc.com

Sterling silver perfume bottle, Middle East, possibly Persia, 20th century, faceted six-sided bottle and large diamond-form stopper with chased foliate decoration, hallmark on base, approximately 8 troy oz., 5 1/2" high. **$240**

Skinner, Inc., www.skinnerinc.com

Viennese enamel perfume bottle, circa 1866-1872, maker's mark "RL," double gourd form, upper register decorated with arabesques above scene of classical figures in landscape, champlevé mounts, 5 1/4" high. **$923**

Skinner, Inc., www.skinnerinc.com

Two Wedgwood blue jasper perfume bottles, England, 19th century, each octagonal form with applied white classical figures in relief, solid pale blue, unmarked, 3 5/8" high and 2 1/2" high. **$240**

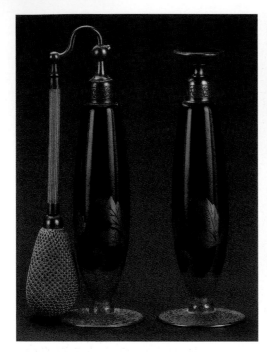

Heritage Auctions

Heritage Auctions

Two English porcelain figural perfume bottles, late 19th century, one of boy holding dog with removable head, other with courting couple in front of tree with removable ornament, 3 1/4" high. **$313**

Two Devilbiss Manufacturing Co. perfume bottles, circa 1920-1930, each of glass with black interior enamel, gilt foliate decoration to body and raised on gilt circular foot, one with atomizer, marks: DE VILBISS, 7 1/2" high (with atomizer). **$163**

Heritage Auctions

Schneider Le Verre Francais glass Lézards perfume bottle and atomizer, Charles Schneider Glassworks, Épinay-sur-Seine, France, circa 1924-1926, spherical perfume of yellow glass with violet overlay, acid-etched in Lézards pattern, gilt metal atomizer cap with gold silk covered hose, bulb, and tassel; marks to glass: Le Verre Francais; marks to atomizer cap: BREVETE S.G.D.G., MARCEL, FRANCK, MADE IN FRANCE; 5 1/2" high. **$750**

Heritage Auctions

Dutch rock crystal and gold perfume bottle, 10k gold engraved hinged lid to top, maker unknown, Netherlands, circa 1865, marks: oak leaf, 3 7/8" high. **$375**

Heritage Auctions

Victorian cut glass and silver perfume bottle, ovoid bottle with silver rim and flip-top lid with scrolling decoration, Walker & Hall, Sheffield, England, circa 1908-1909, marks: lion passant, crown, W&H (in flag); 5 5/8" high. **$88**

Heritage Auctions

St. Louis cased glass perfume bottle with stopper, circa 1987, marks: SL 1987 (signature cane), 6 1/4" high x 2 5/8" diameter. **$813**

Heritage Auctions

Pair of French cased glass perfume bottles, circa 1970, with millefiori canes to base of bottle and stopper, 5 7/8" high x 3 1/8" diameter. **$150**

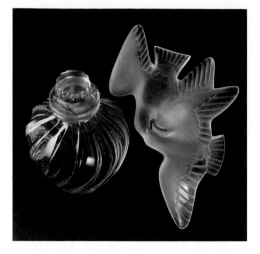

Heritage Auctions

Lalique glass L'air Du Temps Pattern sealed perfume bottle, 20th century, with two stoppers, clear and frosted double-dove stopper and secondary stopper for storage, created for Nina Ricci, marks: Lalique® France, 12 1/4" high. **$1,000**

Heritage Auctions

Pair of English porcelain figural perfume bottles, late 19th century, anchor mark, 3 5/8" high. **$313**

Heritage Auctions

◄ *Chinese cased glass perfume bottle, early 20th century, cased red to clear Peking glass with carp decoration, moss agate lid, 2 3/4" high.* **$188**

Petroliana

Petroliana covers a broad range of gas station collectibles from containers and globes to signs and pumps and everything in between.

As with all advertising items, factors such as brand name, intricacy of design, color, age, condition, and rarity drastically affect value.

Beware of reproduction and fantasy pieces. For collectors of vintage gas and oil items, the only way to avoid reproductions is experience: making mistakes and learning from them; talking with other collectors and dealers; finding reputable resources (including books and websites), and learning to invest wisely, buying the best examples one can afford.

Marks can be deceiving, paper labels and tags are often missing, and those that remain may be spurious. Adding to the confusion are "fantasy" pieces, globes that have no vintage counterpart, and that are often made more for visual impact than deception.

How does one know whether a given piece is authentic? Does it look old, and to what degree can age be simulated? What is the difference between high-quality vintage advertising and modern mass-produced examples? Even experts are fooled when trying to assess qualities that have subtle distinctions.

There is another important factor to consider. A contemporary maker may create a "reproduction" sign or gas globe in tribute of the original, and sell it for what it is: a legitimate copy. Many of these are dated and signed by the artist or manufacturer, and these legitimate copies are highly collectible today. Such items are not intended to be frauds.

But a contemporary piece may pass through many hands between the time it leaves the maker and wind up in a collection. When profit is the only motive of a reseller, details about origin, ownership, and age can become a slippery slope of guesses, attribution, and—unfortunately—fabrication.

As the collector's eye sharpens, and the approach to inspecting and assessing petroliana improves, it will become easier to buy with confidence. And a knowledgeable collecting public should be the goal of all sellers, if for no other reason than the willingness to invest in quality.

For more information about petroliana, consult *Warman's Gas Station Collectibles Identification and Price Guide* by Mark Moran.

Victorian Casino Auctions

Nineteen vintage one-quart Tydol and Veedol metal motor oil cans, in original Tydol cardboard box. **$200-$1,800**

Showtime Auction Services

Red Crown Gasoline and Polarine self-framed beveled edge tin over cardboard sign, copyright 1913, Standard Oil Co., depicting women drivers, repaired nail hole at top and some scratches otherwise very good condition, 19 1/4" wide x 27 1/2" high. **$14,000**

Victorian Casino Auctions

Vintage electric Imperial Mobiloil metal and glass wall mount clock by C.J. Hug Co., Inc., Highland, Illinois, 15" diameter. **$350**

Matthews Auctions

Trico Wiper Blades petroliana display, metal with hinged marquee, 11" high x 18" wide. **$150-$350**

Matthews Auctions

Rickenbacker Authorized Flat Rate Service double-sided porcelain sign with company motto of "A car worthy of its name," in reference to company's founder, Eddie Rickenbacker, highly decorated World War I pilot; small chips at mounting holes, small scratches in hat, 16" high x 30" wide. **$25,000-$35,000**

Matthews Auctions

Mohawk Gasoline single-sided tombstone-shaped neon sign, mounted on new can, neon in working condition, 52" high x 44" wide. **$20,000-$30,000**

Matthews Auctions

Flying A Gasoline globe in glass screw base, minor wear at bottom edge on both sides, body in good condition, 13 1/2" diameter. **$600-$1,000**

Victorian Casino Auctions

▲ *Vintage gas/service station island metal Mobloil display with six glass oil bottles with spouts, pre-1938, with original porcelain sign.* **$500-$1,200**

United Motors Service neon and porcelain oval sign, includes original crate, circa 1950s, sign 37" long x 24" wide. **$1,600-$3,000**

Clipper Gasoline double-sided oval porcelain porcelain sign, scratches throughout, chip at bottom of field, large chip in word "Clipper," 60" high x 30" wide. **$30,000-$40,000**

Caminol product, Beacon Ethyl Gasoline single-sided porcelain sign with die-cut lighthouse-shaped design, circa 1940, light scratches at bottom of "n," 48" high x 30" wide. **$40,000-$60,000**

Heritage Auctions

Edgar Church Texaco Fire-Chief Gasoline ad illustration, 1932, approximately 10" high x 10.5" wide overall. **$287**

Victorian Casino Auctions

Large Shell Oil embossed die-cut seashell porcelain sign, 48" high x 48" wide. **$1,000-$4,000**

Victorian Casino Auctions

Sunoco Motor Oil light-up store display stand, original spout bottles in carriers, "Mercury Made" motto, company formed in 1890, carrier circa mid-1940s, holes in porcelain sides for light to show through. **$1,000-$2,500**

Victorian Casino Auctions

Fleet-Wing Gasoline Motor Oil tin sign, M.C.A. 5-47 with wood framing, one of the earliest examples of promotions used by this company since it was established in 1956, 71" high x 35" wide. **$500-$1,500**

Matthews Auctions

Rare Saxon Motor Cars display sign, small chips at hanging holes, reverse with spiderweb cracks in middle of field, marked Ohio Valley Enameling Co., Huntington W. Va., 18" high x 18" wide. **$1,200-$3,000**

Victorian Casino Auctions

Tiolene Oil round double-sided porcelain curb sign, "Property of the Pure Oil Company" embossed on cast iron base, states "Guaranteed 100% Pure Pennsylvania Oil-Permit. No. 37," The Pure Oil Co., excellent condition, 27" wide x 66" high. **$500-$2,000**

Matthews Auctions

Wyeth Tires single-sided porcelain curved shield-shaped sign, marked "Wyeth Hdw. & Mfg. Co. / St. Joseph, Mo. U.S.A." and "Burdick Consumer building. Chicago and Beaver Falls, Pa.," small chips along top edge, 22" high x 18" wide. **$20,000-$25,000**

Matthews Auctions

Wolf's Head Motor Oil, founded in 1879, oil can graphics, round thermometer with glass face, slightly soiled, marked Pam Clock Co., 12" diameter. **$210-$500**

Matthews Auctions

Oilzum Motor Oils, "The Cream of Pure Pennsylvania Oil" with logo display sign, light paper marks, reverse has chip in lower field, 24" diameter. **$2,100-$4,300**

Victorian Casino Auctions

Specialized Lubrication Service self-framed porcelain sign with metal hanging brackets for display, includes "As Recommended By Motor Car Manufacturers," 36" wide x 64" high. **$600-$1,800**

Matthews Auctions

Sav'n Sam's Regular Gasoline with logo, stations operated primarily in Northern California, die-cut sign, 10" diameter. **$1,600-$2,500**

Victorian Casino Auctions

Three Gilmore Lubricant related items: one five-pound grease can, one two-pound grease can, and one "Gilmore Record Breakers" license plate topper, part of the promotional service program of this company between 1900 and 1945. **$300-$1,500**

Victorian Casino Auctions

Phillips 66-Battery Service vertical embossed self-framed tin sign with wood backing, 18" high x 72" wide. **$500-$1,800**

Matthews Auctions

Texaco embossed gas pump price box, metal, incorporates series of levers and ramps to aid in manual adjustment of prices, 7" high x 10" wide x 1" deep. **$375-$600**

Photography

By Noah Fleisher

Fine art in general took it in the gut when the economy, and the art market, tanked in 2008. Of the various markets that fell within the umbrella of fine art, few saw its fortunes fade faster than vintage and contemporary photography.

Unless the name on your pictures was Mapplethorpe, Avedon, Weston, Sherman – or among the handful of photographers who transcended – then the value of your pieces fell, precipitously in some cases.

It's been a bit of a slog coming back, but five years later there is a sign of stirring in the photography market.

Burt Finger is the owner of Photographs Do Not Bend (PDNB) Gallery on Dragon Street in Dallas (PDNB.com), the center of the city's Design District, and is a longtime recognized expert from his 18 years in his gallery championing both individual artists and collectors.

Noah Fleisher

"Photography, like the other disciplines, has been a struggle since the recession," he said, "but since this year (2013) it seems things are moving forward. Good pieces between $1,000 and $50,000 are selling again. People have some new-gained confidence from what's been going on and there's a new-found equilibrium between buyer and seller."

That's good news for collectors and dealers alike, though the market still favors buyers at auction a little more, with a large concentration of offerings all at once giving collectors a chance to get good buys on a great many pieces in the middle range. Unless you really know your stuff, though, buying photographs at auction can be a daunting world to just jump into.

That is where dealers like Finger come in. While he's in the business of selling photography, like the best of his ilk, he does not approach it from the financial standpoint. His is an artist's eye, and he curates from inspiration; he educates from a love of the imagery and its meaning. He's the sort of dealer who embodies the ethics you want when you are looking for guidance starting or propping up a collection.

In fact, a few weeks after talking with Finger and visiting him at his Dallas gallery, I found myself in conversation with a longtime client (and now friend) of Finger's – a lawyer from Dallas – who related the following assessment of Finger:

"When I first started thinking about collecting, back in the mid-1990s, I wandered into Burt's gallery. I didn't have much discretionary income back then, but he took the time and talked with me and soon was sending me home with books and catalogs, pointing me to shows and specific artists and galleries. He was more like a teacher than a dealer. Soon I was ready to start buying."

He noted that he recently purchased his first William Eggleston. That would be music to any good dealer's ears, and business.

NOAH FLEISHER received his Bachelor of Fine Arts degree from New York University and brings more than a decade of newspaper, magazine, book, antiques and art experience to his position as Public Relations Director of Heritage Auctions, one of the country's foremost auction houses. He is the former editor of *Antique Trader, New England Antiques Journal* and *Northeast Antiques Journal,* is the author of *Warman's Modern Furniture,* and has been a longtime contributor to *Warman's Antiques and Collectibles.*

Where does Finger see the market right now, besides on the rebound? He casts a philosophic glance on where it stands.

"Collectors and collections have to move forward," he said, "and there's definitely a shift forward right now as a new generation ages in and the previous generation moves up. While the 1940s and 1950s were very popular a decade ago, right now vintage pieces from 1960s and 1970s are very attractive to collectors – the '70s in particular."

Another element that the world of photography has had to contend with is the lightning quick progress of technology.

How does photography keep up and stay relevant in a world where iPhones and applications can imbue any photograph with any range of effect that photographers used to have to study years to master?

"A good camera does not make someone an artist," Finger points out. "I'm not concerned with it being 'digital photography,' I'm concerned with the finished product. I think the bar has been changed, it's risen. We have photographers now [who] are thinkers, [who] buy into a whole concept."

Finger cautions against getting too stuck on a particular era or artist, however, as you'll miss opportunities to learn, and to collect, in a variety of venues. A good relationship with a dealer prepares you for gallery buying, but it will also get you set to enter the auction market and to look for hidden gems in the corners of markets, shops and shows all over the country, if not the world.

"It's a thrill to be expansive rather than reductive," he said. "Find out what your interests are individually, not what someone tells you. When it comes to photography it has to be something you really love, not an investment. You are going to live with this image."

Heritage Auctions

▶ *Irving Penn (American, 1917-2009), "Harlequin Dress, Lisa Fonssagrives-Penn," 1950, platinum-palladium, 1979, 20 3/4" x 19". Verso: signed, titled, dated, and numbered 27/30 in pencil, edition and Penn/Condé Nast copyright credit reproduction stamps.* **$131,450**

PDNB Gallery, Dallas

◀ *Thomas Herbrich, "Elephants on a Bridge," 1998, gelatin silver (baryt print), 4" x 6".* **$400**

PDNB Gallery, Dallas

▲ *Delilah Montoya, "Stephanie vs Holly, Sandia Casino," 2003, gelatin silver print, 8" x 10".* **$900**

Heritage Auctions

◄ *John Humble (American, b. 1944), "Santa Monica Blvd at Highland Hollywood, Jan. 17, 2000," chromogenic, 2000, 22 5/8" x 18 7/8", signed, titled, dated, and numbered ed. 1/15 in ink in margin on recto.* **$1,250**

Heritage Auctions

Ansel Adams (American, 1902-1984), "Portfolio V (Ten Photographs)," 1936-1960, gelatin silver, 1979, 19 1/2" x 15 1/2", ed. 72/110. Each signed in pencil on mount recto; artist's portfolio stamp with title, date, and number in ink on the verso. Portfolio printed by Parasol Press, Ltd., New York. Colophon and case included with lot and the following photographs: "Pinnacles, Alabama Hills, Owens Valley, California," 1945; "Mudhills, Arizona," 1947; "Lone Pine Peak, Sierra Nevada, California, Ca.," 1960; "Moon and Clouds, Northern California," 1959; "Forest and Stream, Northern California," 1959; "Petroglyps, Monument Valley, Utah," 1958; "The Black Sun, Tungsten Hills Owens Valley, California," 1939; "Woman Behind Screen Door, Independence, California, Ca.," 1944; "White Stump, Sierra Nevada, California, Ca.," 1936; "Pipes and Gauges, West Virginia," 1939. **$43,750 for the set**

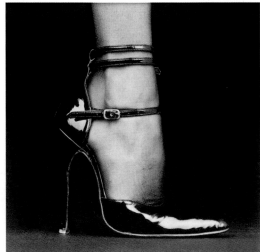

PDNB Gallery, Dallas

▲ *William Eggleston, "Pinball Machine (Troubled Waters)," 1980, dye transfer, 20" x 16".* **$40,000**

Heritage Auctions

◄ *Robert Mapplethorpe (American, 1946-1989), "Shoe (Melody)," 1987, gelatin silver, 1988, 40" x 40", ed. 1/2. Verso: signed and dated in ink.* **$47,800**

Heritage Auctions

Richard Avedon (American, 1923-2004), "Nastassja Kinski and the Serpent," 14 June, 1981, gelatin silver, printed 1982, 28 3/4" x 42 3/4", ed. 4/200, signed and numbered in pencil on mount and mat, artist's copyright stamp verso. **$74,500**

Heritage Auctions

Berenice Abbott (American, 1898-1991), "Five Changing New York Photographs," 1935-1938, vintage gelatin silver, 10" x 8" each. Federal Art Project, Changing New York stamp, titled with annotations in pencil on verso: "Seventh Avenue Looking South from 35th st., 1935; Murray Hill Hotel, Spiral, Park Ave and 40 st., 1935; Manhattan Bridge Looking Up, 1936; Canyon, Stone and William st., 1936; Broadway to the Battery, 1938." **$25,000 for the set**

Heritage Auctions

▶ *Alfred Eisenstaedt (American, 1898-1995), "Children at a Puppet Theater, Paris," 1963, gelatin silver, 1989, 13 3/4" x 20 3/4", signed and numbered 25/250 in ink on recto; notations in pencil on verso.* **$17,500**

Heritage Auctions

▼ *Marilyn Minter (American, b. 1948), "Solaris," 2010, chromogenic, diasec mounted, 2010, 40" x 30", edition of five. Verso: signed in ink on label.* **$20,315**

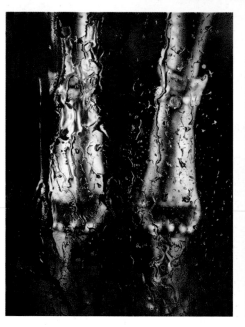

Heritage Auctions

▲ *Brassaï (French, 1899-1984), "Couple d'Amoureux dans un Petit Café, Quartier Italie," circa 1932, gelatin silver, printed later, 10 5/8" x 8 1/2", signed in ink in margin; titled and annotated pl. 78 page 71 in pencil; date in ink; with artist's copyright and Tirage de l'Auteur stamp on verso.* **$18,750**

PDNB Gallery, Dallas

◀ *Rhondal McKinney, "Untitled" (869, Champaign County, Illinois, 1980), gelatin silver, 8" x 10".* **$4,000**

Heritage Auctions

Henri Cartier-Bresson (French, 1908-2004), "Henri Matisse in Venice," 1944, gelatin silver, printed no later than 1974, 9 3/8" x 14 1/8", signed in ink on recto. **$10,000**

Heritage Auctions

Annie Leibovitz (American, b. 1949), "John and Yoko, New York, December 8," 1980, dye destruction, 1980, 13 7/8"" x 14". Recto: titled, dated, numbered, and inscribed John and Yoko, December 8, 1980 New York AP 14 for Ron Cooper Love, Annie Leibovitz in ink. **$26,290**

Heritage Auctions

Cindy Sherman (American, b. 1954), "Untitled (Lucille Ball)," 1975, Fujicolor Crystal Archive print, 2001, 10 3/8" x 8 1/4", signed and dated in ink on verso. **$23,750**

Heritage Auctions

▲ *Ormond Gigli (American, b. 1925), "Girls in the Window," 1960, chromogenic, 2010, 23 3/4" x 24", ed. 78/100, signed and dated in pencil mount recto, signed, titled, dated, and numbered in pencil verso.* **$8,750**

Heritage Auctions

◄ *Francesca Woodman (American, 1958-1981), "Untitled, from Angel Series, Rome," 1977-1978, gelatin silver, estate print, 3 1/4" x 3 1/3", ed. 15/40, signed and numbered in pencil by George and Betty Woodman with PE/FW stamp on verso annotated No.297 in pencil on verso.* **$6,250**

Heritage Auctions

Andre Kertesz (Hungarian, 1894-1985), "Chez Mondrian, Paris," 1926, gelatin silver, printed later, 13 5/8" x 10 1/4", signed and dated in pencil on the verso. **$6,875**

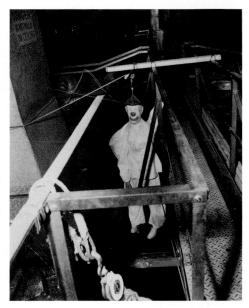

Heritage Auctions

Weegee (American, 1899-1968), "Untitled (Clown Dummy Hanging)," from "Group of Thirteen Photographs," circa 1940-1956, ranging in size. **$7,500**

Heritage Auctions

Don Hong-Oai (Chinese, 1929-2004), "Morning Work," circa 1984, bromide, 20" x 16", signed in pencil with annotations and artist's stamp on verso. **$6,875**

PDNB Gallery, Dallas

Nickolas Muray, "Frida Kahlo," 1939, carbon print, 22" x 18". **$6,500**

PDNB Gallery, Dallas

◄ Chris Verene, "Josh and His Girlfriend," 1993, C-Print, 24" x 20". **$12,000**

PDNB Gallery, Dallas

▼ John Albok, "New York Scene (Sidewalk Race)," 1945, vintage gelatin silver, 7" x 9". **$4,000**

Heritage Auctions

▲ Julie Blackmon (American, b. 1966), "Floatie," 2006. Pigment ink print, 31 3/4" x 31 3/4", ed. 10/10, signed, titled, and dated in ink in margin. **$5,469**

Heritage Auctions

► Imogen Cunningham (American, 1883-1976), "Ruth Asawa's Wire Baskets and Their Shadows," 1956, vintage gelatin silver, 9 1/2" x 7 7/8", artist printing notations in pencil on verso. **$5,938**

Heritage Auctions

O. Winston Link (American, 1914-2001), "Coaling Locomotives, Shaffers Crossing, Virginia," 1955, gelatin silver, 1995, 15 1/2" x 19 1/4". Verso: signed in ink with artist's copyright stamp NW 691. **$5,677**

Heritage Auctions

Edward Weston (American, 1886-1958), "Pepper (No. 14)," 1929, vintage gelatin silver, 8 3/4" x 7 1/2", ed. 9/50. Recto: signed, dated, and numbered, verso: titled. **$50,788**

PDNB Gallery, Dallas

Gregori Maiofis, "Photorealism," 2008, Bromoil, 29" x 30 1/4". **$5,000**

PDNB Gallery, Dallas

Jimmy Katz, "World of Wonders Banner, Florida," 2007, digital C-Print, 29 1/8" x 39 1/8". **$3,000**

Heritage Auctions

▶ *Man Ray (American, 1890-1976), "Portrait of André Breton (in Front of Giorgio Chirico's Painting 'The Enigma of Day')," 1930, gelatin silver, print date unknown, 8 1/4" x 5 7/8", signed in pencil in image on recto.* **$17,500**

PDNB Gallery, Dallas

Jeffrey Silverthorne, "Dougie, Jackie and Rollin," 1972-1976, vintage gelatin silver, 16" x 20". **$4,000**

PDNB Gallery, Dallas

Earlie Hudnall, Jr., "Hip Hop," 1993, gelatin silver, 20 x 16". **$3,000**

PDNB Gallery, Dallas

Michael Kenna, "Chrysler Building, Study 2, New York, New York," 2006, sepia tone gelatin silver, 8 1/2" x 7 3/4". **$3,000**

PDNB Gallery, Dallas

Bill Owens, "McDonald's Modern Day Care Center," 1976, gelatin silver, 11" x 14". **$4,200**

PDNB Gallery, Dallas

▲ *Teun Voeten, "Zabul Exfil, Zabul Province, Afghanistan, August 2004," C-Print, 24" x 36".* **$3,000**

PDNB Gallery, Dallas

▶ *Mario Algaze, "Cotton Candy, San Angel, Mexico D.F.," 1981, gelatin silver, 20" x 16".* **$2,500**

PDNB Gallery, Dallas

Jesse Alexander, "1000 Kilometer Rennen, Nürburgring," 1959, gelatin silver, 8" x 8". **$2,000**

Heritage Auctions

Eve Arnold (American, 1913-2012), "Marilyn Monroe, Rehearsal in The Desert, Nevada (Set of Misfits)," 1960, platinum, printed later, 9" x 13 3/8", ed. 97/100, signed and numbered in pencil in margin, one of 24 images from "Year of Tibet Portfolio," edition of 100, January 2006. **$2,500**

Heritage Auctions

Dennis Stock (American, 1928-2010), "Audrey Hepburn While Filming 'Sabrina'," 1954, gelatin silver, printed later, 14" x 9 1/2", ed. 20/200, signed, titled, dated, and numbered in pencil in margin on recto. **$2,375**

Heritage Auctions

Alfred Eisenstaedt (American, 1898-1995), "Nurses of Roosevelt Hospital, New York City," 1937, gelatin silver, 1993, 12" x 8 7/8", ed. 27/250, signed and numbered in ink in margin; titled, dated, with Time-Life Photo lab credit annotations in pencil on verso. **$2,500**

PDNB Gallery, Dallas

Wu Jialin, "Shuifu," 1987, gelatin silver, 20" x 16". **$2,000**

PDNB Gallery, Dallas

Esteban Pastorino, "ΔHMAPXEION," Skopelos, Greece, digital C-Print, 16" x 20". **$1,800**

PDNB Gallery, Dallas

George Hurrell, "Ann Sheridan," 1939, gelatin silver, 15" x 19". **$1,600**

PDNB Gallery, Dallas

Peter Brown, "Wray, Colorado," 2005, C-Print, 18" x 22". **$1,500**

Heritage Auctions

▲ *Lee Miller (American, 1907-1977), "Pablo Picasso, Cannes," 1958, gelatin silver, estate printed 1984, 10" x 9 7/8", ed. 21/30, signed and numbered by Susanna Penrose in pencil with artist's archive stamp on verso.* **$1,250**

Heritage Auctions

◄ *Michael Kenna (British/American, b. 1953), "Big Sur Beach, California," 1978, gelatin silver, 1979, 5 3/8" x 8 1/2", signed and dated in pencil on mount recto; titled and dated in pencil on verso.* **$1,250**

PDNB Gallery, Dallas

▲ *Misty Keasler, "Damaris on his Bed (Guatemala City Dump)," 2003, C-Print, 24" x 20".* **$900**

PDNB Gallery, Dallas

Keith Carter, "Uncertain, Harrison County," 1985, gelatin silver, 16" x 20". **$1,200**

Quilts

E ach generation made quilts, comforters and coverlets, all intended to be used. Many were used into oblivion and rest in quilt heaven, but for myriad reasons, some have survived. Many of them remain because they were not used but stored, often forgotten, in trunks and linen cabinets.

A quilt is made up of three layers: the top, which can be a solid piece of fabric, appliquéd, pieced, or a combination; the back, which can be another solid piece of fabric or pieced; and the batting, which is the center layer, which can be cotton, wool, polyester, a blend of poly and cotton, or even silk. Many vintage quilts are batted with an old blanket or even another old, worn quilt.

The fabrics are usually cotton or wool, or fine fancy fabrics like silk, velvet, satin, and taffeta. The layers of a true quilt are held together by the stitching, or quilting, that goes through all three layers and is usually worked in a design or pattern that enhances the piece overall. The term "quilt" has become synonymous with bedcover to many people, and we include tied quilts, comforters and quilt tops, none of which are true quilts in the technical description.

Quilts made from a seemingly single solid piece of fabric are known as wholecloth quilts, or if they are white, as whitework quilts. Usually such quilts are constructed from two or more pieces of the same fabric joined to make up the necessary width. They are often quilted quite elaborately, and the seams virtually disappear within the decorative stitching. Most wholecloth quilts are solid-colored, but prints were also used. Whitework quilts were often made as bridal quilts and many were kept for "best," which means that they have survived in reasonable numbers.

Wholecloth quilts were among the earliest type of quilted bedcovers made in Britain, and the colonists brought examples with them according to inventory lists that exist from colonial times. American quiltmakers used the patterns early in the nation's history, and some were carried with settlers moving west across the Appalachians.

Appliqué quilts are made from shapes cut from fabric and applied, or appliquéd, to a background, usually solid-colored on vintage quilts, to make a design. Early appliqué quilts dating back to the 18th century were often worked in a technique called broderie perse, or Persian embroidery, in which printed motifs were cut from a piece of fabric, such as costly chintz, and applied to a plain, less expensive background cloth.

Appliqué was popular in the 1800s, and there are thousands of examples, from exquisite, brightly colored Baltimore Album quilts made in and around Baltimore between circa 1840 and 1860, to elegant four-block quilts made later in the century. Many appliqué quilts are pictorial—with floral designs the predominant motif. In the 20th century, appliqué again enjoyed an upswing, especially during the Colonial Revival period, and thousands were made from patterns or appliqué kits that were marketed and sold from 1900 through the 1950s.

Pieced or patchwork quilts are made by cutting fabric into shapes and sewing them together to make a larger piece of cloth. The patterns are usually geometric, and their effectiveness depends heavily on the contrast of not just the colors themselves, but of color value as well. Patchwork became popular in the United States in the early 1800s.

Colonial clothing was almost always made using cloth cut into squares or rectangles, but after the Revolutionary War, when fabric became more widely available, shaped garments were made, and these garments left scraps. Frugal housewives, especially among the westward-bound pioneers, began to use these cutoffs to put together blocks that could then be made into quilts. Patchwork quilts are by far the most numerous of all vintage-quilt categories, and the diversity of style, construction and effect that can be found is a study all its own.

Dating a quilt is a tricky business unless the maker included the date on the finished item, and unfortunately for historians and collectors, few did. The value of a particular example is affected by its age, of course, and educating yourself about dating methods is invaluable. There are several aspects that can offer guidelines for establishing a date. These include fabrics; patterns; technique; borders; binding; batting; backing; quilting method; and colors and dyes.

For more information on quilts, see *Warman's Vintage Quilts Identification and Price Guide* by Maggi McCormick Gordon.

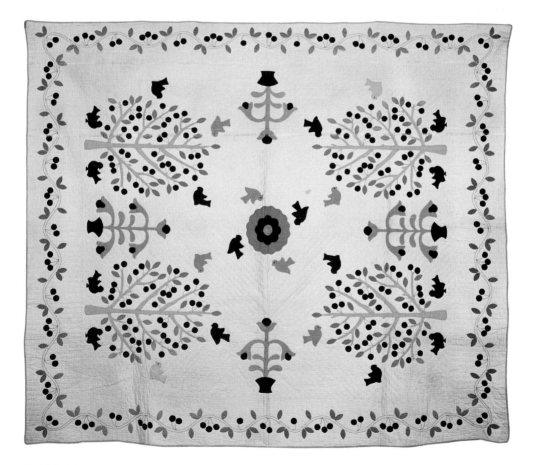

Pook & Pook, Inc.

Appliqué Bird and Cherry Tree quilt, early 20th century, 89" x 77". **$533**

Pook & Pook, Inc.

▶ *Pennsylvania pieced Star of Bethlehem quilt, inscribed Clarence J Spohn 1907 born in Oley July 25 1901, 75" x 77".*
$152

Pook & Pook, Inc.

▶ *Pieced crib quilt, early 20th century, mounted, 37"x 36".*
 $122

Pook & Pook, Inc.

▼ *Pieced Star and Block quilt, mid-20th century, 70" x 92".* **$593**

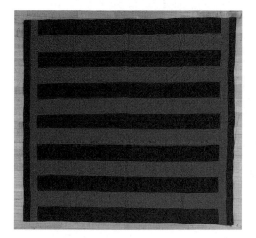

Pook & Pook, Inc.

Pennsylvania bar quilt, 20th century, 76" x 73". **$243**

Pook & Pook, Inc.

Pennsylvania bar rainbow quilt, 20th century, 85 1/2" x 76". **$395**

Pook & Pook, Inc.

Agriculture & Manufactures jacquard coverlet, signed S. Harris 1827, 72" x 90". **$213**

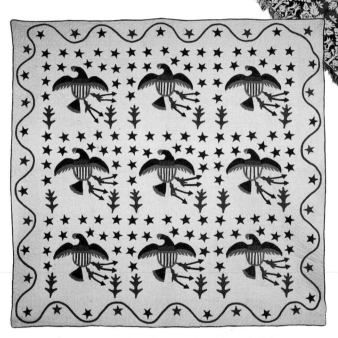

Pook & Pook, Inc.

▶ *Pennsylvania jacquard coverlet, dated 1836, inscribed Emanuel Ettinger Aaronsburg Centre Co Penna, 93" x 77", together with another, inscribed "JH March Manufacturer Salona Centre Co Penna 1838," 91" x 77".* **$711**

Pook & Pook, Inc.

◀ *Appliqué Eagle and Star quilt, late 19th century, 84" x 82".* **$2,133**

Skinner, Inc.; www.skinnerinc.com

◀ *Pieced cotton Roman Cross pattern quilt, American, hand-stitched with 35 blocks of red calico printed squares and rectangles arranged in zigzag design around central white cross on off-white ground, one cross embroidered with name Mary Buckley Nutting, blocks separated by red calico-printed grid, bordered with white and red calico border, backed with off-white muslin, one corner of reverse stitched "ARK 1836," quilted with outline, chain, and shell designs, approximately 104" x 82".* **$420**

Pook & Pook, Inc.

◄ *Appliqué Pride of Iowa variation quilt, circa 1880, 74" x 77".* **$1,067**

Pook & Pook, Inc.

▼ *Broderie perse friendship quilt, inscribed Sarah V. C. Quick 1844 on central panel, surrounded by 116 floral and bird appliqué chintz blocks, many with signatures, 97" x 87". Provenance: The McCarl Collection.* **$15,405**

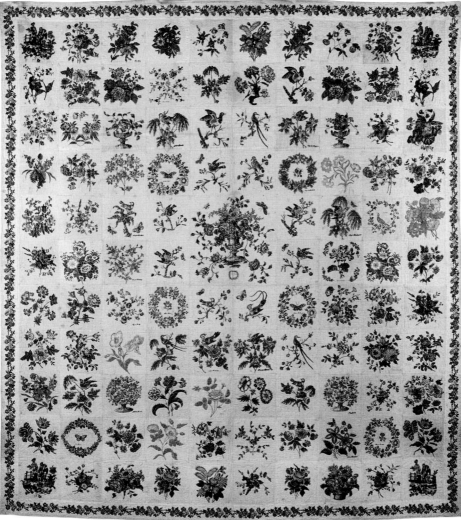

Pook & Pook, Inc.

▼ *Pieced crib quilt, late 19th century, mounted, 33" x 34".* **$356**

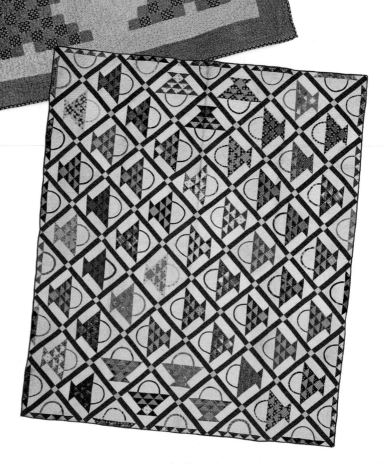

Skinner, Inc.;
www.skinnerinc.com

▶ *Pieced and appliqued cotton Cherry Baskets pattern quilt, American, late 19th century, with 44 baskets and 22 partial baskets composed of multicolored printed and woven cotton triangular and square segments on off-white ground separated by red diamond grid intersecting with light blue printed squares, edged with red printed fabric and backed with off-white muslin, quilted with outline, hearts, and parallel line stitches, minor toning and stains, approximately 94" x 82".* **$960**

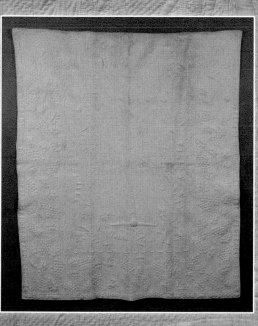

Skinner, Inc.; www.skinnerinc.com

Tree of Life whitework trapunto quilt, American, circa 1820, white homespun cotton quilt face and backing joined together, with quilting stitched in design centered with large tree surrounded by flowering branches, grapevines, and scallop and chain borders, motifs stuffed with cotton batting from loosely woven fabric backing, imperfections, 92" x 78".
$1,722

Skinner, Inc.; www.skinnerinc.com

Pieced and appliqued cotton Oak Leaf and Berries pattern quilt, American, late 19th/early 20th century, 16 blocks of Oak Leaf and Berry pattern, each with four red and green stylized oak leaves with intersecting stylized berry branches in red, green and orange solid colored fabrics, on off-white ground enclosed with red border, edged and backed with off-white muslin, quilted with diamond pattern and diagonal lines, minor toning and stains, approximately 78" x 76". **$510**

Skinner, Inc.; www.skinnerinc.com

Pieced cotton Turkey Tracks pattern quilt, American, late 19th/early 20th century, hand-stitched quilt with 18 blocks of four green and maroon solid-color Turkey Track motifs and gold square, on off-white ground, alternating with blocks of off-white quilted feathered wreaths, with gold and maroon edging and backed with off-white muslin, further quilted with diamond grids and zigzag lines, minor toning, fading and stains, approximately 83" x 76". **$240**

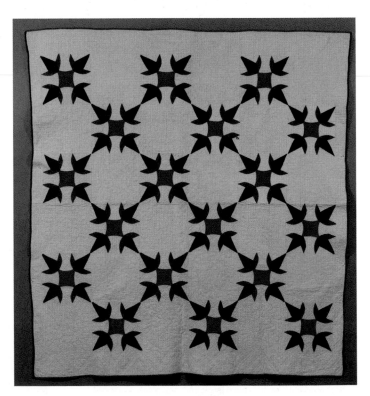

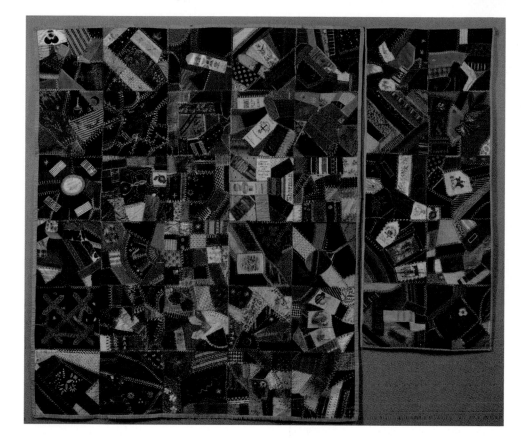

Skinner, Inc.; www.skinnerinc.com

▲ *Victorian embroidered silk and velvet crazy quilt and table runner, American, circa 1890s, quilt and matching runner composed of squares of pieced silk and velvet fabric segments, several printed silk presidential candidate ribbons, organization ribbons, and images of women, each outlined with contrasting embroidery, some segments with embroidered motifs including butterflies, fans, flowers, fruit, and balloons, several segments with painted details, edged in blue and white silk, backed with brown cotton sateen, 58 1/2" x 70", 23 1/2" x 56".* **$720**

Pook & Pook, Inc.

◄ *Pieced pinwheel quilt, late 19th century, 90" x 94".* **$2,252**

Pook & Pook, Inc.

▲ *Elaborate pieced and embroidered quilt, early 20th century, titled "The Homestead," signed F. Cochran, depicting busy farm scene with animals and figures and Illinois Central Railroad in background, 73" x 90". Provenance: Sotheby's, 1983 cover lot.* **$7,703**

Skinner, Inc.; www.skinnerinc.com

▶ *Pieced and appliquéd cotton Washington's Plume pattern quilt, American, late 19th century, hand-stitched quilt with eight solid red scrolled plumes radiating from eight-point star hub with border of 13 singular plumes appliquéd to off-white ground, edged and backed with off-white cotton fabric, quilted in diamond pattern, shaped to fit four-poster bed, fading, light toning, fraying on edges, approximately 82" x 82".* **$180**

Records

By Susan Sliwicki

Values for records — much like those for other collectibles — are dependent on a mix of factors, including condition, rarity, overall demand, market trends, and past sales results. Here are some key points to remember as you buy, sell, and value your records.

Discern the record's quality, which is not the same thing as condition. Quality relates to the materials that were used in the first place. When 78 RPM blues records were pressed in the 1920s to 1930s, manufacturers used either stock shellac or laminated discs. Stock shellac discs had a lower-quality playing surface, which made them prone to more noise at playback, while laminated discs (which were used by labels including Columbia and OKeh) featured a higher quality playing surface.

Likewise, quality can vary for vinyl records. For 12" records, the low end of the scale is 120 gram vinyl (4.23 ounces), with 150 grams (5.29 ounces) considered a "heavy" weight, and anything pressed on 180 grams (6.35 grams) or more deemed audiophile grade. The higher the weight, the higher the quality and durability.

Be ruthless when you assess condition. Goldmine magazine established (and continues to follow) the Goldmine Grading Standard, which determines how well a record, cover, or sleeve has survived since its creation. These are high standards, and they are not on a sliding scale. A record or sleeve from the 1950s must meet the same standards as one pressed today.

Rarity does not guarantee value. You thought you bought a copy of Lynyrd Skynyrd's "Street Survivors" album; the cover and labels were correct, after all. But when you put it on the turntable, you discovered the A-side was actually Steely Dan's "Aja." Or maybe the labels were wrong, but the music was what you thought you bought. Or perhaps you bought a still-sealed record that advertised one group on the cover and contained a completely different artist's album inside. These types of scenarios happened more often than

Gotta Have Rock and Roll

"Autoamerican" album cover signed by Blondie band members Debbie Harry, Chris Stein, Clem Burke, and Jimmy Destri in blue felt-tip pen, very good condition, vinyl included. **$60**

SUSAN SLIWICKI'S favorite childhood memories are of hours spent hanging out with her oldest brother, who let her listen to his collection of albums, including Pink Floyd's "Dark Side of the Moon" and Deep Purple's "Machine Head," in exchange for her silence as long as the record was still spinning on the turntable. A journalist by trade, Sliwicki brought her two greatest passions — words and music — together when she joined *Goldmine* magazine in 2007 and became its editor in 2011.

you might think at a record pressing plant. While these records are snowflakes, they don't possess the types of errors that draw big bucks from collectors; if anything, they negatively impact value. Depending on the music fan, these errors may only be a source of frustration, because the listener was anticipating "What's Your Name" and got "Black Cow" instead.

A record can be old without being valuable, and vice versa. Head to a garage sale, a thrift store or a relative's attic, and chances are good you'll find some old records. We're not saying you'll never find a beauty or two in the mix, but you're far more likely to find copies of Frankie Yankovic's "40 Hits I Almost Missed," Tom Jones' "Live In Las Vegas," and Glenn Miller's "The Carnegie Hall Concert" (worth $5 or less apiece) than a rare 78 RPM of Charley Patton's "High Water Everywhere" Parts 1 and 2 on the Paramount label, which sold for $5,000 in March 2012. Condition, quality, demand and rarity are far more important than age when determining value.

The laws of supply and demand rule. Meat Loaf's claim that "Two Out of Three Ain't Bad" doesn't count if the missing No. 3 is demand. No demand means no value; it doesn't matter how fine or rare the record is unless others want to buy it and own it. Supply figures in, too. A quality record in great condition that also is in great supply means buyers deem what the market is worth.

Trying to sell a record but not getting the price you seek? *Get a second, third or more opinion* on the record in question. Has your record gotten a better grade than it deserves? Is it a first pressing? Or is it a reissue or a counterfeit? Are similar-condition copies selling for wildly different amounts on the Internet or with other dealers? This will give you a better picture of what you have, what it's worth, and how in-demand it really is.

If you feel a dealer is offering an unfair price, make a counter offer. If the dealer shows no interest in negotiating, ask why he or she arrived at the price offered. Keep in mind that reputable dealers offer what they feel are fair prices, based on the costs and risks they assume for the items they acquire.

Collect what you love and what you can afford. Don't raid your 401(k) account to buy a too-good-to-be-true rarity under the guise that it is an investment. Enjoy the thrill of the chase within your budget, buy the best that you can afford, and always take time to appreciate what you have, from super-cool sleeves and covers to great-sounding music.

Backstage Auctions

The Beatles, 1975-1982, sealed promotional vinyl and BBC LP. **$211**

Goldmine's Record Grading Guide

Record grading uses both objective and subjective factors. Our advice: Look at everything about a record — its playing surface, the label, the record's edges, the cover and/or sleeve — under a strong light. If you're in doubt, assign the record a lower grade. Many dealers grade records, sleeves, or covers and sometimes even labels separately. The grades listed below are common to vinyl records, including EPs, 45s, LPs and 12" singles.

MINT (M): Perfect in every way. Often rumored, but rarely seen. Never played, and often still factory sealed. Never use Mint as a grade unless more than one person agrees that a record or sleeve truly is in this condition. Mint price is best negotiated between buyer and seller.

NEAR MINT (NM OR M-): Nearly perfect. Looks and sounds like it just came from a retail store and was opened for the first time. Jackets and sleeves are free of creases, folds, markings, or seam splits. Records are glossy and free of imperfections. Many dealers won't use a grade higher than NM, implying that no record or sleeve is ever truly perfect.

VERY GOOD PLUS (VG+) or EXCELLENT (E): Except for a few minor things — slight warps, scuffs, or scratches that don't affect playback, ring wear on the labels, a turned up corner, cut-out hole, or seam split on the sleeve or cover — this record would be NM. Most collectors, especially those who want to play their records, are happy with a VG+ record, especially if it's toward the high end of the grade (VG++ or E+). Worth 50 percent of NM value.

VERY GOOD (VG): Many of the imperfections found on a VG+ record are more obvious on a VG record. Surface noise, groove wear, and light scratches can be found on VG records. You may find stickers, tape or writing on labels, sleeves, and covers, but no more than two of those three problems. VG records are among the biggest bargains in record collecting. Worth 25 percent of a NM record.

GOOD (G), GOOD PLUS (G+), or VERY GOOD MINUS (VG-): Expect a lot of surface noise, visible groove wear and scratches on the vinyl, as well as more defects and repairs to labels, sleeves, and covers. Unless the record is unusually rare, G/G+ or VG- records are worth 10 to 15 percent of the NM value.

POOR (P) and FAIR (F): Records are cracked, impossibly warped, or skip and/or repeat when an attempt is made to play them. Covers and sleeves are heavily damaged, if they even exist. Unless they are incredibly rare, P and F records sell for 0 to 5 percent of the NM value (if they sell at all).

Backstage Auctions

The Ramones, 1977, "Leave Home" signed album cover. **$295**

Backstage Auctions

The Band, 1970, fully signed "Music From the Big Pink" album. **$885**

Christie's

Single-sided, 7" acetate record, "Strawberry Fields Forever," 1966, with white EMI disc label inscribed in black ballpoint pen in unknown hand, "3:10, Strawberry Fields, 95 RP [Ron Pender], 16-12-66, The Beatles, 2," with white paper sleeve. Provenance: From the collection of Red Ronnie. **$6,746**

Backstage Auctions

Led Zeppelin, 1973, fully signed "Houses of The Holy" album cover. **$10,890**

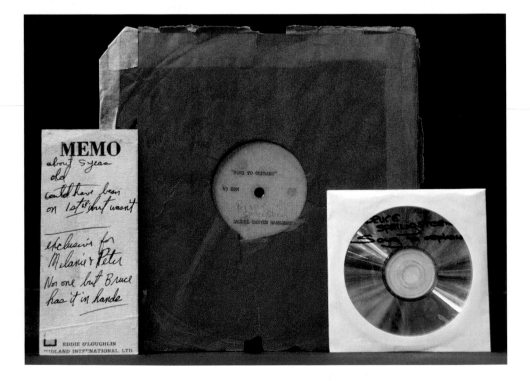

Backstage Auctions

Bruce Springsteen, 1973, "Song to Orphans," rare live acetate. **$1,182**

Meat Loaf, 1977, "Bat Out of Hell," set of two unique record reels. **$753**

◄ *B.B. King signed "Midnight Believer" album cover in blue felt-tip pen, fair condition, cover warped, vinyl included.* **$125**

▲ *Roxy Music's five original members – Brian Ferry, Brian Eno, Phil Manzanera, Andy McKay, and Paul Thompson – signed "For Your Pleasure" album cover in silver paint pen and blue felt-tip pen, very good condition.* **$405**

◄ *Cheech Marin and Tommy Chong signed "Greatest Hit" album cover in blue felt-tip pen, very good condition, vinyl included.* **$175**

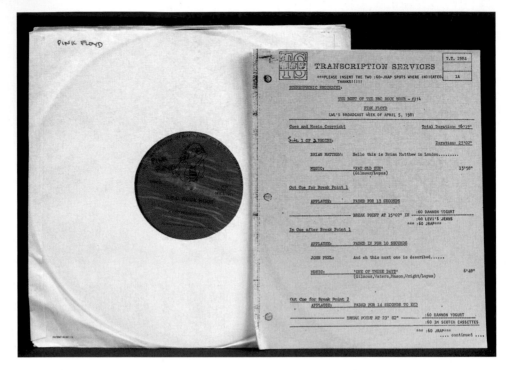

Backstage Auctions

Pink Floyd, rare "The Best of The BBC Rock Hour" radio broadcast, vinyl, with paperwork from BBC Transcription services detailing the air date, cues, advertising spots and content. **$177**

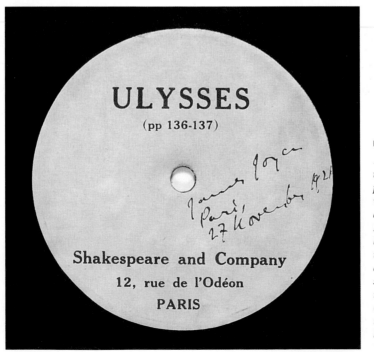

Hakes Americana and Collectibles

12" single-sided 78 RPM recording of "Ulysses," pp 136-137, with printed white paper label signed and dated "James Joyce/ Paris/27 November 1924," label unbrowned, shellac unscratched, record appears unplayed, modern sleeve within custom half morocco gilt slipcase. Joyce (1882-1941) was an Irish novelist and poet best known for his 1922 work "Ulysses." **$43,750**

Gotta Have Rock and Roll

Journey rock band members, including Steve Perry, Neal Schon, and Ross Vallory, signed "Escape" album cover in various felt-tipped and paint pens, very good condition. **$175**

Hakes Americana and Collectibles

"Batman Theme" b/w "Nelson's Riddler" 45 RPM record and glossy picture sleeve, performed by The Nelson Riddle Orchestra for original TV series, near mint condition. **$387**

Backstage Auctions

Poco, 1975-1978, lot with recording reel for stereo single version of "Heart of the Night" and 10" mono acetate for "Heart of the Night" and 7" Columbia Record Productions test pressing for "Makin' Love." "Heart of the Night" appeared on Poco's "Legend" album, released in late 1978, and was the band's best-selling release. "Makin' Love" was part of 1975's "Head Over Heels" album. **$237**

Heritage Auctions

Multicolored vinyl pressing for The Rolling Stones' 1969 LP "Let It Bleed" (London NPS-4), originally intended for a few record label executives only, excellent condition. **$5,625**

Record Price for 78 RPM

A longtime collector and dealer set a new record for the amount paid for one 78 RPM disc on eBay.

John Tefteller of Grants Pass, Oregon, submitted the winning bid of $37,100 to buy Tommy Johnson's "Alcohol and Jake Blues" b/w "Ridin' Horse." Graded by the seller as being in very good++ condition, this copy of Paramount 12950, recorded in 1930, is one of only two known and verified copies. Tefteller owns the only other known copy. He owns Tefteller's World's Rarest Records (www.tefteller.com) and Blues Images (www.bluesimages.com).

A Columbia, South Carolina collector picked up the record a few years ago at an estate sale. When he opened the auction Sept. 18, 2013, he had placed a starting price of $499.99 on the lot. Bidding crossed the $10,000 mark within 24 hours of the auction's opening; by the time the auction closed Sept. 25, 2013, the eight bidders had placed a total of 29 offers.

"He absolutely did not realize what he had and how rare it was until he put it on eBay. Within the first few hours of being listed on the auction site, another collector tried to stop the sale by offering the seller $4,000 for the record. Fortunately, he let the auction proceed and I was able to win it in the final moments," Tefteller said.

A Delta blues singer and guitar player from Mississippi, Johnson made just five records for Paramount in 1929 and 1930. His legend has grown over the years, and his Paramount records are considered Holy Grails for blues collectors. Johnson also made three records for the Victor label, but enough copies have survived that the Victor discs tend to sell for $1,000 to $5,000 apiece. Johnson died Nov. 1, 1956, in Crystal Springs, Mississippi.

Tefteller released Johnson's songs from his first copy of Paramount 12950 on the CD accompanying the 2009 edition of his "Classic Blues Artwork from the 1920s" calendar series. He plans to sell that first copy of Paramount 12950 to offset his new purchase, and Tefteller expects to remaster and re-release the songs from his newly purchased copy on the CD that accompanies his 2015 Blues Calendar.

Tefteller specializes in collecting records on the Paramount label, which was run out of a furniture factory in Port Washington, Wisconsin, from the early 1920s to the early 1930s.

"The original masters for these recordings were all destroyed by World War II. The only way we can hear them now is to rescue the few remaining commercial copies, which are in private homes," Tefteller said. "We have to seek out the best or only copies that exist today and remaster from those."

Historians recognize Paramount as the most innovative and creative independent record label from that time; as a result, collectors seek out its releases. There are a number of legendary Paramount records that are still missing in action, he added.

"Find me the missing Willie Brown or J.D. Short on Paramount label, and you will see me writing really big checks." Tefteller said.

▲ *Seven-inch Emidisc acetate pressing of 1968 Mark Bolan T. Rex songs "Child Star" and "Debora," written on and decorated by Bolan and his wife, June Child, A-side reads "Regal Zonophone / Child Star (Bolan) / From LP, my People were Fair and had sky in their hair but now their (sic) content to wear stars on their brows / Tyrannosaurus Rex/Produced by tony visconti" in two separate hands, with drawings; B-side reads "Regal Zonophone / DeGorah (sic) / Bolan/Tyrannosaurus Rex / producted by tony visconti."* **$750**

◄ *Motown gold record award presented to Michael Jackson to commemorate sale of one million copies of Jackson 5 single "I'll Be There" in 1970, dragon etching on "gold" record produced by Disc Award Ltd.* **$3,200**

Rare promotional single for The Beatles' "Ask Me Why" / "Anna" (Vee-Jay Special DJ No. 8), near mint condition. Reportedly, as few as five copies of this promotional 45 were produced in 1964. There was never a commercial release combining these two songs, although they both appeared on the more common version of "Introducing The Beatles" LP and on Vee-Jay EP. **$35,000**

Gotta Have Rock and Roll

Band members Eddie Van Halen, Alex Van Halen, Michael Anthony, and Sammy Hagar signed cover of "5150," in blue felt-tip pen, very good condition, vinyl included. **$200**

Gotta Have Rock and Roll

The Who's guitarist Pete Townshend signed "Who's Next" album cover in black felt-tip pen, cover only, very good condition. **$175**

Gotta Have Rock and Roll

Ozzy Osbourne's "Diary of a Madman" album cover signed and inscribed "Much love, Ozzy Osbourne" in silver paint pen, very good condition, vinyl included. **$90**

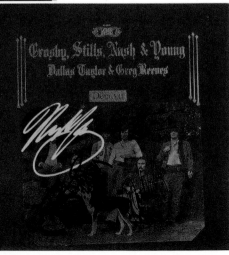

Gotta Have Rock and Roll

▶ *David Crosby, Stephen Stills, Graham Nash, and Neil Young signed "Déjà Vu" album cover in blue felt-tip pen, black felt-tip pen, and silver paint pen, cover only, very good condition.* **$1,283**

Backstage Auctions

U2, vintage and rare vinyl collection, including "BBC Rock Hour No. 410," which was scheduled to air March 6, 1983. **$143**

Gotta Have Rock and Roll

Beach Boys band members Brian Wilson, Mike Love, Al Jardine, Bruce Johnston, and David Marks signed "Endless Summer" album cover in blue felt-tip pen, Marks also inscribed lyrics to "Fun Fun Fun," very good condition. **$656**

Gotta Have Rock and Roll

The Raspberries members Eric Carmen, Wally Bryson, Jim Bonfanti, and Dave Smalley signed cover for "Raspberries" album in black felt-tipped pen. **$125**

Gotta Have Rock and Roll

Monkees band members Davy Jones, Micky Dolenz, and Peter Tork signed cover of self-titled album, in black felt-tip pen, very good condition, vinyl included. **$175**

Gotta Have Rock and Roll

REO Speedwagon cover for "You Can Tune a Piano But You Can't Tuna Fish" album signed by band members Kevin Cronin, Neal Doughty, Gary Richrath, and Bruce Hall. **$70**

Backstage Auctions

The Sweet, 1977, original acetate lot, on acetate dated 11-3-77, songs include "Dream On," "Love is Like Oxygen" (with a note next to 6:49 run time to use edited version), "California Nights," "Strong Love," and "Fountain." "Level Headed" original acetate lot. 45 RPM acetate dated 12-5-77 features "Love is Like Oxygen" with run time of 3:46. **$196**

Gotta Have Rock and Roll

Original Guns N' Roses demo tape from 1985, personally owned by group's guitarist, Slash, who wrote "Guns & Roses Demo 85" in blue ballpoint pen on cassette insert with hand-drawn gun and roses, very good condition, tape contains rare and unreleased recordings. **$1,000**

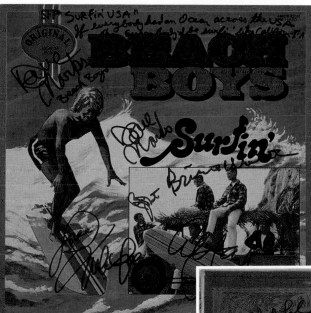

Gotta Have Rock and Roll

Beach Boys "Surfin'" album from Success for Pleasure label, signed in blue felt-tipped pen by Beach Boys Brian Wilson, Mike Love, Al Jardine, Bruce Johnston, and Dave Marks (twice), with inscribed partial "Surfin' USA" lyrics, very good condition, vinyl included. **$405**

Gotta Have Rock and Roll

▶ *Grateful Dead original band members Jerry Garcia, Bobby Weir, Micky Hart, Phil Lesh, Bill Kreutzmann, and Brent Mydland signed album cover for 1967 eponymous debut, in black felt-tipped pen, very good condition, vinyl included.* **$977**

Science & Technology

By Eric Bradley

Grouping science and technology in a collecting genre is a relatively new theme, although these unique objects have been highly sought after for decades. Scientific models, diagrams and lab equipment are now hot collectibles, thanks to a boost in the Steampunk design movement and the rise of "geek chic."

It's cool to be smart and it's a cool collector who has at least a few fascinating objects devoted to mankind's pursuit to knowing more about the world we live in. From books to microscopes to calculators and even quack medical devices, this collecting category spans several object classes.

Increasingly, auction houses are pursuing this trend with specialty-themed sales. Bonhams, Heritage, Skinner, and even Sotheby's have all offered major technological auctions, many with strong results. However, the undisputed leader in this category is based in Germany. Auctin Team Breker, located in Cologne, offers several sales each year on office antiques, photographica and film. The sales are just one more example of how auction houses are seeking to cater not only to what collectors collect, but how collectors collect.

Trends in this area are likely to be centered on the dawn of personal computing. The first personal computer sold to the public was Simon, a hulk of wire and cabinetry holding a simple mechanical brain. It debuted in 1950 for $600 ($5,723 in today's dollars) and was able to perform addition, negation, greater than, and selection. It's rare for these early computers to come to market, however, when they do collectors and investors take notice.

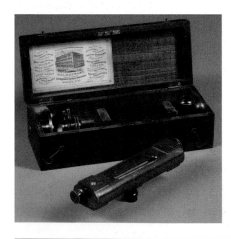

A rare 1976 Apple I computer brought $374,500 at a June 2012 auction. Similar models don't sell for nearly as much money, with provenance, condition and exposure key to an object's auction value.

Rare examples aside, collecting scientific and technology collectibles is a very affordable hobby and one that stands an excellent chance to grow as today's tech-savvy youth become the nostalgic collectors of the future.

Skinner, Inc.; www.skinnerinc.com

W. & L.E. Gurley drainage or farm level, Troy, New York, circa 1883, 8 1/2" green-painted body, four-screw leveling base, ball and socket joint with staff mount, wood adjusting bar, in mahogany fitted case with label. **$123**

ERIC BRADLEY is public relations associate at Heritage Auctions, the world's third largest auction house. He is former editor of *Antique Trader* magazine and is the author of *Antique Trader 2014 Antiques and Collectibles Price Guide*, America's no. 1-selling guide to the antiques and collectibles market. An award-winning investigative journalist with a degree in economics, Bradley has written hundreds of articles about antiques and collectibles and has made several media appearances as an expert on the antiques market at MoneyShow San Francisco, on MSN Money, Nasdaq.com and on AdvisorOne.com. His work has received press from *The New York Times* and *The Philadelphia Inquirer*.

Bonhams

George III inlaid mahogany banjo barometer, J. Ronchetti, Manchester, early 19th century, typical form, spirit level dial inscribed J. Ronchetti, 1 St. Ann Place, Manchester, 58 3/4" high. **$938**

Skinner, Inc.; www.skinnerinc.com

Mahogany veneer stick barometer, Charles Wilder, Peterboro, New Hampshire, circa 1860, peaked shaped crest over hinged glazed door over silvered metal with stamped marks WOODRUFF'S PAT. JUNE 5 1860/C. WILDER PETERBORO N.H., above thermometer with scrolled bulb, over molded and paneled monument base, 38 1/4" high. **$2,040**

Pook & Pook, Inc.

▲ *Hepplewhite mahogany stick barometer, circa 1800, signed P. Gally Cranbrook, 39 1/2" high.* **$1,422**

◄ Pook & Pook, Inc.

Georgian mahogany book press, mid-19th century, 14 1/2" high x 17" wide. **$474**

Victorian Casino Antiques

▶ *Scale model metal K-W Hit & Miss gas engine on wood mount, Pat. 1914, P.M. Research Inc., Wellsville, New York, 10" high.* **$1,008**

Skinner, Inc.; www.skinnerinc.com

W. & L.E. Gurley engineer's transit, Troy, New York, circa 1900, 5 1/2" silvered compass marked as above, fleur-de-lis representing north, scale divided in four quadrants, dual spirit levels, enclosed horizontal scale with vernier divided 80-90-80, A-frame supports with 11 1/2" scope, rack focusing, horizontal silvered scale, on four adjustable screw feet, in fitted mahogany case with label, tripod instrument 14" high. **$492**

Skinner, Inc.; www.skinnerinc.com

Dutch horizontal sundial, 18th century, 5 1/4" x 6" brass plate signed Engel Brecht, sliding gnomon in aperture to set against scale either side of days of month, bordered by engraved Arabic numeral hour scale, second gnomon (lacking plummet) with engraved latitude scale, edge of plate with Roman numerals representing hours, all on three knurled adjustable feet. **$3,000**

Pook & Pook, Inc.

English mahogany banjo barometer, 19th century, signed A. Peduzzi, 38 1/4" high. **$237**

Pook & Pook, Inc.

New Jersey brass surveyor's transit, circa 1805, inscribed Daniel Dod Mendham, with original fitted case, 13 1/4" long. **$2,252**

Pook & Pook, Inc.

Walnut megalethoscope viewer, labeled Charles Ponti, circa 1870, turned-leg base with 12 slides, 23" high x 35" long. **$2,673**

Pook & Pook, Inc.

French iron book press, 20th century, signed Mon Cabany Fend, 12" high x 14" wide. **$304**

Skinner, Inc.; www.skinnerinc.com

18th century brass sector, Paris, France, marked P. Le Maire Paris, with plumb bob window, hinged at 45-degree angle, "Half the Kings Rule" scale, 6 1/2" long closed. **$246**

Victorian Casino Antiques

▼ *Early Angldile springless automatic scale, style no. 420, no. 22749 by Angldile Computing Scale Co., Elkhart, Indiana, restored in green with pinstriping and etched glass tray, top mirror attached.* **$1,872**

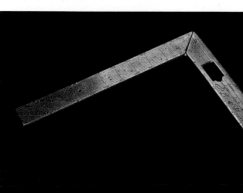
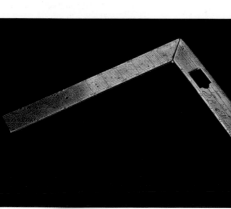

John Bryne 4" brass refracting telescope, New York, 1880, with 59 1/2" main tube, rack focus single-draw eyepiece, engraved J Bryne New York 1880, seven additional eyepieces and prism in velvet-lined and cased box, lens shade, original lacquered surface, fitted in original pine case, with associated wood and cast iron tripod, tripod 60" high. **$3,900**

The Byrne telescope was built in 1880 by noted telescope maker John Byrne, who started as an apprentice of telescope maker Henry Fitz in 1847 and worked with him until Fitz's death in 1863. He then began making Byrne-signed telescopes. Byrne included many innovations in his telescopes, one of which was used by the well-known astronomer Edward Barnard to discover several comets.

Pascal Hubert gilt case coach watch, Roven, circa 1740, chased decorated case, dial with raised porcelain Roman numerals, single blued steel hand, raised decorated center and winding hole, swing-out chain fusee brass movement engraved Pascal Hvbert A Roven, crown wheel escapement, pierced balance cock, silvered regulation dial, Egyptian pillars and decorative multi-medallion vest pocket chain, 70 mm. **$4,800**

Johan Schrettegger brass pocket sundial, Augsburg, Germany, circa 1750, folding hour ring, latitude scale, gnomon, and level, central compass, maker's signature on bottom, in associated octagonal card case, 2 1/2" diameter. **$984**

Japanese "Big Eye" naval binoculars in original wooden chest, marked March 1933, manufactured by Japan Optical Industries Co., Ltd. for nighttime naval attacks, cast body painted gray, front rings painted black, brass eyepieces, binoculars 26 1/2" long x 17 1/2" wide, case 29 3/4" long x 19" wide. **$5,700**

Nickel-plated brass and steel wheel-cutting engine, Switzerland, 20th century, footed and bow-powered tool with 3 3/4" indexing plate with 18 rows for cutting various numbers of teeth, pivoting steel arm with curved finger loop, cutter adjusts on two axes, with thumbscrew fasteners, 6 3/4" high. **$2,040**

Two brass and steel rounding-up tools, Switzerland, 19th century, 6" and 7" handwheels with turned wood handles, knurled thumbscrews, cutter assemblies, and horizontal dovetail slides, both mounted on wood stands, 9" high. **$840**

Pook & Pook, Inc.

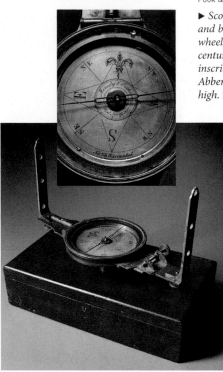

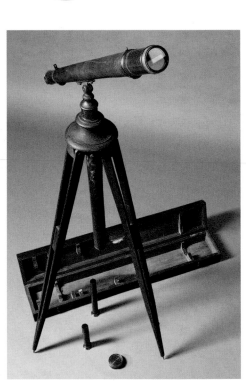

▶ *Scottish mahogany and brass spinning wheel, late 18th century, with plaque inscribed S Thorp Abberley Inv., 47 1/2" high.* **$1,659**

Skinner, Inc.; www.skinnerinc.com

Meneely & Oothout vernier surveyor's compass, no. 976, West Troy, New York, circa 1840, 6 1/4" silvered dial marked as above, fleur-de-lis representing north, scale divided in four quadrants, dual spirit levels on main plate, vernier scale divided 0-30, 7 1/2" sighting vanes, in mahogany fitted case, instrument 15 3/3" long, with tripod. **$840**

Skinner, Inc.; www.skinnerinc.com

Pocket barometer and compass, 19th century, brass-cased John Browning London 942 pocket barometer with silvered dial, brass-cased compass with cardinal points, fleur-de-lis representing north, blued hands marked S and N, both housed in leather-clad fitted boxes. **$360**

Skinner, Inc.; www.skinnerinc.com

Maison Lerebours and Secretan 2 1/2" telescope, Paris, France, second half 19th century, 41" leather-wrapped main tube, rack focus, single-draw eyepiece engraved Secretan Paris, two additional eyepieces in lengths of 8" and 12", with adjustable brass-mounted wood tripod and fitted wood box. **$1,800**

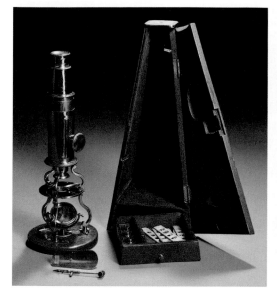

Skinner, Inc.; www.skinnerinc.com

Culpepper microscope in box, rack and pinion focus body tube above circular stage with undermounted spring slide clips supported above concave mirror by three scroll supports, pyramidal mahogany case with accessories drawer with spring stage, fish box, forceps, six bone slides, three numbered objectives and other parts, box 12 1/2" high. **$861**

Skinner, Inc.; www.skinnerinc.com

Brass Bausch & Lomb microscope, late 19th century, no. 55923, with triple nosepiece, rackwork coarse focus on tube, micrometer fine focus on pillar, plano/concave mirror, stage diaphragm, in wooden box, scope 12" high. **$360**

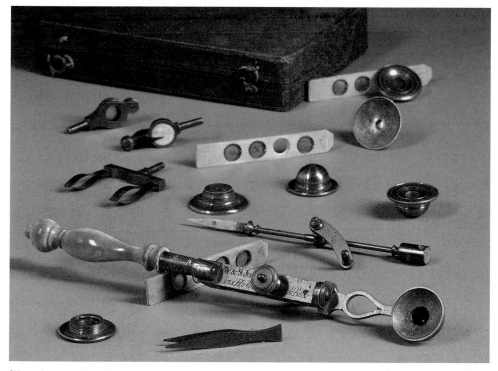

Skinner, Inc., www.skinnerinc.com

W&S Jones brass botanic microscope, 19th century, turned ivory handle, collapsible brass body engraved W&S Jones, 135 Holborn, London, additional eyepieces and attachments, all housed in pebble finished leather case. **$3,120**

Julien P. Friez anemometer recorder, Baltimore, Maryland, circa 1926, with Seth Thomas clock mechanism marked Belfort Observatory, connected to 4" drum with paper recording sheet by dual piston and corkscrew arm, housed on cast iron bed under hinged glass top, U.S.N. No. 126-42, 15 1/2" wide x 13 deep x 9" high. **$480**

J.H. Dallmeyer binocular microscope, London, lacquered brass, eyepieces with rackwork adjustment, single objective marked 1/4" Ross, London, Wenham prism, rim of circular stage divided into one-degree intervals 0-360, X and Y adjustments, plano/concave mirror, on V-base marked J. H. Dallmeyer, London, 1877. **$3,198**

W. & L.E. Gurley engineer's surveyor's transit, Troy, New York, circa 1858, 5 1/2" silvered dial marked as above, fleur-de-lis representing north, enclosed horizontal scale with vernier divided 0-30, spirit level, A-frame support with 10-in scope, rack focusing, spirit level on arm, on four adjustable screw feet, in mahogany case with label, instrument 11 1/2" high. **$900**

Brass noon cannon sundial, 19th century, brass base with brass gnomon in shape of bird above sunk compass, dual spirit levels, 1 1/4" cannon, two arcs with calendar scale on one, supporting 2 1/4" magnifier, base 3" diameter. **$1,230**

Skinner, Inc.; www.skinnerinc.com

Set of 19th century weights and measures with variety of stamp marks, including crown, set in walnut block, set by Fisher Scientific Co. in fitted box, with variety of other sized weights. **$270**

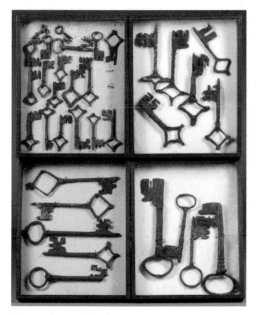

Skinner, Inc.; www.skinnerinc.com

Collection of 12th-15th century keys, Continental, most having thin bits with simple steps and clefts, pin and barrel shanks, circular and lozenge-shaped bows, 33 keys housed in walnut frames, 2" to 10" long. **$1,080**

Skinner, Inc., www.skinnerinc.com

W. & L.E. Gurley reconnaissance transit, Troy, New York, circa 1895, 3 3/4" silvered dial marked as above, engraved star representing north, scale divided in four quadrants, enclosed horizontal scale with vernier divided 0-30, A-frame supports with 8 1/2" scope, rack focusing, vertical silvered dial, on four adjustable screw feet, in fitted wooden case with label, instrument 10" high. **$780**

Swann Auction Galleries

Jean Charles Perrinet d'Orval, "Essay sur les Feux d'Artifice pour le Spectacle et pour la Guerre," Paris, 1745. **$461**

Skinner, Inc.; www.skinnerinc.com

Seven varied iron locks, Continental, 18th century, including chest locks, some with working mechanisms and keys, 5" to 14" long. **$1,200**

Skinner, Inc.; www.skinnerinc.com

"The Graphotrope" carte-de-visite display, William Walker & Co., New Haven, June 1866, walnut viewing box with pair of dome-shaped glazed windows, split turned corner columns and center divider, paper label attached to hinged lid stating Manufactured by William Walker & Co. New Haven, Patd. 1866, top section rotates on iron pillar mounted on raised plinth, with 27 tin-framed photographs, 8 1/2" high. **$1,800**

Skinner, Inc.; www.skinnerinc.com

Western Union Edison-Type 3-A universal ticker, no. 4590, Electrical Industries, New York, with brass supports flanking telegraphic receiving mechanism, twin alpha-numeric rollers and tape-feed mechanism over twin electro-magnets, on circular cast iron base with gilt Western Union Telegraph Co. label, glass dome, wood base, mechanism 10" high. **$5,100**

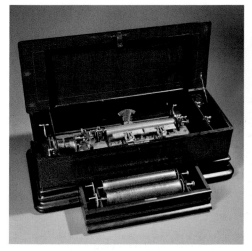

D. Allard & Co. nickel-finished 13" cylinder musical box, Geneva, Switzerland, with brass bedplate, dual combs and damascened zither attachments, interchangeable cylinders, fast/slow knob, tune plate marked D. Allard & Co. MANUFrers Geneva, with eight tune selections, burl walnut veneered case with marquetry, string inlay, and ebonized trim, drawer with two additional cylinders, box 35" long. **$3,075**

World War II 70mm handheld aerial camera, model KE-28A, Chicago, circa 1942, including body with shutter speeds from 1/30 to1/1000, f-stops from 2.8 to 32, crosshairs and dot aiming finder, 6" coated lens, red and yellow bayonet mount filters, in foam-lined aluminum carrying case, 11" high x 11 1/2" wide x 12" deep. **$420**

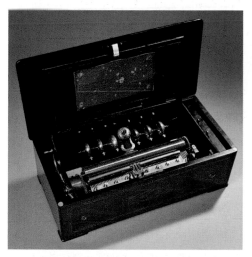

B.A. Bremond Mandoline Organcleide cylinder musical box, Geneva, Switzerland, no. 15872, with brass bed plate, 15" cylinder playing 12 airs, two-part comb, seven exposed bells, center bell engraved Bremond Manufacturer Geneva, governor-cock stamped BAB, tune sheet inside lid, housed in rosewood veneer case with marquetry, banded inlay and ebonized trim, box 26" long. **$3,240**

Brunsviga midget calculator, Grimme, Natalis & Co., Braunschweig, Germany, circa 1900, brass plate upper section marked Brunsviga-Midget, System Trinks, with nine setting levers, operating and clearing cranks, lower carriage with 1-18 digit product or result register, 1-10 revolution register, clearing cranks, all on composite base, instrument 12" long. **$270**

Silver

 ilver has been known since ancient times and has long been valued as a precious metal, used to make ornaments, jewelry, tableware and utensils, and coins.

Pure silver is too soft to be fashioned into strong, durable, and serviceable utensils. Therefore, a way was found to give silver the required degree of hardness by adding alloys of copper and nickel.

Silversmithing in America goes back to the early 17th century in Boston and New York and the early 18th century in Philadelphia. Boston artisans were influenced by the English styles; New Yorkers by the Dutch.

Silver-plated items are made from a base metal coated with a thin layer of silver.

For more information on sterling silverware, see *Warman's Sterling Silver Flatware*, 2nd edition, by Phil Dreis.

Mark Mussio, Humler & Nolan

English Sheffield pearl-handled dessert set consisting of 12 7 7/8" knives and 12 6 1/2" forks, knife blades engraved with elaborate designs, forks also with designs, handles ridged, each piece engraved 2685, presentation wood case with inlay on top, inside fabric nipped and tucked, card from "The Olde Silver Smythe, from the antique collection of Lemon & Son, Est 1828, Louisville, Ky" stating, "This set original English Sheffield, Early Victorian, Georgian influence, register number 2685," excellent condition.
$225

Mark Mussio, Humler & Nolan

Sterling goblet chalice with gold wash and double knob stem, base embossed with wheat stalks, cattails, and pine boughs, impressed "Sterling" near rim with shield logo, inscription on base rim, "In memory of Ellen Blair, donated by the children" with names, normal wear to gilding, 10" high. **$200**

Kaminski Auctions

Rare and important early American repoussé coin silver tea set by WI Tenney, 251 Broadway, New York, active 1806-1848: large tea server, 12" high; covered sugar, 11" high; covered creamer, 8 7/8" high; waste bowl, 6 1/2"; decorated in grape vines, leaves and bunches of grapes, 132 troy oz. **$4,750**

Mark Mussio, Humler & Nolan

Reed & Barton Hampton Court sterling coffee and tea service, six pieces, handled tray 17 1/2" x 24 1/4", 9" coffee pot and 7 1/2" 36-oz. teapot, each with ivory insets in handles, 6" covered sugar, 4 7/8" creamer with gold wash interior, and 3 3/4" open waste bowl with gold wash interior, all impressed "Reed & Barton Sterling, Hampton Court" along with bell or horseshoe logo and 660 or 661 numbers, 185.8 troy oz. **$4,600**

Mark Mussio, Humler & Nolan

▶ *Unger Art Nouveau sterling silver hand mirror embossed with side portraiture of maiden centralized within ruffled poppy flowerhead with poppies on handle, marked "Sterling 925" with company conjoined logo, normal usage dings, original beveled mirror, 9" long.* **$200**

Pook & Pook, Inc.

▼ *Gorham sterling silver centerpiece bowl, repoussé and pierced bird and floral border, 4 1/2" high x 14 3/4" diameter, 45.9 troy oz.* **$1,337**

Mark Mussio, Humler & Nolan

▼ *Sterling silver EJB Co. hinged box with carved carnelian puppy, marked "Sterling" with conjoined EJB Co. initials, 1437 impressed on bottom, interior bound by wood, minor usage dings, 3" high x 3 3/8" square diameter.* **$500**

Pook & Pook, Inc.

Tiffany & Co. sterling silver chrysanthemum pattern bowl, 2" high x 9" diameter, 12.9 troy oz. **$425**

Pook & Pook, Inc.

Charles II silver caudle cup, hallmarked RL, London, circa 1670-1671, with relief lion and goat decoration, 4" high x 4 1/4" diameter, 8.0 troy oz. **$2,066**

Pook & Pook, Inc.

French Napoleonic silver on bronze jewel casket, circa 1870, inscribed L. Oudry, with Alexander the Great portraits and recumbent lion finial, 6" high x 8" wide. **$415**

Pook & Pook, Inc.

Pair of German 800 silver gilt candelabra, 19th century, inscribed on base "Albertus von Ohlendorff & Frau," base decorated with coat of arms and medallion, inscribed "1858 4 Septbr 1883," 23" high, 170.5 troy oz. **$4,977**

Pook & Pook, Inc.

Continental silver footed bowl, 19th century, 6" high x 7 3/4" wide, 9.4 troy oz. **$444**

Pook & Pook, Inc.

Danish sterling silver tankard, circa 1950, bearing touch of Carl F. Christiansen, 8" high, 41.1 troy oz. **$1,154**

Pook & Pook, Inc.

Philadelphia coin silver six-piece repoussé tea service, mid-19th century, bearing touch of Thomas Fletcher: coffee pot, teapot, hot water pot, sugar bowl, waste bowl, and creamer, all engraved McIntosh, fitted mahogany storage case, 223.7 troy oz. **$10,073**

Pook & Pook, Inc.

Joseph Seymour & Co. sterling silver three-piece tea service, 34.3 troy oz. **$652**

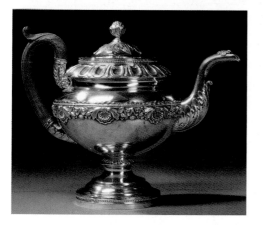

Pook & Pook, Inc.

Philadelphia coin silver covered sugar and creamer, circa 1835, bearing touch of R. & W. Wilson, 9 3/4" high and 6 3/4" high, 37.2 troy oz. **$889**

Skinner, Inc.; www.skinnerinc.com

Late Federal period coin silver teapot, Philadelphia, 1815-1830, Thomas Fletcher & Sidney Gardiner, maker, bulbous form with acanthus leaves to spout and lid, register of shell and scrolls to body, flared circular foot, marked "FLETCHER & GARDINER, PHILA." to underside, surface irregularities, some corrosion to silver elements, 10 1/2" high, approximately 52.0 troy oz. **$2,706**

Skinner, Inc.; www.skinnerinc.com

Sterling silver and mixed-metal lidded jar, Gorham, Providence, Rhode Island, 1880, monogrammed on underside, fruit finial, gold-washed interior, body decorated with mixed-metal crabs and lily pads, 3 1/2" high, approximately 3.4 troy oz. **$1,353**

Bonhams

American silver soldered six-piece tea and coffee service, Tiffany & Co., New York, circa 1873-1891 and later: 14" high kettle on stand, teapot, coffee pot, cream jug, covered sugar bowl, and waste bowl, together with Elkington & Co silverplate dish. **$1,875**

Bonhams

Mexican sterling silver four-piece tea and coffee service with matching two-handled tray, marked Anexo, 20th century, further marked "La Colonial": 11 1/4" high coffee pot, teapot, cream jug, covered sugar bowl, and 24 1/2" long tray, approximately 185 troy oz. **$4,375**

Bonhams

American sterling silver three-piece tea service by R. Wallace & Sons Mfg. Co., Wallingford, Connecticut, early 20th century: 8" high x 9 3/4" long teapot, covered two-handled sugar bowl, and cream jug, approximately 38 troy oz. **$688**

Bonhams

American sterling silver repoussé-decorated bowl, Reed & Barton, Taunton, Massachusetts, 20th century, Francis I, 2 1/4" high x 11 1/4" diameter, approximately 21 troy oz. **$525**

Bonhams

American sterling silver circular reticulated footed cake stand, Meriden Britannia Co., Meriden, Connecticut, retailed by Theodore B. Starr, New York, first quarter 20th century, monogrammed "JK," 2 1/2" high x 15" diameter, approximately 28 troy oz. **$2,125**

Bonhams

 American sterling silver shell-form footed fruit dish, Reed & Barton, Taunton, Massachusetts, 1941, grape-cluster feet, 2" high x 11 3/4" wide, approximately 24.5 troy oz. **$875**

Bonhams

◄ *American hammered sterling silver Arts & Crafts ice bucket by Shreve & Co., San Francisco, first quarter 20th century, monogrammed "BMR" and dated 1929, 7 1/4" high, 10" long with handle down, approximately 26.5 troy oz.* **$1,875**

James D. Julia, Inc.

▲ *Silver and jade Fabergé figurine in form of winged lion's body with woman's head adorned with tall hairpiece, green jade platform with silver frame and four silver ball feet, hallmarked on lion's rear leg reverse "R," "A," and "88," bottom hallmarked with same two hallmarks and Fabergé mark, very good to excellent condition, 4 1/4" high.* **$1,126**

James D. Julia, Inc.

▶ *Large sterling flower basket, Whiting Mfg., pierced decoration and attached handle, marked on bottom "Sterling 4347" with date mark "1915," no monogram, very good condition, clear glass insert damaged, 18" high x 11" at widest, 29 troy oz. total.* **$1,185**

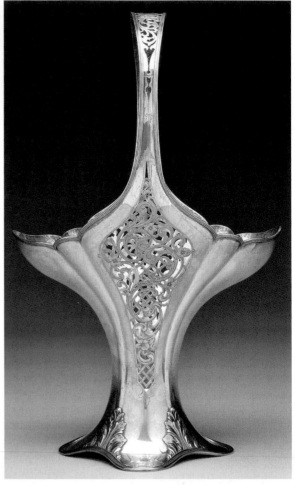

James D. Julia, Inc.

Georg Jensen sterling silver bowl designed by Henning Koppel in 1950, wide flaring body with applied modern foot, signed on inside of foot "HK Georg Jensen Denmark Sterling 980 A," very good to excellent condition, 15" diameter x 6 1/2" high. **$18,368**

Bonhams

American sterling silver Art Nouveau foliate-decorated three-piece place setting by Gorham Mfg. Co., Providence, Rhode Island, 1899: mug, bowl, and 7 3/4" diameter plate, bowl and plate monogrammed "MCA," approximately 33 troy oz. total. **$1,750**

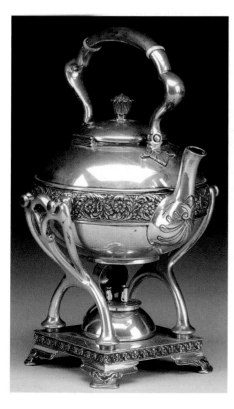

Bonhams

▲ *American sterling silver floral repoussé-decorated bowl, William Wilson & Son, Philadelphia, circa 1900, with later glass liner, 3 1/4" high x 10 1/2" diameter, approximately 20 troy oz.* **$625**

James D. Julia, Inc.

◄ *Tiffany & Co. three-part sterling silver teakettle on stand, base marked "Tiffany & Co. 3448 Maker's 9964 Sterling Silver 925/1000 M" (Edward C. Moore, 1873-1891), inscribed on base bottom "Oct 7th 1891"; round teapot with hinged lid with midpoint roll dyed band of flower heads and leaves, swing handle, and decorative knop, stand marked identically with same number, plain burner also marked with same number, fancy script initial monogram, very good condition, 13" high x 8 1/2" at widest, 55.4 troy oz.* **$2,429**

Bonhams

American sterling silver Art Nouveau floral-decorated footed bowl by Shreve & Co., San Francisco, first quarter 20th century, rim and foot decorated with continuous bands of irises, 6" high x 10 1/4" diameter, approximately 28 troy oz. **$1,500**

Bonhams

▲ *Chinese Export silver humidor marked CC, probably Canton, mid-19th/20th century, 3 1/2" high x 8 1/2" wide.* **$2,000**

Skinner, Inc.; www.skinnerinc.com

Edward VII six-piece sterling silver tea service, London, 1909-1910, Hunt & Roskell Ltd., maker: kettle on stand with burner, coffeepot, teapot, two-handled sugar bowl, creamer, and waste bowl, each with large pear-shaped bodies with engraved, chased, and applied rustic scenes of peasants merrymaking in style of Teniers, raised on four scrolled feet; sugar, creamer, and waste bowl with gold-washed interiors, sugar and creamer with handles formed as drunken revelers on branch; kettle, teapot, and coffeepot with ivory heat stops, finials formed as revelers with barrel, and eagle-head spouts joined to body by grotesque masks; fully hallmarked throughout with serial numbers 2950-2955, kettle on stand 17" high, approximately 257.6 troy oz. total. **$25,200**

Kirk & Son sterling silver repoussé-decorated covered dish, Baltimore, 1896-1924, decorated all over with various flowers and foliage, floral-decorated handle to center, 8 3/8" diameter, approximately 22 troy oz. **$1,800**

Jenkins & Jenkins sterling silver repoussé-decorated bowl, Baltimore, 1908-1915, decorated all over with various flowers and foliage, engraved on underside "Quincy Bent Jr./April 3rd 1911," 5" diameter, approximately 6.9 troy oz. **$360**

Tiffany & Co. sterling silver vine base center bowl, bottom marked "Tiffany & Co. Makers Sterling Silver 23886," round plain bowl supported by branch/vine reticulated base, no monogram, very good condition, 4" high x 8 1/2" diameter, 26 troy oz. **$1,580**

Sciarrotta sterling silver bowl, handmade with stylized leaf design around scalloped edge, feet made of six sterling silver rings, bowl signed on side "Sciarrotta Handmade Newport, RI Sterling," very good condition with four minor dents to interior, 9 1/2" diameter x 4 3/4" high, 28.5 oz. total. **$770**

Sterling silver punch bowl, 20th century, J.E. Caldwell & Co., retailer, pierced rim and foot decorated with floral garland amid scrollwork, body with additional engraved floral designs and armorial, bowl pushed into stem with dents around joint to stem, 6 1/4" high x 14 1/2" diameter, approximately 75.7 troy oz. **$4,800**

Gorham sterling silver oval footed reticulated basket with fixed center handle, ends decorated with scallop shells, base marked with Gorham mark, "Sterling A8419" with date mark of 1912, no monogram, very good condition, 19" high x 12 3/4" x 8 1/4", 22.3 troy oz. **$608**

Space Collectibles

By Noah Fleisher

Human conquest of the cosmos has the ability to inspire humans like little else and, in the brief time we've been slipping these surly bonds, we've done remarkably well, all things considered. In the cosmic sense, this spans but a blink of a blink. We've walked on the moon, sent craft to mars to explore the surface, sent satellites hurtling headlong into the unknown of the Milky Way beyond our system and we've taken pictures of the beginning of time. These are but baby steps for which future generations will be grateful because they will enjoy the fruits of this early labor.

Little wonder then that the pieces, parts, ephemera and personal memorabilia associated with America's space program – the men and women who, in large part, made science fiction a reality – have made collectors of all sorts sit up and take notice.

Noah Fleisher

"The supply of the really important items is certainly finite," said Howard Weinberger, Senior Space Consultant for Heritage Auction Galleries in Dallas, and CEO of Asset Alternatives. "The old saying is that if you collected all the personal items from the six missions that landed on the moon, all of it would fit in a small suitcase."

Weinberger is talking about the cream of the crop, the things that the Apollo astronauts took special pains with to make sure they were on the lunar surface and spent time in the vacuum of space. The rest of the field – from souvenir patches, parts and models, autographs and well beyond – has as much room for variance of budget as a collector could wish and a plethora of material that – like the very subject it covers – can sometimes seem infinite.

Unlike so many categories of collecting, the market for space memorabilia is still being established. The subject has long been popular, but the ability to get the very best of The Right Stuff was not there until recently, as many of the astronauts themselves – or their families, if they've passed on – have realized the value, both historic and financial, of their accomplishments. The more that the remaining original astronauts release key pieces of their extra-terrestrial lives, the more established the market will become.

One of the most important things space collecting has going for it is its appeal, said Weinberger. The steady increase in prices at auction since he's been working with Heritage shows just how broad this appeal is.

"I think it's a function of the fact that people are now aware that these items can be bought," said Weinberger, who is among the few with the connections to bring the choicest pieces to auction. "The genre is unique because the demographic, in my opinion, is among the top three to five potential demographics for collecting."

Meaning there's almost no soul on this planet who doesn't know about, and isn't at least

NOAH FLEISHER received his Bachelor of Fine Arts degree from New York University and brings more than a decade of newspaper, magazine, book, antiques and art experience to his position as Public Relations Director of Heritage Auctions, one of the country's foremost auction houses. He is the former editor of *Antique Trader, New England Antiques Journal* and *Northeast Antiques Journal,* is the author of *Warman's Modern Furniture,* and has been a longtime contributor to *Warman's Antiques and Collectibles.*

peripherally fascinated by, space travel.

"Show a baseball card, a comic book or a regional American quilt to a woman in Asia," Weinberger said, "and it won't translate. If you go back to 1969, to Apollo 11 and the first moon landing, you have the entire planet watching. Everyvbody remembers where they were when Neil Armstrong walked on the moon, or when Allan Sheppard went up with Mercury."

The broad scope of potential buyers is indeed as varied as the material, as a few minutes with the following pages will show. As the field sorts itself out, it is tough to break down into categories. The astronauts, and all the workers at NASA – from the men who walked on the moon to the guys who swept up at the end of the day – were all aware from the beginning of the historic nature of their pursuit – and it potential value.

This prospective worth, then, necessitates at least an attempt at breaking the hobby into categories. According to Weinberger, this is not something that should be done by item type, but rather by mission type and purpose.

"There's not a lot of the very best stuff, so there is a hierarchy of sorts that has evolved," he said. "The highest rung is for items that actually landed on the moon and went on the surface. Then it's something that landed on the moon but didn't leave the capsule. After that it's memorabilia that flew to the moon but only stayed in orbit. From there it's about things that flew in space, things that were strictly in earth orbit, and things that didn't fly in space but are of a personal nature belonging to the astronauts, or having their autographs."

Within these several categories, however, again there can be a striking difference in price depending on the name and the program it's associated with.

Whatever level a collector is looking at to get into the market for space memorabilia, the most important thing is authenticity, especially at the high end. In fact, Weinberger said, if it comes from an astronaut's personal collection, a signature and/or a letter of authentication is of paramount importance.

"No matter what it is, even if it's purchased personally from an astronaut, it has to be certified," he said. "The most desirable certification is having the signature on the item itself. If it has that, and a letter as well, then so much the better."

The most important thing to get started is not a broad general knowledge of what's out there, but to simply have a passion for it no matter how much cash you can put in. You can buy autographs, first-day covers or specially minted Robbins medals that flew on every Apollo mission. You can spend a few hundred or a few hundred thousand dollars; either way, it's an accessible market.

"You can start with something basic," Weinberger said. "The overall amount of memorabilia related to space is endless."

It's a good thing, then, that the enthusiasm of collectors, especially for something as inspiring as space travel, seems to be equally as endless.

All images courtesy Heritage Auctions

Neil Armstrong's training-used beta cloth boots (pair) with original tagging from Apollo 11, part of four-piece inflight coverall garment Apollo astronauts wore while in command module; likely worn by Armstrong during the training process based on date of manufacture and general light wear and accumulated material on Velcro. **$10,000**

Mercury-Atlas 6 (Friendship 7) flown $1 bill signed by John Glenn, with signed certificate of authenticity; Series 1957 $1 silver certificate, serial number A31941854B, flew with Glenn on three-orbit mission, Feb. 20, 1962; signed "J H Glenn, Jr" and "Terry Thompson" (likely launch crew member) to left of Washington's portrait; apparently 52 pieces of U.S. currency ($1 and $2) flew with Glenn on this historic flight. **$20,000**

Apollo 11 flown crew-signed commemorative cover, C-54, color-cacheted "NASA Manned Spacecraft Center Stamp Club Official Commemorative Cover of the First Manned Lunar Exploration" signed by Neil Armstrong, Michael Collins and Buzz Aldrin. Cover flew to the moon on first manned lunar landing mission. Affixed to cover is 8¢ Apollo 8 stamp (Scott #1371) with Aug. 11, 1969, cancellation at Webster, Texas; stamped beneath cancellation is text: "Delayed In Quarantine At / Lunar Receiving Laboratory / M.S.C. - Houston, Texas." Provenance: From the personal collection of Mission Command Module Pilot Michael Collins. **$46,875**

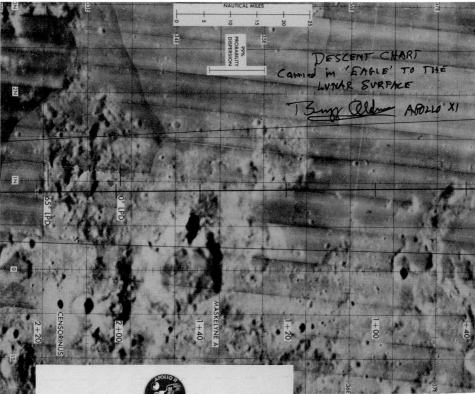

Apollo 11 lunar module flown descent navigational chart page, 8.5" x 10.5" map printed on heavy photographic paper, showing area around Mare Tranquillitatis (Sea of Tranquility) with craters Maskelyne A and Censorinus labeled along with grid and descent path. Provenance: Originally from personal collection of mission lunar module pilot Buzz Aldrin, signed and certified, with signed letter of authenticity. **$29,875**

Apollo 11 crew-signed Washington D.C. Evening Star "Apollo Edition" newspaper front page from July 21, 1969, above headline are signatures of crew: Neil Armstrong, Buzz Aldrin, and Mike Collins in red ink. **$5,625**

▼ Apollo 1 crew-signed color NASA photo with period provenance, 10" x 8" litho print, of astronauts Edward H. White II, Virgil I. Grissom, and Roger B. Chaffee in flight suits at a table behind model of original CM-012 command module; signed in black felt tip. Originally designated AS-204, the first mission in the Apollo manned lunar landing program was scheduled for launch on Feb. 21, 1967. A tragic fire during a "plugs-out" launch simulation on Jan. 27, 1967, claimed the lives of the three astronauts aboard. **$10,000**

APOLLO CREW
Astronauts Edward H. White II, Virgil I. Grissom and Roger B. Chaffee
Prime Crew for NASA's First Manned Apollo Flight

NEIL A. ARMSTRONG

Neil Armstrong-signed white spacesuit color photo, 8" x 10" NASA lithograph print, first man on the moon posed in pressure suit and holding his helmet, against lunar backdrop, signed Neil Armstrong in black felt tip. **$4,688**

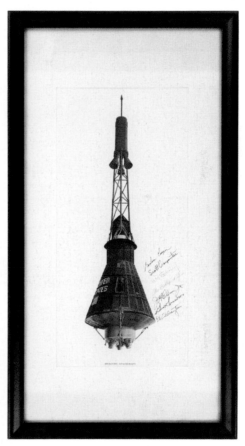

Apollo 11 flown American flag on crew-signed presentation certificate, framed; 5.75" x 3.75" silk U.S. flag mounted to 10" x 12" color certificate printed with: "This Flag Traveled to the Moon with Apollo 11, the First Manned Lunar Landing, July 20, 1969 / APOLLO 11 / July 16-24, 1969 / Armstrong - Collins - Aldrin"; printed on lower area is Apollo 11 mission insignia above crew's signatures; at bottom are printed immortal words Armstrong spoke as he stepped onto moon's surface: "One small step for a man, one giant leap for mankind"; 13.25" x 16.25" framed. **$71,875**

Rare McDonnell Mercury Spacecraft lithograph signed by all seven Mercury astronauts, 8.5" x 17.5" color image of Mercury capsule with escape tower atop, NASA's Group One astronaut signatures to right of capsule area: Gordon Cooper, Scott Carpenter, W M Schirra Jr, Alan B. Shepard, Jr, J H Glenn, Jr, Gus Grissom, and D K Slayton; matted and framed, 14.5" x 26.5" overall. **$81,750**

Neil Armstrong's childhood toy airplane and signed photo of his family home, 601 W. Benton St., Wapakoneta, Ohio. Armstrong's family moved to the house in 1944 and stayed there until 1964. **$10,755**

▲ Apollo 11 flown silver Robbins Medallion, 28mm sterling silver, one of 450 flown aboard Apollo 11, first manned moon landing, July 16-24, 1969, with crewmembers Neil Armstrong, Michael Collins, and Buzz Aldrin. Provenance: Originally from personal collection of Mercury Seven astronaut Wally Schirra, Serial Number 416, with letter of authenticity. **$33,460**

▶ Apollo 17 lunar module flown commander's metal right-side armrest with label on top, "Pull Down Armrest to Release From Stowed Position," around which mission commander Gene Cernan certified and signed, 7.25" x 10.75" x 7" overall, including brackets. Apollo 17 was the last of six manned lunar landings. Cernan, the last person to step foot on the moon, used armrest inside lunar module Challenger for more than three days while on lunar surface. Provenance: Originally from personal collection of Cernan. **$31,070**

Training-used A7L integrated thermal micrometeoroid garment by ILC with astronaut Jim Irwin tagging, likely used in Irwin's early training or possibly as backup lunar module pilot for Apollo 10, International Latex Corp. tag, garment only covers torso and has no connectors, helmet, gloves, or boots. **$53,775**

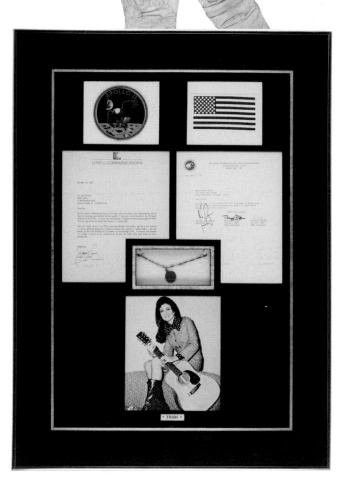

Apollo 11 flown French 20 franc coin and necklace in framed display with crew-signed letter of authenticity, necklace flown by Neil Armstrong in his own Personal Preference Kit; gold coin appears to be of "rooster" type minted between 1899 and 1914 in France, inside bezel and on gold necklace, matted with mission patch, Beta cloth flag, copies of letters of provenance, photo of original owner folksinger Trish Butte; necklace given to her friend James Lovell who helped get it placed into Armstrong's PPK for Apollo 11 mission; after their return, necklace was returned to Butte with typed letter on NASA letterhead, as follows: "Dear Trish: This letter is to confirm the fact that your 20 Franc coin and chain were carried onboard the Apollo 11 spacecraft during its historic mission. With best wishes," signed by Neil Armstrong, Buzz Aldrin, and M. Collins. **$23,900**

Apollo 11 lunar module flown toothbrush and sleeve originally from personal collection of mission lunar module pilot Buzz Aldrin, light blue Lactona S-19 model "Tooth Tip" toothbrush, used throughout mission, including in lunar module Eagle while on moon, 6.5" long, with original 8" x 1.5" plastic pouch. **$22,705**

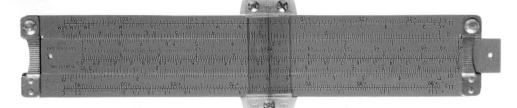

▲ *Buzz Aldrin's Apollo 11 slide rule flown to moon, Pickett Model N600-ES (Eye Saver) Log Speed Rule, six-inch pocket rule with 22 five-inch scales; N600-ES sold for $10.95 in 1969.* **$77,675**

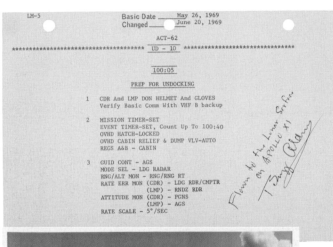

◄ *Apollo 11 lunar module flown Activation Checklist with handwritten notations by Neil Armstrong, 8" x 5.5" two-sided page numbered ACT-62 & ACT-63, printed on cardstock and three-hole punched; book was taken to and used on lunar surface by both Aldrin and Armstrong during landmark moon landing on July 20, 1969; this page is tabbed "Prep for Undocking" with notations from Armstrong on verso, signed letter of authenticity from Buzz Aldrin included. Provenance: Originally from personal collection of mission lunar module pilot Buzz Aldrin, signed and certified.* **$55,268**

Christa McAuliffe signed color photo with STS-51-L Mission Patch, 8" x 10" Kennedy Space Center color glossy of STS-4 liftoff with info stamp on verso, signed: "To Ron- / May your future be limited / only by your dreams / S. Christa McAuliffe / 51-L"; includes embroidered STS-51-L mission insignia patch, excellent condition. **$1,375**

Buzz Aldrin's 1923-S Peace silver dollar flown on moon mission aboard Apollo 11 as part of his Personal Preference Kit (PPK). **$31,070**

Astronaut Gene Cernan's Apollo 17 lunar module flown Fisher AG-7 space pen used during flight and carried by Cernan in spacesuit pocket onto surface of moon. Cernan was the last man to walk on the moon; he used the pen throughout the Apollo 17 mission, including on the lunar surface. **$23,900**

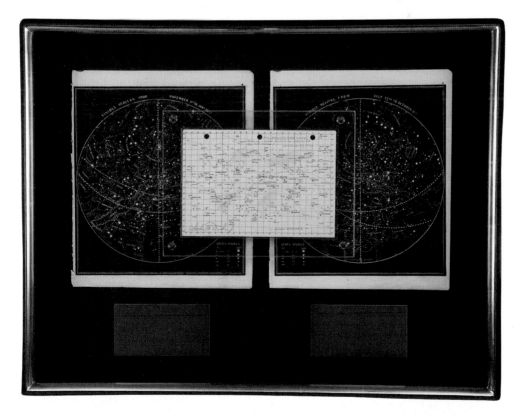

Apollo 16 lunar module flown star chart and G&N dictionary star list originally from collection of mission lunar module pilot Charlie Duke, certified and signed; spent three days on moon in lunar module Orion during flight of Apollo 16, April 16-27, 1972 with crewmembers John Young, Ken Mattingly, and Charlie Duke; black smudges on chart are lunar dust. **$22,705**

Sports

Sports and sports memorabilia are eternally intertwined. Since sports began, there have been mementoes to draw in audiences, attract attention to the games or invite future fans to the stadiums. And because the games tend to evoke fond memories, many times those mementoes are kept for a long time. Sports memorabilia is our connection to sporting events we remember and the players we loved to watch.

Today, sports memorabilia is used for more than simply waking up the memory bank or providing a connection to the past. These items are also increasingly used for home or office décor, as well as investments. Sports collectibles are more accessible than ever before through online auctions, with several auction houses that dedicate themselves solely to that segment of the hobby. Provenance and third-party authentication is extremely important when investing in high-ticket sports collectibles. In today's market, high-quality and rare items are in most demand, with a heavy nod toward stars and Hall of Famers. Condition is everything – keep an eye toward temperature, humidity, and exposure to sunlight with pieces in your collection.

SCP Auctions

◄ *New York Yankees stained glass from old Yankee Stadium, 45 1/2" x 80 1/2".* **$6,245**

Legendary Auctions

▼ *1963 NFL Championship press pin, 1" tall on heavy metal, originally presented to a member of the press present at Wrigley Field in Chicago for the 1963 NFL title game won by the Bears, 14-10.* **$149**

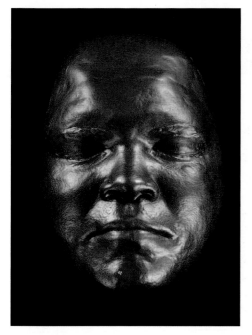

Legendary Auctions

Muhammad Ali Life Mask, full-scale cast approximately 8 1/2" x 6 1/2" x 4" deep, composed of Ultra-Cal casting cement finished with "tribute gold" and "antiquing overlay." **$209**

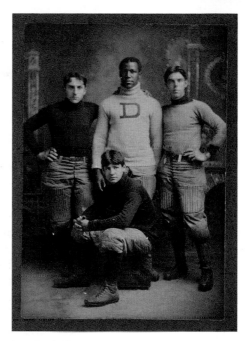

Legendary Auctions

Vintage cabinet photo featuring four players from Dartmouth College football team, circa 1900, 5" x 7". **$388**

Legendary Auctions

1948 Chesterfield Cigarettes ad featuring Baseball Hall of Fame ballplayers Joe DiMaggio, Lou Boudreau, Jack Kramer, Ben Hogan, and Frankie Albert. **$209**

Legendary Auctions

◄ *1912 baseball figurine cast-iron doorstop, engraved notation reading "O.C.F. 1912," 14 pounds, approximately 17" high.* **$388**

▲ *1940s Homestead Grays Negro League pennant.* **$985**

▶ *Roberto Clemente 1962 bobble head, white base, with box.* **$1,938**

▼ *1866 copy of* Haney's Base Ball Reference *by Henry Chadwick.* **$1,422**

▼ *Mickey Mantle 4" x 4" commemorative plate signed with metallic gold paint pen by sports artist Robert Stephen Simon.* **$316**

Robert Edward Auctions

▲ *1885 St. Louis Browns advertising display produced for International Tailoring Co., 20" x 13 1/2".* **$1,185**

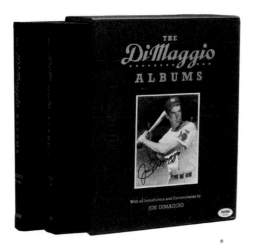

SCP Auctions

Joe DiMaggio, The DiMaggio Albums, *signed case with unsigned books, 1932-1941 and 1942-1951.* **$385**

Robert Edward Auctions

"The White Sox March" sheet music, 1907, 10 1/2" x 13 1/2". **$356**

1912 New York Giants World Series program. **$711**

▲ *Babe Ruth "Home Run Special" ball with original box, circa 1930.* **$1,541**

▼ *1953 Satchel Paige Coca-Cola advertising sign, 11 3/4" x 14 3/4".* **$8,295**

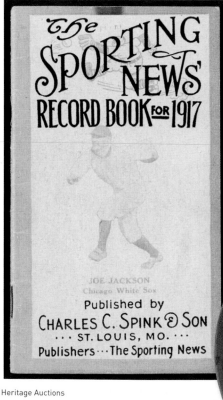

1917 The Sporting News Record Book featuring Joe Jackson, 3" x 5 1/4". **$370**

▶ *1961 Green Bay Packers 4" pinback button.* **$91**

1958-1959 Harlem Globetrotters program featuring Wilt Chamberlain. **$105**

▲ *1948 Exacta Babe Ruth watch with original box, plastic holder, two inserts, and original band.* **$855**

Cap Anson original oil painting by artist Grant Smith, 20" x 20". **$1,028**

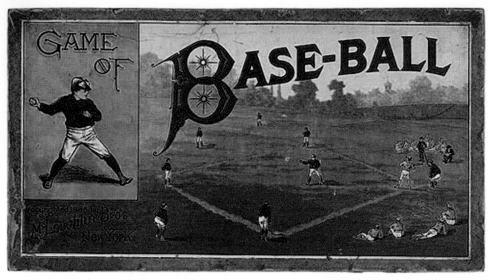

Robert Edward Auctions

1886 McLoughlin Bros. Game of Base-Ball. **$2,252**

Memory Lane, Inc.

Muhammad Ali and Joe Frazier signed fight poster, Madison Square Garden, Jan. 28, 1974.
$943

Legendary Auctions

1914 B18 blanket of Walter Johnson, high-grade felt, 5 1/4" sq. **$210**

Legendary Auctions

▲ *John L. Sullivan bronze sculpture by Ferdinand G. Rebechini (1923-2003), 24" high, 31 pounds, signed "F. Rebechini" on base.* **$2,271**

Collect Auctions

◄ *Dan Marino Best talking football player toy, signed by Marino.* **$51**

Memory Lane, Inc.

1966-1967 Green Bay Packers Super Bowl I team-signed football, 45 signatures. **$5,900**

Toys

Toy collecting has gone through dramatic changes over the years, but the premise of collecting remains the same—holding onto something from childhood that brings a smile to your face every time you see it.

Toys are fun. There are no hidden messages when it comes to toys. They are produced for entertainment, and while they can also be quite valuable, that is not the driving force behind collecting toys.

If you collect now, during a challenging economy and high gas prices, you're doing it as a passion. And that's what toys are all about, a piece of nostalgia that can grow into a fascination that fills rooms in houses and provides endless stories for relatives and friends.

Over the past few years, one aspect of the hobby is becoming apparent: More people are becoming acquainted with toys and their values than at any other point in American history, thanks to the exposure the hobby has garnered from the collectible-based reality programs broadcast on television.

The best weapon in the battle for equitable prices for toys is acquiring knowledge: Education is power. Learn about the toy and its backstory, know its manufacturer and date of production, as well as its importance in the realm of popular culture.

When estimating the value of a toy, you must first evaluate its condition. Mint toys in mint packaging command higher prices than well-played-with toys whose boxes disappeared with the wrapping paper on Christmas day. Mint is a rare condition indeed as toys were meant to be played with by children. Realistic evaluation of condition is essential, as grading standards vary from class to class. Ultimately, the market is driven by buyers, and the bottom line final value of a toy is often the last price at which it is sold.

For more information on toys, see *Toys & Prices*, 19th edition, by Mark Bellomo.

James D. Julia, Inc.

▶ *Ives nine-pin skittles set, late 19th century, wooden pins covered in lithographed paper with detailed faces, legs and hats painted in gold pinstripes, set patented in 1885, comes with what appears to be original wooden ball with red, yellow and blue stripes, overall very good condition, few small repairs to brims of hats, 12" high.* **$1,495**

James D. Julia, Inc.

German Indian skittles container with braves, polychromed in bright colors with intricate molding to facial features, original paper label on underside marked "Made in Germany" with most likely six-digit product number, stamped tin wheels, pins affixed to wooden platforms, overall very fine-plus condition, paint is largely intact with no restoration and/or repairs, 29" long. **$16,100**

James D. Julia, Inc.

Ives clockwork horse head perambulator, circa last quarter 19th century, paper label on rear and on box indicates patent date of 1873, boy simulates movement by pulling and pushing wooden propeller rods, fine original condition including partial cardboard box with label, minor soiling to clothing, papier maché head with vertical crack and separation at seam, tin wraparound by boy has broken solder point on left side, approximately 8" long. **$25,300**

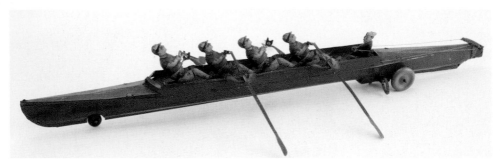

Noel Barrett Auctions

Five-man racing scull tin toy, lithographed, four oarsmen and coxswain, clockwork mechanism propels boat as oarsmen row, unmarked but German, possibly Gunthermann, very good to excellent condition, 21" long. **$4,250**

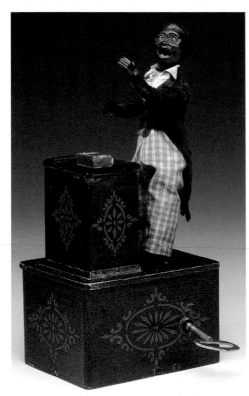

James D. Julia, Inc.

Ives clockwork preacher, late 1800s, wooden box polychromed in orange-red finish with yellow and brown accents, black figure has inset black glass eyes and wire-rimmed glasses; when wound and activated, toy leans forward, slamming right hand on podium while turning head from side to side; very fine to near mint all-original unplayed-with condition, clockwork mechanism in working order, lacking one small screw from left foot and wire from mechanism to body that enables figure to turn head, clothing overall in pristine condition, approximately 10" high. **$4,025**

James D. Julia, Inc.

Women's rights advocate clockwork toy attributed to Automatic Toy Works, late 19th century, gutta percha head and inset glass eyes, original clothing, natural stained box; when mechanism is activated, woman leans forward, slamming hand on podium, then rises up, turning her head; overall very fine original condition, clockwork mechanism is functional, 4" wide x approximately 10" high x 5" deep. **$5,750**

Noel Barrett Auctions

Bicycle race toy, hand-painted tin, depicts three early bicycle riders, each with different colored striped shirt, which race in circles to finish at lithographed tin "Arrivie" flag, powered by central clockwork mechanism, very good to excellent condition, some paint wear to figures, 11 1/2" diameter. **$3,000**

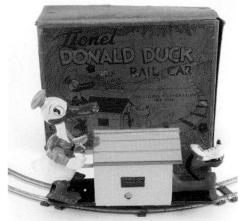

Noel Barrett Auctions

Lionel Donald Duck rail car, No. 1107 clockwork hand car with painted composition Donald and Pluto and full circle of track in original illustrated box, toy in excellent condition, box in good condition with some light staining and one side apron detached, car 10 1/2" long. **$1,300**

James D. Julia, Inc.

George Brown Orion clockwork locomotive, tin boiler painted dark blue with yellow cab and red roof, heavily stenciled, clockwork mechanism concealed within boiler; when wound, toy propels forward and small wheel under engine cab allows train to proceed in various directions, overall good to very good condition, 9 1/2" long. **$4,025**

James D. Julia, Inc.

Kilgore T.A.T. three-engine passenger plane with ribbed fuselage and wing; this particular plane came in two colors, green with yellow wing or red with yellow wing; plane susceptible to damage/hairline cracks at rear rivet junction, overall good to very good condition with some surface oxidation to left wing tip, right wheel cover is older iron replacement, 13 1/2" wingspan. T.A.T., which stands for Transcontinental Air Transport, was founded in 1928 and later merged with what became T.W.A. **$1,380**

James D. Julia, Inc.

Boucher "Polly-Wog" speed boat with double cylinder outboard motor affixed to rear, steam mechanism contained within hull and covered with aluminum sheath and three air ventilators, constructed mainly of wood, name "Polly-Wog" emblazoned on sides along with manufacturer's name, sheath covering engine is polished aluminum, three ventilators are stamped brass, complete Boucher decal affixed to aluminum sheathing, original finish, some flaking to "Polly-Wog" decals on either side, overall very good to near excellent condition, 23" long. **$1,438**

Noel Barrett Auctions

Painted tin Boer War clockwork toy by Gunthermann depicting soldiers of late 19th and early 20th centuries, figures go back and forth, khaki-clad Boer soldier waves rifle at Brit behind brick barricade, very good condition, some paint wear, 10" long. **$3,750**

James D. Julia, Inc.

German shepherd skittles with open back containing eight assorted animals pins, ninth pin is clown, aka "the king pin," original flat paint, all animals with glass eyes, overall very good condition, some animals show wear, 21" long. **$1,150**

James D. Julia, Inc.

Early American tin clockwork horse-drawn fire pumper, untouched all-original condition, gilt stenciling largely intact, overall white horses retain significant amount of original paint, tin driver missing, mechanism intact and in working order, overall fair to good condition, approximately 15" long. **$4,025**

Noel Barrett Auctions

Bing fire house and tractor, lithographed tin house with opening doors and two clockwork fire trucks with lithographed tin clockwork tractor, very good to excellent condition, house 8 1/2" x 6 1/2". **$475**

Noel Barrett Auctions

Burning house with firemen automaton, paper and paper maché-covered wood with internal clockwork mechanism; two firemen operate hand pump while third climbs ladder into burning building; house of lithographed paper on wood with painted flames, upper windows glazed with red stained glass, from back there is access to interior candle holder for added realistic flame and illumination; probably French origin, possibly by Decamps, very good to excellent condition, 19" high, base 10" x 13". **$950**

Noel Barrett Auctions

Mills coin-operated stereo viewer, wooden cabinet with cast hardware, legs, marquee mounts, viewing port, owl head-form side handles reflect use of owl in early Mills logos, internal clockwork mechanism wound by crank inserted in front drops 15 stereo images of partially clad and unclad women, additional 49 original cards including bubble dancer series, cast iron latticework on mirrored doors, excellent condition, 48 1/2" high x 20" wide x 17" deep. **$3,250**

Noel Barrett Auctions

Martin Tireless Blacksmiths Les Forgerons Infatigable, scarce first period Martin rubber-band-powered toy dating to 1883, painted tin figures astride lithographed tin cylinder alternately hammer plate mounted between them with raised letters F. M., good to very good condition, paint losses and general wear, 7" long. **$4,000**

Noel Barrett Auctions

Althof Bergmann camel bell toy, painted tin with carriage bells mounted on camel, heart motif cast iron wheels, large front wheels mounted off-center to create up and down motion as toy is pulled along, excellent condition, 9 1/2" long. **$1,100**

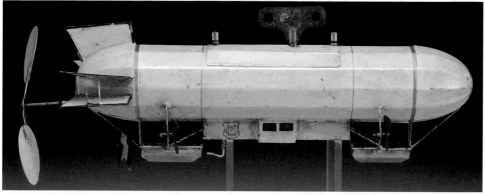

James D. Julia, Inc.

Marklin zeppelin, early part of 20th century, second largest size zeppelin Marklin produced; when toy is activated, rear propellers spin; clockwork mechanism functional, overall very good condition with possible restoration, 15" long. **$4,600**

James D. Julia, Inc.

Buddy L bus with open louvered hood vents, dual spare tires, opening doors, dual real wheels, headlights, extra reinforcement on underside of roof, good to very good all-original condition with uniform chipping/ paint loss, 28" long. **$2,645**

Noel Barrett Auctions

Lionel 400E engine and tender, American steam profile 4-4-4 electric locomotive with copper trim, "Standard" motor with oil tender with six-wheel trucks, both black, very good to excellent condition, some chipping on center wheels, 32" long. **$1,000**

James D. Julia, Inc.

1929 Gendron Jordan Playboy pedal car with crisscross front bumper, two glass and metal headlamps, license plate, wood grille with hand-painted design and "Jordan" on grille, radiator cap, two side lamps, driver side-mounted spare tire with partial cover, adjustable steering wheel, lithographed dashboard with simulated gauges, simulated brake lever on driver's side, large disc steel rims with thin rubber tires, luggage rack on rear, overall very good condition with some minor dents, top of hood displays paint oxidation/loss, 50" long. **$3,300**

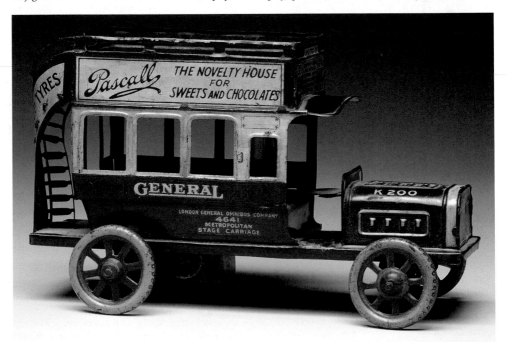

James D. Julia, Inc.

German tin lithographed double-decker bus manufactured by Bing for English market, advertising on sides, rear staircase, and front façade, very fine-plus condition, 7 1/4" long. **$2,300**

Noel Barrett Auctions

Ives Gauge I 3240 locomotive, dark green painted cast iron, American profile electric engine with dark gray painted tin roof, very good condition, some wear, 15" long. **$1,000**

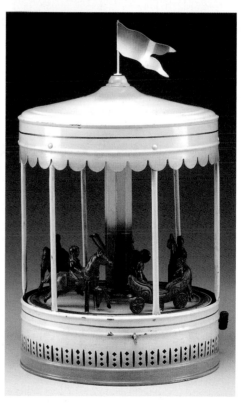

Noel Barrett Auctions

The Pittsburgh House architectural model, circa 1890, Victorian miniature rendition of Carpenter Queen Anne style with decorated gables and finials, sunburst panels, layered window cornices, double level porch railings, overhangs that outline each gable, original multicolored finish and brightness, excellent condition, approximately 38" high, 27" x 27". **$16,000**

The late Joe Daole and Patsy Powers (founders of the Toy Museum of Atlanta) found this structure in Pittsburgh. It was thought to have been one of a series of models of houses of architectural merit made for an exhibition around the turn of the last century. It does not open so is not a dollhouse.

James D. Julia, Inc.

German hand-painted tin windup carousel, circa late teens/early 1920s, four lithographed animals with riders and chariot with passengers, cream with gold pinstriping, airbrushed with blue, mauve, green, and orange; when toy is wound and activated, it proceeds in counterclockwise fashion while music plays; all-original overall very fine-plus to near mint condition, 15" high x 9" diameter. **$1,150**

James D. Julia, Inc.

Ives fire house with pumper, late 19th or early 20th century, large japanned cast iron façade with wooden cabinet trimmed with cast iron window frames with two-horse cast iron pumper; when activated, bell rings sounding alarm, front doors open, and fire pumper bolts down inclined ramp of firehouse; all original, very fine condition with working mechanics, remnants of paper label on roof, aged stress crack to roof, 8 1/2" wide x 12" high x 16 1/2" long, pumper 14" long. **$5,750**

James D. Julia, Inc.

Early Rock & Graner live steam launch, early German live steam toy, circa late 19th century, open launch with live steam mechanism located in center hull, elaborate bow figurehead accents center striped, decaled section along with railed walkway and fenced-in steam motor area, hull bottom and decking with copper finish with black band at top of left and right sides, live steam motor with copper wash and black smokestack, overall good to very good condition, possible areas of restoration, 16 1/2" long. **$10,925**

James D. Julia, Inc.

"Bico Bus to Joyville" double-decker bus, German manufacture for English market, passengers on upper level with standing attendant; when toy is wound and engaged, attendant moves from front to back as if collecting fares; finely lithographed, rear staircase states, "That is the way to Toyland," 8 1/4" long. **$2,300**

James D. Julia, Inc.

Tin lithographed Lyons' confectionery delivery truck, probably originally filled with candy as rear door is removable, circa 1920s, most likely of English manufacture, right and left sides lithographed as is rear door advertising product, overall very good condition, 7" long. **$4,830**

James D. Julia, Inc.

Bentley pedal car, fully restored, pneumatic tires with spare, louvered side vents, leather seat, faux rag top, spring suspension, battery-operated headlamps, opening driver's side door, fold-down split windshield (missing one piece of glass), wood runningboards, Shell oil can affixed to right runningboard and winged Bentley logo above front grille, near excellent condition with minor paint chips, 59" long x 24" wide x 23" high. **$5,175**

James D. Julia, Inc.

Early American tin bell toy with drummer boy and horse, attributed to Althof Bergmann, drum of impressed molded tin with stars in pattern, convex styled base with cast iron heart-shaped wheel spokes, original paint except for white and flesh tone on figure and red on horse (saddle band) and possible enhancement to yellow, overall good to very good condition, approximately 10 1/2" long. **$3,163**

James D. Julia, Inc.

Buster Brown and Tige German windup toy; when toy is wound and activated, Buster Brown or Tige will climb pole, drop, and reverse figure will climb; overall good to very good condition, minor solder repair on rear of toy, 13" high, base approximately 4" x 4". **$4,485**

Noel Barrett Auctions

George Brown circus hoop toy, painted tin, scarce and desirable form of late 19th century toy, designed to be rolled across floor, excellent professionally restored condition, 8 1/4" diameter. **$2,000**

James D. Julia, Inc.

Pedal airplane in blue with yellow highlights, steel wheels with rubber tires, removable wings and folding back wings, steel steering wheel, leather seat, and wooden propeller (replaced), overall good to very good condition, likely an early repaint, 40" long. **$1,093**

James D. Julia, Inc.

Rooster skittle set, multicolored papier maché rooster with glass eyes riding on four cast iron wheels painted gold, nine-pin set in form of chicks dressed as clowns, some minor chips on one side and old crack on left side, chicks in near excellent condition, 19 1/2" long x 15 1/2" high. **$14,950**

Noel Barrett Auctions

Three magnetic action toys, Magnetic Dancers (phonograph) by National Co. in original box: lithographed paper dancers with three metal templates for different dances powered though attachment to record player, along with similar action toy with celluloid house flywheel and painted celluloid figures (dancing couple, chimney sweep chasing boy, clown and pig, and duck) and English-made "skating rink" with die cut paper skaters (one bent), very good to excellent condition, box 4" square. **$400**

James D. Julia, Inc.

Buster Brown and Tige windup German tin bell ringer, 4" platform with Buster Brown and Tige standing at pole; when mechanism is activated, jointed arms on either figure ring bell; untouched all-original condition with uniform wear, approximately 8" high. **$1,955**

James D. Julia, Inc.

Rare Buster Brown tin windup toy, hand painted, winking left eye, holding ball in each hand; when activated, arms swing about, giving illusion of juggling; mechanism tested and functional, all-original paint with uniform paint loss throughout, overall good to very good condition, 6 1/2" high. **$1,323**

James D. Julia, Inc.

Rare Red Top arcade cab, stamped "Red Top Cab Co.," enameled with red upper frame and roof with white body and black chassis, iron wheels painted gray with white interiors and red hubcaps, all original except inset iron spare tire, which has been repainted white with red hubcap, 6 3/4" long. **$1,035**

James D. Julia, Inc.

Arcade flat top Yellow Cab, original, rubber stamped "Yellow Cab" on passenger doors, orange iron hubs and rubber tires, overall very fine-plus condition, 8" long. **$1,265**

Swann Galleries

Maurice Sendak, Todd McFarlane, "Where the Wild Things Are" action figures, complete set of six, new in original boxes, signed by Sendak and McFarlane in blue marker on front cellophane covers, original F.A.O. Schwarz price stickers still attached, boxed figures include Max and Goat Boy, Aaron, Bernard, Emil, Moishe, and Tzippy, each roughly 8" high; figures debuted at New York City F. A. O. Schwarz toy store on Oct. 12, 2000, and sold out in a single day. **$1,320**

James D. Julia, Inc.

Rare Father Christmas tin windup toy, German manufacture, circa 1920s, finely lithographed detail particularly to facial features, standing on embossed snow-covered mica mount; when mechanism is activated, he raises his arms with small decorated Christmas tree in one hand and sack of toys in other; overall very good-plus condition, some minor scraping on right side of figure where arm brushed up against body, heavy deterioration to toy sack, 6 1/2" high. **$1,725**

James D. Julia, Inc.

Large Fallows horse and rider platform toy, hand-painted boy rider atop full-bodied tin black horse on green stepped wheeled base with ruffled half circle kick plate at rear, overall very good condition, 15" long x 12 1/2" high. **$1,380**

James D. Julia, Inc.

Hubley Lockheed Sirius plane, 1930s, open cockpit with pilot and co-pilot, "Lindy" cast into left wing, right wing cast "NR-211," early paint restoration, 8 1/2" long. **$1,495**

James D. Julia, Inc.

Arcade Reo with large nickel-plated grille with attached headlights, dual mounted spare tires, rumble seat, both front and rear bumpers intact, Arcade label still present on interior of rumble seat, original nickel-plated spoked wheels, overall very good-plus condition, wear to edges of roof, one spare tire appears to have been replaced, 9" long. **$1,610**

James D. Julia, Inc.

German tin Hessmobile sedan, flywheel-type mechanism engaged by cranking car from front and lifting lever to engage drivetrain rear wheels, lithographed in dark blue with pinstriping and highlighting, tin-spoked wheels, chauffeur dressed in goggles, helmet, and uniform, near mint original condition, 8" long. **$1,495**

◄ *Gilbert Erector set, zeppelin with box, scarce, all-original fabric, original box with colorful labeled lid, label with tape repairs, built up mooring mast, no additional parts in box, very good to excellent condition, zeppelin 54" long.* **$1,300**

James D. Julia, Inc.

Barking French papier maché bulldog, glass eyes and flocked covering; dog opens mouth and barks when leash is pulled; overall good condition, 17" long. **$1,150**

Noel Barrett Auctions

Bradley Historiscope and Electrical Wonder Book, early lithographed paper panorama toy, turning crank displays hand-colored images of American history from Columbus to Cornwallis surrendering to Washington, with Parker Bros. Electrical Wonder Book, Chiromagica Q & A toy, very good to excellent condition, panorama 8" wide. **$1,000**

Noel Barrett Auctions

Martin Mysterious Ball, painted and lithographed tin; pull string to wind, ball rolls up spiral and when it reaches the top the ball pops open and acrobat appears; very good to excellent condition, wear to ball exterior, 14" high. **$1,300**

James D. Julia, Inc.

Large Japanese race car #42, late 1950s tin plate version of Troy Ruttman's Indianapolis 500-winning "Agajanian Special," chrome steering and suspension, full exhaust, radiator with "A" forming front fender, front rubber tires marked "Special Racer Gem," fine lithography with multitude of advertising, overall very good-plus condition, minor paint chips, some darkening to chrome pieces, minor corrosion to joint seams, 18 1/2" long. **$1,610**

Noel Barrett Auctions

Mandeville musical girl at spinning wheel, fabric-dressed girl with bisque head and wood hands operates treadle that spins wheel while she pulls back and forth on yarn with right hand while turning her head back and forth from wheel to hand, on lithographed paper-covered wood base, hand operated by crank, very good to excellent condition, some paper loss, 19" high, base 15" x 9" x 5". **$1,100**

James D. Julia, Inc.

Schoenhut Dutch Boy & Girl Jolly Jiggers, Dutch garb, papier maché heads, overall very fine all-original condition with minor wear/chipping to faces of both figures, approximately 12" high. **$1,208**

World War II Collectibles

In the 65 years since the end of World War II, veterans, collectors, and history buffs have eagerly bought, sold and traded the "spoils of war." Actually, souvenir collecting began as soon as troops set foot on foreign soil.

Soldiers from every nation involved in the greatest armed conflict mankind has known eagerly sought items that would remind them of their time in the service, validate their presence during the making of history, and potentially generate income when they returned home. Such items might also be bartered with fellow soldiers for highly prized or scarce goods. Helmets, medals, Lugers, field gear, daggers, and other pieces of war material filled parcels, which were mailed home or stuffed into the duffel bags of soldiers who gathered them.

As soon as hostilities ended in 1945, the populations of the defeated nations quickly realized that they could make money by selling souvenirs to their former enemies. This was particularly true in Germany and Japan, which hosted large contingents of occupying U.S. soldiers and troops from other Allied nations. The flow of war material increased. Values became well established. For instance, a Luger was worth several packs of cigarettes, a helmet, just one. A Japanese sword was worth two boxes of K-rations, and an Arisaka bayonet was worth a chocolate Hershey bar.

Over the years, these values have remained proportionally consistent. Today, that "two-pack" Luger might be worth $4,000 and that one-pack helmet $1,000. The Japanese sword might fetch $1,200 and the Arisaka bayonet $85. Though values have increased dramatically, demand has not slackened. In fact, World War II collecting is the largest segment of the militaria hobby.

For more information on World War II collectibles, see *Warman's World War II Collectibles Identification and Price Guide*, 2nd edition, by Michael E. Haskew.

German Leitz 10 x 80 artillery ranging binoculars, mechanically sound with clear optics, manufactured by E. Leitz, no dates visible but green color indicates early World War II or pre-World War II usage, excellent condition. **$300**

Japanese officer's sword with old blade, 38" overall length with 24 7/8" bright polished blade with wavy temper line, blade has a few minor flaws, unsigned tang, World War II officer's mounts with old iron tsuba with gold highlights, steel scabbard has paint wear on edges with heavy chips near drag, with red and brown sword knot. **$2,390**

▶ USAAF flying helmet group: leather A-11 flying helmet in excellent condition with avionics, Type A-14 soft rubber oxygen mask with straps, and pair of AN-6530 flying goggles with clear lenses and soft rubber. **$435**

Signed Japanese flag with GI translation, cotton with cotton corner reinforcements, GI wrote English translations beside Japanese kanji, 23 1/2" x 26 1/4". **$165**

Red and white woven Hitler Youth armband, white diamond center with black woven swastika, no RZM tag. **$85**

Luftwaffe sword with aluminum fittings, faint signs of abrasive wear, no damage or focused areas of wear, no rips or tears in leather, minor age wear, belt hanger still present and undamaged, blade shows minor greying throughout, with etched trademark of E.F. Horster, crossguard marked "Ju3" and "18," JU-3 probably the unit, 18 likely a property number. **$860**

◄ Rare gorget worn by members of elite SA Feldherrnhalle Standarte, shield finished in aluminum color with finished border, centrally placed SA Feldherrnhalle eagle with gilt finish, chain similar in design to that used by Feldpolizei but with brighter finish; reverse is maker marked on chain holding tabs, "RZM," "M1/83," which was license assigned to Willy Annetsberger of München, original wool backing is still present but shrunken and pulled out of crimped bottom edge. **$6,400**

▶ Kelly Hicks-certified ET64 helmet with classic ET SS decal, original green paint, authentic chin-strap and liner, "period-scrape" with remnant of original decal beneath post-war applied political decal, SS decal 100% intact with light abrasions, paint mostly present, light dome wear, supple liner. **$6,950**

Spanish Cross in bronze without swords, separately attached eagles with cut-out swastikas, reverse has tapered pin with original hinge and catch, dark blue leatherette-covered presentation case with collared rectangular button closure. **$1,635**

Standard of III Battalion of Artillery Regiment 26, crimson silk cloth with silver fringe on three sides, both faces with hand-embroidered black army eagle on field of cream-colored silk surrounded by silver-embroidered oak leaf wreath on Iron Cross, 51 cm x 69 cm (without sleeve). The 26th artillery regiment took part in the campaign in France and the occupation of Belgium and France. On the Eastern Front, it fought at Smolensk, Moscow, Vyasma, Rzhev, Orel, the Don Bend, Kursk, Tschaussy, Mogilev and Kholm. **$41,325**

Luftwaffe observer's watch, black clock face with minute and inner hour circles, luminous indices, blued hands with applied luminous material, vestiges of grey paint on housing, laterally marked "Fl 23883," cover with exterior stamping "H5297" and interior "Beobachtungsuhr - Bauart DUROWE - Gerät-Nr. 127-560 Bl - Werk-Nr. H 5297 - Anforderz. Fl. 23883 - Montage Wempe," gilt works Nr. "5297" calibre D5 Durowe (Deutsche Uhren-Rohwerke) by Laco with 22 jewels, Guillaume balance wheel and Breguet balance spring. **$3,445**

Army lightweight service M2A2 gas mask, 1944 dated black rubber mask with light amber lenses, pliable hose, and filter with 95% gray paint, dark olive drab canvas carrier stenciled "U.S." with Chemical Corps markings, anti-dimming stick. **$75**

▲ British-made canteen set for U.S. troops, khaki and light olive web canteen cover with "U.S." stencil, lift-the-dot snaps, interior flap with BroadArrow proof, "1943" maker's date stamp, and "BRITISH MADE" stamp, includes 1944-dated cup and canteen with black plastic cap. **$90**

▶ World War II AAF B-2 shearling cap, brown finished exterior and white fleece interior with turned ear and neck cape, front with large bound brown leather visor, interior with AAF woven nomenclature label listing size medium. **$145**

U.S. Fleet Admiral's flag attributed to Chester Nimitz, blue wool bunting with five sewn stars, heading white canvas with four brass grommets, stenciled "Fleet Admiral" with number 6, engraved plate bearing inscription "Chester W Nimitz Fleet Admiral" affixed to heading, flag slightly faded with wear to each corner of fly end, 41 1/2" x 60 1/2". **$7,780**

Indian Army long service and good conduct medal, 11th Sikh Regiment, silver planchet with crowned profile of George VI on obverse, impressed on rim, "138 WATER CARRIER UTTAM SINGH, 3-11 SIKH R." **$130**

▲ Army artillery visor cap made by Peküro for member of Afrika Korps, private purchase piece, doeskin wool top and early silvered eagle, cockade, and wreath, dark green wool band, piped with bright red wool, well-worn, patent leather chinstrap shows some dryness, visor has thumb wear to reverse, interior has damaged sweatshield with original owner's name and unit information: Gefreiter Jakob Jourdan, 1./Artillery Regt. 33; part of 15th Panzer Division, integral unit of Rommel's Afrika Korps. **$515**

World War II AAF 369th bomb squadron patch. **$450**

▼ Luftwaffe Short-Range Day Fighter Clasp, silver award, instituted Jan. 30, 1941, recognizing 60 combat missions, unmarked, tombac example retains 90% frosted silver finish on obverse with black winged arrow device, pinback reverse. **$895**

U.S. Navy sports gear, 33 3/4" hickory bat with "Hillerich & Bradsby Co. / A&B / No. 102 / Louisville, KY" oval brand and "U.S.N. / Soft-Ball" markings; ball appears never to have been used, marked with "Sporting Goods Inc." trademark and "Official Day and Night Soft Ball / 12A / Kapok Center / U.S. - 1945"; baseman's mitt has "Spalding" maker's logo in script on strap with "U.S.N." embossed at base of palm; fielder's glove has "USMC" with maker's lot numbers. **$325**

Soviet World War II Model 1936 combat helmet, Winter War and early combat helmet with short comb crown reinforcement, retains 90% olive painted finish, interior with variant black rubberized fabric German-style liner with thick gray horsehair padding, dirty and worn but pliable brown leather chinstrap. **$625**

SS field cap, reversible from spring to autumn camouflage, both sides printed in "blurred edge" camouflage material, separately sewn-in national eagle and death's head in green on black backing on spring pattern side and in brown on black backing on autumn pattern side. Provenance: SFC John P. Conlon's unit overran a German field hospital in Czechoslovakia in 1945. When exploring the hospital, he found this field cap outside in a pile of discarded uniforms and took it as a souvenir. **$13,775**

Index

Heritage Auctions

Three Murano glass perfume bottles with stoppers, 20th century, tallest one 11 3/8" high. **$531**

Pottery Appreciated

Pigeon Forge
ampbell
McCoy
ley Gonder
Teco **Owens** Doo
American Encaustic Tiling Com
urley Winter Motawi **Coors**
Zane Stangl **Grueby** Tren
Robinson Ransbottom Weatley **Alhar**
Avon Faience Hull **Nicodemu**
rd **Weller** Van Briggle M
ch Art Pottery Com
Zanesville Majolica **Door** Hamilto
rk Brush McCoy **Pauline Pot**
Hartford Campbell
Roseville Katrich
Ford Kensington Art Tile Com
hardt Tiffany **Marblehead**
Mosaic Saturday Evening Gi
well Teco Moravian
er **Rookwood**
California Art Tile Com
Galloway **Cambridg**
ington Shawnee Niloak
Newcomb
& Reed **Camark** Ephrai
Grindley Pardee Wo
mmon Ground Clev
Unzicker Broth
Cowan Fa
Revere Pottery Pewabi
ce Fulper Clark Stoneware
Kensington M

Every Piece Counts

BELHORN
AUCTIONS

BelhornAuctions.com | (614) 921-9441

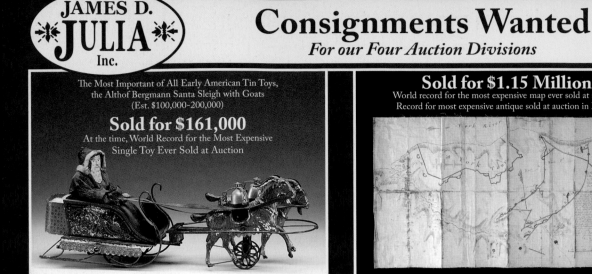

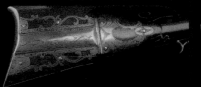